GREAT SHARK STORIES

"The shark was not an accident. He had come up from deep down in the water as the dark cloud of blood had settled and dispersed in the mile-deep sea. He had come up so fast and absolutely without caution that he broke the surface of the blue water and was in the sun."

That should be enough to drive you back to Ernest Hemingway's *The Old Man and the Sea*, from which the above passage was excerpted for this superb collection of fiction and nonfiction pieces by outstanding authors. The nonfiction includes an account of the great white *Carcharodon carcharias* of *Jaws:* the performance of a mechanical shark off Martha's Vineyard was intercut with live footage shot off Australia's Dangerous Reef, resulting in the unforgettable creature who terrorized millions.

Great
Shark Stories

●

Edited by
Valerie and Ron Taylor
with Peter Goadby

BANTAM BOOKS
TORONTO · NEW YORK · LONDON

GREAT SHARK STORIES

*A Bantam Book / published by arrangement with
Harper & Row Publishers, Inc.*

PRINTING HISTORY
Harper & Row edition published June 1978
Bantam edition / August 1978

Contents

VIII. GAME FISHING FOR SHARKS

IX. SHARKS THAT ATTACK

X. FICTION

Publishers' Foreword

The selections in this book were made by Valerie and Ron Taylor, with the assistance of Peter Goadby. These three individuals are among that limited group of people who have spent their lives studying the sea and its inhabitants.

Ron Taylor is considered the foremost photographer of sharks in the world. His wife, Valerie, is an equally well-known photographer and is famous for her lack of fear of and her affinity for the creatures of the sea. People think of the Taylors in conjunction with sharks because of their association with the two outstanding films on the subject, *Blue Water, White Death,* and *Jaws,* for both of which they did the live shark photography. But they have also made films about sharks other than the great white shark as well as about sea lions, leopard sharks, sea snakes, whale sharks, and rare shells. Their underwater television series "Ron and Valerie Taylor's Inner Space" has been shown all over the world and a new one is now in preparation.

Valerie Taylor has provided the introduction to this book, its sections, and its selections, as well as excerpts from her diaries and two magazine articles. These demonstrate that not only is she skilled at diving and underwater photography but also a writer worth reading. Those who have seen her in her films know that she is also a beautiful woman—and Ron Taylor is a handsome man.

While the Taylors are primarily divers, Peter Goadby is primarily a big-game fisherman, whose articles on the subject have appeared in periodicals all over the world and whose books have been well received. He also acts as a consultant to manufacturers of game fishing equipment in both Australia and the United States.

Together, these three Australians know as much about sharks as can be known—and have had more real experience with them than most others, living or dead.

THE PUBLISHERS

Introduction

About ten years ago, a survey was conducted in Australia in an attempt to establish which word had the greatest impact on the largest number of people.

Researchers tested words like rape, death, murder, sex, love, snake, poison. To their surprise, it was the word *shark* which aroused the public's emotions more than any of the others.

At the time, I thought that it must have been because of the large number of attacks that have occurred in Australian waters, for Australians are very conscious of sharks.

But I realize, now, that Australians are not alone in their hatred and fear of sharks. The film *Jaws* brought forth an almost universal reaction against these large fish. They had, to most people, been a distant threat, not likely to be encountered at the local beach, but in the wake of the film a type of mass hysteria seemed to grip whole communities and once popular beaches were deserted.

Men took to the oceans armed with shark-catching equipment. The old saying, "The only good shark is a dead one," became a new law. Around Australia, great white sharks were slaughtered by the hundreds for their teeth, most of which were sold in the United States for up to twenty-five dollars each.

An American promoter offered one million dollars to an Australian diver to swim into a steel cage with a great white shark. He was to kill it with an explosive-tipped spear while the TV cameras rolled and the world watched. I believe that there would have been very little danger involved. The diver would probably have had to swim around in front of the shark to make it look exciting.

Trapped sharks have only one desire—to escape. Sharks, particularly large dangerous ones, don't take kindly to living in captivity and are, generally, already half dead on reaching a holding tank. As for starving the shark to make it more dangerous, sharks can go quite happily for months without eating.

The whole thing must have sounded like a bad joke to anyone who knew anything about sharks and their behavior. To the general public, though, it seemed that the diver was brave and probably more than a little mad to even contemplate such an impossible task. Fortunately, this little piece of stupidity has not taken place and although, at the time of this writing, still planned for the future, seems doomed to failure, simply because it will be so difficult to find and keep alive a shark suitable for the stunt.

My husband, Ron, and I have worked with sharks in their natural element for over twenty years and, without intending to, we have acquired a reputation as shark experts. "Shark expert"—it sounds very important, but it is hardly an apt description. So little is known about the sharks that inhabit our oceans that I don't think there is anyone who can justly claim the title.

A scientist who works with a certain species of shark over a period of years would become an expert on that particular species, but could hardly be called an expert on sharks in general. Ron and I know, from observation, a certain amount about a dozen different types of shark. Of the other four hundred-odd species we know very little, or nothing. This hardly qualifies us as experts.

Our main claim to fame is the work we have done with the great white shark, *Carcharodon carcharias,* the fish that ate its way to worldwide hatred in *Jaws.* The interest aroused by Peter Benchley's book and the later film brought us a continuous flood of mail. Selling shark pictures became big business for us, and we had plenty of them.

Books and magazines devoted to sharks and their habits flooded the market. I walked into a big bookstore in Sydney recently to see no less than seventeen recent publications on sharks staring down at me from the shelves. Nine of them had a photograph taken by us on the cover, two of them without permission or payment. Some of these books were excellent, but most were full of exaggerated, often false, accounts of shark attacks. It doesn't matter, the public laps them up—the more gore the better.

What is this sea creature that seems to have captured the imagination of so many people so completely?

Sharks were an ancient species when the dinosaurs walked the earth. They outlived the dinosaurs as they did countless other creatures that evolved, multiplied, dominated, then vanished, leaving only fossil remains to let us know that they ever existed at all. Yet, through all this time, sharks prospered. Their unique bodies were so well designed that there appears to have been very little change in their shape since prehistoric times.

Most sharks are not dangerous to man. Some do not have teeth in the true sense, but hard, bony crushing plates, suitable for grinding and eating shellfish. Others feed on the smallest creatures in the sea. Many do not grow longer than a few feet. Of the larger sharks considered dangerous to man, only about ten species have been known to attack without provocation.

Of these, only members of the family Carcharinidae (whites, whalers, Zambezi, bull) and the tiger shark attack man on anything like a regular basis. In the Caribbean, there have been reports of unprovoked attacks by the hammerhead shark, but throughout the rest of the world this species seems to be innocent of any attacks on man.

The key to many attacks is provocation. Any shark, even one without teeth, will try to defend itself if hooked, speared, or otherwise molested. This is perfectly normal; any living creature, man included, will do the same.

When we were asked to assemble a collection of shark stories, with this book in mind, I thought it sounded like a fairly easy project. A friend of ours, big-game fisherman Peter Goadby, had the most extensive library of shark stories in Australia. Fortunately, I had access to this library. With Peter's help and advice, Ron and I chose the stories we liked and thought most suitable, but this was just the start.

It soon became apparent that there was a certain sameness in stories about big-game fishermen catching sharks. The account of a tiger shark hooked and fought to the boat in Hawaii, when written down, bears a strong resemblance to a description of the same species hooked and boated in the Indian Ocean. The real differences in each story—how the fish was played, what breaking strain line was used, and so on —would be apparent only to a game fishing enthusiast. By the time I had read a dozen game fishing stories, I realized that I could never choose between them, so I asked Peter Goadby to choose for me, as he is the expert in the field, not I.

My next problem was finding and sorting out the shark attack stories. There are many books on the subject. However, the authors' accounts are similar. They could hardly be otherwise, for the facts regarding a certain shark attack can be altered only in the manner of writing, not in content.

I found many books on sharks to contain identical information presented in different styles, although often the conclusions drawn by the various writers differed widely. In any case it made selections limited. But, eventually, with the help of many people, I arrived at a final choice.

One thing that stands out in the final selection is how differently two people can think about a shark. A great deal of this has to do with the circumstances of the contact, but, even so, the variations of opinion are amazing and interesting.

If I seem to favor stories about skin divers and

sharks, I guess it is only natural. As a professional diver, I feel that accounts of a man or woman, often armed with nothing more than a camera, confronting a potentially dangerous shark in its home, make exciting reading.

It is interesting to note that the diver who knows the fish in its natural state under water has a completely different picture than a surface fisherman has. That is, I feel, because line fishermen rarely see sharks except as desperate, half-crazed creatures fighting for their lives on the ends of lines. Divers see them as they really are—the perfect fish, beautiful, swift, sure of themselves, masters of their environment.

Even when confronted by a great white shark in the open water, Ron and I were struck by the tremendous terrifying beauty of the creature as it passed, turned, and passed again. We did not, at the time, consider it a threat to us; only afterward was the potential danger of the situation fully realized.

No fisherman can ever experience that feeling. Theirs is a different feeling—the thrill of the strike; the satisfaction of subduing a large, potentially dangerous fish with their own skill and strength. This is the epitome of pleasure and excitement to a game fisherman and his crew.

To a diver, it is the smooth, silent passing of death itself, swift as a swallow, smiling a joyless smile; later, climbing onto a rock and sitting shivering in the sun, looking at one's companions alive and whole and laughing with relief, yet excited just the same. I cannot imagine a finer experience.

I have attempted to look at sharks from all points of view, for interest in sharks, today, is not limited to divers and game fishermen. I believe that just about everyone wants to know a little more about them.

I am often asked why sharks attack people. This is a difficult question to answer, simply because there are probably as many reasons as there are shark attacks. Dr. H. David Baldridge, in his book *Shark Attack,* states that approximately 4 percent of all shark attacks are due to hunger. That leaves 96 percent which must have other causes. The reasons for some are apparent. Most obvious is a shark attacking a diver who is spearing fish.

A bleeding, struggling fish is the natural prey of a shark, which will move in very quickly for the kill. Usually, when it sees a big, ungainly creature already in possession of its potential prey, the shark will leave. Some may hang around, in which case it is wise to stop spearing fish.

On rare occasions the shark attacks. A very hungry shark, following the scent of blood or the vibrations of a dying fish, would quickly fall into a feeding pattern. This means that it has made up its mind to eat even before seeing the food source.

It would seem that once you have seen the shark, the chance of attack is slight. It may be significant to note that, to the best of my knowledge, no skin diver who has been attacked by a shark ever saw the shark before he was bitten.

Only once have I had trouble with a shark after I had seen it. It was one of a pack of about twenty. All the other sharks were circling at a respectful distance, except for one bad-tempered female. She circled close, faster and faster, ignoring the baits on the sand. I knew what was coming and braced myself. Suddenly she sped straight at me, and just before she struck, her jaws and pectoral fins dropped. I rammed my camera into her mouth, and after about 30 seconds (it seemed like hours) of mad punching, kicking, and yelling, my companion speared her in the gills.

This may indicate another reason for attack, a shark which is mad, an observation that F. A. Mitchell-Hedges also makes in his book *Battles with Giant Fish*. I have seen thousands of sharks, but only one which behaved in this way. The water was very clear, so it was not a case of mistaken identity, which may often be the case with swimmers or waders in dirty water, such as is found in harbors and estuaries. Here the shark is unable to see because of poor visibility. There may be something in the water which upsets its sense of smell, perhaps human urine. It may then bump or bite the object merely to discover what the obstruction is. Sharks don't have hands and have to feel with nose or teeth. If the object is a human leg, we have a shark attack. This theory gains credibility from the fact that in these types of attacks, the victim, though mauled, is rarely, if ever, eaten. Personally, I would never go swimming in dirty water which is adjacent to an ocean.

Before shark meshing reduced attacks on surfers off Australian beaches (there has never been an attack on a meshed beach), every summer saw a number of unfortunate incidents involving sharks biting swimmers. Some victims were just bumped or cut by fins, some lost limbs and others lost their lives. A possible reason for this type of attack could be that the shark is just swimming along in a normal fashion and suddenly finds itself among a lot of large, unusual creatures. Not having experienced this type of situation before, the animal may panic. During that panic, it would bump anything hindering its escape to open water and may even bite it.

I am also asked why a shark will single out a swimmer in the center of a crowd. This question is almost impossible to answer. I don't really think that a shark has any more reason for selecting one individual from a large crowd than a bird has for eating one grape from a bunch or a human for taking a particular egg from a carton. It is just one of those things. But once a shark selects a victim and continues the attack, it is almost always on the same person. This is true of most carnivores. A cheetah will run past a dozen impala before bringing one down. If the first attack only wounds and the impala escapes, the cheetah will continue after the wounded animal, regardless of the number of others nearby.

Surfboard riders, waiting for a wave with their legs hanging down on each side of the board, look very vulnerable from beneath. A shark with even a slight amount of curiosity must feel compelled to investigate. If I were a surfboard rider, I would paint two mean-looking eyes on the bottom of my board. Sharks don't like being looked at. An eyeless object would possibly be worthy of inspection and perhaps a nibble by a passing shark.

The sharks that I have been writing about up to now are the whalers, Zambezi, bull sharks, and their cousins. These are the sharks responsible for most of the attacks on humans. However, there is one shark which is quite different, the "Great White Death." Great white sharks have different personalities and behavior patterns than all other sharks. They are the end of the food chain.

Whites eat almost anything. Nothing eats a white shark, except a bigger white shark, but even these huge fish don't swim around attacking everything in their paths. They choose their prey as nature intended they should, from the slow, the sick, and the old. I hate to say it but, in the water, a human looks very much like a slow, old seal. These mammals are one of the staple foods of the great white. What appears to be an unprovoked attack by a white could well be brought about by the awkward movements humans make when swimming.

All this is just theorizing. I do know that some species like certain colors; some sharks are attracted to unusual vibrations and smells; some are attracted by specific patterns. All that I can say with certainty is that sharks are predictable only in that they are unpredictable. Each different attack could be caused by a different reason or they could all be triggered by similar causes. I don't know. No one really knows. There are so many variables that to go into them all would require a book twice this size and even then we wouldn't know.

What can you do if menaced by a shark? I can only repeat the advice that I give my nephews when they go out on their surfmats. I make them put the blue side down. I won't let them swim in dirty water or on a rising tide during the late afternoon. I have told them that if they are ever in the water with a shark that appears menacing to put their heads under the water (even without a face mask) and look at the shark.

They may not be able to see the shark very well, but the shark doesn't know that. Having your dinner look you in the eye can be disconcerting, and for sharks, it is worrisome. They are not accustomed to this sort of reaction when they approach. Being animals which work on instinct, not reason, it generally becomes difficult for them to make a decision.

Anything which keeps the shark off-balance is a help. If contact is made, make as much noise as possible. Punch and kick, especially at the eyes and gills; this seems to act as a deterrent in many cases. Everything should be tried. Fight, don't just give in and let the shark do as it pleases.

I would like to say that I am grateful to Peter Goadby, who helped with the selections and advice; Chris Wright, who corrected my mistakes and somehow managed to type up a decent introduction from my bad handwriting. My publishers deserve a special word of appreciation for being so patient with me when I was late for deadlines or out of contact for weeks at a time.

My darling husband, Ron, with whom I have shared all my diving experiences, deserves a gold medal. He remained calm despite my disappearances, rages, and weeks of preoccupation at my desk, reading and writing.

I hope everyone is happy with my work, Harper & Row and K. S. Giniger in particular, because they had faith in my ability when I felt that I had neither ability nor faith.

Valerie Taylor

Great
Shark Stories

I

STARS OF
THE SILVER
SCREEN

●

The best-known shark movies ever made are Peter
Gimbel's documentary *Blue Water, White Death*
and Zanuck-Brown's *Jaws*. Both had a shark as the
main attraction. There the similarity ended as far as
the finished product was concerned. "Bruce," of
Jaws fame, was a giant mechanical monster, while
the white shark in Gimbel's film was the much
smaller real thing. My husband, Ron, and I were
fortunate enough to work on both these films and
for us, as far as the filming went, there was little
difference. Our job was to film live great white sharks
for both *Jaws* and *Blue Water, White Death*. The
same locations were used on both occasions and, for
all we know, even some of the sharks could have
been the same.

Great whites appear to have territories in which
they hunt, and the same sharks could have very easily
visited the filming locations for both films. Although
the location, method of attracting sharks, and time
of the year were similar, Ron was required to shoot
quite different film actions. In *Blue Water, White
Death,* everything is shown as it happens. Everybody
involved appears on film. Much is made of the
cages, baits, boats, and people on board.

1

When filming for *Jaws,* all those things were still present, but they could not be shown. The shark was not supposed to be swimming around our boat and cage off Dangerous Reef, Australia, but trailing a different boat on the other side of the world, near Martha's Vineyard. This made filming much more difficult because sharks don't follow a script. Ron would feel himself lucky if he managed to shoot two or three scenes in a day without getting any of our gear in the picture.

More recently, we were required to film great white sharks for the Dino De Laurentiis production *Orca.* Once again, cage bars were not allowed in the picture. This was, by far, the most difficult filming job we have ever attempted. The script was simple enough and all arrangements were normal, but the shark never came in to perform. Week after week, we waited without completing our filming. A great deal of money was spent with very little return. Dangerous Reef did not live up to its reputation as the home of the great white shark. With one exception, the few sharks we did attract performed poorly or did not perform at all.

Professional shark fishing coupled with big-game fishing for great whites had taken its toll. Dangerous Reef, at the time of this writing, can no longer be considered a sure thing for anyone who wants to film or observe great white sharks.

Fortunately, the great white sharks of Dangerous Reef still live, on the silver screen. They have been seen by more people in more countries than any other shark in the world. Their fame is, without doubt, widespread. *Blue Water, White Death* and *Jaws* have made great whites the most famous sharks in the world and, unfortunately, the most feared.

1

From *Blue Meridian: The Search for the Great White Shark*

PETER MATTHIESSEN

Reading Peter Matthiessen's words takes me straight back to the time when we were working with those fine Americans on the film *Blue Water, White Death*, sharing with them sad and happy days in pursuit of the great white shark.

It was the highlight of my life. Nothing that I have done before, or since, has meant so much to me.

Blue Water, White Death did not turn out to be a million-dollar home movie, as Matthiessen feared—it is the best underwater documentary ever made. It will be a long time, if ever, before anyone else produces a comparable film.

Peter Matthiessen, in his book *Blue Meridian*, tells of the film from its beginnings in New York to the final shooting at Dangerous Reef, off the South Australian coast.

He tells of the time spent waiting for sharks which never came; of the fruitless five months spent crossing the Indian Ocean; of the despair when the producers thought that the shark would never come; of the elation and excitement when one, finally, did appear. This excerpt describes the sighting of the first white shark.

Ron and I never doubted that the waters of Dangerous Reef would provide all the shark action

that was needed. We had filmed there before and all
that we needed was patience.

Since Matthiessen wrote *Blue Meridian,* between
twenty and thirty rare great white sharks have been
caught in the area. They have been taken not because
of man's fears of the silent killer lurking in the depths,
but to satisfy a fad, caused by *Jaws,* of wearing a
shark's tooth around the throat. Great whites have
become profitable.

And Dangerous Reef has become a place of death
not only for the great white but for our charter vessel,
the *Saori,* too, which was later beaten to pieces
against the cliffs of Wedge Island, within sight of the
Reef. The last time I was there, her remains could still
be seen protruding above the surge.

●

On the radio this morning one of the tuna captains
with a white-shark charter party out of Port Lincoln
had some disturbing news: in his last three trips to
Dangerous Reef he had raised only one shy white
shark, and it would not come near the boat. "Not like
it used to be," the radio voice said. "They're being
slowly killed out, I reckon, like everything else in the
world." This man blamed the gill-netters for the disappearance of the sharks and certainly commercial netting is a factor. Like other large predators of land and
sea, the white shark will not survive long without the
protection that it is unlikely to receive from man, and
possibly the Australians are correct in the opinion
generally held here that the species is nearing extinction. I am happy that our expedition has no plan to
kill one except in self-defense.

There are recent reports of white sharks farther
north in the gulf and to the west of Cape Catastrophe,
and there is a feeling aboard that the *Saori* should
pursue these sightings. Pursuit might relieve the strain
of waiting and improve morale, but chasing works no
better with fish than it does with anything else; better
to pick one likely place and chum the hell out of it,
day and night. By the time the slow *Saori* got the cages

to the scene of any sighting the shark might be twenty miles away, and even if a shark were present, there is no guarantee that water clarity would be adequate, or that the shark would approach the cage. Possibly inshore sharks have a hunting circuit, moving from point to point as wolves do, but more likely they move at random taking prey as chance presents and congregating now and then at likely grounds like Dangerous Reef. Instinctively, I agree with Captain Arno, who is relieving Captain Ben over this weekend. Arno is a wonderful bent old salt with white broken bare feet that never sunburn; offered grog, he smites the table, crying out fiercely, "I will!" Says Arno, "Sharks have a head and a tail, and they keep swimming. Nobody knows where the shark goes. I reckon they don't know where they are themselves."

Although these days are painful for Gimbel, they are almost as hard on Rodney Fox, who must choose the fishing grounds and baiting techniques that will bring the missing sharks. Rodney performs his duties with efficiency and style, but his casual air of cocky indifference is deceptive. If anything, he takes too much of the burden upon himself, and tends to construe the discussion of alternatives as implied criticism. For those aboard with a long interest in the sea and sharks, such discussions are fun and ease the strain, but giving a hearing to amateur opinions is hard on Rodney's nerves in a nervous time. Rarely does he permit the strain to show but sometimes, muttering "Too many cooks . . .!" he lies face down on the deck, feigning deep sleep, and one day he actually took refuge in the hold, refusing to come out to eat his lunch.

Nevertheless, Rodney says, he has never worked with a nicer group of people. I feel the same, and so does everyone else; even Lipscomb and I, who often disagree, manage to disagree in a friendly manner. After a year and a half, this film crew is truly a unit, and its strength is mutual affection and acceptance; each man knows precisely what can be expected of the man beside him and demands no more, because those who fail in one respect have made it up over and over in others. As relationships have grown, the people have become more self-sufficient. Even the hearts game, a loud nightly event aboard the *Terrier,* has given way to books and chess and backgammon.

There are other changes, in the crew's youngest members especially. A new confident Cody is so loose that he threatens to join the extroverts while Lake has arrived at a new awareness in his dealings with others. One day on the deckhouse, watching for sharks, Peter said, "Remember when I wrote you that I didn't really care about this film? Well, that's all changed—I do."

By now everyone cares about the film quite apart from his own investment in it, if only because everyone cares about Peter Gimbel, who has his life's work on the line. A great part of the suspense of waiting for "Big Whitey," as the near-mythical ruler of these silent seas has become known, is the knowledge that his failure to appear could be fatal to the film. Therefore the ship is quiet. Against these stark horizons, even the throb of hard rock music has a thin, tinny ring.

More than once I went ashore and prowled the tide pools. I have spent hours of my life crouched beside tide pools, watching the slow surge of simple organisms still close to the first pulse of life on earth. On Dangerous Reef are gaudy giant limpets, and companies of blue, black, and banded periwinkles, and the green snail and a brown cone and a very beautiful cream volute with zigzag stripings; also rockfish and the great fire-colored rock crabs that grow enormous in the deeps, and a heart-colored sea anemone, and a garden of hydroids, barnacles and algae. In every tide pool the seal pups played, and others lay on the warm rocks in a sleep so sound that they could be petted without awakening. When at last one did come to, it would stare for seconds in bare disbelief, then bleat in dismay and flop away at speed over the rocks.

In the white surge along the shore, the seals rolled endlessly, turning and twisting, whisking clean out of the water in swift chases or ranging along, the sleek, sunshined dark-eyed heads held high out of the sea. A small surge would lift them out onto the granite where, groaning, they dozed on the hot rocks in rows. The old bulls, though graceful in the water, were less playful; they stationed themselves on underwater ledges like old mighty sentinels and let the white foam wash around them. Onshore, competitors were driven off in heaving neck fights that were mostly shoving contests; the animals swayed their heavy heads and necks in the way of bears, to which among land mammals they are most closely related. Sea lions are agile on the land and a golden-maned bull protecting a cow and a new pup drove me up onto high ground. One cow was raked drastically on her hind end and right hind flipper by the parallel black lines of an old shark bite, and it was noticeable the the young never left the shallows and that even the adults kept close to the reef edges when not off at sea.

At noon today the *Sea Raider* brought word that an eleven-foot white of thirteen hundred pounds had been hooked at Cape Donington, where the *Saori* had anchored two nights before. Psychologically this news was painful, but the water clarity at Cape Donington is awful and we could not have worked there. And at least it was proof that the species was not extinct.

In a letter to a friend this morning, Valerie wrote that no shark had been seen, but that she expected a twelve-or thirteen-footer to turn up at about 2:00. At 2:20 Peter Lake and Ian McKechnie saw a fin in the slick, some fifty yards behind the ship: the spell was broken. We dragged on diving suits and went on watch, but the fin had sunk from view in the still sea. A half hour passed, and more. Then, perhaps ten feet down off the port beam, a fleeting brown shadow brought the sea to life.

Suspended from a buoy, a salmon was floated out behind the boat to lure the shark closer. Once it had fed at the side of the boat, it would be less cautious; then, perhaps the engine could be started and the cages swung over the side without scaring it away. But an hour passed before the shark was seen again. This time a glinting rusty back parted the surface, tail and dorsal high out of the water as the shark made its turn into the bait; there was the great wavering blade exactly as Al Giddings had described it and the thrash of water as the shark took the salmon, two hours to the minute after the first sighting when Stan Waterman cried, "Holy sweet Jesus!"—a very strong epithet for this mild-spoken man; he was amazed by the mass of shark that had been raised clear of the water. Even the Australians were excited, try as they would to appear calm. "Makes other sharks look like little frisky pups, doesn't it?" cried Valerie with pride. Then it was gone again. Along the reef a hundred yards away, the sea lions were playing tag, their sleek heavy bodies squirting clean out of the water and parting the surface again without a splash, and a string of cormorant, oblivious, came beating in out of the northern blue.

Gimbel, annoyed that he had missed the shark, was running from the bow; he did not have long to wait. From the deckhouse roof, I could see the shadow rising toward the bait. "There he is," I said, and Rodney yanked at the shred of salmon, trying to bring the shark closer to the ship. Lipscomb, beside me, was already shooting when the great fish breached, spun the sea awash and lunged after the skipping salmon tail; we stared into its white oncoming mouth. "My God," Gimbel shouted, astounded by the sight of his first white shark. The conical snout and the terrible shearing teeth and the dark eye like a hole were all in sight, raised clear out of the water. Under the stern, with an audible whush, the shark took a last snap at the bait, then wheeled away; sounding, it sent the skiff spinning with a terrific whack of its great tail, an ominous boom that could have been heard a half-mile away.

For a split second there was silence, and then Lipscomb gave a mighty whoop of joy. "I got it!" he yelled. "Goddamn it, I got it!" There was a bedlam of relief, then another silence. "Might knock that cage about a bit," Rodney said finally, hauling in the shred of fish; he was thinking of the baits that would be suspended in the cage to bring the shark close to the cameras. Gimbel, still staring at the faceless water, only nodded.

Just after 5:00 the shark reappeared. The late sun glistened on its dorsal as it cut back and forth across the surface, worrying a dead fish from the line. There was none of the sinuous effect of lesser sharks; the tail strokes were stiff and short like those of a swordfish, giant tuna, and other swift deep-sea swimmers. This creature was much bigger than the big oceanic sharks off Durban, but for a white shark it was not enormous. Estimates of its length varied from eleven feet, six inches (Ron always plays it safe and underestimates, said Valerie) to fourteen feet (Peter Gimbel: "I saw it alongside that skiff and I'm certain it was at least as long—I'm certain of it!"), but much more impressive than the length was the mass of it, and the speed and power. "It doesn't matter what size the bastards are," Rodney said. "A white shark over six feet long is bloody dangerous."

The day was late. In the westering sun, a hard light of late afternoon silvered the water rushing through the reef, and nearer the blue facets of the sea sparkled in cascades of tiny stars. More out of frustration than good sense, the choice between trying to film the shark immediately and trying to lure it to the baits alongside, in the hope of keeping it nearby overnight, was resolved in favor of immediate action. The motor was started up and the cages swung over the side, and the cameramen disappeared beneath the surface. But the great shark had retreated, and did not return.

By dark the wind exceeded 25 knots, and went quickly to 30, 40, and finally, toward 1:00 in the morning, to 50 or better—a whole gale. On deck, I lay sleepless, rising every little while to check the position of the light on Dangerous Reef. The reef is too low to make a windbreak, and even close under the lee, the *Saori* tossed and heaved under heavy strain. But Captain Ben, who knew exactly what his ship would do, slept soundly below. Toward 3:00 the wind moderated, backing around to the southeast, where it held till daybreak.

This morning the wind has died to a fair breeze. Waiting, we sit peacefully in the Sunday sun. The boat captains hand-line for Tommy-rough, a delicious small silver relative of the Australian "salmon." Others tinker with equipment, play chess and backgammon, write letters and read. Peter Lake has put a rock tape on the sound machine, and on the roof of the pilothouse, overlooking the oil slick, I write these notes while listening to The Band. Onshore, for Jim Lipscomb's camera, Valerie in lavender is baby-talking with baby seals, and I hope that most if not all of this sequence will die on the cutting-room floor. Unless it points up the days of waiting, such material has no place in the climax of the film; it will soften the starkness of this remote reef as well as the suspense surrounding the imminence of the white shark. Stan and Valerie, with a background of lecture films and a taste for amateur theatrics, share Jim's appetite for "human-interest stuff," which might yet reduce this film to the first million-dollar home movie.

Toward dark another shark appeared, a smaller one, much bolder. Relentlessly it circled the ship, not ten feet from the hull. On one pass it took the buoyed tuna at a single gulp.

Since it passed alongside, the size of this shark could be closely estimated: all hands agreed that it was between nine feet and ten. But if this was accurate, the shark yesterday had been larger than thought. Rodney now said that it was over twelve, Valerie, between thirteen and fourteen, and Gimbel thought that it might have been sixteen feet: "I thought so yesterday," he said, "but I felt foolish, with everyone else saying twelve." I thought thirteen feet seemed a conservative minimum. In any case, it had twice the mass of tonight's shark, which was plenty big enough. As it slid along the hull, the thick lateral keel on its caudal peduncle was clearly visible; the merest twitch of that strong tail kept it in motion. Underwater lights were lit to see it better, but this may have been a mistake; it vanished, and did not return the following day.

On January 26 the *Saori* returned to port for water and supplies. There it was learned that four boats, fishing all weekend, had landed between them the solitary shark that we had heard about on Saturday. The *Saori* could easily have hooked two, but what she was here for was going to be much more difficult. Meanwhile, a sighting of white sharks had been reported by divers working Fisheries Bay, west of Cape Catastrophe on the ocean coast, where three whites and a number of bronze whalers had been seen schooling behind the surf; the bronze whaler, which may be the ubiquitous bull shark, *C. leucas,* is the chief suspect in most shark attacks on Australia's east coast.

On the chance that the shark school was still present, we drove out to the coast across the parched hills of the sheep country. Over high, windburnt fields, a lovely paroquet, the galah, pearl gray and rose, flew in weightless flocks out of the wheat; other paroquets, turquoise and black and gold, crossed from a scrub of gum trees and melaleuca to a grove of she-oak, the local name for a form of casuarina. Along the way were strange birds and trees in an odd landscape of windworn hills that descended again to the sea-misted shore. From the sea cliffs four or five whalers were in sight, like brown ripples in the pale green windy water, but the white sharks had gone.

2

The Filming of *Blue Water, White Death*

VALERIE TAYLOR

On May 4, 1969, Ron and I began what was to be one of the most exciting two days we have ever experienced. Had the events that I wrote about not been substantiated by the film *Blue Water, White Death,* I would have been hesitant to submit the story for publication. It all seems so incredible. This action was recorded near the beginning of the filming, when we were following the whaling fleet out of Durban, but to Ron and me it was the highlight of the six months we spent on the film.

Although, in the finished film, the great white sharks were considered to be the stars, it was the oceanic whitetips which were responsible in my opinion for our most dangerous and exciting moments.

Even now, seven years later, I can still close my eyes and fill my mind with that blue, bottomless ocean full of gray torpedo shapes circling, ever circling.

I can see the dead whale floating in a cloud of blood. I can see my companions, ugly awkward shapes surrounded by the deadly beauty of a hundred sharks. I can see our whale catcher, the *Terrier VII,* silhouetted on the surface far above.

I feel sure that each of us there was driven by a different need . . . I know that if I had said that I was afraid, that I didn't want to do it, not one person would have criticized, but the thought never crossed my mind. I did what they did, even though I felt that we would probably be killed.

The excitement of what we planned to do was all-consuming. It left no place for fear or misgivings.

This segment from my diary is part of a much longer story from an unpublished book. I believe it to be the ultimate in shark adventure. It is nothing to do with my writing—it's just the events that happened as I put them down at the time.

The men with whom I shared this experience are still my dear friends and I think of them often with the affection and respect that can only come from the sharing of a profound experience, each relying on the other with complete faith.

I consider myself lucky and my life richer because of this adventure 80 miles from the South African coast, under the Indian Ocean.

●

A.M.

We have just dropped off yesterday's whale completely unused at the flencing station, and are now looking for another. Unfortunately the weather is still awful—overcast, squalls, and rough seas. Poor Peter Gimbel, he has so many problems without worrying about the weather.

later P.M.

Things improved rapidly during the day. The wind dropped away, the sun came out and we found a whale with sharks. There was still a heavy swell running, but I prefer a swell to a short chop. I watched as the cages were lowered. There was less fuss than usual. The whale was bleeding well. How sad it looked in death! Another innocent victim of man's greed.

Peter Gimbel had worked out a plan of action for us divers. I was to try to swim among the sharks while Stan, Ron, and Peter filmed not only me but each other. Peter also wanted extreme close-ups of the sharks feeding.

We went down in the cages. The plan worked very well until halfway to the whale. Suddenly, as if on call, the sharks lost interest in the whale on which they were feeding, and became overwhelmingly attracted to us. We were completely surrounded by the gray marauders as they converged upon our tight little group, bumping and nuzzling.

From every direction they came. I was conscious only of myself, my companions, and the sharks. All else in the world was forgotten. I beat them off furiously with the powerhead, hitting the eyes and jabbing the gills with all my strength.

Peter, Stan, and Ron kept their cameras rolling. There was no need to look for the action; it was everywhere. I thumped and whacked as fast as I could. Stan said afterward, he filmed a giant shark nuzzling my head. I remember feeling my hair being pulled and looking up to see an ugly snout and gaping jaw directly over my head. The sight gave me quite a shiver. I am glad someone filmed it.

Part of Peter's plan was to film, in close-up, sharks feeding on the whale, but we never made it. The sharks beat us back every time.

Ron finally killed, with his own powerhead, one shark that persistently came too close. It died a beautiful death, shuddering down in ever-decreasing circles, bumping several of its comrades in the process. Both Stan and Peter filmed this action.

We ran out of film and air after what seemed a very short time and returned to the *Terrier VII* for more of both. It was warm on the deck and I savored the crew working around us, but within 15 minutes we were all back with the sharks and into the action again.

This time, for some reason, the sharks were definitely less aggressive. I wanted to test my powerhead and tried my hardest, without success, to kill one. I had been given a different powerhead than what Ron and I normally use in Australia and although I left an indentation on the shark's head, and once took a piece right out, the thing refused to detonate.

Via sign language, I was told all the things I was doing wrong but was rather pleased when Peter Gimbel, trying the same stunt, using my powerhead, met with similar success. (It was later discovered the cartridge was wet, so I didn't feel too badly.)

Finally, between us all we must have hit the whole fifty or sixty sharks at least once because one hard look, a shake of the fist, and they would shy away, rolling their eyes and jamming their gills tightly shut. Peter got all the shots he had planned except close-ups of the sharks feeding. They did get some film of sharks swimming into the blood and hitting the whale, but clarity was poor and the action confused.

The magazine in Peter Gimbel's camera jammed for the umpteenth time. The poor guy, he was so upset by it and I don't blame him. Jamming magazines are causing a lot of trouble. However, five rolls of good action came through okay.

We still have the whale and all systems are go for a night dive.

Tuesday, June 5, 1969

At last I have the energy and strength to write again. It was a long night and even longer day. We entered the water about 12:39 A.M., Peter Gimbel first, then myself; Stan and Ron came later. The water felt cool and refreshing. It revived me and I felt less tired. As the bubbles cleared, I lowered the cage a few feet and took my first good look. It was our privilege to gaze upon a scene of death and life, more horrible, more primeval than any I had seen before. We had entered a bygone age. No time machine could have done it better. The carnage around us had not changed, nor did it look different to how it had been and looked a million years ago.

The whale's mutilated body streamed blood and guts into the current. Huge sharks, fifty, one thousand, I couldn't count them, swirled in a frenzy around the carcass.

Where had they come from, these savage survivors from a bygone age? What ocean depths had hidden them from view during the day only to spew them forth in the darkness of night? I couldn't even guess.

Pale against the black water, they swam with their mouths agape, some carrying great hunks of torn flesh, gulping and swallowing without missing a beat of their powerful tails. One, larger than the rest, moved through the pack, cutting a path between his lesser fellows. He hit the whale with tremendous force, shuddering his way into the torn belly until only his vibrating tail and anal fins showed. Blood flowed like a green mist, obliterating the writhing body.

Stewart's lights hung like giant suspended stars, some 20 feet below our cage. Moving with the surge, their beams swung back and forth revealing, then losing, countless graceful bodies. One even larger shark could be seen moving in and out along the perimeter of illumination. I strained my eyes in its direction. Could it be the longed-for great white?

Something about the bobbing brilliance suddenly attracted this shark. It moved up from the fluttering darkness without haste, completely sure of its place. Peter and I watched in awe as this giant among giants carefully took the lights in its tremendous jaw, obliterating their brightness and plunging our world into darkness. Time and time again it mouthed the lights, feeling with its teeth the steel casings surrounding them. Curiosity suddenly satisfied, this great monster with the night black eyes and pale striped body passed our cage and circled several times before disappearing into the blackness. We didn't see the tiger shark again.

It was at least 15 feet and possibly 17 feet long. Its head looked to be the width of our cage. It was, next to the harmless whale shark, the largest I had ever seen.

By now Ron and Stan were entering their cage—

ghostly shadows in a web of buckling steel. It was a relief to be able to descend fully. The heavy surface swell created a pitching motion that was becoming most unkind to my middle region. Almost immediately our troubles started.

Our light, which had been pulled over to us, proved extremely difficult to handle. The cage's tethering rope seemed longer than the power cable and it took all my strength to keep hold of the thing. We were tied to the *Terrier* which didn't help matters much. Her rise and fall in the heavy swell was many times that of the whale. Peter, realizing my difficulty, helped me pull a length of cable into the cage. He then hooked it around the valve on the spare air cylinder. This put tremendous strain on the valve, but we did manage to light and shoot several scenes before the strain became so great that it endangered the cage.

It then became another battle to extract the cable. We finally lost our light altogether when, in spite of our combined efforts, it pulled completely away from the cage, all but dragging us out the open door.

Ron and Stan were having even greater problems. Their light cable had almost immediately become entangled around the whale. From there, it was twisted around the buoyancy tanks on our cage. They, like us, had been unable to hold their light after the first minute or so.

Unknown to us they were having even greater dramas on board the *Terrier*. Stewart Cody, seeing our problem, had leaped into a zodiac, cut the cages from the *Terrier,* and, with exceptional thought and courage, proceeded to untangle the twisted mess.

The milling sharks were a constant hindrance. Fortunately, we in the cage didn't realize our predicament. I wondered why we were unable to see the whale anymore and why the light was fading and why the steady, familiar beat of the ship's engines had vanished, never realizing our cages were no longer tethered to anything but adrift at night surrounded by feeding sharks under the Indian Ocean. Not a comforting thought when one thinks about it. However, what one doesn't know doesn't hurt.

Somehow, Stewart sorted out the incredible mess, tethered us back to the whale, and eventually returned our lights to us. Peter, with his usual presence of mind, jammed our cable in the cage door. This gave me better freedom of movement and I could hold the light much steadier. The light was so heavy and awkward and I needed both hands to keep it under control and to point it in the general direction Peter was filming. Even more difficult was to maneuver the lights into the correct position and hold them there. Mostly, I judged my direction by watching the side of the camera housing and endeavoring to keep my light coordinated with this.

It was during one of our more difficult moments that a 10-foot oceanic whitetip chose to entangle itself in the connections at the top of our cage. An exciting few moments followed as we were buffeted from side to side. Terrified by the unaccustomed restrictions, the shark struggled frantically until finally it thrashed its way free. Peter gave me a look that said, "What's next?" What came next was something completely unplanned.

Somehow, during the confusion, both cages had drifted close into the whale. Ribbons of mutilated intestine streamed through the cages as they clanged together right where the sharks had ripped open the whale's belly. Ron was struggling frantically to keep his cage free of the jawbone. I could hardly see him for blood and gore which turned the surrounding water into a sort of raw soup. Although I knew it was impossible, I felt I was smelling, breathing, and tasting the stuff. I don't know how we eventually left the whale, perhaps the surface crew towed us away, but it was so pleasant to be away from that torn smelly hulk, I felt almost happy.

Peter showed me his pressure gauge. It read 0. I still had 900 pounds left but that didn't help Peter much. Stan signaled from the other cage that his air was low also. Both he and Ron had shot a 400-foot roll of film. The zodiac picked them up first. As they left the water, the sharks, as though signaled, attacked the whale with, if possible, renewed fury. There is no doubt that they are far more active at night. Our cage, by now, was well away from the whale. In the darkness, I could hear the ship's engines coming closer. Suddenly, without warning, a tremendous shock vibrated the cage. We had drifted into the *Terrier*'s hull. God, do those cages take a hiding when alongside the rolling ship.

Peter handed out his camera and, although out of air, came down and made his "after you" sign. This, I felt, was extremely thoughtful, because if there is any difficulty in my getting through the top hatch, he is always on hand to give me a good push in the rear. This night, however, I didn't want to go. The zodiac was in an impossible position for me to reach and I hung grimly to the cage as it ground into the ship's hull. Eventually someone leaned down and dragged me back on deck, an exhausted, trembling wreck.

I heard how the cages had nearly been lost when cut adrift from the *Terrier*. Stewart's quick thinking had saved us. He had the captain maneuver the vessel into a position down current to pick us up. Without this quick thinking, we could possibly still be going.

I managed to snatch three hours' sleep. More than Peter and Stan had, I would say. Peter had obtained permission from the Durban-based whaling company to keep the whale for another twelve hours.

We were up at daybreak. For once, the weather was really with us. Nothing could have been kinder than the oily swell and clear skies. We were in the water by 8:30 A.M. The sharks were still there, all of them. By now, dozens of albatrosses had gathered on the scene, their round white chests and ungainly web feet making a comical contrast to the fat sleek sharks in our underwater world. I tried to touch an albatross on the foot, but he bent down and gave me such a nip I forgot the idea immediately. Ron, I noticed, tried the same thing and was nipped also. Almost as bad as the sharks, those birds; just as well they are not underwater swimmers.

We were now working completely out of the cages. Sharks bumped and jostled around us. Many were 10 to 12 feet in length and very fat. The blue sharks were even longer and by far the most beautiful with their slender blue bodies and big black eyes. I was feeling very tired but pushed and poked sharks to the best of my ability. Also, my right arm was beginning to ache from the constant jarring as I hit the sharks. An old skiing injury to the elbow didn't help much either.

Ron was testing the powerheads. We needed to know that they would work properly if there was an emergency. He hit several sharks without much result. The powerheads we have on this trip use a weaker cartridge than the ones we use in Australia. None of the sharks appeared to die. In fact they all kept swimming and feeding in fine style. Then Ron tried something else. Something he had often wondered about. Would it be possible to kill one with a knife?

I guess it's a question that all divers would like to know the answer to. Using the ship's grinder, Ron had a hollow razor-sharp double edge on his diver's knife. An 8- to 9-foot whitetip swam directly over Ron's head. Ron plunged in his knife up to the hilt. It slid down the throat between the pectoral fins and laid open the belly. His victim swam down into the vast blue nothing beneath us, leaving a trail of smoky green blood in its wake. Encouraged, Ron experimented further, having a stab at every shark unfortunate enough to swim within his reach. He soon discovered that even his super sharp knife would not penetrate the top of the shark's head at all or the back or any part other than the soft underbelly.

Around lunchtime, I went down in the cage with Peter Lake. Unknown to me, the tethering rope attaching us to the whale had chafed through and we did a dazzling descent to around 80 feet before I realized what had happened. I pulled down the air holder to stop our descent but nothing happened. The cylinder had exhausted its air supply. I became very frightened. There was a frantic turning on of air and switching around of dials which, thank heaven, caused us to rocket ahead of a massive stream of bubbles back to the surface. Peter Lake and I drifted along for a while, then someone noticed us and came in a zodiac to tow us back to the whale. What did my diving companions think of all this? Why, he simply thought I was giving him a bit of fun; he wasn't alarmed at any time though he did wonder why we went so deep. A perfect example of what you don't know doesn't worry you!

It was around 3:30 P.M. when we had our last and most spectacular dive. I arrived rather late on the scene, having had to change tanks after my dive with Peter Lake. Also, I took time off for rest and a coffee break. The whale was little more than a heap of torn, stinking flesh. The sharks, somehow sensing that soon the end would come, seemed to be making the most of what time was left. If possible, they attacked the whale with even greater vigor.

As I swam down, an incredible sight greeted my eyes. Peter Gimbel had, perhaps because it was the last chance, chosen now as the time to film his much-deserved close-ups of the sharks' teeth tearing into the whale. He was swimming up through the clouds of blood protected by Stan, who was fighting a terrific battle with his exhausted powerhead. Further down, Ron was sitting on top of a cage running off the last of his film. I moved in to help Stan, my weariness forgotten in the excitement. It looked like a suicide mission. Dozens of feeding sharks milled around us, diving into the whale, then swimming out again, huge lumps of oily flesh hanging from their maws, blood flowing from their gills.

Some hung on to the carcass, shuddering their way through flesh and sinew, tearing, gulping, swallowing in a continuous spasm of gluttony. Peter was filming about three or four feet from the heads of a group of feeding sharks. I whacked, hit, and thumped as hard and as fast as I could. A quick glance at Stan showed him to be doing the same. We formed a triangle with Peter facing the whale, Stan and myself facing outward. A shark banged me so hard on the shoulder I nearly dropped my powerhead. Peter filmed away calmly as though the sharks were toothless minnows, carefully lining up his shots to get the best action.

Another shark about 7 feet in length bumped me gently in the side. The first I knew of it was when it hit me. He actually mouthed my waist and a terrible tingle went over my body, but he apparently decided I was not what he wanted and moved on into the whale. At one stage, I rubbed against a feeding shark. Its vibrating body next to mine felt terrible, like some primitive shuddering monster in a nightmare. It was, I think, my only moment of fear during the entire time I was diving out from Durban in the Indian Ocean. Even then, I think it was less fear than revulsion.

Suddenly, for a moment, I realized how close I was to the bait, what was going on around me and how out of place I was. Peter Gimbel seemed to like it up there in the gore and blood, he took so darn long getting those last few close-ups.

Finally, he gave his little "film's out" sign. I took one last look. Sharks, hundreds of them, milled in the vicinity of the whale. Out and down as far as we could see their ominous shapes glided silently to and fro, already gorged to the hilt, but reluctant to leave the banquet. Ron swam up to join us. We entered our cages and ascended. Our trip back in time was over.

We reentered our present-day world, tired, hungry, cold, but elated. No one else in the world had done what we had done. Without the film, it would have been unbelievable. While unsuiting on board, Ron told a horrifying story. During the time Peter, Stan, and I were up with the whale, Ron was filming from the top of his cage when a large shark rammed him on the side of his head with its nose. The blow was so hard Ron went dizzy, saw stars, and fought to regain consciousness. Had he blacked out completely, he would have fallen off the cage and sunk into the depths without any of us being aware of what had happened. The water here is 2 miles deep. I would never have seen Ron again.

My arm ached from hitting sharks—in fact everything ached. It was a relief to get rid of the scuba tanks. Stan came up with a good theory as to why we were still alive. He reasoned, and very well, too, that the sharks, after realizing we were not easy prey although still curious, came to accept us just as some more marine creatures that had come to the feast. There were albatross, rainbow runners, kingfish, and three species of shark, so why not humans? Certainly, there was enough whale for everyone.

I crashed into bed, an exhausted mess, immediately following dinner—only sleep eluded me. Every time I closed my eyes and even when they were open, all I could see were sharks swimming toward me, around me, nuzzling me and, in my mind, I wearily beat them off. At 9:30, I was still, in my mind, fighting a thousand sharks. They plagued me, gave me no rest. Ron was tossing around, too, as though he had a shark in bed with him. I called, "What are you doing?" and he said, "Fighting sharks." We both took tranquilizers and finally slept.

3

From *Jaws*

PETER BENCHLEY

Peter Benchley's best seller *Jaws* needs little introduction. The excerpt chosen takes place shortly after the shark hunt begins. Anyone who has ever sat in a dirty little fishing boat, surrounded by burley, waiting for a shark could not help but be touched by the truth and power of Benchley's descriptions.

Reading it, I heard the sounds and smelled the smells, for this segment is true to life. It really is like this. He describes to perfection a situation that Ron and I have experienced many times.

The shark is there and the waiting men know it, but they are powerless. They must wait on the shark; he, not they, controls the situation.

Be it the first time or the thirtieth, it is always the same when you see the great white shark approaching the cage. Hooper staring enthralled, impelled to flee but unable to move, captures the feeling perfectly.

I am amazed how clearly Benchley has reproduced my exact feelings and given them to a fictitious man in a fictitious situation. Of course, our sharks have always been repelled by the cage within which we work. Even the largest of them dislikes the feel of metal against teeth.

Benchley makes his fish completely believable, then gives it a brain which can think to plan the destruction of three men. No wonder that this shark

24

inflamed the imagination of so many people, causing the beaches to be deserted and thousands of sharks to be slaughtered in a frenzy of mass hatred.

The general public believed all sharks could think and act according to a plan and they became afraid. I believe that this is part of the key to the success of *Jaws* and the fascination it has for the general public.

●

At eleven-thirty, Brody was startled by a sharp resonant *snap*. Quint leaped down the ladder, across the deck, and on to the transom. He picked up the harpoon and held it at his shoulder, scanning the water around the stern.

"What the hell was that?" said Brody.

"He's back."

"How do you know? What was that noise?"

"Twine snapping. He took one of the squid."

"Why would it snap? Why wouldn't he chew right through it?"

"He probably never bit down on it. He sucked it in, and the twine came tight behind his teeth when he closed his mouth. He went like this, I imagine"—Quint jerked his head to the side—"and the line parted."

"How could we hear it snap if it snapped under water?"

"It didn't snap under water, for Christ sake! It snapped right there." Quint pointed to a few inches of limp twine hanging from a cleat amidships.

"Oh," said Brody. As he looked at the remnant, he saw another piece of twine—a few feet farther up the gunwale—go limp. "There's another one," he said. He stood and walked to the gunwale and pulled in the line. "He must be right underneath us."

Quint said, "Anybody care to go swimming?"

"Let's put the cage overboard," said Hooper.

"You're kidding," said Brody.

"No, I'm not. It might bring him out."

"With you in it?"

"Not at first. Let's see what he does. What do you say, Quint?"

"Might as well," said Quint. "Can't hurt just to put it in the water, and you paid for it." He put down the harpoon, and he and Hooper walked to the cage.

They tipped the cage on to its side, and Hooper opened the top hatch and crawled through it. He removed the scuba tank, regulator, face mask, and neoprene wet suit, and set them on the deck. They tipped the cage upright again and slid it across the deck to the starboard gunwale. "You got a couple of lines?" said Hooper. "I want to make it fast to the boat." Quint went below and returned with two coils of rope. They tied one to an after cleat, one to a cleat amidships, then secured the ends to the bars on top of the cage. "Okay," said Hooper. "Let's put her over." They lifted the cage, tipped it backward, and pushed it overboard. It sank until the ropes stopped it, a few feet beneath the surface. There it rested, rising and falling slowly in the swells. The three men stood at the gunwale, looking into the water.

"What makes you think this'll bring him up?" said Brody.

"I didn't say 'up,'" said Hooper, "I said 'out.' I think he'll come out and have a look at it, to see whether he wants to eat it."

"That won't do us any damn good," said Quint. "I can't stick him if he's twelve feet under water."

"Once he comes out," said Hooper, "maybe he'll come up. We're not having any luck with anything else."

But the fish did not come out. The cage lay quietly in the water, unmolested.

"There goes another squid," said Quint, pointing forward. "He's there, all right." He leaned overboard and shouted, "God damn you, fish! Come out where I can have a shot at you."

After fifteen minutes, Hooper said, "Oh well," and went below. He reappeared moments later, carrying a movie camera in a waterproof housing, and what looked to Brody like a walking stick with a thong at one end.

"What are you doing?" Brody said.

"I'm going down there. Maybe that'll bring him out."

"You're out of your goddamn mind. What are you going to do if he does come out?"

"First, I'm going to take some pictures of him. Then I'm going to try to kill him."

"With what, may I ask?"

"This." Hooper held up the stick.

"Good thinking," Quint said with a derisive cackle. "If that doesn't work you can tickle him to death."

"What is that?" said Brody.

"Some people call it a bang stick. Others call it a power head. Anyway, it's basically an underwater gun." He pulled both ends of the stick, and it came apart in two pieces. "In here," he said, pointing to a chamber at the point where the stick had come apart, "you put a twelve-gauge shotgun shell." He took a shotgun shell from his pocket and pushed it into the chamber, then rejoined the two ends of the stick. "Then, when you get close enough to the fish, you jab it at him and the shell goes off. If you hit him right —in the brain's the only sure place—you kill him."

"Even a fish that big?"

"I think so. If I hit him right."

"And if you don't? Suppose you miss by just a hair."

"That's what I'm afraid of."

"I would be, too," said Quint. "I don't think I'd like five thousand pounds of pissed-off dinosaur trying to eat me."

"That's not my worry," said Hooper. "What concerns me is that if I miss, I might drive him off. He'd probably sound, and we'd never know if he died or not."

"Until he ate someone else," said Brody.

"That's right."

"You're fucking crazy," said Quint.

"Am I, Quint? You're not having much success with this fish. We could stay here all month and let him eat your bait right out from under us."

"He'll come up," said Quint. "Mark my words."

"You'll be dead of old age before he comes up, Quint. I think this fish has you all shook. He's not playing by the rules."

Quint looked at Hooper and said evenly, "You telling me my business, boy?"

"No. But I am telling you I think this fish is more than you can handle."

"That's right, boy? You think you can do better'n Quint?"

"Call it that if you want. I think I can kill the fish."

"Fine and dandy. You're gonna get your chance."

Brody said, "Come on. We can't let him go in that thing."

"What are *you* bitchin' about?" said Quint. "From what I seen, you just as soon he went down there and never come up. At least that'd stop him from—"

"Shut your mouth!" Brody's emotions were jumbled. Part of him didn't care whether Hooper lived or died—might even relish the prospect of Hooper's death. But such vengeance would be hollow—and quite possibly, unmerited. Could he really wish a man dead? No. Not yet.

"Go on," Quint said to Hooper. "Get in that thing."

"Right away." Hooper removed his shirt, sneakers, and trousers, and began to pull the neoprene suit over his legs. "When I'm inside," he said, forcing his arms into the rubber sleeves of the jacket, "stand up here and keep an eye. Maybe you can use the rifle if he gets close enough to the surface." He looked at Quint. "You can be ready with the harpoon . . . if you want to."

"I'll do what I'll do," said Quint. "You worry about yourself."

When he was dressed, Hooper fitted the regulator on to the neck of the air tank, tightened the wing nut that held it in place, and opened the air valve. He sucked two breaths from the tank to make sure it was feeding air. "Help me put this on, will you?" he said to Brody.

Brody lifted the tank and held it while Hooper slipped his arms through the straps and fastened a third strap around his middle. He put the face mask on his head. "I should have brought weights," said Hooper.

Quint said, "You should have brought brains."

Hooper put his right wrist through the thong at the end of the power head, picked up the camera with his right hand, and said, "Okay." He walked to the gunwale. "If you'll each take a rope and pull, that'll bring the cage to the surface. Then I'll open the hatch and go in through the top, and you can let the ropes go. It'll hang by the ropes. I won't use the flotation tanks unless one of the ropes breaks."

"Or gets chewed through," said Quint.

Hooper looked at Quint and smiled. "Thanks for the thought."

Quint and Brody pulled on the ropes, and the cage rose in the water. When the hatch broke the surface, Hooper said, "Okay, right there." He spat in the face mask, rubbed the saliva around on the glass, and fitted the mask over his face. He reached for the regulator tube, put the mouthpiece in his mouth, and took a breath. Then he bent over the gunwale, unlatched the top of the hatch and flipped it open. He started to put a knee on the gunwale, but stopped. He took the mouthpiece out of his mouth and said, "I forgot something." His nose was enclosed in the mask, so his voice sounded thick and nasal. He walked across the deck and picked up his trousers. He rummaged through the pockets until he found what he was looking for. He unzipped his wet-suit jacket.

"What's that?" said Brody.

Hooper held up a shark's tooth, rimmed in silver. It was a duplicate of the one he had given to Ellen. He dropped it inside his wetsuit and zipped up the jacket. "Can't be too careful," he said, smiling. He crossed the deck again, put his mouthpiece in his mouth, and kneeled on the gunwale. He took a final breath and dived overboard through the open hatch. Brody watched him go, wondering if he really wanted to know the truth about Hooper and Ellen.

Hooper stopped himself before he hit the bottom

of the cage. He curled around and stood up. He reached out to the top of the hatch and pulled it closed. Then he looked up at Brody, put the thumb and index finger of his left hand together in the okay sign, and ducked down.

"I guess we can let go," said Brody. They released the ropes and let the cage descend until the hatch was about four feet beneath the surface.

"Get the rifle," said Quint. "It's on the rack below. It's all loaded." He climbed on to the transom and lifted the harpoon to his shoulder.

Brody went below, found the rifle, and hurried back on deck. He opened the breach and slid a cartridge into the chamber. "How much air does he have?" he said.

"I don't know," said Quint. "However much he has, I doubt he'll live to breathe it."

"Maybe you're right. But you said yourself you never know what these fish will do."

"Yeah, but this is different. This is like putting your hands in a fire and hoping you won't get burned. A sensible man don't *do* it."

Below, Hooper waited until the bubbly froth of his descent had dissipated. There was water in his mask, so he tilted his head backward, pressed on the top of the faceplate, and blew through his nose until the mask was clear. He felt serene. It was the pervasive sense of freedom and ease that he always felt when he dived. He was alone in blue silence speckled with shafts of sunlight that danced through the water. The only sounds were those he made breathing—a deep, hollow noise as he breathed in, a soft thudding of bubbles as he exhaled. He held his breath, and the silence was complete. Without weights, he was too buoyant, and he had to hold on to the bars to keep his tank from clanging against the hatch overhead. He turned around and looked up at the hull of the boat, a gray body that sat above him, bouncing slowly. At first, the cage annoyed him. It confined him, restricted him, prevented him from enjoying the grace of underwater movement. But then he remembered why he was there, and he was grateful.

He looked for the fish. He knew it couldn't be sitting beneath the boat, as Quint had thought. It could not "sit" anywhere, could not rest or stay still. It had to move to survive.

Even with the bright sunlight, the visibility in the murky water was poor—no more than forty feet. Hooper turned slowly around, trying to pierce the edge of gloom and grasp any sliver of color or movement. He looked beneath the boat, where the water turned from blue to gray to black. Nothing. He looked at his watch, calculating that if he controlled his breathing, he could stay down for at least half an hour more.

Carried by the tide, one of the small white squid slipped between the bars of the cage and, tethered by twine, fluttered in Hooper's face. He pushed it out of the cage.

He glanced downward, started to look away, then snapped his eyes down again. Rising at him from the darkling blue—slowly, smoothly—was the shark. It rose with no apparent effort, an angel of death gliding towards an appointment foreordained.

Hooper stared, enthralled, impelled to flee but unable to move. As the fish drew nearer, he marveled at its colors: the flat brown-grays seen on the surface had vanished. The top of the immense body was a hard ferrous gray, bluish where dappled with streaks of sun. Beneath the lateral line, all was creamy, ghostly, white.

Hooper wanted to raise his camera, but his arm would not obey. In a minute, he said to himself, in a minute.

The fish came closer, silent as a shadow. And Hooper drew back. The head was only a few feet from the cage when the fish turned and began to pass before Hooper's eyes—casually, as if in proud display of its incalculable mass and power. The snout passed first, then the jaw, slack and smiling, armed with row upon row of serrate triangles. And then the black, fathomless eye seemingly riveted upon him. The gills rippled—bloodless wounds in the steely skin.

Tentatively, Hooper stuck a hand through the bars and touched the flank. It felt cold and hard, not clammy but smooth as vinyl. He let his finger tips caress the flesh—past the pectoral fins, the pelvic fin, the thick, firm genital claspers—until finally (the fish seemed to have no end) they were slapped away by the sweeping tail.

The fish continued to move away from the cage. Hooper heard faint popping noises, and he saw three straight spirals of angry bubbles speed from the surface, then slow and stop, well above the fish. Bullets. Not yet, he told himself. One more pass for pictures. The fish began to turn, banking, the rubbery pectoral fins changing pitch.

"What the hell is he doing down there?" said Brody. "Why didn't he jab him with the gun?"

Quint didn't answer. He stood on the transom, harpoon clutched in his fist, peering into the water. "Come up, fish," he said. "Come to Quint."

"Do you see it?" said Brody. "What's it doing?"

"Nothing. Not yet anyway."

The fish had moved off to the limit of Hooper's vision—a spectral silver-gray blur tracing a slow circle. Hooper raised his camera and pressed the trigger. He knew the film would be worthless unless the fish moved in once more, but he wanted to catch the beast as it emerged from the darkness.

Through the viewfinder he saw the fish turn towards him. It moved fast, tail thrusting vigorously, mouth opening and closing as if gasping for breath. Hooper raised his right hand to change the focus. Remember to change it again, he told himself, when it turns.

But the fish did not turn. A shiver traveled the length of its body as it closed in on the cage. It struck the cage head on, the snout ramming between two bars and spreading them. The snout hit Hooper in the chest and knocked him backward. The camera flew from his hands, and the mouthpiece shot from his mouth. The fish turned on its side, and the pounding tail forced the great body farther into the cage. Hooper groped for his mouthpiece but couldn't find it. His chest was convulsed with the need for air.

"It's attacking!" screamed Brody. He grabbed one of the tether ropes and pulled, desperately trying to raise the cage.

"God damn your fucking soul!" Quint shouted.

"Throw it! Throw it!"

"I can't throw it! I gotta get him on the surface! Come up, you devil! You prick!"

The fish slid backward out of the cage and turned sharply to the right in a tight circle. Hooper reached behind his head, found the regulator tube, and followed it with his hand until he located the mouthpiece. He put it in his mouth and, forgetting to exhale first, sucked for air. He got water, and he gagged and choked until at last the mouthpiece cleared and he drew an agonized breath. It was then that he saw the wide gap in the bars and saw the giant head lunging through it. He raised his hands above his head, grasping at the escape hatch.

The fish rammed through the space between the bars, spreading them still farther with each thrust of its tail, Hooper, flattened against the back of the cage, saw the mouth reaching, straining for him. He remembered the power head, and he tried to lower his right arm and grab it. The fish thrust again, and Hooper saw with the terror of doom that the mouth was going to reach him.

The jaws closed around his torso. Hooper felt a terrible pressure as if his guts were compacted. He jabbed his fist into the black eye. The fish bit down, and the last thing Hooper saw before he died was the eye gazing at him through a cloud of his own blood.

"He's got him!" cried Brody. "Do something!"

"The man is dead," Quint said.

"How do you know? We may be able to save him."

"He is dead."

Holding Hooper in its mouth, the fish backed out of the cage, sank a few feet, chewing, swallowing the viscera that were squeezed into its gullet. Then it shuddered and thrust forward with its tail, driving itself and prey upward in the water.

"He's coming up!" said Brody.

"Grab the rifle!" Quint cocked his hand for the throw.

The fish broke water fifteen feet from the boat, surging upward in a shower of spray. Hooper's body protruded from each side of the mouth, head and arms hanging limply down one side, knees, calves, and feet from the other.

In the few seconds while the fish was clear of the water, Brody thought he saw Hooper's glazed dead eyes staring open through his face mask. As if in contempt and triumph, the fish hung suspended for an instant, challenging mortal vengeance.

Simultaneously, Brody reached for the rifle and Quint cast the harpoon. The target was huge, a field of white belly, and the distance was not too great for a successful throw above water. But as Quint threw, the fish began to slide down in the water, and the iron went high.

For another instant, the fish remained on the surface, its head out of water. Hooper hanging from its mouth.

"Shoot!" Quint yelled. "For Christ's sake, shoot!"

Brody shot without aiming. The first two shots hit the water in front of the fish. The third, to Brody's horror, struck Hooper in the neck.

"Here, give me the goddamn thing!" said Quint, grabbing the rifle from Brody. In a single, quick motion he raised the rifle to his shoulder and squeezed off two shots. But the fish, with a last, vacant gaze, had already begun to slip beneath the surface. The bullets plopped harmlessly into the swirl where the head had been.

The fish might never have been there. There was no noise, save the whisper of a breeze. From the surface the cage seemed undamaged. The water was calm. The only difference was that Hooper was gone.

"What do we do now?" said Brody. "What in the name of God can we do now? There's nothing left. We might as well go back."

"We'll go back," said Quint. "For now."

"For now? What do you mean? There's nothing we can do. The fish is too much for us. It's not real, not natural."

"Are you beaten, man?"

"I'm beaten. All we can do is wait until God or nature or whatever the hell is doing this to us decides we've had enough. It's out of man's hands."

"Not mine," said Quint. "I am going to kill that thing."

"I'm not sure I can get any more money after what happened today."

"Keep your money. This is no longer a matter of money."

"What do you mean?" Brody looked at Quint, who was standing at the stern, looking at the spot where the fish's head had been, as if he expected it to reappear at any moment clutching the shredded corpse in its mouth. He searched the sea, craving another confrontation.

Quint said to Brody, "I am going to kill that fish. Come if you want. Stay home if you want. But I am going to kill that fish."

As Quint spoke, Brody looked into his eyes. They seemed as dark and bottomless as the eye of the fish. "I'll come," said Brody. "I don't guess I have any choice."

"No," said Quint. "We have no choice." He took his knife from its sheath and handed it to Brody. "Here. Cut that cage loose and let's get out of here."

4

The Filming for *Jaws*

VALERIE TAYLOR

This story is taken straight from my diary. If differs considerably from the picture that Carl Gottlieb paints in *The Jaws Log*. He was at a disadvantage, having to rely on information acquired long after we had finished the live shark shooting.

I wrote every day, sometimes twice a day, about what actually happened. This story is not complete. I stuck to the main points, leaving out the small everyday happenings. It tells without alteration or glamorization how we went about filming the great white shark and how some of the difficult scenes of the sharks attacking the cage were obtained.

When we were shooting the live shark footage, none of us had any idea that the film would be such a tremendous success. To Ron and me it was just another filming job, our eighth at that time, involving great white sharks.

It was the first time that Ron had to work to a script. Fortunately it was not the final script, so there was some leeway with the action.

For editing purposes, a series of shots showing the shark swimming toward and away from the camera was required. Cage bars were not to be shown. This meant that to film these sequences, Ron had to work out of the cage.

Working outside of the cage is not as dangerous as it sounds. Ron always stays next to the door, so, if need be, he can slip inside in a few seconds. It becomes more dangerous when there are two or more sharks circling because only one can be watched at a time, but Ron believes taking the occasional risk to be part of his job, and he is always very careful.

Even so, during the *Jaws* filming, Ron miscalculated and actually pushed himself away from a shark by ramming his camera against its mouth. It was one of the two dangerous incidents that occurred. The other is described in detail here.

●

A ribbon of harsh granite boulders break the ocean's surface about 14 miles off the South Australian coast. Over a hundred years ago, explorer Captain Matthew Flinders first observed these bleak, spray-washed outcrops.

Flinders considered the area a hazard to future shipping and as a warning to all who dared venture forth upon the southern ocean, he named the place Dangerous Reef.

Today, this name means more than just a hazard to shipping. It is a warning to all. Inhabiting the cold, gray waters surrounding Dangerous Reef, *Carcharodon carcharias,* the great white shark, hunts his prey. An attacker of all who dare cross his path, this giant survivor from a bygone age has become to man the epitome of terror in the sea.

Over the last ten years, my husband, an underwater cameraman, has hunted the white shark with his camera, capturing on film the most dramatic and exciting scenes of shark behavior ever recorded. Ron does not consider the shark an indiscriminate killer, but a poor dumb brute goaded by an unsatiable appetite into awe-inspiring eating feats.

The great white is nature's garbage man: efficient, inexpensive, and nonpolluting. His job is to keep the oceans free from large masses of garbage; be it a dead whale or a cardboard box, the great white devours all, leaving the oceans cleaner with his passing. Man, with all his knowledge, could never do the job as well.

Early in 1974, Ron and I started preparing to film white sharks once again. The Zanuck-Brown company planned to produce a film version of Peter Benchley's best-selling novel *Jaws* for Universal Studios.

Zanuck-Brown were going all out to make the shark a living, thinking star attraction. Ron was to shoot real whites in their natural element for intercutting with a man-made mechanical giant.

Smaller cages were especially constructed. A former American jockey, Carl Rizzo, was to be sent across as a stuntman and Carl was to double for the full-size actor, who would be working with the main production crew in the United States.

The villain of *Jaws* is a 26-foot white shark and this is not as outlandish as it sounds. The largest white shark ever seen was taken in South Australia, and supposedly measured over 36 feet. Twenty-foot great whites are uncommon, but still seen off the South Australian coast.

Big-game fishermen have not landed any white sharks larger than 18 feet. They have been hooked over 20 feet in length, but a shark that size is so strong and heavy, the game fisherman would need a crane to winch it in. The shark portrayed so realistically by Mr. Benchley in *Jaws* could easily be a true animal. There is certainly no proof to the contrary.

Ron and I arrived in Port Lincoln, South Australia, on February 12, 1974. Our good friend Rodney Fox had everything organized for the filming expedition. He had bought a sick horse from a farmer; it was slaughtered and the carcass prepared for use as shark baits. He had also ordered six bins of minced tuna heads, which we would use to try and burley in the shark.

The 35-foot *Trade Wind* had been chartered for several weeks, and Dick Leach was our skipper. We like working with Dick; he is cheerful, hard-talking, and a fine seaman.

The Americans arrived in Port Lincoln on the thirteenth. Jim Hogan, our production manager, had been rushed across as a replacement for his contemporary,

Frank Arrigo, who had suffered an unexpected heart attack shortly after arriving in Sydney.

With Jim was little Carl Rizzo. At first, I found Carl shy and hard to communicate with. He had been a good jockey and now trained racehorses. Sometimes he doubled for children on horseback in feature films, which was how he became a stuntman.

Carl had been sent to double under water for the main actors. He had never been scuba diving in the ocean—his entire experience consisted of a couple of brief lessons in an enclosed pool. Hollywood had sent him to us, this gentle little man, and we were supposed to bundle him into a cage, tie baits to the bars, lower the cage into the icy turbulent southern ocean and then wait for the sharks to attack. I guess that is the sort of stuff Hollywood lives on, but to us, who knew sharks and the ocean so well, it all seemed incredible.

On the sixteenth, we were finally ready to leave. There had been a holdup in the arrival of the American cages, which had delayed us two days. We left the Port Lincoln wharf by midday, Rodney leading the way in his 19-foot fiberglass abalone boat, *Skippy*. It was a pleasant trip to Dangerous Reef. The sun shone and a brisk southeasterly wind whipped the southern ocean into a living carpet of white and blue.

The lee at Dangerous Reef was hardly a lee at all. A sloppy swell was running as usual around the point and made the *Trade Wind* toss in an annoying fashion. Dick anchored in 37 feet of water. The chum buckets were lowered and a dozen bloody baits strung in an appetizing fashion along the hull. It was an uncomfortable anchorage, but we had no choice and settled down to wait.

On the reef itself hundreds of Australian sea lions could be seen. Many had little dark brown babies, newly born. These sea lion pups are a favorite source of food for the white pointer. They are not born swimmers and have to be taught by their mothers. During the learning-to-swim period, the little pups are extremely vulnerable. Nature's culler, the great white shark, patrols the breeding colonies, ever ready to strike down the weak, the slow, or the unwary.

Early on the seventeenth, our first white shark moved up the burley slick. Ron loaded his 35-mm Camaflex. The cage was rolled over the stern and Ron, sleek as a seal in his black wetsuit, climbed down onto the duckboard. The shark was a good one, 13 feet long and unafraid. He came straight in to feed. The script calls for him to be scarred around the nose, so while he was busy chewing the prop, Rodney, using my lipstick, reached down and painted on a few scars. Ron shot 400 feet of film, then changed cameras.

Next, I went down in the cage, dressed like the scientist in the film, and Ron did a roll of over-the-shoulder shots. The rough surface conditions made everything very difficult. By the time my tank had run dry, I was bitterly cold and rather battered. It was hard work in the cage. The surge tossed it around in a most aggravating fashion, making it impossible for steady photography. Around midafternoon, the shark became bored with us and left.

The following day was marred by a steady drizzle. However, to everyone's great joy, a new shark came in and we began to tease him with the baits. Ron immediately went down in the cage. The shark action was not good, but at least it stayed around, swimming in a slow smooth pattern, back and forth, back and forth.

The *Trade Wind* pitched like a mad thing; the wind blew like ice from the South Pole. My nose told me the baits were beginning to ripen rather well. Only the shark seemed unaffected by the weather and the rolling boat. Ron decided he wanted Carl down in his smaller cage. Getting Carl ready was difficult. He was not used to the movement of the boat. It was Rodney's job to get Carl in and out of his cage, which, for the purpose of the film, was attached to the abalone winch on Rod's boat. I felt from the start that Carl, a rank beginner, could never handle the rough conditions, but he was being paid to try and try he did.

Dick and Rodney lowered Carl into the small cage,

but no sooner had he disappeared under the surface, they had to pull him back because water had entered his mouthpiece. Three times Carl tried to go down in his cage, without success. The water was just too rough for a beginner. Finally Ron abandoned the idea—he would have to wait for calmer conditions.

One week and not much luck later, on February 26, we were anchored again, in the same position. The sea lions watched our arrival with the look of someone who had seen it all before. Weather conditions were still not good at Dangerous Reef, but at least it was sunny.

While the men were eating lunch, I wandered out onto the deck and started throwing minced tuna into the water. After about ten minutes, a 13-foot shark appeared just under the surface and started cutting to and fro through the burley. I called, "Shark," and threw some blood in his path.

Rodney leaped up from the table, followed by everyone else, but in his great hurry to see the shark, his finger somehow became jammed behind the cabin's narrow sliding door. No one could squeeze past, and Rodney could not free his finger. I looked back to see Rodney blocking the door with his body and yelling a few choice words. I thought some great catastrophe was about to happen, but at that moment Rod's finger came free and the men spilled out onto the deck.

Everyone immediately leaped into action, lunch forgotten. Here is what I wrote in my diary at the time.

"The big shark liked blood. He moved closer. Tasting the water. More minced tuna was thrown in and Ron's cage lowered. Carl's smaller but much heavier and stronger cage was manhandled into position next to Rodney's boat. It was held in place by a hand-operated abalone winch. Carl was suited up and helped into his cage. Conditions were calmer now than they had been for weeks. The shark seemed afraid of the divers. He was approaching no closer to the cages than 8 feet. From the deck we could see the brute circling around. It is terribly frustrating to be down in the cage watching and waiting, every nerve concentrating on the shark, wondering from what direction he will come, then having him pass swiftly as a swallow, too far away for decent photography. On deck we can see the shark long before Ron. I tried to will him closer to the cages. I think we all did, but the beast paid no heed to our silent thoughts and kept his distance. He was tied to us by his instinct to feed, by our trails of blood and horsemeat baits, yet he hesitated in his approach until, finally, Ron, frustrated, surfaced and climbed back on board. Carl was also brought to the surface. He had managed very well, only the shark had performed poorly. Ron and Carl had been on deck a few minutes, when a new shark appeared. He came straight and strong, fearing nothing. This was the type of shark we had been waiting for. A shark who moved, thought, and behaved like the fish Peter Benchley had written about so convincingly in his book.

"Ron's cage bounced as the fish attacked the flotation tanks. Immediately Ron put on a fresh scuba tank, asking Carl to do the same.

"The shark circled closer. We could all see Ron, six feet down, sitting on top of his cage filming, a rather risky method he had been using for some time in an effort to get shots without bars in the foreground. I was frantic that he should take such a chance. By now, there were three sharks around. Ron couldn't look everywhere at once. He was gambling on the other sharks remaining cautious while he concentrated on filming the more aggressive newcomer. Several times, watching from the deck, we saw Ron push the shark in the mouth with his camera.

"I loaded a .303 army bullet into the powerhead on my speargun and placed it within easy reach. Then I told Greg Dean, the assistant, if there was any trouble, I would jump in with the gun and that I expected him to help me in the water. Greg said, 'Sure,' and he meant it, too.

"Later Ron explained how his scuba harness had become hooked in the wire mesh, stopping him from moving inside the cage when the shark attacked. Not used to aggression, particularly in the form of a cold, hard camera housing, the white gave way and, no doubt, pondered this strange series of events before instinct forced him to try again.

"Eventually, Carl was ready to dive. Dick helped him into Rodney's 19-foot runabout, *Skippy*. Rodney was busy adjusting Carl's mouthpiece when our new shark swam around *Skippy*'s stern. The beast cut close to the hull, bumping the steel ropes attaching Carl's cage to the winch. Feeling the unfamiliar metal cable against his nose, the shark lunged blindly forward, pushing his great pointed snout further between the cables. Water flew. The *Skippy* rolled onto her side, dragged down by a half a ton of fighting fish. A huge head rose above the spray twisting and turning, black maw gaping in a frenzy of rage and pain. Triangular teeth splintered as they tore the restricting metal. The brute dove, his cycle tail whipping the air six feet above the surface.

"Carl stood frozen with shock. As Rodney pulled him back, the tail brushed Carl's face. Had Rodney been two seconds slower, the little stuntman would have been killed, his head crushed into pulp.

"Suddenly, I awoke from my spellbound trance and ran for the movie camera. Greg Dean grabbed his still camera. We both started shooting. Jim, who was holding an inch and three quarter sisal rope attached to *Skippy* had the thing snap in his hand, throwing him off-balance back into the burley drum. How Jim held against a pull so hard it could break a new 1,000-pound breaking strain rope I don't know and neither does he, but many unusual things happened in that short space of time. Under the strain, the winch began to bend. The great white shark's body crashed into the hull. The noise was incredible, splitting wood, thrashing water, cage against boat, shark against boat.

"Again and again the fish tried to dive, mindless of the havoc above, striving only for freedom in the cold dark depth below. Water was slopping over the deck. The winch bent further. There was a loud cracking. Suddenly, the *Skippy* sprang upright, minus her winch and part of the decking.

"A last mighty splash, then shark, cage, winch, and deck vanished in a boiling, foaming swirl. Had Carl been in the cage, he too would have vanished with no possible chance of survival.

"The *Skippy* sat quietly like a wounded bird. We also were silent, for there seemed little to say.

"Underwater from his cage, Ron had filmed the whole thing, starting when the shark swam around the motors. At first, Ron thought Carl must be in the cage. It wasn't until the shark, still entangled with the cage and winch, spun twisting in agony toward the ocean floor that he realized Carl must be safe.

"The writhing mess was headed straight for Ron, who had a few moments of real fear before the whole lot plowed into the bottom only feet away, stirring the sediment into a billowing mushroom of obliterating sand. Ron continued to film and captured the shark suddenly darting away from the turbulence. By a miracle, it had struggled free.

"Somehow Ron managed to retrieve the cage and winch, tying both onto his own cage, so all could be dragged back to the *Trade Wind*. He actually moved his cage along by putting his hand through the bars and pushing on the ocean floor. It was a slow and painful process. Two more sharks hovered like vultures, following Ron's every move. Whether just curious or waiting the chance to attack, Ron couldn't say, but they stayed close, forcing Ron to remain in the cage for twenty minutes until the whole lot was physically dragged aboard by the men."

Jim Hogan was as pleased as anything with the action. We played about a bit more with the sharks until it became too dark for good photography.

I cooked a big dinner, which was rather a celebration, then we headed back to port.

Jim left the following day with the film. He wanted it processed in Sydney, then sent to Universal in Los Angeles, so the director, Steve Spielberg, could see what had been shot up to date.

On the afternoon of March 5, we received word from Hollywood to try and shoot more shark footage.

As the cages had been repaired and Rodney's boat was seaworthy, the following morning we once again put to sea.

As we left we heard a report on the radio news that the abalone divers were complaining publicly about us burleying in sharks. An abalone diver had been attacked and killed in South Australia by a great white shortly before, and this, understandably made the other abalone divers very nervous. Frustrated by the bad weather and frightened by the recent shark attack, a small group of divers had, it seems, decided to blame us, at least in part, for their misfortunes.

We arrived at Dangerous Reef around midmorning. Four drums were evenly spaced in front of the area where we usually anchor. It appeared they had been set to catch sharks. One had a small, very dead bronze whaler still attached. The drums were only of 12-gallon capacity, far too light to seriously hold a white, but certainly capable of hooking one and hurting him enough to make him very annoyed. It was obvious that the abalone divers were out to give us trouble.

We received a radio message from Jim Hogan telling us to quietly pack and return to Port Lincoln. We dropped all our baits and headed back. Later, we read in the local paper that the abalone divers claimed to have scared us off and that, if we ever returned to film sharks, they would follow us around dropping baited hooks next to us, wherever we were trying to work.

On April 5, exactly fifteen days later, we were anchored at Dangerous Reef once again. Rodney had spoken to the abalone divers, explaining what we were trying to do. Provided we killed the white sharks after we filmed them, they promised to leave us in peace. We had no alternative but to agree to this request.

Three days and no sharks. Ron was becoming worried that he would not have any sharks to film, so we decided to make an all-out effort. The burley flow was doubled, producing an incredible feeding frenzy among the small fish around the stern. Dick and Rodney fished constantly, dragging in one quivering trevally after the other.

Still no sharks came, so we waited, watching the slick for the telltale sign of a fin breaking the surface. It seemed that now we were paying for our good luck and good sharks with no luck at all.

On the morning of April 12, Ron was up before daybreak, searching the slate gray water. No black fin cut the swell, all our baits hung untouched. We had sent an invitation across the ocean, our feast was waiting, we as hosts were waiting, but the guests declined to attend. The last of the minced tuna heads floated away. We could not go to find the shark, he had to come to us and, if he refused, we could do nothing about it.

By midmorning, we started to pack up the gear. Rodney cut the baits loose. I watched them sink slowly to the ocean floor, surrounded by a thousand small fish. The big fish we wanted so badly had not come; there was nothing else to be done. We headed home across the sunlit sea. Pacific gulls cried their farewells. They had fed magnificently on our baits and were sad to see us leave. The sea lions I love to watch played on. They cared nothing for us, our hopes, our failures.

There is a charisma about this cold lonely place, where the gentle sea lions live out their joyous lives and "the White Death" patrols the cold green depths.

II

ADVENTURE

●

Many of the excerpts I have chosen for this book are related to adventure in one form or the other. Several stories were written by people who seek adventure in its purest form. By this I mean they will deliberately organize or seek out the unusual or exciting for their own enjoyment rather than scientific gain, sport, or commercial enterprise.

Francois Poli writes about his Central American adventures as well as those of other people he met during his travels. You only have to read his book to realize that excitement was to him the sap of life.

On the other hand, the Americans who paid a lot of money to go down in cages to see white sharks were adventurers of a different kind. They did not seek out adventure themselves but paid to have someone else plan and organize it for them.

Ron and I have adventures nearly every time we go diving, and my two-year-old nephew had an adventure riding on a train for the first time. Everyone experiences adventure at some time, for the feeling of adventure is, for the most part, entirely in the mind. What one person takes for granted could be extremely exciting to another, so what adventure really means is hard to define.

However, the stories I have chosen are about adventure for adventure's sake, which is something few people know how to find in this busy, overcrowded world.

5

From *Sharks Are Caught at Night*

FRANCOIS POLI

It is an established fact that sharks can be found well into freshwater streams as much as 300 miles from the sea, but there is only one place where sharks are completely adapted to fresh water, Lake Nicaragua in Central America.

Without doubt, these sharks were once inhabitants of the salty oceans. Lake Nicaragua was at some time connected to the sea and sharks journeyed to the lake in search of food. Possibly because of a sudden change in the earth structure, the lake was cut off from the sea. Those sharks trapped in the lake gradually evolved into freshwater sharks as the composition of the water changed.

Poli's stories about the lake, its sharks, and the Indians who live along the shore are fascinating. That these sharks will attack and kill people is undisputed, but I am doubtful that a man without mask and fins, armed only with a knife, could successfully attack and kill a shark.

I know that it crops up time and time again in accounts of sharks ("A Passage of Islands" is another instance in this book), but a shark, particularly one of the Carcharinidae family—whaler, blue, bull shark—when endangered, would have so much strength and agility that no mere human armed with a knife could hold it.

It is also all but impossible to penetrate the hide

49

of a shark with a knife, except in the soft underbelly, and I doubt that a diver, without a mask, could see well enough to find this vulnerable area in the time the shark would allow him before it escaped.

Poli seems to lead an adventurous life. His book is fast-moving and exciting. He is a man who takes life in his stride and has the capacity to make people feel and see what he saw and felt, through his writing.

●

Throughout the trip the scene was always more or less the same: a collection of wooden cabins, a few cement buildings, women in brightly colored stuggs, and beyond the dwellings, an area—usually small—of cultivated fields. Surrounding all, the bush.

Seeing these villages cut off from the rest of the world, one might well wonder where the Indians got the banknotes with which they paid Alvarez for his merchandise. In fact, many of them went off every day to work in the mines or forests of the interior.

The lumbermen carted the logs to the shores of the lake, rolled them into the water, and lashed them together, and then convoyed the great rafts to San Carlos, poling themselves along like gondoliers.

One village we called at had been the scene of a grim drama about six months before. An Indian had rolled some logs into the water and was lashing them together when he lost his balance and fell in. A shark bit off his leg, and by the time the wretched man had been brought ashore, he had lost three-quarters of his blood. He died a few hours later, while the shark continued to hover near the scene. A second Indian dived, attacked the shark with a knife, and succeeded in killing it with only slight injury to himself.

"Then," said Alvarez, "they opened up the shark's stomach, took out the Indian's leg almost intact and buried it beside his body."

The village that marked the end of our trip was situated on a rocky slope a mile or two inland. When we tied up at the point nearest to it we had been away from San Carlos for rather more than five days, and most of our stock was still unsold.

We were to stay here three days, going back to sleep on board at night, except for the Nicaraguan, who always slept with the Indians. It was on one of these evenings that the ex-convict told me his real reason for staying in this part of the world. The afternoon had been spent in selling the last of the stock, and for the first time I had seen Alvarez paid not in cordobas but in gold. The old man who handed him the little transparent bag of nuggets was the chief of some thirty Indians who had settled at this point on the lake. This tribe did not live in wooden cabins but in huts built of stone and beaten earth, in which two large openings were made opposite each other, as is usual in the tropics, to create a permanent through-draft. The head man lived apart, in a most surprising house: a proper white villa, as out of place in this landscape as a radio-mast in a documentary film on the Stone Age.

Architect and masons had come from Managua to build it. Alvarez himself brought the somewhat scanty furniture from San Carlos, also the enormous electric fan that was installed in the middle of the largest room. As he was unable to bring electricity at the same time, a mechanic had to be fetched from Costa Rica to fix up a complicated arrangement of pulleys and gear-wheels by which the fan could be worked. During the hottest part of the day, young boys from the village took turns at sitting on the seat provided and pedaling diligently away on bicycle pedals to keep the fan moving.

All this represented a little mountain of nuggets. But nuggets were plentiful enough. One had only to look at the fabrics and jewelry with which the women were adorned to see that this village was very different from the rest.

These descendants of the Sumo Indians did not even till the soil. They had no scruples about fishing for shark—but why should they bother? Gold brought them everything they wanted.

It was about gold that Alvarez made up his mind to talk to me that evening. Was it because he had rather overdone the rum that afternoon, during his palaver with the Indians, or because he felt we knew each other well enough by now for him to speak more freely? As I listened to him I could hardly recognize the fat, placid man of the preceding days. His permanent smile had gone and there was a strange glow in his eyes.

From his place in the stern of the *Lucitron* he gazed intently at the shore, and with a movement of his hand he indicated the village, where one by one the lights were going out.

"Five years ago," he said, "those people were like the rest. No villa, no nuggets, nothing. Ragamuffins. Then they found gold. We don't know who discovered the mine; probably the old man. Since then they've all lived on it. Of course they haven't declared it—which proves two things: one, that they're not such fools as they look, since they know the government might cheat them, and two, that it must be very well camouflaged.

"People have tried to find it, naturally. They've come from San Carlos and Managua to explore the hills. The Indians let them do it every time. And every time the prospectors went away empty-handed. It might be different if the government interfered, but for the moment . . ."

He was silent. After a moment, hitting the edge of the boat gently with his open hand, he added:

"So that's how it is. I've decided not to leave the country until I've got my hands on that treasure. I don't know how I shall do it; I'm trying to work something out. If there is a way I shall find it."

When Alvarez lay down to sleep that night, my watch showed that it was after two o'clock. For two hours the ex-convict had sat in the same position, nervously clasping and unclasping his hands and smoking silently, his eyes riveted to the shore.

When I woke with the first rays of the sun he had been up for a long time and was talking to his assistant, who had just come aboard. It was time to leave for San Carlos.

For this strange convict-pedlar it was just the end of a trip; for me it was the end of my travels. The two Germans who had brought me to San Carlos must already be waiting to take me back to Managua, where I was to catch the plane for New York and Paris.

We had been traveling along our return route for some time when we came in sight of the cove: a sort of tiny fjord penetrating the land for about twenty yards or so. It was the *playa de los muertos,* the beach of the dead. The name dated from the time when the Indians of these parts, according to a now obsolete custom, threw their dead to the sharks. The water there was unexpectedly clear and very deep.

I was now to hear the last and most extraordinary shark-fishing story of my whole journey.

"Nobody knows just when it happened," said Alvarez.

"About thirty years ago, I believe. The chap who built this house was a Dutchman, and he came here for one thing: to catch sharks. But not ordinary sharks. He wanted the ones that fed on the corpses which the Indians threw into the water; they were thrown in wearing all their jewelry, so you can see why. As soon as the ceremony was over, the Dutchman cast his lines in order to recover the gold and emeralds from the sharks' stomachs. It was a mad idea, because, after all, there's more than one shark in the lake. All the same, they say he made a tremendous pile. Between burials he used to throw in the bodies of animals he killed in the mountains, hoping that the same sharks would come into the creek for this bait too. Then one day the Indians discovered what the fellow was up to ..."

Alvarez cast his eyes round the horizon and added:

"So then they set fire to the house. And cut the Dutchman's throat."

6

The Great White Shark Expedition

VALERIE TAYLOR

On February 5, 1976, a group of four American adventurers arrived at Port Lincoln, South Australia. These men had paid four thousand dollars a head, plus air fares, in the hope of seeing a great white shark in its natural element. Carl Roessler, from See and Sea Travel in San Francisco, had organized the trip.

Ron and I were there to shoot underwater film of the proceedings for a television station in Adelaide, South Australia. It seemed incredible that someone would pay to do what we were normally paid for, but I guess it just goes to prove what charisma these sharks have.

All of the visitors were divers and underwater cameramen. The operation plan was that they would sleep ashore coming via a fast boat to the chummed area every day. Ron and the diving boat's skipper, Dick Leach, and I stayed out on location, constantly keeping the chum flowing and, if they came, the sharks around.

It turned out to be a most successful trip, even by our standards. We had never had so many sharks, and such fine weather before. For everyone, the trip was a great success. The four divers were elated by the experience and went home very happy with their adventure.

The poor great whites did not fare so well. All the publicity given by the media to the expedition focused
54

the attention of shark hunters on the area. During the five months following, at least twelve great whites were caught because of the high price their teeth would bring. Twelve sharks is a lot to take from one area and it will be a long time before the great white sharks return to Dangerous Reef in anything like their former number.

It is interesting to note that this idea of taking paying tourists down in a cage was decided upon before the film *Jaws* brought white sharks to the attention of the general public.

I have chosen the first section from my diary covering the first sighting of a great white by the Americans and how they reacted.

A similar trip for the following year had to be canceled because of adverse publicity, an unfavorable reaction from the abalone divers, and, most of all, because of the lack of sharks.

After the See and Sea trip, Ron and I made two expeditions back to Dangerous Reef trying to film whites. Our success was limited and we finally had to finish the shooting in Western Australia.

•

February 3, 1976

Had dinner with the Americans last night. There are four of them—Carl Roessler, John Bell, Dr. Ted Roulison, and John Fudens.

They seem to be pleasant fellows. Ron and I are accompanying them on their venture. They have each paid See and Sea Travel four thousand dollars for the trip. This doesn't include their air fare from the United States to Australia. Someone must be going to do well out of it. One thing's for sure, it's not us.

We have to pay our own way down, but I, for one, wouldn't want to miss out. It's probably the first time anywhere in the world that tourists have paid for the chance of going down in a cage and seeing sharks swimming around.

The idea was born about one year ago when the head of Sea and See Travel, Dewey Bergman, was visiting Australia.

Dewey is an old friend. We were dining together when I mentioned that seeing white sharks from a cage could be an interesting tourist attraction. Dewey really sat up and took notice. Ron said we had a friend in South Australia who could arrange everything and so the idea was started.

Things have been moving toward a climax ever since. I wonder what they all think they are going to see. It really is incredible, four thousand dollars to look at a great white.

We are leaving Sydney for Port Lincoln the day after tomorrow.

February 6, 1976

Well, we made it. Boy! Those Americans sure hustle along. What a bunch of live wires. They all seem to be in a mild state of panic.

I have been asked at least ten times what I think the weather might do or if I think the sharks will be there. My guess is as good as theirs, but Ron and I haven't paid all those dollars to see a shark so I guess we can afford to be more relaxed.

There has been a fair amount of publicity given to this tour by both the press and television. Considering the problems we have had in the past with abalone divers, it doesn't seem wise, but it's not my trip so I can't say much. Guess I will just play it by ear and see what happens. Anyway the weather looks good so they could be in luck.

1:30 P.M.

Ron and I are on the *Trade Wind* once again. The Americans are on Bill Zealand's boat, *Temptation*. Bill is the same as ever, happy and quick off the mark. Actually his boat looks a bit crowded.

There are the four Americans; Rod Fox; Bill; his

deckhand, John; and three guys from Channel 10 who are going to shoot a documentary on the whole thing, from start to finish.

Dick, Ron, and I have our boat to ourselves. It was a rough trip out and the anchorage is very rolly.

The Americans are all waiting, cameras in hand, for "Whitey." They must expect him to rise from the sea and start performing, at any minute.

I wonder how long this enthusiasm is going to last.

I feel rotten. I got a bit seasick on the way out and it's sticking with me. The Americans had a practice at climbing in and out of the cages. They all seem in high spirits.

February 7, 1976 A.M.

The *Temptation* returned to Port Lincoln, leaving Dangerous Reef at 5:30 P.M.

Dick, Ron, and I are staying out here on the *Trade Wind* to keep the all important burley slick going.

Had a terrible night. The wind came from all directions. There was little sleep for any of us. Dick had to move the *Trade Wind* twice.

It looks a good morning though. Calmed right off. Boy! Those Americans are lucky. Our breakfast is coming on the *Temptation* so I am keeping one eye on the horizon.

7:30 P.M.

No sharks today. The Americans are becoming somewhat downcast.

Sometimes we have waited a week or more for a shark, a piece of information that did little to cheer our visitors up.

It's not an easy game. If it was, a lot more people would be doing it, but I feel a bit sorry for those Americans; they have come so far and spent a lot of money. The thought of failure must be like a nightmare to them.

February 8, 1976

A calm night was enjoyed by all, and we have just had an enormous breakfast. It's a beautiful still morning and I can see the *Temptation* fast approaching. Dick has just said, with some regret, "Our peace and tranquility is about to be shattered."

We are hoping for some fresh baits. There is the feeling of a shark around. It's about time, third day out and a good burley slick going day and night.

7:30 P.M.

Three sharks came. How lucky can you be! When the first one arrived, the excitement was electric.

All the Americans were shooting either movies or stills. Rod Fox was shooting stills. Bill Zealand and Dick Leach, our two skippers, were shooting stills. The Channel 10 boys were shooting movies. Ron and I were shooting movies.

That poor shark. He must have wondered what kind of creature this wall of black eyes looking at him belonged to. Every pass of the boat was heralded by the excited cries from the Americans and a dozen clicking cameras. Never was a shark so photographed.

His first confident approach became more hesitant when the cages were lowered. It was obvious all these objects in the water made him nervous. Undaunted, the Americans, with great excitement, suited up and prepared to dive.

Never have I met a group of guys who could ask so many questions. They wanted to know everything we had ever learned about whites and how to photograph them. Questions and answers were shouted back and forth.

The shark rammed into the far cage. Everyone yelled and cheered. From our boat, it looked chaotic and probably was. But the visitors were so happy it made us natives happy just watching them.

The water was red with chum as the divers entered the cages. By now a second shark had joined the first.

Both were circling. Each had taken a bait. I thought the Americans must be getting some good footage. Several times the sharks banged the cages spraying water over the people on the deck.

Ron was hanging off the duckboard filming as best he could. The Americans came up to reload their cameras. It was a joy to see how pleased they were. Every move and pass of the sharks was discussed and described.

By the time they went back, there were three sharks swimming around. It was getting late, for the sharks had not arrived until midday. Filmable light was dropping off rapidly. Still the Americans stayed down, squeezing every moment possible from the experience. The sun was sinking very low when they finally decided to call it a day.

"Did you think it was worth the money and effort?" I asked John Fudens.

"Without any doubt, without any doubt at all," he answered.

"I never dreamed a living creature could be so impressive," Dr. Ted just sort of stood there and said in his quiet way. "It was a great experience, I'll never forget it; those sharks are the most beautiful things I have ever seen."

7

From *Shark: Unpredictable Killer of the Sea*

Thomas Helm

Thomas Helm is one of those rare adventurers with the skill and discipline to put his experience into words. In *Shark: Unpredictable Killer of the Sea,* Helm tries to tell the complete story of a shark, giving its origin and history.

Dramatic accounts of shark attacks on man and even more dramatic accounts of man's attacks on sharks are recorded in Helm's racy style. The segment I have chosen deals mainly with man attacking sharks.

This in itself is not unusual. Man has attacked thousands more sharks than sharks have attacked man. What is unusual is the horrible crude ways Helm and the men he writes about thought up to destroy sharks.

I cannot feel anything but disgust for someone who would feed a perforated can of Drano to any living creature, be it shark or elephant. At least feeding the shark hand grenades brought about an unexpected (by the shark) but sudden death. The end of the story, where a loaded shark swam under their rubber raft, was a just, as well as humorous, finale to that adventure.

Helm wrote *Shark: Unpredictable Killer of the Sea* in 1961. I like to believe that the average saltwater fisherman does not dislike sharks today with the same intensity as he did seventeen years ago.

Whether you like sharks or not, Helm's book is full of interest and adventure and easy to read.

•

Shark fishing comes in for its share of rules, especially where game sharks are concerned. The average saltwater angler dislikes the whole shark clan with such intensity that he will go along with almost any method of fishing that succeeds in taking just that many more sharks out of the sea. I once knew some fishermen who evolved a novel and exciting way of catching sharks. They got several dozen of those heavy, five-gallon gasoline cans, called "Blitz cans," that were standard equipment on the tail end of World War II Jeeps. The fishermen painted the cans bright yellow and attached a long, heavy steel leader to each handle. On the other end of each leader was a powerful shark hook baited with dead sting rays, chunks of overaged beef, partly spoiled fish, or anything else available that would whet the appetite of a shark. When the tide began to ebb, the shark hunters carried the cans out to the pass and tossed them over the side. Then they chummed the water with several buckets of beef blood bought from a local slaughterhouse. If luck was on their side, which it usually was, one of the yellow cans would soon begin to bob up and down in the water; then it would skim along the surface while, undoubtedly, the shark that had taken the baited hook tried to figure out what was preventing him from swimming in his normal manner.

On a good day there would sometimes be as many as two dozen yellow cans skittering this way and that across the surface while fishermen tried to run them down in outboard-powered skiffs. When the men caught up with a can, the shark was hauled in and killed with either a club or shotgun. It was all great sport and everybody but the sharks enjoyed himself. This game might still be going on if a concerned Chamber of Commerce had not called in key mem-

bers of the group and requested that they find some
other form of piscatorial entertainment. The sight of
so many sharks being caught—and some of them
were man-eater size—so close to shore was having an
adverse effect on the summer vacationists, who came
from other states to enjoy a couple of weeks of swimming in the surf. The club reluctantly disbanded, and
I have often wondered what became of all those yellow Blitz cans. Of course, the idea was not original,
since Mississippi River folk have been "jugging" for
catfish in the same manner for years. In that area,
however, the floats are gallon jugs, the quarry is catfish, and tourists do not panic when they see a man
chase down a floating jug and pull in a harmless but
appetizing catch.

Izaak Walton leagues and other fishing clubs are
found all around the world. For the most part, these
clubs are for groups of fishermen who enjoy sitting
around a hot stove regaling one another with wild
tales of the monster musky, bass, trout, or sailfish
they once hooked. In recent years shark-fishing clubs
have started to organize; small in number, they are
dedicated strictly to the sport of catching sharks.

Such shark-fishing clubs are worldwide, with
branches springing up in Australia and Africa and
along the southern coasts of the United States. I am a
member of one organization, which is known as the
Palm Beach Sharkers. This club, founded in August
of 1959, is currently headed by tall, angular Morry
Vorenberg, who spends his daylight hours operating
his gift shop at the foot of the West Palm Beach Mu-
nicipal Pier. Once he closes the doors to his shop,
Vorenberg and his fellow Sharkers are almost certain
to be found near the end of the long pier, which
stretches out towards the Gulf Stream.

The club members limit the size of their tackle to
nothing larger than a 9/0 reel loaded with seventy-
two-pound test line, and as a rule the action is fast
and furious. Seldom does the club assemble for a bout
with sharks that real excitement does not develop.
There was the night when a large tiger shark had been

caught and was fought up to the pier. He was hit with a couple of well-placed slugs from a .45–.70 rifle, and then one of the members went down the side of the pier to slip a heavy rope noose around the "dead" shark's tail so that he could be hauled up and photographed.

The shark was roped all right, but suddenly he came back to life and clamped his jaws around the pier brace on which the roper was standing. In the confusion the man fell with a splash right beside the enraged fish. There was bedlam for the next few minutes. The fishermen on the pier began scrambling over the side to help their companion, but he was nowhere to be seen. Everybody was wielding a flashlight and yelling. When it seemed certain that the shark had taken his revenge by swallowing their fellow member, the men heard a shout some fifty yards back toward shore.

It was the fisherman. He had swum along underwater, weaving in and out of the pilings with the skill and speed of a porpoise, until his lungs had run out of air. When he came up for a breath, his hands closed on a timber and he hauled himself to safety. In the meantime, the rope tied onto the shark's tail had become tangled in the underpinnings of the pier, and when the excitement subsided, he was hauled up for observation and photographing. Everybody thought it was a good night's work—everybody, that is, except the roper. He cast a furtive glance at the shark's mouth, which resembled the open end of a tooth-studded barrel, and vowed that he would never again deliberately place himself in such close contact with an angry shark.

Sometimes the Palm Beach Sharkers come up with a real mystery. Morry Vorenberg once caught a hammerhead that measured nearly ten feet in length. As is the practice, he split it open to examine the stomach contents. Inside he found what appeared to be the intact pelvic bone of a human. Deciding that this was a matter for the police, he called in the local constabulary. At first there was excitement and interest from the police department, but this was followed by a news blackout. Vorenberg was never able to get any information about the mysterious bone; he never even knew whether the coroner had remanded it to pathological examination. The Sharkers are still scratching their heads over this one.

Not long ago the Palm Beach Sharkers almost demolished the fishing pier. If for nothing else, the story is worth recounting in order to demonstrate the power of a big shark when he gets excited. For several days a hammerhead, estimated to be no less than sixteen feet in length, had been cruising around the pier. Now and then he would pick up a fisherman's bait, but the instant he felt the hook he would take off for the Gulf Stream like a runaway submarine, snapping the line short when the reel was empty.

Out of sorts as a result of losing their expensive tackle, the Sharkers decided to forgo their regulations temporarily and catch the monster at all costs.

Accordingly, several hundred feet of new manila line measuring three-quarters of an inch in diameter was secured to an eight by eight-inch upright stanchion on the railing and a hand-forged shark hook nine and a half inches long and four inches across the bend was made fast to the line with a length of chain. The hook was baited with a large bonito and tossed out into the water. Almost immediately, the giant hammerhead came to the bait. As everybody waited expectantly, he engulfed it in his jaws and started to swim away. When the Sharkers felt the time was right, they grabbed the manila rope and set the hook with a vicious jerk.

For a moment the shark stood motionless in the clear green water; then he lunged ahead and the hard new line began hissing over the side. In a matter of seconds all of the slack was gone, and with a rending crack, some thirty feet of stout timber was torn from the pier railing. That was the last anyone saw of the huge hammerhead or the pier railing.

It is a marvelous experience to catch a big shark and fight him into submission, and those saltwater anglers who have not known this thrill have missed a lot in fishing. The Palm Beach Sharkers are several dozen men from many walks of life who have discovered that big fish and good companionship can be highly rewarding. They have found, too, that catching big-game fish from a pier is just as much fun as spending a hundred dollars per day for a charter boat that goes out to deep water.

Out in the Pacific, prior to World War II, military men often found themselves hard pressed for some form of entertainment. Those of us who had an abiding love for fishing were often the lucky ones if we were willing to exert ourselves. We could be sure of finding a little excitement if we picked up our heavy rods and went down to some palm-fringed cove and baited up for sharks. I caught so many in the years that I knocked around from one island to another that I gained some kind of reputation. I was forever coming back with a shark-fishing tale or the jaws from one of the big fish.

The zaniest shark-fishing escapade I ever became involved in started with two cases of overaged hand grenades, a hijacked side of beef, and a flight to Palmyra Island.

VP-12 was a PBY (Catalina Flying Boat) squadron operating out of Kanehoe Bay on the Island of Oahu. The skipper of the squadron was a grand old naval flight officer named Buckley, and he had a sort of magic touch with his mob of pilots, crew chiefs, and radiomen. He kept the men on their toes during working hours but allowed them free rein when they were off duty.

A few months prior to that infamous day of December 7, 1941, our squadron drew an assignment of flying torpedoes down to a submarine refueling base on Palmyra Island, which is one of the Line Islands, along with Christmas, Baker, and others. The 960-mile flight to the southwest was long and monotonous, and when we got there all we could do was sit around and play poker and wait for orders to return to base.

It was on one of these trips that a Marine sergeant, who was stationed at Palmyra, was told to dispose of two cases of hand grenades that had remained in storage longer than the naval ordnance manual recommended.

The sergeant would no doubt have loaded them into a skiff and carried them to deep water to be dumped had not one member of our crew asked to be allowed to throw a few of the grenades out into the lagoon just to see the explosions. The sergeant granted the permission, and before the third grenade was tossed we noticed several sharks cutting the surface with their dorsal fins as they scurried about picking up the stunned fish that had been upended by the blasts. From that point on, things moved ahead in a hurry. As well as torpedoes, we always brought to the Marine detachment some fresh beef and hams, recent movies, and cases of soft drinks, beer, and candy bars. On this trip one of the sides of beef somehow happened to get "mislaid," and the next morning the Marine sergeant and four of us from the squadron were out of bed, shaved, and well up the beach to a small lagoon by the time the bugler sounded reveille. With us went the "mislaid" side of beef, the two cases of grenades, and a seven-man rubber life raft "borrowed" from one of the PBYs.

Palmyra is the epitome of the average adventurer's dream of a real tropical paradise. Seen from the air, it resembles little more than a discarded shoestring cast out on the water. Seen from the ground, however, it is found to be a group of some fifty tiny islets, rectangular in shape, from east to west. Surrounding these palm-studded sand dunes, which are little better than six feet about high tide, is a barrier reef of coral. Palmyra is about five and a half miles long and little better than a mile wide. The largest islet covers no more than forty-six acres. Some of the smaller ones are just little mounds of coral sand with perhaps a palm tree growing in the middle.

The deep water in the lagoon was still and clear in the early morning light as we began to prepare for our bizarre fishing trip. While one of our group set about the task of inflating the raft and making it ready for sea, the rest of us busied ourselves unpacking the hand grenades and cutting the beef into chunks that would fit the hungry jaws of sharks. When everything was ready, we loaded our equipment on board, scrambled into the raft, and shoved off.

We started by throwing chunks of beef into the still lagoon as we paddled away from shore. Soon the sharks began to appear. Some were little five-footers but others were considerably larger. We teased them with small scraps and pieces of bone until there were several dozen sand and blue sharks milling around, making rushes for anything we threw in the water. A hand grenade was tied onto the next chunk of beef with a piece of string, and a length of strong fishing line was made fast to the ring. After heaving the offering well out to the side of the raft, we watched it sink slowly toward the sandy bottom. A shark spotted it, and a second later he had picked it up. Right then the string was pulled and the countdown was started: ". . . seven, six, five, four, three, two, one and *blammo!*"

One instant the shark was angling away with a big chunk of smelly beef in his gullet and the next he was without a head.

With diabolical enthusiasm we blew the heads off of shark after shark. Instead of catching on to our scheme, the remaining ones became more excited in their feeding. Some even began feasting on the decapitated members of their tribe. As long as the fishing line was attached to the ring on the grenade, we had some measure of control over where the explosion would take place; but in the excitement we began short-circuiting the procedure and pulling the pin an instant before the chunk of beef was tossed. The system worked fine for a while, but then the unexpected happened. Over the side went a chunk of beef with a live grenade attached. A passing shark engulfed it but, instead of swimming away, he drifted towards the raft, perhaps hopeful of picking up another handout.

"Get us away from him!" somebody yelled. "He's gonna explode right under us!"

The shark, oblivious to his impending doom, drifted closer and closer even though we dug the water furiously with the aluminum paddles. We counted off the seconds before he would explode . . . five, four, three, two, one! There it was! The shock wave hit the raft, flipped it over, and spilled us into the lagoon along with the chunks of bloody beef and unused hand grenades. All around us were dozens of hungry sharks. I shall never understand why, but nobody was hurt, and in less than two minutes we were scrambling up on to the sandy beach. We sat around and waited until the raft drifted ashore. When we had it deflated, we strolled back into the compound. The sergeant casually announced that the two cases of grenades had been disposed of according to orders.

California fishermen recently came up with an equally diabolical method of killing sharks. It is a well-known fact that a shark will swallow almost anything, and the fishermen found that a can of Drano was a particularly potent weapon. The method is simple and effective, if not very sporting. The can of Drano is punched full of holes and either stuffed inside the body cavity of a dead fish or tied to a chunk of spoiled meat. Once the sodium hydroxide (caustic soda lye) in the Drano begins to mix with the acid in the shark's stomach, he dies quickly. Often he churns about the surface in a wild frenzy while his insides are being burned out.

8

From *Heaven Has Claws*

ADRIAN CONAN DOYLE

Adrian Conan Doyle was born with a spirit of adventure and a zest for life. In his book *Heaven Has Claws,* Doyle tells of an expedition he made, with his wife, to the Indian Ocean looking for ancient cities, exploring coral reefs and islands.

The scene of the action is this excerpt is near Kilwa Kisiwani Island, south off the coast of Tanganyika. It takes place shortly after a native told Doyle a story about a huge shark he had seen the previous evening.

The man had been wading in the shallows of a channel between the islands of Kilwa Kisiwani and Songa Manara when the shark had attempted to reach him; he was only a few feet from the shore and managed to scramble to safety. This shark was known to patrol the area and had supposedly eaten the crew of a small dhow that had capsized.

Doyle set out to catch the shark. His tale of subsequent events, though short, is beautifully told and paints a vivid picture in the mind of a still and warm night, a tropical island, and death lurking beneath deep black waters. It is a man-hunts-shark story with a difference, and one full of as much mystery as any of Doyle's father's stories.

•

From the first I had determined to get there, to this island with a name like the thrum of a harpstring, to

69

this island with a secret. And now, with the slackening of the wind, my opportunity had come.

"Allah! Allah! Allah!" chanted the crew in unison with the hoisting of the anchor chain. Slowly the jungled mounds of Ras Mashindo slid away and passing down the long stretch of inland water we reached the open sea. On the way along the coast we took a severe buffeting and in the Lindi Sewa channel the following swell towered high above our stern. When I see this kind of thing, I always realize how much I like the land. A few hours later, however, we were safely round the point and our anchor rattled down in relatively calm waters.

A hundred yards distant on our port side lay Songa Manara, a long low island of feathered palms and thick bush, broken by huge coral outcrops hung with lianas and creeping vines. Two clumps of very high and massive trees rose in the background. On our starboard was the little island of Sonya Ya Kati and between the two lay the blue waters that were reputed to be the swim of the man-eater.

It was necessary to get some fresh food, so we ran out the rods and within a few minutes Anna had a heavy strike, the fish plunging deep and then coming in on the reel after a half-hearted fight. It turned out to be a striped Rock Cod, weighing 45 pounds. Shortly after, I caught his grandson and then in quick succession, three more of the same ilk, averaging about 5 pounds each. There was a lull and then a tremendous strike on Anna's rod which bent almost double as the line whizzed under the boat. After playing the fish really magnificently, she topped the performance by actually landing it without the gaff, which had been broken in the struggle. Again it was a Rock Cod, all mouth and spiky fins, and it tipped the scales at a few ounces over 90 pounds. This we impaled on a shark hook and, attached to a line that had been tested at 3,000 pounds, the succulent corpse drifted away into deep waters.

The sun blazed from a cloudless sky and as we had

tasted nothing cooler than warm water for the past week, we welcomed the arrival of a Songa native bearing two wild pineapples and a basket of fresh mangoes. When we mentioned the great shark, he confirmed its existence adding several details that enabled me to hazard a guess as to its precise species.

"How big is it?" I asked.

"Like that," he replied, pointing to his 30-foot canoe. "It is a terrible fish, Bwana-Mkouba," he went on. "When it passes, it is like a dhow rushing with the wind in its sail, and it is striped like the lion of India."

The best part of the day being over, we had steeled our minds against the temptation to burst headlong into the bush in search of the ruins, feeling that the project was altogether too important and that it should await the next day when, with our equipment ready and some working hours before us, we could give ourselves wholeheartedly to the task.

The afternoon crawled away in a miasma of heat, spiritually relieved by a really marvelous concert of birds amid the trees of Songa Manara.

One species gave vent to an exquisite warble while another would chime in with a single ringing note resembling exactly the striking of a gigantic wine glass and, in the pauses of the music, arose a voice of an obviously low-bred fellow whose contribution consisted of a series of clacks and tinkles as though he was counting his loose change. At length, with two white-headed fish eagles circling overhead and Anna's 90-pound fish glimmering below, the whole ship fell asleep.

We awoke to a world of darkness. The stars were almost obscured by heavy banks of cloud and at one point only, where a faint luminosity gave promise of a moon to come, was the jungle discernible as a jagged black outline. Specks and patches of phosphorescence drifted past in the dark waters, but in no way comparable with the extraordinary spectacle which we had witnessed in the lagoon of the coral island. We had run out our rods from the stern and were just on the point of settling down to a comfortable bout of fishing and smoking when, from the velvet darkness of the midchannel, there arose a sound which froze us.

It was far away, that reverberation, as though some vast body had broken surface and was plunging toward us through the water. We listened intently and the silence was so complete that I could hear a slow drip from the aft tank. Black silence and . . . yes, there it was again and nearer, and then again, much closer still and now we could hear an indescribable noise, between a grunt and a hiss, followed once more by the crash of water and yet again as the surface of the channel was ripped savagely apart. I can find no words to portray the impression of overwhelming malevolence conveyed by the thunderous plunges and splashes of the unseen thing which was rushing upon us through the darkness.

Grabbing a powerful torch, I turned the beam full upon the direction of its approach, and quite suddenly there appeared in the circle of light a high burst of foam like the wave of a speedboat, then a grayish flash as a huge body, at least 25 feet in length, turned slightly and with a roar of water plunged into the depth. The hissing noise was so loud that the comparison of a Westinghouse brake passed through my mind. The creature broke surface again in a burst of foam and, as it drew level with us, it appeared to slow and, for an instant, the thought arose whether it was contemplating an attack on the bait or on the boat! Then at tremendous speed the succession of splashes and flurries tore away into the distance. The thing had passed.

It was a trifling incident, perhaps, and yet for the first time I saw Anna frightened. I can say this because she is a woman of rare courage proven on numerous occasions by that combination of tough living conditions and very real physical danger that searches out the weak spot in a man's or woman's character and sends them scuttling for security. Even when collecting reptiles in the Cameroons, she had assisted me by handling living snakes as part of the day's work, but she would fish no more that night after the passing of the scarcely seen shape, and donned a jacket against the coldness which had crept over her. Until midnight we sat and listened and stared over the black waters while far below, the bait, untouched and ignored, gleamed like a green lantern. Personally, I have no doubt that we witnessed nothing else than the passage of the huge man-killing shark. "And when it passes, it is like a dhow rushing with the wind in its sail . . ."

The dry hissing grunt, which incidentally bore not the faintest resemblance to the "blow" of a whale, does puzzle me, however, and the only explanation that I can offer is that the noise was caused by the suction of the monster's tail when plunging. Be that as it may, it was altogether horrific, and I shall long remember the tearing welter of foam rushing past us in the darkness of the narrow channel and on into the night like Death late for an appointment.

III

SHARK BEHAVIOR

●

Shark behavior, like child behavior, is a subject of interest to many people. Dr. Eugenie Clark has devoted many years of her life to the study of sharks and the way they behave under different situations. A diver as well as a scientist, Dr. Clark has been able to observe sharks in the open ocean, which must be a great asset when studying behavior patterns. Of course, much of her work has to be done with captive sharks. A shark in the open ocean will hardly stay around long enough for someone to photograph it, let alone conduct prolonged experiments.

It is not only the scientists and researchers who assist in the gathering of information on sharks. Anyone who observes these fish for a length of time must learn something about their behavior patterns. For instance, big-game fishermen know that pelagic sharks favor small school fish as bait. Some game fishermen are so familiar with the way different sharks behave when hooked, that they can tell what species is on the line and roughly how much it would weigh—all this without seeing the shark and, most of the time, quite correct in their estimate.

Two different people can watch the same shark and come to two different conclusions as to what they believe the shark is doing or why he is doing it. Also there is the possibility they could both be wrong. It's going to take many more years of study before complete behavior patterns begin to emerge. All information concerning sharks is of value, whether it comes from a famous scientist or a rock fisherman.

Ron and I have been fortunate in having spent considerable time working with gray nurse sharks (sand bar tigers in the United States). During the day, they behave in a quiet, sluggish fashion but become extremely active at night when they have to hunt for food. This is a simple observation regarding the behavior of a certain species of shark. Although we didn't consider ourselves to be shark experts, like most experienced divers, we do have a certain amount of knowledge about the behavior of sharks we most commonly see. These simple, everyday traits of the sharks are fairly easy to define and are by now common knowledge among people who work with sharks.

The big question mark regarding shark behavior is one asked by millions of people. Why do they attack? Nobody really knows for sure. It is a phenomenon still being studied extensively by scientists in all countries where attacks occur. It's a question that has no simple answer and I feel one that can never be answered in full.

Shark behavior is still mostly a mystery whose surface has only been scratched. These stories I have chosen are a very mixed collection. About the only definite thing to be found by reading them is that shark behavior is completely variable.

9

From *Sharks, Sea and Land*

"SINBAD"

Sharks, Sea and Land (reprinted from *Temperance World!*) is a tiny booklet, published by the Blackfriars Printing and Publishing Company in 1889. It is a collection of old stories about many different sharks, including one chapter on land sharks of the human variety.

I have selected a section dealing with a shark which, like the tiger shark in the Australian shark arm case (see Part IX), was instrumental in bringing a crime to the attention of the authorities. It is amazing what a shark will swallow, as the case recounted by Mr. Wylie here proves.

That the attitudes of the sailor toward sharks has not changed is apparent from this story. Although the credibility of these stories leaves a lot to be desired, the old-fashioned manner of their telling makes a delightful contrast to the more serious accounts appearing in this book.

No doubt, most of the incidents related here did happen, after a fashion. Most shark stories have a true beginning. It is just that in the telling and retelling, the sharks grow longer and the men become braver.

•

Some few years ago a shark's jaw was to be seen at the Jamaica Admiralty Court. Inquiring the history of it, the following legend was told. During the great war with France in the early part of this century, our men of war had much work to do in the West Indies, as contraband of war was often carried in neutral bottoms (i.e., ships), and it was necessary that all suspicious craft should be searched. For this purpose cutters were rigged out, and junior officers placed in command, with orders to cruise and overhaul the papers of every ship they fell in with. One of these cutters, the *Sparrow* by name, was commanded by a Mr. Wylie, his cruising-ground being off Cape Tiburon, a promontory on the Island of St. Domingo. One day the *Sparrow* chased and overhauled an American brig, whose cargo, coupled with other circumstances, produced such a suspicion of her being enemy's property, that Wylie thought it proper to put a prize crew aboard her and sail her to Port Royal for examination.

On her arrival there the American skipper swore so positively through thick and thin, "as only an American can," to the truth of the papers which he produced, that the court was induced to set him at liberty; thereupon the Yankee commenced a prosecution against Lieutenant Wylie, claiming demurrage for the detention of his vessel.

Whilst the case was pending, a small tender, commanded by Midshipman Titton, arrived off Port Royal. Being a friend of Wylie's he went on board the *Sparrow* and was astonished to find him "down in the dumps" and low spirited. Inquiring the cause, he heard of the trouble his friend was in at the idea of the ruinous damages which would be awarded against him on account of the Yankee.

Titton, on hearing the name of the skipper of the brig and the nature of her cargo, told his friend to be under no apprehension, for the brig was yet a fair prize.

He then explained that, whilst cruising in his tender near the position where the *Sparrow* had chased the vessel, and much about the same time, they had caught a large shark. On its being cut open by one of the men they were surprised to hear him sing out, "Stand by to receive your letters, my boys, for here's the postman come on board"; handing out at the same time a parcel of papers from the shark's stomach. As they were but little injured by the digestive powers of the monster, Titton retained them and the jaw as curiosities.

On comparing them with a manifest of the brig's cargo, they appeared to be the real papers of the American, which he had, when pressed in the chase, thrown overboard, and the shark had swallowed them. They proved beyond a doubt that the cargo was French.

Wylie was in high glee. The two friends proceeded at once to Kingston with this new conclusive evidence, but all further investigation was rendered unnecessary, for the skipper of the brig was so thunderstruck on hearing the circumstance (believing it to be a visitation from heaven for his perjuries) that he absconded, and the vessel after all was condemned to the *Sparrow*, with a result that Wylie got £3,000 as his share of the prize money. Titton sent up the jaw of the shark to the Admiralty Court at Jamaica with his compliments, observing that he considered it a capital collar for all neutrals to swear through in future.

THIRD FISHERMAN: Master, I marvel how the fishes live in the sea.
FIRST FISHERMAN: Why, as men do a-land; the great ones eat up the little ones.
                                    Shakespeare's *Pericles*

My readers have already heard that sharks will swallow any kind of garbage, but I fear the following will be too much for their credulity, although affirmed by several well-known names: Ruysch, one of the most trustworthy of the old naturalists, writes "that a man in mail (*Homo loricatus* he calls him) was found in the stomach of a white shark." Blumenback, one of the most celebrated naturalists of modern times, records that in one case a whole horse was found, and Basil Hall, an eminent naval officer, relates that from the stomach of a white shark, which he saw caught, there was taken the whole skin of a buffalo, besides a quantity of other articles which had been dropped overboard in the course of the previous week. There is also a story told at St. James, St. Helena, of a shark having been stranded, and on the fishermen opening it, they were horrified to find the body of a full-dressed artilleryman.

The French name for shark is *requin*. As my readers are doubtless aware, this word is probably derived from the Latin *requiem,* and signifies that if a man fall into the sea among sharks, his comrades may repeat for him the usual prayers for the dead. It is seldom, if ever, that a man who is so luckless as to fall amongst shark appears again; a shriek is heard, a moving mass if seen under the surface and a fin above it; the next wave that breaks against the ship-side is crimsoned, and the horror-stricken seamen know that their messmate has gone to that bourne from which no traveler has returned.

Ancient mariners had a superstition that the spirits of their departed messmates entered into the bodies of the stormy petrels, or Mother Carey's chickens.

That white sharks have very large mouths, and, if not capable of taking in a whole horse or buffalo, are sufficiently large to take in a man, is proved by the following: H.M.S. *Flora* was, some years ago, stationed at the island of St. Helena, and one day a monster shark was caught. The jaws, after the head had been severed from the body, were cleaned and opened to their fullest extent, when they were found capable of taking in the head, shoulders, and body of a lieutenant, a man of twelve stone, without touching any part of him.

The following is a descriptive account of the capture of a shark, as related by M. L. Platt in the *Musée des Sciences*.

"A shark of great size, certainly not less than thirty-five feet in length, had ventured to draw near our vessel. As we were then becalmed, and had nothing to do, we hailed the pleasant burst of excitement, the agreeable relief to our monotonous occupations, which he was likely to afford us. By way of precaution, and to keep him occupied, we flung to him a pair of old boots, which he conscientiously swallowed. However, he as yet required no enticement; for while the calm lasted, and so long as our ship did not make more than three or four knots per hour, the shark never stirred from the wake of our floating palace, where he always expected to see something regal allotted to him.

"While he amuses himself in plunging and diving in the wake of the ship, everybody is in a state of tumult upon deck. We arrange our warlike engines, and make ready for the battle. An enormous fish-hook is attached, by means of a bit of iron chain, to the extremity of a long, stout cable. The bait is a large piece of pork, just such another piece as the monster has already swallowed, while it lay soaking in the sea water in readiness for the crew's dinner.

"At length all is ready. The captain holds in his grasp a well-greased harpoon; the slip-knots of the cable glide with complete ease, and are disposed within reach of the hand. Everybody has collected on the quarter-deck, a sailor flings the hook into the sea, and the fishing begins.

"The shark now ceases to plunge and wheel about the ship; he smells the bait and lazily swims toward the floating piece of pork. He has learned long ago that so small a prey cannot escape him. Immediately that he touches it with his snout, he turns on his side, opens his huge mouth, and swallows it. But at this moment the cable is violently jerked, forcing the fish hook into one of his jaws; two hands catch firm hold of the rope, and begin to tighten it, while the shark plunges about in pain, churning the waters into foam. Sometimes the hook breaks; in such case the game must be recommenced. The shark, with torn and bleeding throat, nevertheless swallows a second bait with equal avidity.

"As soon as we are satisfied that the hook is securely fixed, we draw the animal alongside; the man placed at the post of honor—generally, as in the present case, the captain—vigorously darts the harpoon into his body. It is necessary that the iron should so far penetrate into the flesh that the movable portion form a cross with the axis of the lance. We have two points of attachment, and raise the shark out of the water by means of the cable of the fish-hook and the rope of the harpoon, drawing upon both simultaneously. The animal once lifted from the sea loses a part of his strength, his fins and tail have no longer any point of support. Nothing is easier, while he hangs by the ship's side, than to pass a running bowline round his tail. The three ropes which now hold him fast run quickly over pulleys fixed to the yard-arms, and the shark is speedily landed upon the quarter-deck.

"The prisoner captured, his punishment is not long delayed. In vain are all his struggles; in vain the repeated and heavy blows of his tail, which threaten to crush through the planks. A sailor plunges a hand-spike into his throat, to hold him down, while another severs his tail with an axe. In this mutilated condition he is perfectly harmless and powerless, though a blow from his tail would kill a man, or, at all events, break his thigh. The monster rendered defenseless, we cut open the belly and extract the heart, which is immediately thrown overboard. Sometimes a portion of the stomach is put aside to be eaten; sometimes the animal is stripped of its skin, which is dried, while the dorsal spine is fashioned into a handsome walking-stick. The liver, also, will probably be utilized, being rich in iodized oil."

As we are now on the subject of shark-catching, the following may interest my readers as showing a novel way of destroying sharks. Reverting to the years 1847–49, whilst stationed on the West Coast of Africa in H.M.S. *Blazer,* the shark afforded many hours of amusement to the officers and men in the dreary monotonous days when no sail in sight appeared for us to go in chase of, and hopes of prize-money had gone. On one occasion the ship was anchored off Lagos, in the Gulf of Guinea, where the sharks were so numerous that the act of a man showing his face over the side of the ship apparently brought them to the surface, and to have fallen overboard would have been instant death. One morning the crew were practicing with ball cartridge, when it occurred to the commanding officer that Jack Shark might form a good target, so directions were given for an 8-pound piece of Queen's own (pork) to be suspended from the foreyard arm to within two feet of the water. The ruse answered admirably, causing the greatest excitement. The monsters in quick succession rose one after the other and attempted to seize the bait, ever failing to do so, and in return getting a musket ball through the head. The sport was stirring, and gave the men something to laugh and talk about over their salt horse and weevily biscuits at mealtimes.

Sailors have an idea that the shark will not touch a black man, no doubt from the fearless manner he has of jumping overboard, sharks or no sharks in sight. The British Consul, however, at that desolate place, Lagos, said that scarcely a week passed without some natives being taken away by them, when their canoes were capsized on the bars.

At Greytown, Nicaragua, a dismal place in another quarter of the globe, where leave was prohibited to seamen, from its unhealthiness and the tempting grog-shops, houses held by a class of land sharks, it was customary for one watch (forty men) at a time of the crew of the sloop of war stationed there to be allowed to land for a run on the opposite side of the harbor, taking with them a large well-fitted shark hook, a coil of two-and-a-half-inch rope, and a log of wood for a buoy. Sharks and alligators abounded in that (now closed) harbor. To the left point of the entrance, which is sandy and steep too, like Dungeness Point, our jolly tars would repair, light their pipes, and bait the hook with the invariable Queen's own, a little less rancid than the African rations. When ready, the baited hook, buoyed and fastened to the two-and-a-half-inch rope, would be cast into the water, the current taking it off the point. Presently the buoy would disappear for a second or two. Jack's excitement was intense, and at the boatswain's mate's piping "Stand by," each man would lay hold of the rope, allowing it to slip through his fingers as the shark tugged at the bait. On the buoy disappearing altogether, "Haul taut" was piped, and then "Haul away." In a minute or two a monster of a shark was, much against its will, hauled well up on to dry land out of the water. Pipe "Belay" was sounded, and three cheers given. The men, frantic with delight, surrounded the captive, soon cutting it up into small pieces, which were thrown into the sea for the alligators to devour.

10

From *Lord of the Sharks*

FRANCO PROSPERI

The contradictory opinions regarding shark behavior presented as fact by different shark experts must quickly become apparent to anyone reading this book. In his book *Lord of the Sharks,* Franco Prosperi comments on these differences of opinion.

Naturally enough, being a diver myself, I tend to side with Hans Hass, whose work appears later in this book, regarding the ferociousness of sharks; generally speaking they are not dangerous. Pechuel-Loesche's claims, which will sound to the average reader like a figment of that learned gentleman's imagination, are undoubtedly true. I have often found myself in the water surrounded by whaler sharks and, provided no provocation is initiated, they have, after the first curious examination, gone about their business without confrontation.

Francis Day's observations that shark bites inflicted on fishermen in India are usually caused when the captured sharks are hauled aboard the fishing boats before they have died are perfectly logical and, no doubt, completely factual. I know two Australian spearfishermen, and have heard of many more, who have been bitten by a supposedly dead shark. These bites are rarely severe, but still give fuel to the theory that sharks are attackers of man.

One young man was propping open the jaws of a speared and supposedly dead shark with his knife. The shark twitched, the knife slipped, and the jaws snapped shut on the unfortunate man's hands. A most unpleasant experience, but hardly the fault of the shark. However, the newspaper headlines read, DIVER MAULED BY SHARK.

Lord of the Sharks is an interesting book all around and covers many aspects of sharks and their behavior. I liked the way Franco Prosperi tested Hass's "scream theory." It is interesting that his results were similar to the results I achieved when I tested the same theory.

●

Here is what several authors have had to say on the subject in the past.

First of all let us take that great eighteenth-century traveler George Dixon, who spent a long time in the Pacific and especially among the South Sea Islands. He assures us that thereabouts the shark is not much feared, and says he once witnessed a fight between some Sandwich Islanders and a few sharks over the remains of some pork that the sailors on his ship had thrown into the sea. (This proves that sharks are not the only famished creatures.)

Gesner, however, writing in the sixteenth century, had been less optimistic. His contention was that sharks were certainly man-eaters and that, at any rate, in the tropics, one should never swim in deep water for fear of meeting them. He also quoted the case of a blue shark captured near Marseilles which was found to contain a complete soldier fully armed (an antimilitarist shark, no doubt).

Even a much more recent author, E. G. Boulenger, director of the Zoological Society's Aquarium in London, believes that certain species such as the great white shark attack man, and points out that since the Suez Canal was made these species have come into the Mediterranean, and there are always one or two casualties in the course of the season there among incautious bathers.

But swelling the throng of those who want to rehabilitate the shark and give it once more an honored place in animal society, whitewashing its unsavory reputation, is Peschuel-Loesche, an adventurous writer who has published the interesting experiences he has had in the course of several voyages on whalers in the South Atlantic. He declares that the shark is utterly harmless to man. When swimming he often found himself surrounded by sharks, but neither he nor the people with him ever had the slightest bother with them. He also tells that in the island of Mocha, off the coast of Chile, the local boys, almost completely submerged and armed with strong harpoons, caught coastal sharks as they swam near the shore. As a rule the sharks were not very big, but from time to time there would be a *Carcharias* two or three yards long in their catch.

After a personal experience in the waters of Singapore, to which he has added various other accounts collected in the same area, the naturalist Sir James Edward Alexander infers that sharks are man-eaters and extremely dangerous to bathers even in shallow water. One day he was looking for shellfish in the shallows near a coral reef by the coast when he was suddenly attacked by a school of tiger sharks, and certainly would have been overcome by their repeated assaults if a passing boat had not picked him up just in time. During the fight he lost one boot, part of his trousers, and a piece of his skin was torn off.

Francis Day, on the other hand, covering more or less the same area as Alexander, has made a most interesting and thorough study of the fishes of India and reached completely different conclusions. This writer says that although sharks are much feared by the local fishermen, he never heard of a verifiable case of death caused by the attack of a shark. It is his belief that the sinister reputation sharks have in all the coastal villages is chiefly due to the bites and wounds they inflict after they have been caught, in the confined space of the local fishing vessels, on to which they are hauled before they are dead.

The theories of many other authorities such as Risso, Maast, Couch, Rondelet, etc., might be quoted.

But we would be no nearer to forming a clear idea of the behavior of these animals.

Needless to say, all these accounts have only a relative value; they are hardly ever based on direct experience. The writer has almost never been present personally at the events he records, but is working on vague hearsay, yarns, and legends, seldom confirmed by witnesses, and some of them barely credible.

Fishermen and sailors on every coast and from every land blindly believe the tales that are passed down from one generation to another, and all of them express the most unmitigated hatred of sharks and tell the most horrifying tales about them. But if one presses them for proof, or for exact information, regarding the tragic incidents they describe, one is very unlikely to get anything from them but vague and unsubstantiated answers.

The fact of the matter is that very little is known about the habits of these animals, and that the name they have for cruelty and ferocity encourages loose writing about them. But at the turn of the last century and in the early years of this, when organized shark fishing began, knowledge concerning the shark became less superficial.

The classic exponent of this new category of fishermen is Captain William E. Young. In his famous work *Shark! Shark!,* he describes experiences he has had with sharks in practically every sea. And he too sides with the writers who unhesitatingly condemn sharks as man-eaters. Impelled by an innate aversion to these savage "tigers of the sea" (as he himself calls them), he has devoted his entire life to hunting them.

But perhaps "aversion" is not the right word. There is never any hatred or repulsion in the hunter when he kills his prey. This is how he describes his first encounter with sharks: "There they were, the savage, armored sea tigers which had become my fetish, my totem. I thrilled to the sight, as I leaned there, staring in utter fascination, my throat contracted. Tingling shivers ran up and down my spine, to my fingertips and toes. I wished for a harpoon, a rifle, anything that would give me a chance to make my first shark kill."

Just as the true hunter will often have an exaggerated idea of the value and cleverness of the game he pursues, so does Captain Young see the ferocity and implacability of his prey a little larger than life. He cannot bear anyone to doubt the dangerousness of these lords of the sea, or to think it possible to escape safely from waters infested by them. And indeed he quotes the cases of many swimmers, of whose foolish audacity he disapproves, who never came back from bathing in ill-famed waters. His book is illustrated with horrifying photographs (at any rate in the French edition) of men trapped in those terrible jaws, and he quotes many sensational legends current in the Polynesian Islands of death due to sharks. After so many years' travel and experience, the conclusion he has come to is that sharks attack and eat man, and that to believe the contrary is both false and foolish.

Refraining for the moment from any comment, I pass on to the opinions of Dr. Hans Hass, the well-known marine scientist and one of the pioneers of underwater fishing.

His own passionate interest in the subject has aroused a worldwide interest in marine life, the fascination of which was originally revealed by William Beebe, after he had explored the coral reefs of the Pacific. Hass has been the great popularizer of underwater fishing, the love of which is now widespread among European swimmers. After an early expedition to the Caribbean, he has continued his field work in the Red Sea and the Mediterranean, with particular emphasis on photography.

In these expeditions of his, which started one year before World War II, he frequently met sharks. It was the first time that man had found himself in the shark's own environment, at the mercy of its attacks, which it was thought nobody could resist, with nothing in his hands but a camera and a long harpoon. So that Hass's evidence on this enthralling subject was of paramount importance. Actually Hass did not propose to carry out a scientific investigation of the subject, but nevertheless his testimony is extremely valuable.

What happened the first time Hans Hass found himself gazing into the eyes of a "sea tiger"? Nothing much: for a little while man and beast stared at each other, then they both went their several ways each equally anxious to come safely out of the unusual encounter. But things did not always go so smoothly: sometimes the sharks would lunge dangerously and cause some most unpleasant thrills.

One day Hass and two members of his expedition were hard pressed in just such a situation, when they made an accidental discovery: the terrified cries of one of the party, reverberating in the water, put the shark to flight as though it could not bear the intensity of the unexpected vibrations caused by the latter which affect the shark's abnormally sensitive receiving organs, and utterly terrify it.

But it isn't always as simple as it sounds. When we ourselves tried to put the advice of these Austrians into practice, we didn't always get what we wanted.

After experimenting with the scream theory under water (both when it seemed necessary and when it didn't), with a considerable number of sharks belonging to the various dangerous species, we decided that the terror we aroused was in proportion to the size of the animal.

That is to say, if the shark was young and small, not more than four or five feet in length, one could count on a scream putting it to instant flight, but with the bigger sharks, especially the ones over six or seven feet, it was a very different matter. The animal felt our vibrations, and would shy abruptly every time we screamed, but this did not make it go away, nor stop lunging. The only result of the screams was to irritate it and make it weave around us faster.

To sum up, Hans Hass asserts that a good underwater fisherman, especially if he has a friend with him, so that a lookout is kept for other unexpected attacks, should not be afraid of meeting these lords of the deep. His conclusion, it will be seen, is the exact opposite of Captain Young's.

Naturally as Hass's views are the result of direct observation and of his own personal experience in the shark's natural habitat, they are of far greater value to use than the frequently secondhand accounts reported by Young, Gesner, Alexander, Henglin, and Risso, who all more or less agree in considering the shark a man-eater. Dixon, Pechuel-Loesche, Day, and Wyatt Gill, on the other hand, agree with Hass.

We may reduce the problem to the simple question: "Is the shark dangerous to man or is he not?" but there is no simple answer. All sorts of different conditions may bring about different results when man meets shark. Place, time, and the species of the animal may all be determining factors.

11

The Vanishing Gray Nurse

I wrote "The Vanishing Gray Nurse" for *The Australian Women's Weekly*. Over the years, they have published many of my shark stories, so that I have been able to present the conservation angle to a large number of people.

As always, when I write of sharks being rather nice creatures, not nasty, vicious, man-eating monsters, I receive a sudden flow of letters from readers. Usually, the letters supporting my viewpoint outnumber those condemning what I have said.

"The Vanishing Gray Nurse" created more interest than usual. As I thought it a very ordinary little story, I was surprised at the large amount of mail. I think that it was because every year, in Australia, several people are bitten by sharks. We are probably the most shark-conscious people in the world, and much is made, by the media, of each attack.

Almost always the shark is described as being gray in color. This is not surprising, as most sharks are some shade of gray. So, because of his name, the gentle gray nurse (*Odontaspis taurus*) has become the gray attacker of man to many people.

It is probably for this reason that the article caused so much interest. I had letters from mothers telling me that I was mistaken. One sweet lady used three pages explaining to me that if I didn't change my view I would end up a gray nurse's breakfast. A schoolteacher used it constructively, reading the article to her class of ten-year-olds, and following with an hour's discussion on the points raised.

Most who criticized objected to my describing the gray nurse as timid, harmless creatures saying that I was giving people the wrong impression. I believe that my assessment is correct. There are many hundreds of species of shark and the gray nurse is only one of them. It is a pity that the aggressive actions of a few species are attributed to a shark which would never attack without extreme provocation.

●

Making an acceptable television series is not easy and making one about a particular species of shark in its natural element is, at times, almost impossible. Without years of diving experience, it would be impossible. Ten years ago, large fish life—sharks, rays, groupers— abounded all along the coast of New South Wales. The water was clear, too.

Now, pollution and spearfishing have both taken a tremendous toll. A toll that only someone who has been diving a long time could know. It is unfortunate that newcomers to the sport will never fully realize what they have missed.

Former Australian spearfishing champion Vic Ley, Ron, and myself have recently finished working along the east coast, completing the last of our TV shows. One episode, called "The Vanishing Gray Nurse," could almost have been retitled "The Vanished Gray Nurse." Without our library of stock shots, this episode would have been impossible. The large schools of gray nurse sharks have vanished.

The reason is not hard to find. I can remember seeing a well-known Queensland diver powerhead (an explosive-headed spear, fired from a rubber-powered spear gun) twenty-two gray nurses at Seal Rocks one sunny day nine years ago. He seemed to think he was a superhero and strutted up and down boasting of his great deed. If swimming up to a peaceful unsuspecting creature resting in a gutter and blowing its brains out with a shotgun cartridge makes a hero, I guess he was. In those days, gray nurse were considered to be man-eaters, but even so, the sight of all those sad gray bodies drifting back and forth in the surge was sickening.

Twelve years ago, the gray nurse was blamed for most shark attacks in Australian waters. We genuinely believed we were hunting true man-eaters and brave was the diver who, armed with only a conventional spear gun, sought out these vicious murderers in their own element. The invention of the powerhead served to accelerate the indiscriminate slaughter, but many divers, ourselves included, realized that the gray nurse shark seemed extremely unaggressive and was, in all likelihood, the victim of false publicity. However, killing sharks had become a popular sport.

Whether the hunted was dangerous or not made no difference, it was the name *shark* that counted. Only the lack of available victims has finally slowed the slaughter down.

Nowadays, anyone who thinks gray nurse sharks are dangerous, savage beasts, and that to kill one makes the victor some kind of superhero, needs his marbles rearranged.

During our weeks of searching, the few sharks we did find were in deep water off isolated reefs or islands. They were so afraid of divers that it was almost impossible to film them. Although we didn't plan it this way, the vanishing gray nurse is the story of a tragedy, or to put it more bluntly, a story of man's stupidity. We show how it was, what we did, and how it is now. A common enough theme in today's civilized world.

Ron and I are not innocent either, and to say I killed only a few is no excuse. Our punishment was making this film, knowing what we had done and suffering for it, as we searched the barren surge-swept gutters. It cost us money and precious time, but more distressing was knowing that we had played a part, however small, in the slaughter.

At Nine Mile Reef off the New South Wales—

Queensland border, we found no sharks. Solitary Islands, out from Wooli, New South Wales, were devoid, not only of sharks but almost everything else as well. The gutters at Fish Rock, New South Wales, were also empty, though we had a fleeting glimpse of one lonesome shark in very deep water around the back of the rock.

Further south, at Mermaid Reef, where Vic had seen dozens of gray nurse only a few years before, one frightened shark was sighted and it swam away never to be seen by us again. We had already been to Brush Island and Montague Island further south.

Seal Rocks, 200 miles north of Sydney, was to be the last area we would search. For the first time since we had started filming the series, six cyclone-studded months before, really good weather moved in, from the northeast.

We arrived at Seal Rocks on April 6, 1973, late in the afternoon. Although a big swell was running, we decided to launch our dinghy and do a quick reconnaissance of what we felt to be most lively places to find sharks.

The first place we looked was in the old shark gutter, the same place that superhero conducted his big slaughter nine years before. I really expected to find nothing so when Vic, who had gone in for a quick look, surfaced and said, "There is a shark down there," I was not prepared at all.

There was a big scramble for gear, cameras, and lights. We had to work fast. Already it was late afternoon. Ron was in the water, lights and all, in about ten minutes. I was not far behind. Underwater visibility was roughly 50 feet, but close to the rock where we had anchored, foam caused by the breaking waves cut that distance in half. The shark was hard to see. He blended into the gray rocks and I did not notice him until he moved.

When he saw us he turned and swam away. This shark did not seem afraid of us. He was only a baby. Six feet long and about one year old. (Jack Evans, the owner of the Porpoise Pool at Tweed Heads, has two gray nurse who were actually born in his tank. They were six feet long when a year old.)

We followed the little shark up the gutter. Even down 20 feet, visibility was poor. With what seemed like deliberate casualness, the shark ignored us. We moved without haste. As we neared the rock, the entrance to a cave grew blackly through the haze. Our shark vanished inside, becoming as one with the darkness. We followed. To our amazement, thirteen baby gray nurse sharks materialized in the gloom, beautiful creatures drifting together in complete harmony. I was tremendously excited.

Ron and Vic began filming. It was instantly obvious that the sharks found Ron's camera lights upsetting, for they flicked aside as he approached, thumping their tails loud in the confined space. As we moved further into the cave, one by one, the sharks left, swimming silently away. Delighted with our good fortune we followed, but they had scattered among the tumbled rocks. Ron found one in deeper water and spent some time stalking her, but she was clearly nervous and kept her distance. It was hopeless for stills so I decided to swim back for another look at the cave, while Ron and Vic hunted around in the deeper water. As I neared the cave entrance I saw a little shark also sneaking back. Then, from the turbulent shallows above the cave, another shark appeared and slipped silently into his home. It was rather like playing hide-and-seek— five sharks were already home and within minutes two more arrived. They had certainly given the boys the slip.

Poor little babies, all they wanted was to be left in peace. I could almost see the worried look being sent in my direction as I swam closer. The agitation in the cave seemed to increase, but as long as I stayed outside the sharks remained together. I turned to see Ron approaching with his camera and the lights which disturbed them greatly. A courageous male left the group, swam toward Ron, almost brushing me with his fins. Right up to the camera he went, then suddenly, with a whack of his tail, he was gone. Ron ran off his remaining film and we returned to our dinghy.

By the time we reached the beach, it was almost dark. Vic and Ron wrestled the dinghy through the surf and the backbreaking struggle with gear, cameras, boats, and trailer began.

It is relatively easy to manhandle a 15-foot aluminum dinghy and 40-horse Evinrude motor down a sandy beach, but something quite different to manhandle it up.

We were all pleased with our afternoon's work. After so many disappointments, we finally had success. The following day was really beautiful, but the seas were still fairly heavy, which meant continued poor visibility. Two local boys were going out with us. They were interested in what we were doing and we were interested in the extra manpower when it came to beaching our boat. Also they were really nice guys and, although not divers, had a love of the sea and her creatures that matched our own. We launched the boat without any problems.

When we reached the gutter, Vic hung over the gunwhale for a quick look. There was still a lot of foam around and the surge was a nuisance. He couldn't immediately see any sharks. My heart sank a little, but Ron said, "Get in and have a good look." Vic simply rolled off the boat and vanished. Our guests, John and Greg, were amazed that anyone, let alone someone completely unarmed, would just swim off looking for a pack of sharks.

Ron tried to explain how placid gray nurse are by nature, but I am not sure he was believed completely. In a minute, Vic was back with the good news that our little actors were huddled up into the cave, ready and waiting for the action to start. He claimed they all frowned when he appeared and I could well believe it.

Once again we moved among the sharks and once again they, one by one, left. Actually the only difference to the action of the previous day, was that this time the sharks did not return to their cave. This pleased us, for although we appeared rather pushy in forcing the sharks to vacate their home, we really were doing them a favor. The cave was in shallow water well within the reach of skin divers, and, because of this, the little sharks were very vulnerable. A diver armed with a powerhead could easily kill four or five sharks before they realized something was wrong and swam into the safety of deeper water.

Without harming them, we had taught them that humans were nasty, annoying creatures who should be avoided. Ron had some marvelous closeups of the sharks and I some great stills. Vic Ley, using Ron's second camera, had shot some very acceptable film of Ron and me working with the sharks.

Although we had to be in Sydney by the following evening, we planned one more quick dive before we left. I guess everyone was interested to see if the sharks had returned during the night.

We were up very early and anchored over the gutter. Vic swam down to survey the situation. There were no little sharks. He dove into deeper water. Still no sharks. Although we were not sorry they had left the shallows, Ron still needed a few more shots for the end sequence of the episode.

We sat in the boat for a while wondering where they could be. Vic knew of a cave in deep water about two miles away that he thought sharks might like. Ron decided it was worth taking a look.

We anchored over the area. Ron and Vic donned their gear and did a bump dive to the bottom to reconnoiter the place. They were back in seconds, grins all over their faces.

It seemed incredible, but the sharks were there.

Ron dropped over his lights, started the generator, and down we went. Sure enough, there they were, thirteen familiar little sharks. How they must have hated seeing the three of us again. Their new cave had two entrances: Ron swam in the large one and I squeezed through the back way, putting myself behind the sharks. This time they were not in such a hurry to leave, though the flash of my camera gave one such a fright he banged into Ron, skinning Ron's hand.

They were sharing this cave with a four-foot Port Jackson shark and several red moyongs. As caves go, it was very beautiful. The walls were coated with orange sponge and pink sea tulips hung around the entrance. Eventually, our noisy presence proved too much and, one by one, the sharks reluctantly moved out. When last I saw them, they were swimming slowly down. We followed to well over 140 feet before giving up. Somehow, I think they will return to the orange-walled cave, though I would rather they found a new home, so remote and so deep that no powerhead-wielding diver will ever find them again. Only by doing this will they be completely safe.

"The Vanishing Gray Nurse" is one of my favorite episodes in our "Inner Space" series. Ron and I feel that anyone seeing this film cannot help but feel that the shark has rights too. More, perhaps, than we do, in the underwater world of "inner space."

In July 1977 I sent a letter to Dr. D. Franzois, Director of Fisheries, New South Wales, describing our experiences with the gray nurse shark and the decline in their numbers. I requested that the gray nurse be protected by law from line fishermen and spearfishermen all along the coast of New South Wales. No decision has at this time been reached regarding my request.

12

From *The Arcturus Adventure*

WILLIAM BEEBE

If the name William Beebe means anything to most people, it is in connection with his deep dives in the bathysphere. But this was not his sole area of interest or claim to fame. He did a lot of the early pioneering scientific work connected with underwater exploration.

The Arcturus Adventure is an account of his experiences diving with helmet and hose—hard-hat diving. His experiences recounted here are almost identical to those we have had under similar conditions, the main difference being not in the fish life, but in the unwieldy diving equipment he was using.

Beebe's inquisitive mind and fine sense of curiosity must have played a major part in his success. He was obviously a man who went under the sea to expand human knowledge. Each dive enhanced his own understanding of fish and sharks. I thought his experiments with feeding the shark revealed he was not prepared to take anyone's word for anything. He had to see for himself.

This reflects our own approach to the sea and its creatures. We have seen for ourselves and drawn our own conclusions, which are frequently in opposition with established opinion. We think that each person should have the chance to see for himself, which is why the objective underwater films being made by us and other underwater film teams are so valuable for research and teaching purposes.

•

When I rolled over and looked about, there came to me a vision of the abundance of life in the sea. The cloud of little fishes had gone, even the ubiquitous yellow-tailed surgeons were out of sight for once, and yet from where I sat I could see not fewer than seven or eight hundred fish, not counting the wrasse and gobies which played around my fingers as thickly as grass-hoppers in a hayfield. Out of the blue-green distance or up from frond-draped depths, good-sized grey sharks appeared now and then. Two came slowly toward me, closer with the in-surge and then floating farther off with the out-swing. They turned first one then the other yellow catlike eye toward me, and after a good look veered off. Near to them were playing round-headed pigfish, a few Zesurus swam still nearer, and even small scarlet snappers, the prey of almost every hungry fish or aquatic bird, even these went by without any show of nervousness. The pair of sharks passed on, almost unnoticed, and all the mass of life of this wonder world seemed going smoothly and undisturbed. Far away in the dim distance one of the sharks appeared again, or it may have been another—when, looking around me, I saw every fish vanishing. While I have mentioned what must seem an identical occurrence before, yet this was as different as a great battle is from a street acci-dent. Through copper and glass and air I sensed some peril very unlike the former reaction to the sea lion, and I rapidly climbed a half-dozen rungs, swallowing hard as I went to adjust to the new altitude. Clinging close to the ladder I looked everywhere, but saw noth-ing but waving seaweed. The distant shark had van-ished together with all the hosts of fish, even to the bullying fearless groupers. I was the only living being except the starfish and the tiny waving heads of the hydroids which grew in clusters among the thinner growths of weed, as violets appear amidst high grass. Whether the distant shark was some different, very dreaded kind or whether some still more inimical thing had appeared—fearful even to the strange shark—I shall never know. Five minutes later, fear had again passed, and life, not death, was dominant.

I climbed to the surface at last, my teeth chattering from the prolonged immersion. This water, although in no sense the Humboldt Current, is much cooler than that at Cocos and I became numb and chilled without knowing it. Excitement and concentrated interest keep me keyed up, and the constant need of balance requires that every muscle is taut, and then when I reach the surface and relax, the chill seems to enter my very bones. Fortunately there is always either rowing or pumping to do and this soon warms me.

During my last dive I had noticed five or six new species of fishes and hoping to hook some of the smaller ones, I decided to get some bait. I had the boat backed near shore and at a propitious moment on the crest of one of the lesser swells I leaped off. The scarlet crabs here are remarkably tame, far more so than on any of the other islands, a fact for which I can in no way account. The casual visits of man may be of course ruled out as having nothing to do with it, and yet here birds and fish, the crab's most deadly enemies, are unusually abundant.

With two big scarlet crabs I vaulted back on the crest of another convenient little swell, fortunately just avoiding the succeeding three, any one of which would have tossed our cockle-shell high up on the jagged lava. I found to my disappointment that we had between us only one hook and that a large one. However, I anchored again near the spot where I had last dived and threw over the hook. I immediately caught one of the roundheaded pigfish, about a foot in length. As I was pulling in a second one, a six-foot shark swung toward him and this gave me a hint upon which I acted at once. I pulled in the fish quickly and studied the situation through the water glass. Two sharks were swimming slowly about the very rock where I had been sitting a few minutes before, probably the same individuals who had then been so curious about me. A small group of the pigfish swam around, over and below the sharks as they had done when I

was submerged, sometimes passing within a foot of
the sharks' mouths without the slightest show of emotion, or fear, or otherwise. An angelfish and two yellow-tailed cows passed, and a golden grouper together with two deep green giants of the same species
milled around beneath the boat, cocking their eyes up
at us, now and then.

I baited the hook with a toothsome bit of crab and
lowered it. All the pigfish rushed it at once, and as it
descended, the sharks and groupers followed with mild
interest, almost brushing against it, but wary of the
line. Failing to elicit any more practical attention from
the golden grouper, I allowed one of the pigfish to take
the bait and hook. Then, watching very carefully, I
checked his downward rush, and swung him upward.
He struggled fiercely and like an electric shock every
shark and grouper turned toward him. Without being
able to itemize any definite series of altered swimming
actions, something radical had happened. The remainder of the school of pigfish, while they remained in the
neighborhood, yet gathered together in a group and
milled slowly in a small circle. There was no question
that from being a quiet, slowly swimming, casually interested lot of fish, the three groups—pigfish, groupers,
and sharks—had become surcharged with interest focused on the fish in trouble. I drew the hooked fish
close to the boat, and could plainly see that the hook
has passed only around the horny maxillary. There
was not a drop of blood in the water, and the disability
of the fish consisted only in its attachment to the line.
Yet the very instant the struggle to free itself began,
the groupers and sharks, from being at least in appearance friendly—or certainly wholly disregarding the
pigfish—became concertedly inimical, focused upon it
with the most hostile feeling of an enemy and its prey.

For half an hour I played upon this reaction and
learned more than I had ever seen or read of the attacking and feeding habits of groupers and sharks.
When the struggling began the sharks all turned toward the hooked fish. Not only the one nearest who
must easily have seen it for himself, but two, far off,

turned at the same time instant, and within a few seconds two more from quite invisible distances and different directions. What I saw seemed to prove conclusively that sharks, like vultures, watch one another and know at once when prey has been sighted by one of their fellows. The numerous sharks thus call one another all unintentionally, as when one of our party caught a shark at Cocos, and in an incredibly short time there were seventeen attacking it. On the other hand it must be admitted that sharks differ from vultures as widely as the poles in the matter of scent. Vultures all but lack this sense, while we know that fish have it well developed. But even in the case of blood in the water, it seems to me that diffusion cannot be nearly rapid enough to account for the instantaneous reaction on sharks near and far. The phenomenon is as remarkable in general aspect as the apparent materialization from the air of a host of vultures where a few minutes before none were visible.

Even more than in this problem, I was interested in the exact method of feeding of sharks and groupers. After making sure of the first phase of interest, I allowed a six-foot shark to approach the hooked pigfish. It came rather slowly, then with increased speed and finally made an ineffectual snap at the fish. The third time it seized it by the tail and with a strong sideways twist of the whole body, tore the piece off. The second fish attacked was pulled off the hook, and two sharks then made a simultaneous rush at it. So awkward were they that one caught his jaw in the other's teeth and for a moment both swished about in a vortex of foam at the side of the boat.

I noted carefully about thirty distinct efforts or attacks on the hooked fish, and only three times was I able by maneuvering the fish to get the shark to turn even sideways, never once on its back, as the books so glibly relate. I sacrificed seven pigfish, and then tried to get the golden grouper, but it was too wary. A giant five-foot green grouper, larger than any we had taken thus far, was becoming more and more excited, however, and when I had tolled him close to the surface I let my fish lure drift loosely. One swift snap and the entire fish disappeared, then a single slight nod of the head and the line parted cleanly. The general effect was of much greater force and power exerted in a short space of time than in the case of the sharks. When it comes to lasting power for only a short time, after being landed, however, the groupers fight while the sharks smash and thrash until they are actually cut to pieces.

After this exhibition, without hesitation, I dived in the helmet again in this very spot with no change in the attitude of the sharks toward me. I had had these sharks close to me a little while before, and although my efforts under water seem to me no less awkward and helpless than a hooked pigfish, yet to these so-called man-eaters, there is apparently all the difference in the world, and I was absolutely safe from attack.

Mr. Zane Grey, who, at my recommendation, went to Cocos and the Galapagos, had as his object big-game fishing, and as the following paragraphs will show, he underwent the same experience that we had, both when we were here two years ago on the *Noma,* and now again on the *Arcturus.*

Fishing off Chatham Bay, Cocos Island, he writes in his book *Tales of Fishing Virgin Seas:* "The next hour was so full of fish that I could never tell actually what did happen. We had hold of some big crevalle, and at least one enormous yellowtail, perhaps seventy-five pounds. But the instant we hooked one, great swift gray and yellow green shadows appeared out of obscurity. We never got a fish near the boat. Such angling got on my nerves. It was a marvelous sight to peer down into that exquisitely clear water and see fish as thickly laid as fence pickets, and the deeper down the larger they showed. All kinds of fish lived together down there. We saw yellowtail and amberjack swim among the sharks as if they were all friendly. But the instant we hooked a poor luckless fish, he was set upon by these voracious monsters and devoured. They fought like wolves. Whenever the blood of a fish discolored the water these sharks seemed to grow frantic. They appeared on all sides, as if by magic.

"By and by we had sharks of all sizes swimming round under our boat. One appeared to be about twelve feet long or more, and big as a barrel. There were only two kinds, the yellow sharp-nosed species, and the bronze shark with black fins, silver-edged. He was almost as grand as a swordfish.

"While trying to get the big fellow to take a bait I hooked and whipped three of this bunch, the largest one being about two hundred and fifty pounds. It did not take me long to whip them, once I got a hook into their hideous jaws. The largest, however, did not get to my bait.

"An interesting and gruesome sight was presented when Bob, after dismembering one I had caught, tumbled the bloody carcass back into the water. It sank. A cloud of blood spread like smoke. Then I watched a performance that beggared description. Sharks came thick upon the scene from everywhere. Some far down seemed as long as our boat. They massed around the carcass of their slain comrade, and a terrible battle ensued. Such swift action, such ferocity, such unparalleled instinct to kill and eat! But this was a tropic sea, with water at eighty-five degrees, where life is so intensely developed. Slowly that yellow flashing, churning mass of sharks faded into the green depths."

13

From *Sharks and Other Ancestors*

WADE DOAK

Walter Starck's inventiveness and dedication has opened some of the sea's once closed doors. Nothing is too bizarre or small for Walter to investigate—his studies of sea snakes and sunworshippers in the Pacific led him to band his wetsuit as a shark protection. This was one of his better-known experiments and involved painting white horizontal stripes on his black wetsuit in an effort to frighten sharks away. The idea behind this odd action was that sharks were supposedly afraid of sea snakes, some of which are banded.

Using Dr. Starck's research vessel, *El Torito*, as a base, Wade Doak spent many months diving in tropical areas inhabited by these sharks. His book, *Sharks and Other Ancestors*, describes in detail many of his personal encounters with sharks both dangerous and placid. These are the sort of encounters which eventually happen to any diver who consistently works in the remote reef areas of the Indo-Pacific.

A fine underwater photographer and writer, New Zealander Wade Doak writes about the gray reef shark with an authority that comes only from personal experience.

The gray reef shark, because of its aggressive personality and the fact that in virgin areas it is generally numerous, has become a popular subject for both underwater photographers and thrill-seeking spearfishermen. The latter hunt the sharks with explosive-tipped spears for little more than the excitement of the kill. It is easy to see, from Doak's descriptions of the gray sharks, why they make such good photographic material. They are also excellent subjects for scientific research. Dr. Starck has been studying gray reef sharks in their natural habitat for many years.

After the initial burst of publicity, little more has been heard about the striped wetsuit and it would appear that the idea has not been pursued—which, considering the lack of banded sea snakes in most of the world's oceans, is probably just as well.

Anyone interested in learning more about sharks and their behavior in their natural element would find Doak's book interesting reading. It is obvious that he has had personal experience with the different marine animals he writes about, which makes a refreshing change from the exaggerated viciousness and danger writers with less experience usually attribute to large marine creatures.

●

One of the most graceful and streamlined of the reef sharks, the gray is also one of the most widespread and abundant species around coral reefs and atolls. They often gather in passes where there are dense masses of fish, and dozens of individuals may be seen cruising up and down ready to attack any fish which shows signs of stress.

Up to eight feet in length but usually around five feet, this reef shark is uniformly dark gray, except for the whitish stomach and the black tinge on the trailing edges of its fins. This is especially marked on the upper lobe of the caudal.

The teeth of the upper jaw are broadly triangular; those of the lower jaw narrower. The upper teeth have serrated edges, the serrations more pronounced on the posterior edges of the teeth. The lower teeth have smooth edges. This tooth pattern is an ideal compromise for an all-purpose predator. The narrow, smooth lower teeth are for grasping and holding slippery active prey while the heavier, serrated upper teeth are adapted for cutting up the prey and chopping chunks from larger food items.

The tooth pattern is similar in silvertips and blacktips; the whitetip has tricuspid teeth and is more specialized for catching and holding small fishes without the heavy teeth for cutting up larger prey.

Of the reef sharks the gray is the most dangerous to man. A book on the fishes of Polynesia reports ten recent attacks by grays in French Polynesia alone. One resulted in death, another required amputation, and the others produced deep, semicircular, crenellated wounds, with torn muscles, blood hemorrhage and deep shock requiring rapid treatment.

At Eniwetok in the Marshall Islands Richard Johnson and Donald Nelson, two diving scientists, carried out a series of experiments on gray reef sharks to determine whether they would make attacks on man for reasons other than feeding. Until then the basic assumption in shark deterrent research has been that sharks are motivated to attack men chiefly by hunger. From the new research and Walt Starck's studies it seems apparent that while this may be the case with the largest species such as tiger sharks and white sharks, it is not true for others, especially the gray sharks. Grays often compete for food, and have developed a ritualized threat display which is likely to be of communicative value in their normal social encounters with each other and other shark species. (Just as a dog will raise its hackles and bare its teeth as a threat gesture, and only attack if the threat is ignored.)

It has long been believed sharks would not attack scuba divers when there was nothing to arouse their feeding responses: no blood in the water or wounded fish. However, with increased diving activity in the Pacific and the pooling of information, it is now clear that this is not true. Of the many reported attacks on scuba and skin divers by gray sharks, none involves the shark feeding on his victim. They all bite and run.

Johnson and Nelson analyzed such reports and discovered there were several factors common to each attack which deserved investigation. Often the diver reported preliminary behavior such as in this account by Ron Church: "The shark started a small circle just opposite us and as he came around, his body started turning and twisting and rolling back and forth in the water as he swam. The whole body was being used to swim with, his head moving back and forth almost as much as his tail. He trimmed himself with his pectorals."

The scientists noted reports of five incidents where such behavior led to attacks on men. They then looked for any factors common to these attacks which might explain their provocation. They found that in each case the shark had found its escape route restricted in some way by the divers.

In the case above, Ron Church said the shark had passed between the two divers and the reef wall. The divers had moved toward the shark as it passed and this had apparently released the behavior pattern described. As soon as the threat display was complete the shark rapidly dashed at one of the divers. Jim Stewart, who received two severe bites just above the elbow.

In shark literature it has often been recommended that if a shark seems a menace the diver should stand his ground and act aggressively toward it. This may hold true for big lone predators such as tiger sharks, but it is most dangerous with the reef sharks.

With considerable courage Johnson and Nelson set up a series of experiments on gray sharks to determine and record on film just what the pattern of threat behavior was and to see if it could be provoked by a diver. They conducted a series of ten tests in which a diver (carrying a means of defense which would undoubtedly have been useless), upon seeing an approaching gray shark, swam rapidly at it from twenty feet range. In each of the ten trials the shark made a definite threat display. This lasted from fifteen seconds to one minute and varied in intensity according to the degree to which it was cornered or restricted from escape by different types of reef structure.

As a control the divers did another series of tests where, upon the approach of the shark, the diver made no movement toward it. In every such case the shark made no threat display and left without attacking.

Clearly, if a diver, either by accident or intent, surprises a gray shark and moves toward it aggressively, he risks triggering a pattern of ritualized behavior likely to end in attack, especially if the shark finds its escape routes restricted.

From analysis of slow-speed movie frames, the scientists found the threat display was as follows: the shark begins to swim in an S-shaped path, elongate at first, intensifying to a figure eight pattern as it gets closer to the diver, doubling back on its course and holding its ground. It swims with an exaggerated lateral motion, its body rolling or spiral looping, the pectoral fins severely depressed. The shark's body is gripped with extreme muscular tension, the snout raised, jaws slightly open, and back arched. It is making an instinctive threat gresture to counter the aggressive approach of the diver. Such ritualized behavior must have developed under natural conditions for use in courtship or territorial defense, but in the case of wide-ranging sharks the term *Lebensraum* or living space is more apt than the idea of a precise geographical territory. Many fishes use fin displays and exaggerated swimming movements for threat display against rivals and much the same behavioral pattern is used in courtship.

Walt has used the *El Torito*'s wet submarine to carry such studies further. With its speed, maneuverability, and protection, he has been able to observe provoked attacks by gray sharks on repeated occasions. Once the propeller was seized and the drive pin snapped, necessitating an ascent without power. Another time a shark broke one of the half-inch plastic windows in the rear canopy.

Walt told me that the first gray reef shark attack on the submarine occurred when *El Torito* was at Eniwetok, Marshall Islands.

"We were cruising along the seaward side of the atoll near the outer drop-off, in about seventy feet of water. It was the first day that we'd taken the submarine out to actually use it in the Pacific. Visibility was around 150 feet when we spotted this gray about eighty feet ahead. A large individual for a gray, he was close to seven feet long. His attack behavior was typical of what we saw in subsequent encounters; as we approached him at a distance of perhaps forty feet, he began to swim with a slightly exaggerated lateral motion of the head. This increased as the submarine began to catch up with him. At about twenty-five feet distance, he began to arch his back slightly about two-thirds of the way along, which gave him a rather stiff-bodied appearance. At the same time his pectoral fins angled downward. Instead of being held out to the sides horizontally, they angled down at a 45-degree angle. He was swimming with this stiff-bodied motion, pectorals down, head wagging side to side and moving away from us.

"As the sub continued to gain on him, at a distance of perhaps twenty feet, he suddenly whirled and made a rapid circle around to our left and attacked the propeller from behind. The circle was so fast that if you'd been in the water it would have been virtually impossible to turn around and face him as quickly as he came around. Still moving fast, he came in, hit the propeller, and sheared the drive pin so the motor suddenly revved up. The submarine lost speed and sank to the bottom. He then circled around looking like he might attack again. We didn't have any side windows on then and I was really afraid that he might charge in. If he hit where the window gaps were, he might end up inside, which would be disastrous. Fortunately he didn't and we sat still until he went away. I blew the ballast tanks and came to the surface. When we got back to the island with the sub, I found an old plastic desktop, cut it up and made the side windows that are on now.

"My first thought was that his attack had been directed at the noise and motion of the propeller. However, the next attack occurred in a lagoon pass with a very similar preattack pattern. This time the shark first attacked the body of the submarine and then returned to attack the canopy right at our faces. In all he made five separate attacks. He'd hit in and bounce off and I'd turn the sub and go after him and he'd attack it again. Subsequent attacks involved both the body of the sub and the canopy. The latter seemed to be directed at us inside but, of course, glanced off the clear plastic instead.

"In between these attacks there were a number of sharks we approached which didn't attack. I would say one out of five sharks attacks, and the others just tend to move away with a stiff-bodied motion, managing to swim just a little faster than we're moving.

"In a couple of striking instances, the preattack display became so exaggerated they lost all forward motion in the water and ended up suspended at a 45-degree angle, slashing their heads back and forth, snapping their jaws with pectorals down and back arched. The whole motion is similar to what they do when they are tearing into a large prey to rip a chunk out of it. So I think this preattack display may really be a displaced attack which, in some instances, is carried through to an actual attack. There's a desire to repel a competitor or something that's threatening them but also the opposing drive to attack is displaced by fear. But if the drive to attack becomes strong enough to overcome the opposing fear then the attack is carried out on the sub.

"There doesn't seem to be anything that directs it at any one part of the sub; it's been at the canopy or us inside, it's been at the fiberglass body of the sub and it's been at the propeller.

"The last attack was at Kuop. We were cruising beside a vertical drop-off along the wall of the pass at a depth of about ninety feet. Suddenly I felt something hit the sub. My first thought was that I'd bumped an outcropping of coral rock with a wingtip. I quickly glanced over. It was simply a quick, natural response:

I felt a bump and glanced over because I thought I'd been hit. I could see I was about five feet off the wall.

"I looked back—Al Giddings, the underwater photographer, was in the back seat. He shrugged and looked at me. I thought something had dropped back there—maybe his tank or camera had bumped something. But Al just shrugged and looked at me—and we went along a little way, perhaps thirty feet, when suddenly there was another bump. At this point we were well out from the wall, perhaps ten feet or so. I felt right then that it must be a shark, but I hadn't seen any. There wasn't one ahead of us or above us—apparently it was below us and I couldn't see him. We simply passed over him and he'd attacked. In any case, there was a second bump and I started looking around for a shark.

"Then I spotted him, coming up ahead of us on our starboard quarter. I swung the sub around and he veered to our left, away from the wall. I banked the sub around trying to face him so Al could get some film footage. He suddenly rushed around us again in a complete circle of only fifteen feet radius. I continued to circle around and he went out of my field of vision. There was a third bump and I continued to circle. As I did so I saw this thing glinting in the sunlight and drifting downward like a leaf, sashaying back and forth as it sank. Then I realized it was a piece of the canopy. I turned around and I could see that, on the right hand side, by Al, the lower portion of the window was gone. I pointed to it. Al looked back and quickly stuck his tank there in case the bastard came back and made another attack. In any event the shark by this time had disappeared and we couldn't find him again. We cruised along and saw several more—they went through their usual displays but didn't attack and that was the last actual attack we had.

"Since then I've seen a number of aggressive displays on the occasions that we've used the sub, but I haven't had a chance to do any more real shark-chasing with it. I went at several of them in the channel at

Palau and produced the usual displays. Then out at Osprey Reef in the Coral Sea when we used it I got some displays and a couple of displays at the Marion reefs but in none of these was I close enough to provoke an attack and gain further observation."

At Eniwetok Atoll, Ted Hobson (*Pacific Science, 1963*) conducted a series of fourteen experiments on the feeding behavior of grays, blacktips, and whitetips. He concluded that for these sharks smell is the most effective sense for detecting prey, either injured or just in a state of stress, at a distance. Upcurrent they are able to follow such a stimulus to its source without the help of any other orienting stimuli. It releases a pattern of exploratory behavior in gray sharks which promotes appetite. It takes some other specific stimulus to incite them highly. Despite the curiosity aroused by various stimuli, the approach to an unfamiliar situation is initially cautious but with increasing familiarity this caution will steadily subside.

With a motionless prey the gray's final phase of approach is normally directed by vision. Significant visual cues seem to involve the detection of movement, or contrasting brightness, or both. Visual acuity and the ability to distinguish form were not evident. In one experiment grays showed no preference between a four-inch cube of wood and a similar-sized cake of fish flesh. They accepted equally an intact fish or one with head and fins removed. But when offered the choice of a pair of three-inch fish cubes, one natural and one dyed black with nigrosine dye, in a total of 172 trials under all possible lighting conditions, the black was taken 124 times—seventy-two percent of the total.

Further experiments showed that while gray sharks will initially accept baits such as fish flesh soaked in alcohol, such baits are promptly rejected when the taste is unacceptable.

In another experiment mollusk flesh such as that of the giant clam was paired with chunks of grouper flesh. The baits were taken with equal vigor, indicating a lack of visual discrimination, but the mollusk flesh was rejected almost immediately.

Tests with standard shark repellent copper acetate-nigrosine dye showed it to be ineffective when gray sharks were present in numbers and motivated by food adjacent to the repellent.

14

Great White Death

VALERIE TAYLOR

Several years ago, with the help of my diary, I decided to write down much of the general knowledge that I had accumulated on the "Great White Death."

No doubt my observations and experiences will differ greatly from those of other people who have had the opportunity to study this shark at close range.

However, with very little to go on other than my own observations, I did the best that I could. Not being a scientist, or a professional writer, I am sure that readers with such experience will be able to point out many errors.

I have put into print, however, for better or worse, a collection of incidents and experiences which I hope make interesting reading and may teach people a little about the shark, whose reputation and numbers has suffered so drastically since the release of *Jaws*.

The sharks that I write about are real ones, some of them probably still living, off the South Australian coast. Peter Benchley's monster was the fabrication of an imaginative mind, although he did use the characteristics of the real white with amazing effectiveness.

This piece does not cover all our experiences with the "Great White Death." They would fill a whole book, but there is enough information to give a good overall picture of the sharks and of some of the people who work with them.

●

There is one shark which is the epitome of all man's fears. It is not common or easily found. It is known by many names. *Carcharodon carcharias*. Great White Death. Man-eater.

The Great White Death is the ultimate predator—a superbly designed eating machine. There is no other animal alive which has evolved to the same degree of perfection, essentially unchanged for millions of years.

Its main enemies are others of its kind and, of course, man. At present there are still remote corners of the world, like the cold waters off the South Australian coast, where the Great White Death patrols the ocean in an eternal search for food, as its ancestors have done for sixty million years.

When Matthew Flinders first charted this coast in 1802, he wrote of the hundreds of large sharks that he saw. Their numbers have been declining ever since. Vulnerable because of their fearlessness, they are becoming increasingly rare. To find a white shark today is an uncertain and expensive business. To find one in twenty years' time could be impossible.

We believe that great whites live in a certain territory, despite the generally held opinion that they are ocean roamers. When we seek great whites, we sail into places where we know they live. Dangerous Reef, 19 miles from Port Lincoln is such a place.

In this area, few females are seen. Most of the sharks are males, 11 to 15 feet long. Females are found at Kangaroo Island, 100 miles away. There appear to be fewer of them, and, as is the case with most shark species, they are larger—16 to 20 feet in length.

The largest, all females, are found at Streaky Bay, 186 miles west of Dangerous Reef. These are rare giants measuring up to 20 feet and weighing well over 2,500 pounds. The world record great white was taken here in 1964 by a man named Alf Dean and, although only 16 feet long, it weighed 2,664 pounds.

Big-game fishermen have tried to beat this record and

while several have claimed that they hooked bigger fish, none have been landed.

There are no records available on sightings of really small great whites. Where do the babies live? Small whites are not uncommon around the North American coast, but these are not babies. I have been unable to find scientific records of really small great whites anywhere. Even pregnant females are not common.

The only reference I could find on this was a report that a pregnant female with two fetuses was caught on a line near Kangaroo Island, South Australia. Little is known of their breeding habits, but one thing I am sure of; white sharks are slow breeders and probably live a long time, perhaps hundreds of years. Also, they continue to grow. The largest white shark on record, taken near Port Ferry, Victoria, supposedly measured 36½ feet, but there is some question as to the validity of this claim.

The Great White Death may be an ocean roamer as some experts suggest, and it is probably true in some cases, but our experiences suggest that it is mainly a creature with a defined territory.

I believe that, in the Dangerous Reef area, we have lured some of the same sharks, year after year. In January 1973, all but one of the sharks lured to our chartered boat, the *Temptation*, acted in a way that suggested that they had experienced the cages before. In the past, the sharks had repeatedly attacked the cages. On that occasion, they carefully looked them over, then moved away, concentrating on the baits around the stern of the boat.

Their attitude was disastrous for our film work. Ron was forced to return to his original 1965 method of filming sharks. This meant hanging his unguarded body from the duckboard and filming the marauders as they attacked the lures, only feet away.

White sharks have some interesting habits. To me, the most fascinating is that they raise their heads from the water to investigate the unusual. It is rather nerve-wracking seeing a 13-foot great white carefully watching one's every move, with its head above water.

This unsharklike mannerism could have resulted from hunting warm-blooded creatures which live along the shore. South Australian fishermen tell stories of whites lifting half their bodies clear of the water to grab a sleeping seal from a rock. I see no reason to doubt them, for the sharks certainly do lift their bodies several feet from the water time and time again, reaching for baits pulled well above the surface.

It will not, however, rise from the water six inches to reach a vulnerable human kneeling on a duckboard. It will watch in a most intelligent way. I am not saying that the great white is more intelligent than any other shark, just that its behavior is different.

Apart from its immense size and aggressive disposition, it is this behavior that makes him so special. It is not just the best armed, it is also the oddest shark I have ever met.

Sometimes a shark would swim past the boat without seeming to take any notice, then surprise us all by sneaking back under the hull and grabbing a bait before we realized what was happening.

This never happened with a person, although we all spent a lot of time kneeling or lying at water level and were within easy reach. We were obviously not their normal prey.

Both Ron and I, when working with sharks, try by behavior and dress to make sure that the shark can recognize us as something other than natural food. So far this has worked perfectly, but it is not a proven fact and cannot be recommended as a surefire safety precaution.

The closest call we ever had with a white happened one night about 11:30 when neither dress nor behavior were recognizable. There were three sharks around the boat, coming in one after the other trying for the baits. We were working with Italian film director Bruno Valatti. Bruno had been filming sharks feeding at night.

We had noticed in the past that the usually calm, controlled, daytime great white shark turned aggressive after dark. Our three had performed well for the cameras and I was in the tiny cabin of the *Temptation* when Bruno yelled, "Ron's in, Ron's in the water!" Everything stopped. Everything. I knew that Ron could not survive. He would die, torn to pieces in the cold black southern ocean.

Here is what I wrote in my diary at the time: "18.1.72. Late last night, I nearly lost Ron. At 11:45 P.M. he slipped from Rodney Fox's 20-foot fiberglass boat into the oil slick. There were three big sharks feeding on half a horse. Everyone was stilled with horror, almost like statues unable to move. The wind and current were carrying Rodney's boat away fast. It was very dark and rough. Ron swam after the small boat away from the baits and blood. He wore no diving equipment but being a strong swimmer reached Rodney's boat within 30 seconds and grasped the bow. He tried to pull himself from the water but lacked the strength. Hand over hand, he inched his way around the gunwale, his body from the hips down still immersed. As Ron reached the stern, Rodney helped him up over the motors. Rodney said later Ron virtually flew into the boat. As his legs cleared the surface, a great gray shape loomed up beneath him and the big black eye watched for a second before moving under the stern."

Ron had been helping Rodney anchor the cages away from the *Temptation,* and, while jumping from one boat to the other, had slipped on the oily deck.

The previous day, Ron had spared a white shark, now the favor had been returned. I was in the cage with Ron when it happened.

A beautiful big male, twelve feet long, had been performing well against the bars. Ron was shooting movie, and I, still photographs. Our rather skimpy cage was tethered to the *Temptation* by a slender steel trace which hung an inch or so below the water level.

The shark, which had been circling us about 4 feet down, suddenly came in on the surface. His nose touched the trace and, with a sudden start, the shark flicked back, twisting a loop of steel around his head. Frightened, he dived deep, found himself trapped, and went into a characteristic spin, binding the cable even more firmly around his body.

The cage plunged and bucked like a mad thing. I thought we would be killed. Ron was not using scuba. Fortunately for me, I was.

Sometimes, the cage would be under the water for a minute or more before the flotation tanks pulled us back to the surface, where Ron could grab a quick breath of air.

Not realizing how tangled it was, our friends on board cast the trace off, hoping that the shark would free himself. Our ride became wilder. The trapped shark twirled with incredible suppleness, twisting back, again and again, to bite the wire that held it.

The shark eventually began to tire. Although battered, I started taking stills. Ron, with his usual calmness, had been filming whenever possible. The above-water cameraman had stood and stared without shooting a single frame!

Once the shark became exhausted, it hung head down from the cage, giving only an occasional flutter. We then used Rodney's boat to tow the shark to shallow water in the lee of Dangerous Reef. Ron sat on a rock, and removed the trace from around the shark. The white's expressionless eye seemed to roll back, watching every move. Once the tail was free, Ron gave the shark a push and it swam out into deeper water, then turned in a big circle and returned to where Ron stood.

He pushed it once again toward the open sea. The great tail lashed the water once and, in a flurry of spray, the shark vanished. Only a surface swell marked its path. Ron spared the shark; the following night it was Ron that was spared.

The accidental capture of a white shark may appear a rarity, but almost exactly one year later, on January 2, 1973, it happened again in the same way. This time, to our amazement, the shark was a female, the first that any of us had ever seen in this area.

It is easy to determine the sex of a shark. Males have two large claspers situated between their anal fins. Females do not.

She hung a forlorn sight, completely exhausted from her struggles, her tail securely attached to the cage. Rodney, Ron, and I went into the water to take photographs.

The shark suffered us to crawl all over her. Only once did she break into a violent struggle, sending Rodney and I swimming frantically away while Ron dashed in, camera whirring.

All the while her eyes watched us. She was exhausted, but very much alive and aware of us.

We dragged her into shallow water, tail first. She had suffered severe bruising as the steel wires grated over her body. Anoxia was causing her to roll sickeningly. Once the waves started breaking over her, she recovered quickly and would have swum away but for the restricting coils of metal.

Ron and I were both in the water with her. We jabbed a metal name tag through her dorsal fin, making her the second great white we had tagged. It read: "O'Gower. UNI. N.S.W. 2000 . . . No. 11."

Professor Ken O'Gower is Australia's leading shark researcher and for many years has been tagging sharks to assist in the study of their migratory habits.

Another shark expert, American Thomas A. Lineaweaver III, had asked us to take a great white's temperature—if we ever had the chance. Ever since receiving this request, we had carried two large thermometers around, just in case.

This was the chance. Ron drove a slender knife six inches into the fleshy part of her back, near the spine. He then inserted a thermometer into the wound. The body temperature was 22.55°C. The water temperature was 20.5°C. It is believed that the muscle action of "game fish" generates a certain amount of heat, but the shark had, by now, been virtually motionless for over three hours.

She was becoming anxious to go. I could feel her

tail muscles swimming within themselves. A quick run over with a tape showed her to be 13 feet long—she was quite a big lump of shark.

We set her free. She hesitated for a second, then, with a sweep of her tail, flowed away from us forever.

Six months later, Mr. Peter E. Huggins, a professional shark fisherman from Colac, Victoria, caught our tagged shark. He returned the tag to Professor O'Gower with details as to how she died and how much a pound her flesh brought at the fish market.

One day, some qualified person may be interested enough to research whites in their natural element. I only hope when that day arrives there are enough great whites left to make the study worthwhile.

Whites are reasonably plentiful wherever there are large colonies of seagoing mammals. They may be found around harpooned whales, or attacking schools of fish, but they live near seal colonies.

The white shark acts as nature's culler, sorting out the sick, the old, and the feeble, leaving only the strong and healthy to perpetuate the species.

I have never seen seals chased from the water by a shark, but I have seen a shark chased by a young bull sea lion. This astounding incident occurred the afternoon of January 1, 1973.

A 13-foot shark had swum up the slick and was circling the *Temptation*. To let him know he had found the right place, we threw out several baits. Once the shark arrives it is important to feed him, otherwise he could become bored and go away.

This shark had taken a bait and was beginning to perform well. Ron and I were about to enter the cages when a young bull sea lion swam out from the reef and began to annoy the shark.

It was really quite incredible. The seal would constantly leap through the surface, then dive at the shark. Although concentrating on the tail, the seal darted around the predator's head several times. He gave it no peace. There were seven people watching and we all agreed the bull seal appeared to be following or chasing the shark.

The white shark must have thought so too, because he became more agitated, swimming faster to avoid the seal. Finally, after 10 to 15 minutes, the shark swam away. We never saw him again.

I could hardly believe it. A 250-pound seal had harassed a 1,200-pound shark into leaving the area. We had just spent five days and one thousand dollars enticing the shark to us. Now he was gone, and we had to start all over again.

The victorious young bull swam back to his island, lumbered up the rocks, and plopped down in the sun, where he promptly went to sleep. It appeared that playing with white sharks was all in a day's fun for him.

The most interesting piece of information to emerge from this incredible incident is that even a great white beginning to fall into a feeding pattern can be deterred. The shark had swum possibly 20 miles, or more, following the whale oil slick. On arrival, it must have been hungry and ready to eat, yet, a bothersome little seal had forced it away. One would imagine a white shark tearing the mammal to pieces. We were all waiting for something like that to happen.

I had the feeling that what we witnessed was not an unusual happening, but a course of action used by the Australian sea lions. Ron and I discussed this event for some time, our main interest being that if a seal could harass a big shark like that, could similar behavior by a diver produce the same result? In any and every case where a diver confronted a white shark with aggression, the shark eventually departed.

All the divers I know who've survived an attack by a great white say they never saw the shark before it hit them.

I am not saying that if a potential victim sees the shark before the attack he can frighten it away, just that it appears to be a great psychological advantage to show aggression. Sharks certainly seem to know when they are being watched or threatened. It is something they do not normally encounter in their day-to-day life.

Sharks also learn simple things quickly. There is obvious mistrust of the boat and its occupants. It is always a painstaking business to coax these sharks to feed. Once you do, it is interesting to watch how quickly their subconscious feeding behavior takes over. Having another white feeding around the boat helps a lot. The shark's brain is impregnated by hereditary behavior patterns over which the owner, once the signal is strong enough, has little control. Sharks can also think —and some better than others.

It would be interesting to know at what stage conscious thought is replaced by blind instinct. With whaler sharks this happens very quickly. In most whites, particularly ones who have experienced big-game fishermen, blind instinct seems always to be tempered by either conscious thought or subconscious fear.

In the Indian Ocean, we were filming hundreds of sharks feeding on a harpooned whale. I was kept busy beating them off with a short metal stick. Constantly aiming for the eyes, I must have landed hundreds of blows. Some persisted more than others. After I had jabbed them several times, I noticed an amazing thing. By shaking my stick at a previously hit shark from a distance of up to twenty feet, I could make that shark flinch, jam his gills tightly shut, roll his eye back, and flick away.

This happened with not just one shark, but many sharks. They were mainly oceanic whitetips, 8 to 10 feet long, though one oceanic blue performed in a somewhat similar manner. Within half an hour, these supposedly mindless man-eating predators had learned a simple lesson. If they bumped me, I bumped them back hard, and they did not like it!

I think that white sharks would behave under similar conditions in the same manner. Unfortunately, I will never be able to prove this theory properly, for whites do not bump before they bite. They just bite. Even a gentle nip from a great white is disastrous.

Whites appear to be very afraid of each other. If several sharks have been attracted at the same time, they take turns attacking the cages, never swimming in to-

gether. Should two sharks be on a collision course (and
it does happen), each, on sighting the other, will flick
away at great speed.

In *Blue Water, White Death* there appeared to be
only one great white shark. In fact, there were five all
around the boat at the same time. We could rarely
film them together, because they did not swim together.

One white, several feet longer than the rest, appeared to have an unchallenged right of way. If it approached the bait at the same time as another, the
smaller one always gave way immediately as they were
in sight of each other.

I have never seen a white shark in a feeding frenzy.
Whites take everything in a slow, calculated fashion.
Even when fighting for a bait, the great jaws snapping,
there is perhaps a sudden burst of energy, but no continued frenzy.

They are cannibals by nature and will attack a
wounded comrade with the same impunity as they attack a box, a boat, or even, occasionally, man. Fortunately, man is not a food that they like. I believe most
attacks have been mistakes.

At the time of this writing, there have been only
five positive deaths due to white shark attack recorded
in Australia. Not a very impressive record for a shark,
particularly when compared with the 140-odd attacks
attributed to the bronze whaler, *Carcharhinus macru-
rus,* a smaller relative of the white shark.

On March 12, 1960, Brian Rodgers was attacked by
a 9-foot white pointer (another name for the great
white) during a spearfishing competition near Aldinga
Beach, South Australia. Brian drove off the shark, made
a tourniquet for his injured leg with speargun rubber,
and swam toward the shore three-quarters of a mile
away. He was picked up by divers in a boat and rushed
to hospital where three hundred stitches were inserted
in his torn leg.

Rodney Fox, who was fishing in the same competition, also saw the shark when it circled him several
times. Rodney said he pointed his spear gun at the
predator and felt as though he were pointing a match,

the gun looked so small by comparison. The shark vanished, leaving Rodney shaken but unharmed.

Two years later, on December 10, 1962, during another spearfishing competition, sixteen-year-old Geoffrey Corner met a shark just 14 miles from where Brian had been attacked. Geoffrey's spearfishing competitor, Allen Phillips, dragged the mutilated boy from the shark's maw, but he was dead before reaching the beach.

Exactly one year to the day after Geoffrey's death, Rodney Fox was fishing in the South Australian spearfishing championships, one hundred yards from where Brian Rodgers was attacked. This time Rodney was not so lucky. He did not see the shark until it had his body crushed in its mouth.

Although critically wounded, Rodney fought his way free and was picked up by a nearby safety boat. Rodney survived, where most would have died. His ribs were crushed, his lungs punctured and his liver torn. Only Rodney's physical and mental fitness pulled him through. Rodney decided he was going to live and, although all the odds were against him, he did.

There is a strong possibility that Brian, Rodney, and Geoffrey were all attacked by the same beast. Perhaps the shark was merely trying to deter intruders from its territory or was it a mad ravenous brute trying to kill anything that crossed its path? Unfortunately, the answer is something we will never know.

The last of our friends to be attacked by a great white was Henri Bource. Henri had his leg bitten off at the knee while he was swimming with a group of sea lions. The shark was dragging Henri down by his leg when the shark teeth severed the bone at the knee. As Henri was not using scuba, he is extremely lucky not to have drowned. When the attack occurred, he was not the only diver in the water. His companions beat back the shark with hand spears as it followed Henri to the boat.

In each of these cases, there were other people in the water when the attacks took place. Was it just bad luck or were they the particular victims singled out for some reason? Certainly, carrying bleeding fish on the weight belt increases the chances of attracting a shark.

It is very much to their credit that they are back diving again.

Many years of experience have proved to my satisfaction that sharks do not attack without a reason. Either the victim has unwittingly done something to attract the shark or, as in the case of Raymond Short, who was bitten in shallow water near Sydney, the shark was sick and wounded.

The few whites that I have met accidently have shown a certain curiosity, but no inclination to attack. They have simply flashed past, looked us over, returned for a second look, then disappeared. Had we been spearing fish and the sharks hungry, things may have happened differently.

When a shark's feeding instinct is aroused, they are likely to attack and try to devour anything from a beer can to a 60-foot boat. If animal blood is poured into the water near white sharks, they will swim through the red cloud, jaws snapping with tremendous ferocity. They appear to be feeling with their teeth for the owner of the blood and will usually bite, viciously, the first solid object to cross their path.

Ron and I have had prolonged experience only with white sharks which we have lured with food. They are so rarely seen otherwise, it is difficult to guess what the pattern of their everyday lives is. Food would be the main interest, but, beyond that, little is known about them.

Unfortunately, whites do not take kindly to being trapped in tanks and generally die before any extensive research can be done. The only white I know of kept in captivity constantly bumped the walls of his tank. In nature, they know no restrictions, in captivity they refuse to accept them.

An unexpected feature of the great white is that it does not have to be in motion to breathe. Both of our trapped sharks managed perfectly well hanging motionless, by their tails, for several hours.

A great white is easy to recognize under water, the

most distinctive feature being his round black eye. Unlike other members of his particular family, his serrated triangular teeth are always showing in a sinister smile. The tail is also very distinctive. Most sharks have a tail with the top lobe much longer than the bottom. The great white has a tail with lobes of almost equal length, a modification shared by several other fast-moving sharks and most big pelagic fish.

One trait all sharks have in common is that they can be very unpredictable, and it is this unpredictability that makes them potentially dangerous.

The contrast in behavior between whites and whalers will show what I mean. We had five male whites of roughly equal size and weight swimming around our boat. After a short time, we knew each individually. There was a definite pecking order.

The leader was more aggressive and had the right of way. He took more baits and approached the boat more frequently. Another similar shark circled further away from the boat and took no baits at all. It was hungry or it wouldn't have been there, yet it was timid and appeared to be easily bullied by the others. According to Professor O'Gower, this is not uncommon behavior in some species.

On the other hand the whalers have little or no respect for their leader, at least during feeding. A group of various-sized whaler sharks will attack lures in a mad, mixed-up scramble.

This type of behavior could be the reason white sharks have made so few attacks on man and whalers so many.

Looking at all the records available to me on whites, I discovered a confusing number of theories but little fact. Considering that the Great White Death is the most awesome predator living on earth today, this is rather surprising. Scientists may or may not agree with what I have written here, but the majority of my statements are based on personal experience and the rest on the experiences of personal friends.

IV

SCIENTIFIC

●

The segment from Dr. Eugenie Clark's book, *The Lady and the Sharks,* is titled "Sharks That Ring Bells." It is the only completely scientific experiment concerning sharks that I found suitable for inclusion. In fact, there is very little data available on experiments concerning sharks and their behavior that makes good general reading. The result is that Dr. Clark has a section all her own.

True, I could have included "Sharks That Ring Bells" in the shark behavior section, but it hardly seemed the correct thing to do. The other stories under "Shark Behavior" are mostly odd little snippets about a shark or sharks that came to the author's attention for some special reason regarding their actions at the time. My story about gray nurses came about because we were trying to make a film, not do scientific research into their behavior.

Most of the other scientific books I considered, while not uninteresting to me, concentrated more on describing sharks and where they could be found. For instance, "Leopard Shark, *Triakis semifasciata,* shallow water, eastern north Pacific, five gill slits" and so on. This type of information, while useful to someone who wants to know all the particulars about a certain shark, hardly makes good reading for the general public.

Anyway, Dr. Eugenie Clark is such an unusual person and her work so important to the understanding of sharks, I feel she deserves a special place of her own in this book.

15

"Sharks That Ring Bells"

EUGENIE CLARK

Eugenie Clark is a remarkable woman. She was the founder and director, for the first ten years of its existence of the Cape Haze Marine Laboratory in Florida.

During her period with the lab, it evolved from a tiny, one-woman affair based in a 20 by 12 foot wooden building into one of the most respected institutions of its type in the world.

Although I have had the pleasure of meeting Dr. Clark only once, I feel that I know her and have done so for a long time. She has the inquisitive mind of a good scientist and her research into sharks and their behavior patterns has done much to further man's limited knowledge of these large fish.

The first book of Dr. Clark's that I read was called *Lady with a Spear*. It was enjoyable reading and I found it encouraging that this world-famous marine scientist regarded marine animals not just as objects of research, but as living, feeling, thinking creatures, each with its own personality. *The Lady and the Sharks* is even better. It is full of interesting facts and information presented in an exciting easy-to-read style.

The chapter I have chosen tells how foolish people can be about sharks. Had the four-year-old child dangling its legs in the shark pen been bitten, all blame would, no doubt, have fallen on the shark and Eugenie

133

Clark. The parents ignored No Trespassing signs and crossed a chained-off driveway, but would have aimed their outrage and sorrow at the shark rather than themselves.

The experiments with the lemon sharks ringing bells is fascinating, as is the description of sharks copulating. I am often asked how sharks mate. This is the only time that I have ever read of someone actually watching and recording the event in such fine detail.

Most famous of the experiments, and one which is quoted in other subsequent books on sharks, is that concerned with the training of sharks to ring a bell for food. It may not seem like a very significant or useful achievement, but, prior to this, it was generally believed that sharks had very limited intelligence and could not be trained to do anything. This program proved that they can not only be trained but that they learn fairly quickly.

The same basic program was later extended to test the visual perceptions of sharks. A number of interesting things came out of this—including the fact that some species of sharks are very attracted to strong striped patterns, information that should be passed on to the swimwear designers, and perhaps, Dr. Walter Starck, inventor of the banded wetsuit.

In a later chapter, she calls a special shark friendly. I know that they can be friendly, but generally hate to say it. After *Jaws* most people think nothing nice about sharks, least of all that they can be friendly.

I would like every person who has seen and been frightened by *Jaws* to read Dr. Clark's book for a balanced picture of sharks as they really are. A better book would be hard to find, for it is a warm, quite funny account of an interesting woman in love with the sea.

•

As the lab becomes better known, the problem of unwelcome visitors arose. Once we found an 11-foot tiger shark dead in our pen with the hoop of a large, long-handled dip net jammed over its gills. This was a particularly handsome shark that was living well in our pen and eating huge quantities of shark meat left over from our routine dissections. We couldn't imagine how the naked wire hoop of the dip net, which Beryl had left on the dock until he had time to put a new net bag on it, got into the pen and over the shark's head. Beryl learned how when he was getting a haircut. The man in the next chair was telling his barber.

"That Cape Haze Marine Lab is a dangerous place," he said, and went on to tell how he and his wife went down to look around one day, but nobody was there and the buildings were locked up. They were fascinated by the large tiger shark in the pen and, finding the big hoop with the long handle decided to see if they could make the shark swim through the hoop. As the shark swam close to the dock, the man's wife held on to the end of the eight-foot handle and lowered the hoop directly in the shark's path. The shark swam into it, but the pectoral fins prevented the hoop from getting further than the gill region. "That goddam shark was ready to pull my wife into the water if she hadn't let go the handle," he told the barber. They then hurried away from the "dangerous" lab, leaving the tiger shark to thrash itself to death.

Beryl and I decided we had to take more precautions, and as much as we disliked putting up eyesores, we made No Trespassing signs and put a chain across the driveway to the lab. This discouraged most off-hour visitors, but not the worst kind. As the lab grew, we had to put up stronger warning signs and barbed-wire fencing. Even then, I sometimes caught trespassers in the act when I was working late at the lab or on a Sunday. One Sunday, I looked up from my desk and was horrified to see a child about four years old sitting on the feeding platform dangling his feet in the shark pen. His parents had brought him. They had ignored the signs and climbed the fence. They saw no sharks in the pen and were wandering about the grounds. An 11-foot dusky shark was swimming in the deeper murky water of the pen. Fortunately it had eaten its fill the day before.

One evening, when I had to work very late, I watched as a man, pushing down one barbed wire with his foot and lifting the upper wire with his hand, allowed a pretty girl to step through. I caught up with them as they neared the shark pen and he was saying, "Wait till you see this!" I interrupted their adventure and talked with them. He defiantly told me, "We weren't going to harm your precious sharks." I might have lost my temper except I was stalling for time. I had already called the police.

The couple was arrested. The arrest, announced in the paper the next day, was enough to keep trespassers away for some time.

Another time, a man with three young ladies in his boat pulled up alongside a small pen which held twenty baby sharks we had delivered the day before and were hoping would live. The man began showing off by catching one of the two-foot sharks by the tail, twirling it around his head, and hurling it across the pen while his audience giggled. He quickly started up his motor when he saw me coming out of the lab.

We continued setting our lines for sharks. After a day of diving on the reefs, Beryl would check the shark line on the way back and we might return to the lab with garbage cans of two-inch gobies, blennies, and serranids and a twelve-foot shark. I kept on experimenting and studying abdominal pores and anything else I could learn about the sharks we caught. This led to a series of experiments that ultimately got too much publicity and stuck me with the dubious label of "shark lady."

Somehow my reputation of diving and using a spear to collect fishes (described in my book *Lady with a Spear*) made reporters and writers of magazine articles assume that I collected big sharks by diving and spearing them. Even when I corrected this notion in an interview and stipulated before the interview that I be allowed to see the text of the article before it was sent to press (something popular-magazine writers and editors hate to do), many bloopers got through. In one case, the writer carefully avoided any hint that I dived with and speared the sharks I worked with, but when the art department of the magazine got to work, they sketched a picture of me diving, with a one-rubber arbalete spear gun that would barely hold a mullet, about to shoot the spear into a gigantic shark. This came out as a two-page spread in the magazine.

The things we were learning about sharks and our success in keeping sharks in captivity drew the attention of scientists from various parts of the world who were interested in problems related to sharks. They came from Africa, Germany, Italy, Israel, England, France, Denmark, and Japan to work with us. We were able to expand our research with additional financial help we got in the form of grants from the National Science Foundation, the Office of Naval Research, the American Philosophical Society, and the Selby Foundation.

There are about 250 different species of sharks living in the world, ranging from a cute little deep-water species less than a foot long to the giant whale shark reported to attain 60 feet in length. The largest shark that ever lived was *Carcharodon megalodon*. Its black and gray fossilized teeth, measuring up to six inches, are commonly found on Florida beaches. It probably grew to nearly 100 feet in length and is related to the most dangerous man-eating shark now living, the great white shark, *Carcharodon carcharias*. Fortunately, the white shark grows to only 20 feet.

The wide shallow continental shelf extending about 100 miles out on the west coast of Florida limits the variety of sharks we can catch to about eighteen species. For practical reasons, we had to operate our shark lines within eight miles of shore and had little chance of catching real deep-water or oceanic sharks. We caught three different species of hammerhead sharks, two species of blackfin sharks, several types of small dogfish sharks, and on rare occasions a white shark or a sand tiger shark. But we could count on a good supply of dusky and sandbar sharks each winter, nurse sharks and tiger sharks all year round, and many bull and lemon sharks during the spring, summer, and fall.

Most of the sharks we caught were from 5 to 11 feet long. We measured a few dusky, tiger, and great hammerhead sharks that got into the 12- and 14-foot range and nearly 1,000 pounds, but this size group is uncommon in our records.

Our examinations of the contents of hundreds of sharks' stomachs showed us that our local sharks eat over forty varieties of fish, including eels, some prickly bony fishes (e.g., spiny blowfish and poisonous spined catfish), stingrays, and other sharks. We also often found remains of squid, octopus, shellfish, starfish, crabs, and shrimps, occasionally sea turtles and sea birds, and rarely some porpoise remains. Once we found a yellow-bellied cuckoo and another time a gull with a metal band (which was reported to the amazed bander) in the stomach of the omnivorous tiger shark.

Most of the species we studied seem to mate in the spring and early summer. At this time, the claspers of mature males were red and swollen. Often sperm oozed out of the urogenital papilla,* and on dissection we could see the testes were much enlarged. When we opened the female, we could find wriggling sperm by examining under the microscope smears taken from the vagina, uterus, and tubes leading toward the ovary. On the ovary, large yellow ripe round eggs were nearly ready to break out of their follicles. Shortly after the mating season, the ovary would contain only small white eggs, but the uterus would contain big yellow oval-shaped eggs. These had been fertilized by sperm at some point high in the tubes, and partway down the tubes in the nidamental or shell gland had acquired a soft golden "shell" before settling into spongy pockets in the uterus. Sometimes we found each oval egg had a tiny wriggling embryo on the surface of the yolk.

By plotting the size of these embryos at different months of the year, we could draw their growth curve and determine the gestation period, which varied from

*During copulation, sperm from the urogenital papilla enters a groove in the clasper, which swings into a forward position and is inserted into the female.

eight to fourteen months, depending on the species. The females of most species we studied seem to have a litter of pups only once in two or three years.

The size of the litter depends to some extent on the species of shark. The sand tiger shark has only two young at a time, and these, according to Stew Springer, start feeding before they are born on eggs the mother continues to supply from the ovary. The bull, dusky, sandbar, and lemon sharks have from five to seventeen young at a time; the great hammerhead can have several dozen, and the tiger shark over a hundred. The older the mother shark gets, the greater the number of young she carries when pregnant. We also observed a few "senile" big sharks whose ovaries had apparently stopped functioning.

Our shark dissections, especially on pregnant females, supplied fascinating information on the reproductive habits of some large species of sharks about which little was known previously. The most interesting part of our work with sharks was studying the live animal, working with one individual day after day for long periods of time and getting to know its personality.

One of the most extraordinary sharks I ever got to know was one I gave up for dead the day we caught her in May 1958. She was an adult lemon shark nearly 9 feet long. This was before we devised better methods for bringing live sharks from our setlines in the gulf back to the lab. We towed this shark by the hook she had taken in her mouth and firmly set in her jaw. It was a rough day. She was bounced on large waves in the gulf, and once we got her in the bay, we had to drag her across shallow barnacle flats because of the low tide. All the time, her mouth was being held open by the hook and towline, and water poured into her.

She struggled weakly when we first found her caught on the line. By the time we had her in the large fish pen alongside the lab's dock, she appeared dead. We tried to revive her by "walking" her around the shallow end of the pen—pushing and pulling her gently so that the water would flow over her gills—but she didn't respond.

We finally gave up. It was too late in the day to hoist her onto the dock to weigh, measure, and dissect her. So we tied her limp form alongside the dock, still with the hook and setline in her mouth, and left, intending to work on her in the morning.

When we saw her next, she was a very lively shark, raising a commotion at the end of the dock. We put her into the pen again, in shallow water where she could not struggle too much. We held her down, propped her mouth open with a block of wood, and removed the hook. We had to cut the hook wound open a little wider, in order to back out the barbed hook with long-handled pliers. As soon as we released her, she swam vigorously around the pen and then slowed down to an effortless glide. Only gentle, undulating movements of the end of her body and tail were needed to propel her powerful, streamlined body.

So we began to learn how hardy lemon sharks are, unlike other active sharks, and how well they can adjust to captivity. In the years that followed, we found it easy to bring lemon sharks in from our lines in good condition.

After the shark had spent a day in captivity, we discovered the probable reason for her weakness on the line—seven newborn lemon sharks, each about two feet long, swimming with her in the pen.

It was the first time a shark had given birth naturally at the lab. We had removed many living embryos and near full-term pups from gravid dusky and sandbar female sharks we dissected. Those babies, even when we tried "incubator" methods, seldom lived more than a few days. But we had great hopes for raising the newborn lemon sharks.

The day after they were born, they started feeding. The female and her pups had our large 40 by 70-foot pen all to themselves. In a few weeks, they were eating well and the babies grew noticeably fatter. The sight of a person walking to the corner of the shallow end of the pen, where the young sharks were fed, attracted them almost immediately, and the first piece of cut fish dropped into the water set up a feeding frenzy as the seven young sharks crisscrossed each other and rushed around the feeding area.

Then I made a mistake. Our setlines caught a large male lemon shark, and I thought he would make a good mate for the female. We put him in the pen and he did get along fine with her. But the baby sharks began disappearing one by one. Those healthy young sharks, which would have been ideal for testing the function of abdominal pores because of their small size, were soon all gone.

We were left, however, with a handsome pair of adult lemon sharks that were very responsive to signs of food. We had an excellent opportunity to study their feeding behavior.

At first we threw fish (whole mullet) to them. We used so much mullet to bait our shark lines and to feed the sharks we kept alive that we invested in a storage freezer. It paid for itself with the money we saved buying mullet wholesale, 200 pounds at a time.

In order to watch more closely when the sharks were feeding, we built a feeding platform close to the water. We weighed the amount of food we gave them each day, since I found out that practically nothing was known about the amount of food needed to keep a large shark alive. We could make the sharks come to the edge of the platform and take mullet handed to them. Occasionally a shark would miss and a mullet dropped to the bottom, especially when the shark charged toward the platform with open mouth and the feeder understandably let go of the mullet a fraction of a second early. Then we couldn't be sure which shark got the food.

A bright junior high school student, Tommy Romans, was a regular visitor to our lab and begged us to let him be a volunteer worker and, among other things, to let him feed the sharks. The risk we ran having an "attractive hazard" was unavoidable for our studies, but we could avoid letting a fourteen-year-old boy feed sharks from a platform suspended over the pen. Tommy was very persuasive. It could have been annoying except that he was so pleasant. He started working for us, helping in the weighing, measuring, and dissection of dead sharks. He also looked around for any odd jobs he could do, was quick to grab the hose and scrub down the dock when a dissection was over, sweep out the lab floors, wash our aquariums, empty garbage, help bait hooks on the boat—always showing almost the same enthusiasm and willingness to do these jobs as to join us skin diving. He was a fine diver and loved helping collect small fishes and pulling up the shark line, especially when something was tugging on it. He fed all the little gobies, blennies, serranids, and other animals in the aquarium room, and soon took over weighing and preparing the food for the big sharks.

He watched us feed the sharks. One shark, making a clumsy pass at a mullet, bumped into the feeding platform which at high tide was at water level. (When the tide was extra high, we didn't feed the sharks. A foot could be mistaken for a mullet.) The mullet fell down, and both sharks went after it. The sharks never fought over the food, but even their gentlest movements around the feeding platform stirred up the soft muck on the bottom of the pen, and you could see down only 2 or 3 feet of the 7-foot depth. We couldn't tell which of the two sharks had got the mullet. Also, we now had a big nurse shark in the pen which stayed on the bottom most of the time.

"Why don't we tie a weak string on the mullet until the shark takes it?" suggested Tommy. It was a good idea, and Tommy undertook the task of tying each mullet with a string several feet long and wrapping the length neatly around the fish, so that it could be thrown to the shark like confetti and the strings wouldn't tangle in the bucket of fish. The sharks came quickly to the splash at the surface, and the mullet could then be pulled into a convenient position for camera studies before a shark was allowed to take the food. This method took away the hazard of feeding the sharks by hand; the records of food consumed by each shark became more accurate; and Tommy had won himself the job of feeding them. His interest went deeper. He began borrowing books from our library to take home. And would discuss them with me the next day. I wondered if he was ever getting his regular school homework done.

Dr. Lester Aronson, an expert in animal psychology, came to the lab during the early summer of 1958. "Has anyone ever made a study of the learning behavior of sharks?" I asked him.

Dr. Aronson told us that some experiments on the olfactory sense of small sharks had been done. Plugging a nostril will cause a dogfish to swim in circles toward the unplugged side if a scent of food is in the water. But no sophisticated experiments of the kind done with birds and rats had been tried on sharks. Sharks, being such primitive fish with a primitive brain and poorly developed visual apparatus, were generally considered rather stupid—poor subjects for the classical experiments done with higher animals. "Besides," he said, "they're difficult to keep as experimental animals, and no one has tried putting them into a Skinner box!"

"Our sharks are smart, and, boy, can they see us coming with the food!" Tommy said defending his pets.

Dr. Aronson then encouraged us. "You certainly have a unique and good setup for testing their ability to learn some simple task."

We prompted Dr. Aronson further and before the day was over we had a plan. He suggested that we place a target in the water and train the shark to take mullet from the target in such a way that the shark would bump its nose against it, which would ring a bell. After a long training period, we condition a shark to associate the target with food, and to press the target and ring the bell even when the food was no longer presented along with the target.

Before he returned to New York, Dr. Aronson helped us work out a design for the apparatus to try an experiment in "instrumental conditioning," using the feeding end of the shark pen as a kind of Skinner box.

"I wish I could stay longer and help try to train

those sharks. They do look smart. Don't be discouraged. It may take months, but it really will be something if you can succeed."

At the end of the summer, Tommy hated to leave the lab. Oley Farver, another ex-commercial fisherman, had started working with us. Oley, with Tommy's assistance, had built a longer, stronger, platform with a railing. He also built a special arm to which the target, a 16 by 16-inch plywood square painted white, could be attached during feeding tests. The target could be placed so that it was just below the water surface regardless of the tide, and a firm push on it would close an electrical circuit, causing a submerged bell (an ordinary six-volt doorbell sealed in a metal cylinder) to ring.

Near the end of September, we started a strict training program for the sharks. Every day at 3:00 P.M, Oley and I put the target in the water a maximum of 20 minutes and fed the sharks in front of it, dangling the mullet from a string. At first the sharks seemed wary of the target and hesitated to take the food. But after a few days they could be lured in so close that in order to get the food into its mouth, each shark was forced to press its nose against the target. We increased the intensity of the bell from a weak buzz the first week to a loud ring that could be heard clearly above the water by the end of the second week.

From our feeding records, we were surprised to learn that it took only 15 pounds of mullet a week to keep a full-grown lemon shark of nine feet healthy and active. If we gave them all they could eat, each would take more than 30 pounds at one time, but then they fed poorly or refused food for days. A shark in its natural habitat probably goes weeks, or even months during cold weather, without eating and then may find a huge meal, such as a weakened porpoise or sea turtle, that will keep it going for another long period without food.

In order to keep our lemon sharks in training every day, and to make them repeat pressing the target and ringing the bell as many times as possible each day, we cut the mullet into smaller and smaller pieces until each shark had to ring the bell about six to ten times to get his daily quota of two pounds.

In a few weeks, the sharks were taking food from the target so rapidly that the daily training test was often over in less than 6 minutes. We had to devise a fast way to reload food on the target, for when one shark removed the food the other shark was often directly behind. We attached a thin wire to the center of the target. To each piece of food we then attached a short loop of weak string. We looped all the pieces of food on the end of the wire that reached the platform. As a shark pressed the target and removed the food, the next piece could be released to slide down the wire and be in place on the target as the second shark came.

We could see clearly how wrong was the old belief that a shark has to roll over to take a bite. Even though the mouth is on the underside of its head, the lemon sharks had no difficulty coming squarely at the target and removing the food without rolling. The snout projecting forward over the mouth, however, did make it necessary for the end of the snout to give the target a good bump in the process.

The large nurse shark we also had in the pen occasionally gummed up the training period. It wasn't satisfied with the food we gave it in another part of the pen. It wanted to get in on the act. But the nurse shark, *Ginglymostoma cirratum,* is quite different from the lemon shark, *Negaprion brevivostris*. It belongs to another family of awkward-looking sharks and is slower, more sluggish, and clumsy; it spends most of its time lying on the bottom, often under ledges or in dark caves. The adults are about the same size as lemon sharks (9 feet) but they have tiny eyes with much poorer vision. Our later tests on baby nurse sharks proved they have good vision. But the large nurse shark in the pen with the swift-feeding lemon sharks didn't seem to be able to see the target. Slowly it would pick up the scent of food and, unlike the lemons, could dangle in front of the target in a vertical position, holding this position by waving its broad fanlike pectoral (arm) fins while gently passing its small-toothed, blubber-lipped mouth over the surface of the target. It would smell and feel its way to the food with the help of its barbels, a pair of whiskers on either side of its mouth, and then, by closing its gill slits and opening its mouth, create a vacuum that would suck in the food and break the string, stealing the lemon shark's food without ringing the bell. The nurse shark got in the way so much that sometimes we'd have to poke him on the nose with a stick to get him away from the target so we could get on with the training of the lemons.

After six weeks of feeding the lemon sharks from the target, we gave them the big test. We put the target in the water at the appointed time but with no food on it. The male lemon shark who usually responded first rushed at the target with his mouth open, then swerved aside when he reached it and found no food. The second time, and for eight more times, he came in slowly, looking over the target without touching it, a few times brushing it lightly. Finally, he nuzzled the empty target hard enough to set off the automatic bell, and we quickly tossed out a reward piece of food wrapped in confetti string that hit the water with a splash just to the left of the target. The shark quickly grabbed the food, cutting the string with his teeth. In this first critical test period, he proved he had associated pressing the target with getting his food by repeatedly pushing the empty target and then taking the food tossed to him.

The more timid female lemon shark took longer to respond to the empty target, but within three days both were working the target without hesitation. We had succeeded in "instrumentally conditioning" the lemon sharks. The nurse shark gradually gave up.

We came to know the sharks as individuals. Even though they looked identical from above (except for markers we put on their dorsal fins), it was easy to tell which was the male and which the female by the manner in which they swam, turned, and reacted to the target. The male was bolder, and often when he saw us bringing the target onto the platform, he would cut short his wide-circling swim around the pen, go to a position opposite the platform, and, as the target was being lowered into the water, swim directly at it and push it with force almost the instant it was under water.

The female would hold back until the male had gotten several pieces of food and satisfied his initial hunger before she would alternate working the target with him. She would approach the target from her wide-swimming circle and often press it gently with the side of her head, just barely enough to ring the bell.

We started dropping the reward food farther and farther away from the target, giving the sharks only 10 seconds to get the food after the bell sounded. This was to test their ability to learn to make a correct turn.

For some odd reason, probably having nothing to do with Coriolis force (the effect of the earth's rotation which causes a deflection to the right in the Northern Hemisphere and to the left in the Southern Hemisphere),* the sharks in our pens almost always swam in clockwise circles. After pressing the target, the shark would have to make a counterclockwise turn to be in the direction where the reward food splashed down. They were slow to break their swimming habit.

Usually a shark would press the target, make a clockwise circle, and come back for the food; however, with a time limit of 10 seconds, as we moved the food farther away, they had less chance to reach the food on a clockwise turn than on a counterclockwise turn. After a few long clockwise turns and reaching the food just as the 10 seconds were up and the food was being pulled out of the water, the sharks learned to make the counterclockwise turn.

And they learned something else we didn't antici-

---

*I was somewhat startled when Dr. Lochner, an acoustician working with sharks in South Africa, came to visit the lab and remarked that all the sharks (in his lab's tank) swim in counterclockwise direction. Just a coincidence, probably. The local sea-bottom topography and currents undoubtedly influence a shark's swimming pattern more than the earth's rotation.

pate. It was a dramatic sight for visitors to watch us lower the target into the water, have the shark rush to push the target, make a left turn, then swim 8 feet down the side of the pen and catch the food dropped there as it hit the water. Of course, this is an easy trick to teach a porpoise or a seal, mammals with intelligence on the level of a dog; but for the lowly shark—which some taxonomists consider so beneath the bony fishes in evolutionary development they they won't even classify it as a fish—this was an accomplishment.

I decided to make it more dramatic by training them to take a fast swim way down to the end of the 70-foot pen for their reward food each time they pressed the target. It would also be a good movie sequence for the film record I was trying to make. But as the food was tossed out farther and farther away from the target, it was the female who caught on first that when the bell rang she could get the food faster than the male if she just kept circling the food area instead of going to press the target. When the male pressed the target, the female took his food. Both sharks quickly learned that the one who pressed the target had the least chance of getting the food. They started to hold back from pressing the target, and I had to move the feeding place back nearer the target to continue the experiments.

We made a crude test of an acoustical factor. The sound of the bell cued off the feeder that the shark had pushed the target and the reward food could be tossed out. We suspected that the sharks heard the bell and that its sound had reinforced their learning. What would they do if they pushed the target and the bell didn't ring? One day, when everything had been running smoothly for some days and the sharks were building up excellent scores in our record book, we didn't use the bell.

As usual, the male charged the target immediately and hit it. No bell sounded but we dropped the reward food. The shark turned counterclockwise but slowed down, and then instead of going to the feeding area, he returned to the target. The next time he pushed the target, and for the rest of the test period, it didn't bother him that the bell didn't ring. He pushed the target and went for his food which Sam Hinton says should be called the Nobell Prize.

We continued to run the tests for eight weeks until, just before Christmas, the water temperature dropped below 70°F, and the sharks lost interest in eating and in pressing the target. Then we learned something about their winter "hibernation" and memory.

The water temperature in the pens didn't go up to the seventies again until near the end of February, and the sharks started showing some interest in food again. All during the ten cold weeks, we had tried feeding them every few days just with food on a string. On February 19, we put the target in the water and the two lemon sharks pressed it as though there had never been an interruption in their daily routine with the target. We continued feeding the sharks by making them ring the bell, preparing them for more complex tests.

Dr. Dugald Brown, chairman of the department of biology at the University of Michigan, came to do some experiments at the lab in late April. He was making some complicated physiological tests on isolated pieces of living tissue from a shark's heart, which he kept alive in a high-pressure tube in a saline solution bath. Sometimes he had to check this tissue at odd times. On the night of May 1, near midnight, Dr. Brown went to the lab to check the temperature of the bath containing the muscle tissue. After that, he walked out on the dock with a floodlight to see what the lemon sharks were doing. They were copulating.

The copulation of large sharks has never been witnessed before or since, that I know of. Only small species of relatively slow-moving sharks (like the California horned shark or the European dogfish) have been seen *in copula*—the male partly coiled around the female as they mate while resting on the bottom of an aquarium.

A male shark can easily be told from a female, even in young embryos, by paired modified extensions of their pelvic fins. These sizable claspers are possessed by the males of sharks, rays, sawfishes, and skates, all of which have internal fertilization. During copulation, one of the two pennonlike claspers is rotated into a forward position, inserted into the vagina of the female, and then the unusual head of the clasper is opened as a person might expand one's hand from a fist. Cartilaginous ridges and hooklike spurs form a complex pattern which differs and is characteristic for each species of shark. An experienced shark anatomist can often tell the species of shark by examining just a clasper, the way Dr. Don Rosen, the gonopodium expert on xiphophorin fishes, can tell the species of platyfishes and swordtails apart by just the structural pattern of the male's intromittent organ, part of the anal fin of these aquarium fishes.

Dr. Brown couldn't make out any details from the dock, but he drew a sketch of the lemon sharks *in copula*. "They kept right on swimming in wide circles around the pen. I watched them for one hour."

The sharks were mating side by side, heads slightly apart but the posterior half of their bodies in such close contact and the swimming movements so perfectly synchronized that they gave the appearance of a single individual, a two-headed monster.

The next night, I stayed up with cameras and floodlights ready for use, and for the next week I drafted all reliable friends I could to help take watches through the night, but the sharks did not copulate again. Once, at dusk, the male lemon shark swam unusually close to the female and then sank, frozen in a curled position, to the bottom of the shallow end of the pen for four minutes. The claspers were noticeably pulled to the left side and appeared enlarged and slightly pink. A remora that usually accompanied the female shark was attached to the clasper region of the male shark with its sucking disc. We wondered if some seminal secretion was being released by the male lemon shark and acting as an attractant.

The female paid no special attention to the male during his stops, but occasionally she would stop her swimming and rest alongside the male. Once they both stopped swimming and rested side by side for twenty minutes. Actually, it may be more work for a lemon shark to stop swimming than to swim in slow circles. While swimming, a lemon shark keeps its mouth slightly open, and water passes in and is flushed over the gills and out the five pairs of passive gill openings. The sphincter around the esophagus at the back of the shark's throat is held in a contracted position so water doesn't flow down into the stomach. The esophageal sphincter muscle probably gets tired and opens when a shark, worn out from fighting a hook and line, is towed behind a boat and water is forced down its throat. Very little muscular activity of the shark's body is needed to keep its streamlined body in motion. But when a shark stops swimming, it has to pump water over its gills to keep up an oxygen supply. The muscular apparatus to keep this pump system going and opening and closing the mouth and gill slits looks as if it uses more calories than are needed to keep up a leisurely swim.

All during May, the pair of lemon sharks seemed unusually close and, we imagined, affectionate. They often swam together side by side or in tandem for long periods. Although they ate a little less food at this time, they worked the target very well, and we conducted many kinds of experiments with them, especially on their swimming pattern and ability to hear sounds.

Then unwittingly I made a decision with tragic consequences. I had read in books that since no cones had been found in histological preparations of the shark retina, sharks were color-blind. The retinal rods and a reflecting layer of guanin crystals at the back of a shark's eye were thought to be responsible for the shark's visual acuity in dim light and at night. And sharks seem more darkly poetic if you think of them as crepuscular creatures.

Just for fun, I decided to try a small test of our shark's color blindness. I painted the white target yellow. I figured the sharks would not notice the difference.

The male lemon shark lined himself up and rushed headlong toward the yellow target as Oley lowered it into the water. Two feet from the target, he suddenly jammed on the brakes by lowering his pectoral fins, and did a back flip out of the water, sending a spray of water over Oley, Dr. Brown, and me. All three sharks in the pen began acting strangely, swimming erratically, fast then slow, every which way, bumping into each other as they turned.

The male lemon shark never recovered from this experience. He refused food offered in any way, wouldn't go near even a white target again, and died three months later. His skin wrinkled as he lost weight. His swimming movements changed completely, his body twisted, and he kept his head turned to one side with his body muscles contracted on that side. He swam slowly, always at the surface, his back slightly arched and his tail almost half out of the water. The long upper lobe of his tail flapped on the surface of the water.

"Maybe he sprained his back on that back flip," Oley suggested. But then we noticed that on rare occasions the shark could straighten out.

We felt terrible about his death. For more than a year, he had been a part of our daily activities. We had examined hundreds of sharks by now, but it was very different to put the body of this lemon shark on the dock for a routine dissection. We did this after school hours because Tommy wanted to be there. The shark's liver was shriveled and leathery. We towed the remains of this once beautiful creature some miles out into the gulf and watched it sink.

V

DIVERS
AND SHARKS

●

Divers who work in the areas of the ocean where sharks
are prevalent learn far more about these creatures in a
few months than the most industrious scientist who
never sets foot in the water could ever learn on land.

Sharks in their natural element are truly the most
incredible creatures. Their awesome beauty of shape
and movement defies apt description, for to see a great
shark in the ocean, gliding weightlessly through his
blue world, is not only a visual sensation but an
emotional one as well. The full impact of the
experience can be completely appreciated only by the
people present at the time and to be present one must
be able to dive.

Stories about sharks and divers are always more
exciting than, say, stories about game fishermen and
sharks. For a start, the reader knows that there is no
way the shark is going to attack and eat the fisherman.
In diver and shark stories, however, there is always
the strong element of impending disaster. Divers do get
attacked by sharks and sometimes lose their lives as a
result. In spite of this, many divers, ourselves included,
feel no animosity toward sharks. In fact, we seek them
out whenever the opportunity presents itself. They are
always exciting companions and good photographic
subjects.

Newcomers to the sport of diving are generally

somewhat apprehensive about sharks. This is perfectly normal. It takes time to adjust to something new and sharks are no exception. Actually, the diver who sees sharks frequently is fortunate indeed. We have great difficulty finding them. The only place we know of where potentially dangerous sharks are still very plentiful is the Coral Sea.

Of course, they must also abound in other remote areas but a constant supply of good sharks is no longer common near any heavily populated area. Fifteen years ago, fast-moving pelagic sharks were common all along the New South Wales coast. Today they are a rarity.

Jacques Cousteau and Hans Hass, those pioneers of the sport, must have seen some wonderful sights during their early years in diving. Even I can remember great packs of sharks off the coast as recently as twelve years ago. Now, they, along with most other big fish, have gone and it's only the diver who can know this, for it's only the diver who can see it for himself.

Reading or hearing about an event is never quite the same as seeing it personally. The big sharks of the world are a dying breed. While environmentalists fight for the sea mammals, it is hardly likely that they would side with the sharks whose reputation makes them so unpopular.

16

From *The Coast of Coral*

ARTHUR C. CLARKE

In 1969, Ron and I met Arthur Clarke on board the
Terrier VII off the coast of what was then Ceylon.
Mr. Clarke came aboard while we were trying to film
sharks and marine life on the *Hermes,* a British
aircraft carrier sunk by the Japanese in 180 feet of
water during World War II.

I had read with pleasure many of his books and
meeting the famous man in person left me shy and
tongue-tied, two things from which I seldom suffer.
Not only did I admire Mr. Clarke as a writer of some
of the world's best science fiction but I also respected
him as a diver of great skill and experience. As so
often happens when in the presence of someone you
greatly admire, words failed me.

This segment from his book *The Coast of Coral*
describes something which has happened to a great
many divers, including Ron and me. I am immensely
impressed with the truth and simplicity of his writing.
No exaggeration or false drama, and this from a man
famous for his imagination and dramatic stories of
fiction.

The area where this incident occurred is off the
reef at Heron Island, not far from a place we call the
Bommie. We know the area well. For the past ten
years, Heron Reef has been a national park, but before
this, spearfishing was not only allowed but encouraged.
Clarke's description of the sharks and their behavior,

both swimming free and after being speared, is excellent.

I was also interested to note that a shout from Arthur Clarke had no more effect on the shark than a shout from me, and is another example of one of the classic shark repellents failing.

Clarke's book is fine reading. It is honestly presented from cover to cover, yet retains a flow of excitement and adventure that would hold the interest of any reader.

•

We met no very large fish—above all, no sharks— but we did not expect to do so, for we were inside the boundary of the reef and in comparatively shallow water. When we were quite sure that we had a reasonably good chance of photographing anything that came along, we prepared to make our first dive over the edge of the reef. Mike had made one preliminary reconnaissance under bad conditions some days before. The water was still dirty after a recent storm; he had dived off the dinghy just to have a look around and had climbed hastily back into the boat with a very thoughtful expression.

"It's weird down there," he admitted, "and there's some big stuff moving around. It won't be safe until the water's clearer—you can't see what's coming at you now."

I was content to take his word for it; there was no point in running unnecessary risks by diving in water which was too dirty for photography—and photographs were, after all, the main object of our expedition.

It was about an hour after noon, and on a falling tide, that we rowed out to the reef and tried our luck for the second time. I slipped quietly overboard, with the Leica strapped round my neck, and found myself drifting twenty feet above a dense thicket of stag's-horn coral. The anchor of our boat lay supported in the topmost branches of the petrified forest, with a few small fish playing around its stock.

Visibility was excellent; when, a few seconds later, Mike followed me into the water, we could see each other clearly when we were sixty feet apart. The sun, though it had passed its noonday peak, was still powerful enough to throw patches of dappled light on the coral beneath us.

There were some very large fish moving sedately over the sea bottom, but never venturing far from the shelter of some cave or cranny into which they could retreat if danger threatened. Keeping one eye on Mike, who was prowling around with his spear gun at the ready, I made several dives to the bottom to take close-ups of interesting coral formations. After a while I decided that there was a better way of reaching my goal than swimming, which used up a lot of energy and air. The anchor line provided a convenient stairway into the depths, so I flushed out my lungs, then filled them to bursting, and pulled myself hand over hand down to the sea bed.

When I arrived at the bottom, most of my reserve of air was still intact; I twined my legs around the anchor and relaxed in the water to survey the situation in comfort. I hoped that if I remained motionless for long enough, some of the larger fish would let their curiosity overcome their natural caution.

Nothing whatsoever happened for almost a minute, and I was just about to head back to the surface when the utterly unmistakable shape I had been hoping to see slipped into my field of vision. Thirty feet away a small shark, with a startlingly white tip on its forward dorsal fin, was sailing smoothly above the coral undergrowth. It was no more than five feet long —just about the right size for an introduction to the species. As soon as I had refilled my lungs, I began to stalk it with the camera, and had no difficulty in securing a couple of shots as it passed over sandy bottom and was silhouetted against the dazzling white of pulverized coral.

Then I surfaced and yelled to Mike, who was in the water some distance away. I tried to indicate with my arms the direction the shark was taking, and Mike set off toward it as if jet-propelled. When I again ducked my head under the surface, I had lost sight of the beast, and regretted my missed photographic opportunities. Almost at once, however, there was a flurry fifty feet away, and Mike emerged momentarily to yell, "I've got him."

Ignoring the excellent rule that one should swim quietly on the surface, without making too much of a splash, I stern-wheeled across to Mike at maximum acceleration. When I arrived on the spot, I found him using his gun to fend off a very angry shark, which was turning and snapping on the spear that had passed right through its body below the rear fins. Though its crescent-shaped mouth was only about six inches wide, I did not at all like the way in which its teeth kept grinding together in rage and frustration.

I took two hasty photos, then moved in close (or as close as I cared) with my own hand spear, to help push the beast away from Mike if it showed signs of coming to grips with him. He had swum slowly backward toward the boat, towing the spear with one hand and using the discharged gun to keep the still violently wriggling shark at bay.

We had an acquaintance in the dinghy who had come along for the ride and seemed slightly taken aback when we drew alongside and yelled at him to help haul our captive aboard. He reached down and tried to grab the tail, which was about the only thing he could do—though even this is not recommended in the best circles, since sharks can curl round to snap at their own tails with no trouble at all. They also have skins like sandpaper, which further discourages contact with the bare hands.

We had managed to get the shark halfway out of the water when, in a sudden paroxysm of fury, it succeeded in tearing itself loose from the spear. I caught a final brief glimpse of it shooting away across the coral, apparently none the worse for its encounter. When I surfaced again I found that Mike had climbed into the boat and was doing a dance of rage, accompanied by suitable sound effects, which were being greatly admired by another boatload of spear-fishers, who had now arrived on the scene. He stated, in no uncertain terms, what would happen to this particular shark if he ever met it again, with or without spear gun. He added several footnotes, containing information which would have surprised ichthyologists, about the ancestry and domestic behavior of sharks in general. In fact, he managed to convey the distinct impression that he did not, at the moment, feel very kindly disposed toward sharks.

When we had succeeded in calming him down a little, we went back into the water and did a search for the weight belt he had lost during the battle. After five minutes' hunting, he was lucky enough to find it on a patch of sand, and this did something to restore his good humor. The loss of these weights would have been quite a serious matter, as without them it would have been difficult or even impossible for him to remain in effortless equilibrium at any depth. Though we had brought spares of all our other equipment, we had drawn the line at an extra ten or twenty pounds of lead, which somehow always seems to be even heavier than it actually is.

While engaged in the search for Mike's belt, I had swum a considerable distance against the prevailing current and had noticed that the water "upstream" was much clearer than in the region where we had been operating. So we pulled up the anchor and rowed a hundred yards against the current to try our luck farther round the edge of the reef.

The character of the bottom had changed greatly, even in this short distance. Huge coral boulders, ten feet high, were spaced at irregular intervals through the blue-lit twilight. The water was also considerably deeper and much richer in fish life. Horned rhinoceros fish, coral trout, and groper swarmed beneath us, playing hide-and-seek around the submerged hillocks when we tried to get close to them. I noticed a fine groper, well over a hundred pounds in weight, moving along a valley below me, and surfaced to draw Mike's attention to it. As I did so, a large turtle, moving with surprising speed for so ungainly a beast, shot past me and disappeared into the depths. I had no opportunity of giving any of this information to Mike, however, for no sooner had I broken surface than he shouted, "Shark," and pointed back into the water.

For a moment I wondered if our earlier victim had been rash enough to return. It took only a second's glance to dispose of that theory.

This was a real shark—a good ten feet of ultimately streamlined power, moving lazily through the waters beneath us. His body was a uniform metallic gray, with no trace of markings. He seemed aware of our presence, for he was cruising in a wide arc as if wondering what to do about us. I swam slowly above and behind him, trying to get a picture every time he was in a good position. If I kept moving steadily toward him, I felt quite sure that he would not come at me; indeed, my only concern was that I might make too violent a move and frighten him away. I was far too lost in admiration of this beautiful creature—the first large shark I had ever met in clear water—to feel the slightest sense of alarm.

But then I saw something that made my blood run cold. Mike, apparently thirsting for revenge, had reloaded his speargun. He was getting into position to attack this monster which was bigger than both of us put together.

I shot up to the surface like a rocket, and, as soon as Mike came up for air, yelled at him, "For God's sake —don't shoot." The spearfishers in the boat fifty feet away heard every word; Mike, a yard from me, appeared to be stone-deaf. I followed him all the way down, making all the sign gestures I could think of to try to dissuade him, but it was no use.

Things sometimes happen so quickly under water that often one can never clearly recall the sequence of events. I cannot remember the actual moment when the gun was fired; I can only remember my vast relief when the spear missed, and the shark veered away from its course. It did not, however, show any signs of fright as the steel arrow whizzed past its nose; indeed, it swept round in a great circle and swam toward Mike, who had now reeled in his spear but—luckily—had not had time to reload the gun. As the shark came slowly up to him, Mike suddenly realized that it was about time he did something, and began to shout into the water in the approved textbook fashion. The shark took no notice at all, but continued its leisurely approach. Mike jabbed his empty gun in its general direction; still it came on. Not until it was about five feet away, and Mike could see its myopic eyes staring straight into his face mask, did it apparently decide that this was just another of those annoying and indigestible human beings and swing contemptuously aside. I caught a last glimpse of it, a blurred torpedo lit by the slanting sunlight, as it vanished along the reef.

We climbed back into the boat, and recriminations continued as we rowed homeward. Mike swore, not very convincingly, that he thought I wanted him to shoot the shark. I produced all the witnesses within earshot to prove the contrary, and loudly lamented the masterpieces my camera had lost. "If you must shoot a shark," I wailed, "at least wait until I've finished photographing it."

Looking back on these events from the comparative calm of the present, I am inclined to believe that Mike never actually intended to hit the beast, but merely wanted to express his feelings. He is a dead shot at fish anything more than nine inches long, and it makes no sense at all for him to have missed something that occupied most of his angle of vision when he fired at it. At the crucial moment, his subconscious mind must have decided that this nonsense had gone far enough, and made him deflect his aim.

That evening, as soon as we could borrow the necessary ice from the tourist center, we set to work to develop the color film I had shot during the day. After two hours' work, pouring liquids from one bottle to another and running round with lumps of ice to maintain all the solutions at the right temperature, we knew that our photographic efforts had not been in vain. There was our gunmetal friend cruising over the coral, the undisputed master of the reef.

Undisputed? Well, one day Mike may decide to put that to the test again. I hope he does it when I'm not around.

17

From *Men Beneath the Sea:*
Conquest of the Underwater World

HANS HASS

The romantic figures of the lean, bearded Hans Hass
and his photogenic wife, Lotte, were proof to us that a
dedicated man-and-wife team, and the sea, could be a
way of life perhaps unequaled in this day and age. Hans
Hass courageously records what he saw and believed.
Like Captain Jacques Cousteau, Hass is a pioneer
pacesetter in the underwater world.

Hans Hass has been diving for far longer than Ron
and I, and to me has always been something of a hero
—the man who did the things that the rest of us only
dreamed about. He has been diving and taking
pictures almost since the beginning of skin diving, and
has helped bring the world under the sea closer to the
general public in an enjoyable and easily understood
way through his books and films.

In this segment from his book *Men Beneath the Sea:*
Conquest of the Underwater World, Hans touches on
many subjects familiar to Ron and me, mostly talking
of things which stimulate and excite sharks. One
which must be of interest is that Hans claims some
aggressive sharks can be frightened by loud underwater
screams.

We have experienced limited success with this
method, although the sharks we generally work with
are probably of different species from those Hans has

163

encountered. Sharks are completely unpredictable creatures and what works well on one as a repellent is just as likely to have no effect on another.

Hans refers to us filming *Blue Water, White Death,* "leaving the cages and swimming around quite unconcerned among dozens of excited sharks, tapping them on the snout and treating them quite light-heartedly." This must be how it appears in the film for Hass to mention it that way, but in reality it was quite the reverse. We were all very concerned, not only for our own safety but for each other. Behind my lighthearted taps to the shark's snout was every bit of power and strength that my 126-pound body could muster.

At the time I felt that I was fighting for my life, although afterward, on the deck of the *Terrier VII,* we would all appear elated and happy. This was due to completing the dive without mishap and capturing the action on film.

Hans has based his comments on what seems to be quite solid evidence but was not in fact an accurate interpretation, and does serve to point out the dangers of a writer misinterpreting an event. Nowadays, Hans Hass is more interested in conservation of the marine animals than in filming them and works hard toward the banning of spearfishing on a worldwide basis.

•

As for underwater films, the audience—and hence also the film distributors—are positively disappointed unless at some moment, accompanied by sinister music, the terrible specter of a shark appears. In one of my own films, from which I financed the first *Xarifa* expedition, this was actually a stipulated condition. Every diver who can report being attacked by a shark finds a willing circle of listeners who automatically regard him as a hero. John D. Craig, an American diver and professional film producer, declared: "Every shark that is hungry or angry or both will attack a man." This is simply not true. Cousteau was molested by sharks in the open sea off the Cape Verde Islands during his first visit to the tropics, and this obviously left him in a state of shock. In a book he later declared that the better acquainted one becomes with sharks, the less one knows about them. This story also gained wide acceptance, and is often quoted today as the quintessence of an expert's experience.

In an American film the hero (Gary Cooper) was accused in court by two old maids of being "pixilated" and therefore unfit to testify. The two ladies meant by this that he had a screw loose—but defending counsel had an idea, and asked them if they regarded anyone else as "pixilated."

"Of course," they replied at once, "everybody—except for the two of us."

"Even His Honor the judge?"

"Yes, he's pixilated, too." And the man was acquitted. It is no different with the "unpredictability" of sharks. Of course there are surprises, but they are extremely rare and certainly not characteristic of these creatures. My reply to Cousteau's sibylline pronouncement would be: "The more thoroughly one investigates sharks, the better one knows them."

The behavior of sharks—as of any other creature —is governed by instincts which are activated by optical, acoustic, olfactory, or other stimuli. Konrad Lorenz speaks of a "parliament of instincts" in which, according to the "majority vote" of the moment, now one and then another governs behavior. This means in practice that animals respond more strongly to, or actively seek, first one stimulus then another. A hungry creature responds primarily to those stimuli which make him aware of his prey, one which is amorously disposed will respond primarily to those of his sexual partner. With sharks, there are four groups of stimuli which lead them to their prey.

They can detect disturbances of the water, that is to say, fluctuations in pressure, from a great distance —you can observe this if you drop anchor or dive into the water near the edge of a reef. Often it takes no more than a few seconds before sharks are in sight. However, they usually keep at a considerable distance, make one or two circuits, and then as a rule, if nothing further occurs to excite them, disappear immediately. As I wrote in my first accounts, they behave like "policemen, looking to see what's going on." A dynamic explosion in which fish are stunned or killed also creates a visual stimulus; if it is repeated frequently, sharks snap at fish and associate them with the detonation. In Greece in 1942 we were amazed at how quickly sharks gathered where there was fishing with dynamite. Normally a diver never catches sight of a shark there, but we saw specimens over thirteen feet long.

Sharks are especially sensitive to vibrations of the water caused by the struggles of a fish which is wounded or otherwise in distress. In response to this stimulus, sharks frequently swim in direct attack until they are close to the struggling creature. Every fisherman knows that any fish he catches in the tropics must be landed quickly, or he is likely to lift only a fish head out of the water. The rest, the sharks have snatched away. For underwater hunters, this constitutes—as we found in 1939—a serious danger, and this is how accidents have already happened. The target of such attacks may well be the fish, but if the underwater hunter is holding it, then of course he himself may also get bitten.

Before Jack McKenney became editor of *Skin Diver,* he worked for three years as a diving instructor at Freeport on Grand Bahama, near Florida. In all that time, so he told me, he saw only about fifteen sharks. In the very last week he went fishing with a friend. It was past three o'clock in the afternoon, and they were harpooning fish. A grey shark suddenly appeared. Jack said: "I had my camera with me, and I thought to myself, 'Fine, now at last I'll get a good picture.'" But the shark swam off again. Then Jack harpooned another fish—back came the shark and snapped at it. "I could hear his teeth grating on the hook, and I thought, 'Help!' Then he came straight at me—I only had the harpoon—I thrust it at his head. He swam away and came back again. The third time I missed him, and he

grabbed the harpoon only so far from my hand."
Jack showed me; it was about eight inches. "I almost
had heart failure!" The friend meanwhile had dropped
the net with the fish. Two more grey sharks appeared.
"The one with my harpoon in his mouth probably
thought I didn't taste too good. He swam down and
paid no more attention to anything but the net with
the fish. Meanwhile we swam ashore."

So harpooning big fish in areas frequented by sharks
is not without danger. Even in the Mediterranean there
have been attacks, one of which had a particularly
tragic end. On September 2, 1962, the pioneer Italian
diver and distinguished underwater photographer Mau-
rizio Sarra, harpooning grouper near Terracina on the
Italian coast, was fatally wounded by a shark. Here is
another case:

In the summer of 1964 Al Giddings and French Le
Roy, two outstanding American divers, were diving off
some islands north of San Francisco. They were leading
a team of skin divers who went down in several parties.
Numerous fish were harpooned. Suddenly Al Giddings,
who was just fetching his camera from the boat, heard
shrill screams and saw someone floundering about on
the surface. As quickly as he could, he swam toward
him—and saw to his astonishment that it was not one
of the pupils, but his partner Le Roy. A shark had
wounded him. The sea was smooth, and just as he
got to Le Roy an enormous tailfin appeared directly
underneath the victim. Al Giddings said: "Le Roy told
me later that that was the most terrifying moment for
him, because he could see in my eyes what I saw."
The great shark made another grab at Le Roy's leg,
and dragged him under water. When Le Roy came up
again, Giddings grasped his companion from behind
by his air cylinders, for Le Roy was now flailing wildly
about, as though demented. Giddings had the presence
of mind to release his weighted belt and dragged Le
Roy back to the boat. Every moment he expected a
fresh attack, but none came. Le Roy was pulled on
board, minus a sizable piece of his thigh. A tourniquet

was applied and a helicopter summoned by radio. No one had even seen the shark, for Le Roy was already on the surface when unexpectedly attacked from behind, and Al Giddings lost his diving mask when he rushed to his aid. Here too there is no doubt that the harpooned fish had attracted the big shark, and the smell of blood had made it aggressive. The second stimulus which activates predatory behavior in sharks is the smell of blood. In collaboration with Eibl-Eibesfeldt, I made an exhaustive study of this phenomenon in the Maldives in 1957. Near a steep ridge where we knew there were sharks, we killed some fish and hid them among the corals. In only about five minutes the smell of blood had spread far enough to attract sharks from the open sea outside our range of vision. They behaved in an obviously excited manner, darting about and poking their snouts right under the coral in search of the source of the blood. They were very perseverant and most of them found the hiding place. How utterly this olfactory stimulus dominates the shark is shown by instances where bathers have been bitten and gallant rescuers have brought them out of the water. These rescuers have hardly ever been wounded themselves, for the shark, if it continued to attack, bit only the person already wounded. Our experiments also produced the same results. At first we were wary, but we soon saw that the bleeding fish hidden in the coral, usually only two or three yards from us, were in effect our protectors. Eventually, up to ten sharks were squabbling over the prey and taking not the slightest notice of us. The calmness with which I filmed this scene indicates how safe we felt. True, Eibl-Eibesfeldt declared that the sharks showed more aggressiveness toward him, but this may have been because he was the one who had harpooned the fish and taken them off the spear, so the smell of blood was on his hands.

These observations are important for shipwrecked men. In areas where there are sharks, persons who are bleeding undoubtedly run the danger of being attacked, especially in tropical waters. But uninjured people in the vicinity need not despair; if attacks take place near them, this doesn't in the least mean that they will automatically be the next victims.

In this connection the account of Flight-Lieutenant A. A. Reading, who drifted in the open sea for sixteen hours after coming down east of the Wallis Islands, in the central Pacific, is instructive. When the plane crashed he was unconscious, but his radio officer, E. H. Almond, dragged him out of the aircraft. Almond, however, was unable to salvage the dinghy. The two men tied themselves together with a cord. Almond was wearing only shorts. "In about half an hour," reported Reading, "there were already sharks swimming around us, but for an hour nothing happened. Suddenly Almond said he had felt something bump against his right leg, and it was beginning to hurt. I told him to climb up on my back and keep the leg out of the water, but before he could do so the sharks attacked him again. We were both forced under water for a second." Five sharks now surrounded them, and the water was red with blood. Reading went on: "He showed me his leg; not only was his right foot covered with bites, his left hip also was badly gashed. He didn't feel any great pain, but I noticed how every time the sharks went for him, his whole body twitched. Finally I grabbed my binoculars and struck at the creatures as they swam by. Within a few seconds they attacked again. Once more we were dragged under, and this time I became separated from Almond." Reading received a blow across his right cheek from one of the sharks, but this was all that happened to him. He saw how his companion was hemmed in by the sharks, his head already under water. Then the body drifted away, encircled by sharks. "Every now and then I felt one at my feet. . . ." So Reading drifted for several hours, until at midnight he was picked up by a patrol boat—uninjured. Other accounts of shipwrecked men and of airmen shot down read very similarly. If you consider that sharks are predators and possess a murderous set of teeth, it's really rather surprising how hesitant they are to make use of these weapons. In the case of Reading and Almond, the fact that Almond was wearing shorts may have been significant. He was attacked, but Reading was not; the sharks which swam past so close obviously missed the smell of skin which provoked the attack.

Other stimuli of aggressive behavior may be found in the sphere of optical perception. The assertion that sharks' eyesight is poor has been proved on closer investigation to be false, and they are no longer believed to be color-blind. It used to be claimed that Negroes were attacked less often than men with light skin, but experiments by the American biologist Hobson on Eniwetok Atoll with three different species of shark produced exactly the opposite result. From a raft he lowered into the sea two identical baits, one darkened with a pigment to which, as tests had shown, sharks were not responsive. Out of 172 tests the dark bait was taken first in 72 percent of cases overall, and in 82 percent of cases when the sky was clear and sunny. Admittedly, the observer, who was on the bottom in a cage, pointed out that in the given conditions the black bait was more clearly distinguishable from the background. The sharks always came out of deep water from the same direction, swimming against the current. Certainly these results do show that visual impressions also play a part. If a shark is attracted by pressure waves or smell to within sight of an object, then such stimuli are decisive factors in its predatory behavior. On the other hand, if a shark encounters a diver by chance without its aggressiveness being stimulated by blood or by a flurry of fish, as a rule it keeps well away from him, eyes him, and perhaps cruises round him, then swims on its way.

The final stimulus which governs aggressive behavior in a shark is the taste of the object under attack. Hobson soaked fish in ethyl alcohol for four days and then rinsed them for three hours in seawater. Then he offered them to the sharks together with normal fish, once again lowering them from a raft. In every case both baits were taken—and each time the one that had been rendered tasteless was spat out. So after pressure waves, smell, and optical stimuli have evoked the shark's predatory behavior, it is ultimately flavor which determines whether or not the predator really bites into its prey and swallows it. In earlier accounts it was claimed that sharks would swallow anything, and that even brushes and the like had been found in sharks' bellies. This may well be true when they're gobbling up refuse thrown overboard from ships, but it's probably not the general rule. When Hobson offered the sharks fish made of wood or other material, they simply sniffed at them and turned up their noses.

How then, when all is said and done, must a diver behave if a shark—as happens only in rare and exceptional cases, unless it is actually being hunted—should approach him? It has often been recommended that he keep still; this is what pearl divers do. As with most predators on land, anything motionless scarcely attracts attention, even if it is conspicuous by its shape or color. Back in 1939, in the West Indies, we found that approaching sharks can be put to flight if you swim straight at them. This method may not be to everyone's taste, but it works excellently. In this way I have frightened away even very big sharks, over thirteen feet long. Here again we find the same reaction displayed by land predators. A swiftly and purposefully approaching body inspires flight; man also reacts in the same way.

Another "weapon" which we discovered at that time has even found its way into cartoons. Quite by chance, we discovered that sharks which come storming in at top speed after a fish has been speared can be scared off by shouting into the water. Later on, when investigating the death of the Australian prime minister, Harold Holt, who disappeared in the sea near Melbourne in 1967, I found in his house a framed cartoon which showed him swimming under water and shouting at a shark which bore the inscription "taxpayer." The caption said: "But you can't chase this one away by shouting!" We have observed this effect with reef sharks in the Red Sea, the Indian Ocean, and the Pacific, and many other well-known divers have confirmed our experience—for example, Jim Oetzel, Ron Clark, Rodney Jonklaas, R. H. Burton, and others. Wally Gibbins, one of Australia's oldest and most daring pioneers of diving, had a special method of harpooning sharks, in which he would fasten the head of the spear by a long rope to a tire floating on the surface. The harpooned shark dragged the tire behind it and so exhausted itself, while the divers followed. Naturally enough, Gibbins and his companions were frequently attacked. Gibbins wrote: "You can easily see when things are getting serious from the way a shark behaves. In my experience the best thing to do then is to take your stance and wait until the shark is about six feet away, then suddenly stretch out your arms and legs, and shout. The nearer the shark, the more effective the shout." This tallies exactly with our experience. On the other hand, anyone trying to frighten a shark swimming by at a distance of thirty feet or more is hardly likely to succeed.

True, as we discovered back in 1942, there are exceptions. In Greece, the sharks that came racing along after dynamite explosions did not react at all to shouting. This was because they were accustomed to much louder noises. Nor can it be expected that sharks which frequent the vicinity of public bathing beaches, where people often shout in the water, or those which follow ships and get used to the noise of their screws, will react to shouts. When diving gear is used, the mouthpiece makes it difficult to shout and muffles the sound. With oxygen-recycling equipment, which makes no noise, this is less critical than with compressed-air gear, when air bubbles are regularly emitted into the water. Even the bubbles which suddenly appear with the shout (when a mouthpiece is worn they come out of the corners of one's mouth) may play their part in the deterrent effect. Earlier divers' accounts often mention that sharks are frightened of air bubbles.

We discovered in the Azores in 1953 that the deep-sea white-fin sharks in general do not react to shouts. I observed the same thing in the rare white shark and also the tiger shark. Philippe Cousteau, in a book about sharks written jointly with his father, said that to advise anyone to scare off a shark by shouting was "criminal."

To this I can only say that very many other people have witnessed its effectiveness—with the limitations mentioned above, of course.

Unexpected behavior does occur with sharks just as with any other creature. On many occasions sharks—even quite small ones—suddenly swam at us for no apparent reason. If one then stays still—my wife also has followed this rule—the shark will turn away of its own accord. Obviously this isn't a genuine attack—what would be the motive? I think it's a question of territory. Intruders are deterred and chased out of the domain. Here, too, Hobson's experience is instructive. In many instances he observed that sharks carried out deterrent measures against grouper and snapper which competed for their prey—but also against divers. He called them "warning passes."

A totally unexpected reaction was observed by two American divers, Ron Church and James Stewart, near La Jolla, on the coast of southern California. They were swimming in a channel between two reefs when a shark came straight between them from the direction of the shore. First it turned toward Ron, who photographed it, then toward Jimmy. Once again it was startled and swam off a little way. Then it turned round, looked back, and dashed straight at Stewart and bit him in the arm. This shark was little more than six feet long.

As investigations with land animals have shown, such unexpected reactions occur either when an impulse cannot be worked off or when two impulses run counter to each other and the animal thus becomes confused. Then we get "flash behavior." The energy of thwarted instinctive behavior flashes across, as it were, into other channels. The animal then behaves in a way which is not at all motivated by the actual situation.

I have already pointed out in my earliest books that sharks are very sensitive, indeed almost high-strung. The American biologist Eugenie Clark, who for ten years was head of an institute in Florida dedicated to the study of shark behavior, made an observation which very clearly supports my view. During tests in a water

tank to measure the intelligence of sharks, she trained
a female and a male to strike with their heads a board
lowered into the water, thus setting off a mechanism
which rang a bell. The sharks received their food near
the board—and later at points farther and farther away.
The two sharks, one eight feet and the other ten feet
long, became accustomed to this procedure and regularly rang a bell. "Then," writes Eugenie Clark, "unwittingly I made a decision with tragic consequences."
As it was still debatable whether sharks were color-blind
or not, she painted the white board yellow. When it
was lowered, the male shark raced toward it as usual,
but pulled up suddenly two feet away from it by lowering his pectoral fins, and leaped backward out of the
water. The other sharks in the aquarium thereupon
swam madly to and fro, colliding with each other. The
shark "never recovered from this experience. He refused food offered in any way, wouldn't go near even
a white target again, and died three months later."

A further observation by Clark is no less enlighten-
ing. On July 27, 1958, not far from her institute, a
shark only six feet long bit an eight-year-old boy whose
leg had to be amputated immediately. As she discovered, the accident happened at very low tide, in a
lagoon in which the shark had obviously become
trapped. When low tide came, it could not get back
across the sand bank into the sea. This state of confusion may, she thinks, have been the reason why when
it saw the boy's light-colored legs in the cloudy water, it
swam in biting. This incident could at a pinch be compared with the attack on Jim Stewart—who blamed
his glittering mask as the critical factor.

One species of shark which can perhaps with justification be described as a "killer shark" will almost
certainly be exterminated by man sooner or later—
the white shark (*Carcharodon*). With a behavior pattern different from other kinds of shark, this creature
really is dangerous to man and hence, presumably, is
doomed to extinction. The white shark lives in the open
sea and only occasionally approaches the coast. How

rarely this creature puts in an appearance is shown by the fact that Peter Gimbel, Ron Taylor and Stan Waterman, who were making a film about the white shark, cruised for six months between Africa and Australia and killed countless creatures for bait before they finally managed to entice a specimen out of the deep.

A fatal accident caused by a white shark occurred on June 14, 1959, near the Scripps Institute, in La Jolla. The victim, Robert Pamperin, was a thirty-three-year-old engineer, an enthusiastic underwater hunter and diver. Accompanied by a less experienced friend, he was diving for abalone, which have to be pried off the seabed with a flat iron bar. The bar is pushed quickly under the opened shell before it can close and batten onto the rock. Pamperin was towing along with him an inflated tire, from which hung a bag for the abalone. He was wearing pink swimming trunks, a black face mask, and blue flippers. The two men set out from a rocky headland and went about fifty yards out from shore. Here the partner who was less good at diving decided to work in shallower water. Suddenly he heard Pamperin, about twenty yards away, cry for help. He turned quickly to see Pamperin being thrown straight out of the water, having already lost his face mask. Then the body disappeared under water. Quickly he swam in that direction and looked downward—the visibility was only about twenty-five feet. To his horror he saw a gigantic shark, which he estimated was more than twenty feet long. It was holding Pamperin round his middle in its mouth, shaking him to and fro, and lashing out fiercely with its tail fin. He tried to frighten the beast by shouts and movements, but in vain. Then he lost sight of them both, and swam as fast as he could to the shore, where he raised the alarm. Conrad Limbaugh, diving director of the Scripps Institute, was quickly on the spot with nine volunteers. For four and a half hours they searched the area with diving gear—but without success. Later a helicopter spotted a blue flipper floating on the surface, and Pamperin's tire, with two abalone in the bag, was found drifting in the sea. As

Conrad Limbaugh, at that time perhaps America's most experienced diver, confirmed, fish had been harpooned in the area a little earlier.

On June 14, 1950, I myself was attacked by a white shark near the landing stage of the Sanganeb reef, in the Red Sea eleven miles northeast of Port Sudan. This specimen was thirteen feet long and came steadily toward me, like a machine. I had been filming smaller shark and only saw the creature when it was very close to me. I was at the top of a vertical face of the reef, where I was crouching on projecting coral at a depth of about 50 feet. To lure sharks we had chopped fish into pieces and tossed them into the sea near the edge of the reef. When I noticed the creature, it was already too late to reach for my spear, which was floating above me, fastened to my shoulder by a loop. I gave a scream, as loudly as I could—but this shark did not react, so I was left with only my hands with which to to ward off the great head. It must be emphasized that the creature displayed not the slightest excitement. The light-grey colossus swam quite slowly in a straight line along the wall directly toward me—just as if I were any old chunk of meat it wanted to snap up. When the snout was right in front of me, I punched at the back of its mouth, in the region of the gills. It turned away and circled round. The unexpected movement directed against it had produced the reaction of flight. Then steadily and unswervingly it came at me again—no slower and no faster. In the meantime I had had time to reach for my spear, and I thrust the point at its head. It turned away. Now, however, I was attacked by the other shark, which I had been filming earlier, and which up till then had been only curious but by no means aggressive. It was about ten feet long and wanted a piece of me too—an example of mood transference, of the infectiousness of predatory behavior. I could not possibly defend myself on two sides, so I scrambled up the wall as fast as my flippers would take me, to where my three colleagues, including Lotte, were waiting on the ridge and had witnessed the whole episode. The result of my flight was that the two sharks followed me with equal speed, but we were lucky, for it was just low tide. On the top of the reef the water was barely eighteen inches deep, and all four of us fled into this shallow zone, where the creatures could not follow us. They swam up and down close to the edge, clearly excited; then they calmed down again and disappeared from our sight.

The white shark may possess a differently developed set of innate reactions from other sharks. This could be related to the creature's size, also perhaps to its life in the open sea. For this kind of predator, the motivating stimuli scarcely need to be differentiated, and those inhibitions which would make them approach strange objects with caution are superfluous. It is known from finds of fossilized teeth that the now presumably extinct ancestors of this variety of shark reached the incredible length of over eighty feet. According to reconstructions, the mouth must have been big enough for a man to stand up in. For such a mighty predator, almost anything in the wide ocean that came its way would be potential prey. This would explain why this creature, in contrast to the coastal sharks, behaves so mechanically, and automatically swims up to attack even a being that is strange to it—a human being.

Other species of shark known to have caused fatal accidents in Australia and South Africa are the tiger shark, the mako shark, the blue shark, and the hammerhead. These species too reach a considerable size, and are rarely seen near the coast. Compared to today's figures for traffic accidents on land, however, the danger which these sharks represent is very slight. In both countries, watchtowers have been erected to guard popular beaches; if a sizable shark is sighted, a warning bell is rung. In the last ten years, underwater hunters— especially in the Australian coasts—have killed many sharks, some of them quite large, with shark clubs which have explosive heads. Wide-meshed nets of fine nylon have also proved very effective, for the sharks do not notice them; they get their heads stuck in them, finally becoming so entangled that they perish. Presumably up to 90 percent of the sharks killed in this manner were harmless. Still, whereas Australia previously had two deaths a year to complain of—an extremely small proportion of the hundreds of thousands of swimmers, divers, and surfers—the sharks there have now been eliminated over wide stretches. However, as a bogey, a jealously guarded property of journalism, films, and adventure books, the shark is still an effective box-office draw. This may have been acceptable hitherto, but now, when sporting divers take to the water in such large numbers, things are different. What makes money for one man may endanger others, even cost them their lives.

For, as has been said before, the greatest danger for divers is panic, a reaction inspired by fear. In this sense, misleading information is not only dangerous but actually "criminal." For example, films which Philippe Cousteau has produced with his father include scenes of a regular bloodbath taking place around cages containing divers. Close-ups show how the sharks enticed in this way attack greedily. What else would one expect? This keeps the shark's image as a "bloodthirsty killer" alive and, moreover, satisfies the audience. The danger of such presentations is that with sharks—as with land predators—fear and flight excite interest and aggressive behavior. Although according to present-day experience divers are hardly in danger even when a sizable shark comes in sight, panic behavior can actually attract these creatures and indeed arouse their aggressive instinct.

For this reason it is also important to oppose trick photography. On June 7, 1968, *Life* published a sensational story which showed most convincingly a diver being bitten in the chest by a shark. In Germany this was copied by *Stern* and in Britain by *Weekend Mail*. According to this report the accident had happened during filming off Isla Mujeres, on the Mexican coast. I received letters from there to the effect that not a word of the report was true. It then turned out that these pictures were intended as publicity for a film. A dead shark was fastened to a diver in appropriate positions, and at the same time red dye was released from a bag. Dewey Bergman, an American diver and head of an organization for arranging diving expeditions, spent a whole year clearing up this case, and eventually *Life* had to admit the hoax in the magazine *Skin Diver*. The editor wrote: "What we took to be an unusual picture story proved to be a fabrication. . . ." Typically, however, *Life* never let on about it in its own magazine, nor did *Stern* or *Weekend Mail*. But thanks to this publicity the film, in the making of which the accident was supposed to have happened, was a box-office sellout.

Divers in cages, surrounded by many sharks attracted by blood, were shown in Peter Gimbel's film about the white shark. But to the credit of this film, it must be said that the next scene showed these divers—Ron and Valerie Taylor, Stan Waterman, and Gimbel himself— leaving the cages and swimming around quite unconcernedly among dozens of excited sharks, tapping them on the snout and treating them quite lightheartedly. When Eibl-Eibesfeldt and I ran feeding experiments without cages, we had the same experience, namely that the creatures concentrated entirely on the source of the blood. I do not seek to belittle the extraordinary courage of the divers I have named, for when they took their pictures there were far more sharks about, and besides, they were filming out at sea. Nevertheless, what must be emphasized about all films of this kind is that such orgies of greed represent totally untypical situations, created artificially, which give no information at all about the normal behavior of sharks.

A weapon every diver should carry is a stick about four feet long with a moderately sharp point, which he can fasten to his shoulder by a loop. If the unusual should in fact occur, and a shark should become a nuisance, it can be fended off. To sum up, I can only repeat that as long as he does not spear any big fish, the sporting diver who makes a descent off tropical coasts need hardly worry about being molested by sharks. It is far more likely that he will have the disappointment of not seeing any sharks at all.

VI

SEA GIANTS

●

I often wonder what the early seafarers must have
thought of those giant fish of the sea, whale sharks
and basking sharks.

Imagine being far from land and coming across a
huge sea creature almost as large as the craft on which
you lived. It's true that Thor Heyerdahl had this type
of experience but he also had some knowledge of the
fact that huge sharks did exist and that they were not
considered man-eaters. Even so, meeting a whale shark
proved a terrifying experience for Heyerdahl and his
crew.

No wonder ancient mariners told stories of great sea
monsters who could churn the ocean into a fury as
they passed, and wrecked boats with the flick of a
tail. Superstition was like a religion to the sailors of
old and, many times, upon sighting a great whale
shark, they must have felt their hours to be numbered.

Stories of great fish appear all through history, and,
even today, if we can make a film about some large
sea creature, it is always popular with the buyers and
public alike. In fact, giant sea creatures rate second
to dangerous sharks as popular subjects for a television
special.

Unfortunately, giant sea creatures are not easy to
find. Whale sharks are particularly rare. We have
only seen one in over twenty years. I know professional

fishermen who spend their lives on the sea and have never seen a whale shark.

From reports I have read, it would seem that whale sharks are somewhat more prevalent in the Sea of Cortez. The reason for this, of course, would be the prolific marine life that abounds in this sea. Diving friends have told me that the water sometimes becomes so thick with planktonic life that underwater visibility is less than a few feet. This sounds like an ideal place for the big plankton eaters to live and breed.

The huge basking sharks are found in the Northern Hemisphere. More common than their spotted cousins, the basking sharks are hunted commercially, mainly off the British Islands. It is interesting to me that, as far as we know, basking sharks have never been filmed in their natural element, yet, from all the accounts I have read, they are not only plentiful but, unless molested, extremely docile.

Maybe it's the old story of what is readily available is overlooked in favor of more exciting subjects. I don't think that dirty water would be the problem because P. Fitzgerald Connor writes about the bosun looking over the gunwale and seeing tier upon tier of huge shapes weaving their bodies this way and that. Water clarity must be fairly good to see basking sharks one under the other.

Several small, harmless sharks bear a certain similarity to the whale shark. The little Port Jackson has not only the characteristic hard ridges running along its body but it also lays an egg. Leopard sharks are another similar species and they, too, have a gentle disposition.

It is one of nature's oddities that the largest of all fish is also one of the most gentle and I guess it's just as well. Imagine a whale shark or a basking shark armed with the teeth of a great white and possessing the disposition of a whaler. "Bruce," the *Jaws* shark, would be a baby by comparison and I, for one, would most certainly not be a diver!

18

From *Kon-Tiki*

THOR HEYERDAHL

The *Kon-Tiki* expedition across the Pacific Ocean on a balsa wood raft is one of the epic adventure stories of the sea. The men were brave and resourceful, but Thor Heyerdahl's account of their meeting with a whale shark shows how even men such as these will react to the unknown.

By the time of their meeting with the whale shark, many adventures and near disasters had befallen the raft and its occupants—all were to be expected, as anyone who has made a long voyage on a small craft will know. However, the sighting of a giant whale shark so near to their flimsy raft brought forth emotions in the men ranging from shouting laughter to a desire to kill.

We can understand their feelings, because they believed that their lives were in danger, but it is a fact that the great shark would have become bored with the raft and eventually swum away. It is, in any case, harmless, feeding mainly on microscopic plankton. Erik, by harpooning the creature, actually placed the raft and everyone on board in great danger. Although the shark had not the intelligence to know what caused its pain, it could have quite easily, in its desire to escape, destroyed the raft without even knowing that it had done so.

Few people have ever seen a whale shark and fewer

have had the opportunity to study one at such close range. It seems to me that in attacking it Heyerdahl and his crew made one of their few mistakes during a fantastic voyage that was otherwise in harmony with the sea.

●

It was May 24, and we were lying drifting on a leisurely swell in exactly 95° and 7° south. It was about noon, and we had thrown overboard the guts of two big dolphins we had caught early in the morning. I was having a refreshing plunge overboard at the bow, lying in the water, keeping a good lookout and hanging on to a rope end when I caught sight of a thick brown fish, six feet long, which came swimming inquisitively toward me through the crystal clear seawater. I hopped quickly up on to the edge of the raft and sat in the hot sun looking at the fish as it passed quietly, when I heard a wild war whoop from Knut, who was sitting aft behind the bamboo cabin. He bellowed, "Shark!" till his voice cracked in a falsetto, and as we had sharks swimming alongside the raft almost daily without creating such excitement, we all realized that this must be something extra special, and flocked astern to Knut's assistance.

Knut had been squatting there, washing his pants in the swell, and when he looked up for a moment he was staring straight into the biggest and ugliest face any of us had ever seen in the whole of our lives. It was the head of a veritable sea monster, so huge and so hideous that if the Old Man of the Sea himself had come up he could not have made such an impression on us. The head was broad and flat like a frog's, with two small eyes right at the sides, and a toadlike jaw which was four or five feet wide and had long fringes hanging drooping from the corners of the mouth. Behind the head was an enormous body ending in a long thin tail with a pointed tail fin which stood straight up and showed that this sea monster was not any kind of whale. The body looked brownish under the water, but both head and body were thickly covered with small white spots. The monster came quietly, lazily swimming after us from astern. It grinned like a bulldog and lashed gently with its tail. The large round dorsal fin projected clear of the water and sometimes the tail fin as well, and when the creature was in the trough of the swell the water flowed about the broad back as though washing round a submerged reef. In front of the broad jaws swam a whole crowd of zebra-striped pilot fish in fan formation, and large remora fish and other parasites sat firmly attached to the huge body and traveled with it through the water, so that the whole thing looked like a curious zoological collection crowded round something that resembled a floating deep water reef.

A 25-pound dolphin attached to six of our largest fish hooks was hanging behind the raft as bait for sharks, and a swarm of pilot fish shot straight off, nosed the dolphin without touching it, and then hurried back to their lord and master, the sea king. Like a mechanical monster it set its machinery going and came gliding at leisure toward the dolphin which lay, a beggarly trifle, before its jaws. We tried to pull the dolphin in, and the sea monster followed slowly, right up to the side of the raft. It did not open its mouth, but just let the dolphin bump against it, as if to throw open the whole door for such an insignificant scrap was not worthwhile. When the giant came right up to the raft, it rubbed its back against the heavy steering oar, which was just lifted up out of the water, and now we had ample opportunity of studying the monster at the closest quarters— at such close quarters that I thought we had all gone mad, for we roared stupidly with laughter and shouted overexcitedly at the completely fantastic sight we saw. Walt Disney himself, with all his powers of imagination, could not have created a more hair-raising sea monster than that which thus suddenly lay with its terrific jaws along the raft's side.

The monster was a whale shark, the largest shark and the largest fish known in the world today. It is exceedingly rare, but scattered specimens are observed here and there in the tropical oceans. The whale shark has an average length of 50 feet, and according to zoologists it weighs 15 tons. It is said that large specimens can attain a length of 65 feet, and a harpooned baby had a liver weighing 600 pounds and a collection of three thousand teeth in each of its broad jaws.

The monster was so large that when it began to swim in circles round us and under the raft its head was visible on one side while the whole of its tail stuck out on the other. And so incredibly grotesque, inert, and stupid did it appear when seen full face that we could not help shouting with laughter, although we realized that it had strength enough in its tail to smash both balsa logs and ropes to pieces if it attacked us. Again and again it described narrower and narrower circles just under the raft, while all we could do was to wait and see what might happen. When out on the other side it glided amiably under the steering oar and lifted it up in the air, while the oar blade slid along the creature's back. We stood round the raft with hand harpoons ready for action, but they seemed to us like toothpicks in relation to the heavy beast we had to deal with. There was no indication that the whale shark ever thought of leaving us again; it circled round us and followed like a faithful dog, close to the raft. None of us had ever experienced or thought we should experience anything like it; the whole adventure, with the sea monster swimming behind and under the raft, seemed to us so completely unnatural that we could not really take it seriously.

In reality the whale shark went on encircling us for barely an hour, but to us the visit seemed to last a whole day. At last it became too exciting for Erik, who was standing at a corner of the raft with an eight-foot hand harpoon, and encouraged by ill-considered shouts, he raised the harpoon above his head. As the whale shark came gliding slowly toward him, and had got its broad head right under the corner of the raft, Erik thrust the harpoon with all his giant strength down between his legs and deep into the whale shark's gristly head. It was a second or two before the giant understood properly what was happening. Then in a flash the placid half-wit was transformed into a mountain of steel muscles. We heard a swishing noise as the harpoon line rushed over the edge of the raft, and saw a cascade of water as the giant stood on its head and plunged down into the depths. The three men who were standing nearest were flung about the place head over heels and two of them were flayed and burned by the line as it rushed through the air. The thick line, strong enough to hold a boat, was caught up on the side of the raft but snapped at once like a piece of twine, and a few seconds later a broken-off harpoon shaft came up to the surface two hundred yards away. A shoal of frightened pilot fish shot off through the water in a desperate attempt to keep up with their old lord and master and we waited a long time for the monster to come racing back like an infuriated submarine; but we never saw anything more of the whale shark.

19

Riding a Shark

VALERIE TAYLOR

All divers who love the sport and thrill of adventure must long to meet a whale shark. It is, without doubt, one of the big highs associated with skin diving—and one of the rarest.

When we found our whale shark, Ron had been trying to film sea lions for an episode in a television series called "Skippy, the Bush Kangaroo." The sea lions were swimming and playing close to the rocks in very turbulent water, which was unsuitable for filming. We tried to coax them out away from the breaking waves, but they were having so much fun, they ignored all our efforts.

If they had cooperated and followed us into clearer water we would have stayed with them, instead of giving up and heading back to shore. Fate, which had seemed so unkind, sent us right into the path of the whale shark, and what seemed a failure became one of the greatest successes of our diving career.

Neither Ron nor I are very proud of our initial impulse to kill the creature, but it was at a time when we genuinely believed, along with most other divers, that all sharks were potential attackers and that the only good one was a dead one. Time and much more experience has shown us that we were wrong.

Whale sharks are not common; you could search for a lifetime and never see one. We had never seen one before and we haven't seen another since.

The sight of a 50-foot long shark has different effects on different people, as the short extract from Thor Heyerdahl's book shows. One diver we know, when confronted with a 35-foot whale shark, grabbed his diving companion and held him like a shield before the shark. It is only ignorance that causes such fear. Whale sharks are harmless, gentle plankton eaters, not given to attacking large creatures, marine or otherwise.

Unfortunately, they do have a tendency to scratch their backs on floating objects, such as boats. This habit can be very disconcerting and dangerous for passengers on the boat chosen. In a case like this, the only defense is to move away from the area.

We remember our ride on the whale shark as one of the most exciting and outstanding encounters we have ever had at sea.

●

Ron Taylor, John Harding, our diving assistant, and myself were pounding shoreward through a heavy northerly slop. It was a nasty day and we were returning after an unsuccessful filming trip to Seal Rocks off the New South Wales coast, where heavy seas had made work impossible. John was standing up on the bow of our 14-foot aluminum dinghy trying to keep the nose down and soften the ride when he called out that there was something big and dark in the water ahead.

The boat crested a wave and, suddenly, we could see it, a huge shape moving along just below the surface. A black dorsal fin intermittently broke through the waves. We were all on our feet now staring in amazement. There could be no mistake. It was a shark.

The boys thought, because of its size it must be a white pointer, the most dreaded shark in the world and responsible for attacks on four of our diving friends. Ron decided that, because we had to continue working in the area the next day, we should try to kill it with our powerheads.

There was a mad scramble in the boat as we all frantically searched for our diving gear, bullets, powerheads, and cameras. Ron felt that the best possible method to bring about a quick death would be for him and John to fire simultaneously, both trying for the spine. The water was only around 160 feet deep in this area and, once the shark was killed, it would sink. Ron could then, using scuba, recover it and we could tow our victim into shallow water and take photographs. I was to try to photograph the kill with my still camera.

If the pointer was not killed immediately, the shock of having two .303 bullets enter its body at close range should frighten it into the depths where it would surely die from its wounds. At the very least, we should be able to frighten it away.

The boat was maneuvered into position a few yards ahead of the monster. Ron cut the motor and we all jumped out, abandoning our boat to its own devices. I lay joggling on the surface, apprehensive in spite of the closeness of my armed companions, my eyes straining into the distance.

For a few seconds there was nothing, then, suddenly, like a tanker emerging from a fog, came a head so enormous it hardly seemed real. We hung suspended, powerheads dangling, as yard after yard of beautiful, spotted, streamlined body flowed past. Before our amazed eyes was not the dreaded white pointer which we had foolishly thought to kill, but the largest shark in the world, the rare whale shark. Ron had dreamed of this moment for years and at last it had arrived, five miles out to sea, in a howling northerly gale. It could have been a cyclone for all we cared. Here was our shark, bigger and better than our wildest dreams. For the moment, fate was our friend.

Frantic with excitement, we scrambled back into the boat after photographic equipment. Fortunately, we had both movie and still cameras on board. The boys wanted me to look after the boat, but not on your life. I wasn't missing out on this experience; the boat could look after itself. It wouldn't come to much harm this far out to sea.

At first, we were hesitant as to the best approach. The shark, whom I called Wimpy in spite of her sex (she was a female), was 40 to 50 feet long, 7 or 8 feet through at the widest part, and had a head the size of a double bed. All this was propelled through the water by a mackerel-type tail over 7 feet high. We knew it was a peaceful plankton-eating creature, but she was just so darn big.

I started by hanging onto her dorsal fin, then I moved up to her pectoral fin. She swam placidly on. The only time she showed any resentment to our attentions was when I accidently put my hand in her eye. There was a sudden crash dive to a depth of around 50 feet, then a gradual return to the surface. John and I crawled all over our giant shark acting for Ron's camera. We knew she was the largest ever photographed anywhere in the world. Only three other divers that we knew of had ever photographed whale sharks, and we were familiar with their shots. Ours was by far the largest. To tell her correct size would be quite impossible, as the water visibility made it difficult to see all of her at once.

She seemed to be following a set course. We tried turning her back, but without effect. It was like trying to turn around a locomotive without rails. Some unknown destination beckoned her southward and nothing we puny humans could do was going to make any difference. To her we were no more than parasites sneaking a free ride and that's how she treated us, with complete disdain.

She had a very ugly head but rather beautiful body. Her skin was dark and spotted with white. Like all sharks it was very abrasive. John's legs received a nasty chafing when he rode on her tail. I looked into her mouth. A deep breath and I would have been sucked down that great rubbery-looking cavern without even touching the sides, a thought which made me move away to a safer position. Small parasites skated around her lips, scattering from my path. Like us, they were nothing but a nuisance to be completely ignored.

There were no remoras on her belly, which I thought rather unusual. Most large sea creatures carry these scavengers with them. Hard, bony ridges ran along her sides the length of her body. She was not so smoothly made as other sharks. More like a leopard shark or Port Jackson shark in appearance, only much, much bigger. One swipe from her mighty tail could smash us and our boat into little pieces. We tried riding her in every way we knew how.

John hung onto her tail and I onto John's ankles. With a mighty sweep, I was whipped through the water losing my face mask. After that, I took care to ride on the more static parts of her body. Fortunately for us, the shark was traveling with the wind and current so our dinghy was moving in the same direction. Every so often we would climb aboard our boat and move ahead of the whale shark, her dark shape easily seen even from a distance. Ron would take the opportunity to reload his movie camera, a tricky business in a small pitching dinghy, but the resulting footage would be well worth the effort. A chance like this might never come again. It was a once-in-a-lifetime experience.

We spent three and a half hours and traveled about five miles with our shark, but we could not stay with her forever. The cold was seeping through our wetsuits and into our bones. Lunch was six hours overdue. It was with reluctance, however, that we finally abandoned our shark to head back to shore. Her great black bulk could be seen moving away as we started the motor. I watched until her blackness vanished into the distance, swallowed under the turbulent ocean. Sad that our brief encounter had to come to an end.

It was a long, cold, rough trip back, pounding into the teeth of the gale, but we didn't care. Our recent experiences were really worth it and I, for once, didn't mind the crashing boat and stinging spray. It had been a great day.

20

From *Creatures of the Sea*

WILLIAM B. GRAY

It is rather difficult to find stories about whale sharks. They may be the largest sharks in the world, but they don't seem to attract all that much interest.

William Gray's description of finding and following a whale shark is most interesting—particularly the details of its feeding. He is mistaken in saying that the whale shark gives birth to live young, for they lay a large leathery egg containing a juvenile replica of themselves.

Gray has some doubts about Jonah. Like myself, he cannot see how Jonah could ever have been swallowed by a whale or a whale shark because the gill rakers (or baleen) allow only small objects to pass down the throat.

I like the way Gray observed the shark without molesting it in any way, for he was a man who usually killed or captured marine specimens for display in his acquarium.

•

In spite of the aquarium, the tackle shop and the many visitors to the pier, I had plenty of time for fishing expeditions of my own, either alone or with friends. It was on one of these expeditions, in company with two other anglers, that I saw the largest fish in the world.

The creature which holds this distinction is the whale

193

shark, or *Rhineodon typus,* as it is officially titled. It can reach a length of more than forty feet and a weight of ten to fifteen tons. Because it has a vertical tail and breathes through its gills, it is classified as a fish, but like the whale, which is of course a mammal, it bears its young alive and one at a time. Both whale and whale shark feed on plankton—minute animals sometimes so small that they cannot be seen without a microscope. The whale shark filters plankton from the water by straining it through its fine gill rakers, as do most whales. Its mouth cavity is large enough to hold a man, but its throat is too small to swallow even an object the size of a grapefruit. The teeth are very small, but there are very many of them, so that the jaws are covered with a formation rather like a coarse grade of sandpaper. On a whale shark twenty-three feet long the teeth were found to be two millimeters, or .079 inches long. Certainly neither the whale nor the whale shark would have been able to swallow Jonah!

Whale sharks are solitary creatures which can be found in all the temperate oceans of the world. Since they do not frequent any particular part of the ocean, they can be found quite unexpectedly almost anywhere, except in shallow water near the shoreline. Here they seldom venture. They have no defenses against their enemies except their immensity and the toughness of their hides, which some harpooners and riflemen nevertheless try to pierce. Such "sport" is not very rewarding, for the whale shark is a sitting target which doesn't give the fishermen much chance to show skill; it is of no value, moreover, when dead.

The day we discovered the whale shark, three of us were cruising along the northeast fringes of the Bahamas in search of game fish or interesting exhibits for the aquarium. We were about five miles east of Walker's Key, where the ocean was glassy calm, when one of my friends, who was acting as a kind of lookout, saw a mysterious object two miles away. He suggested that we go toward the spot, where there seemed to be some commotion on the surface.

As I brought the boat in quietly and with caution,

we saw before us a huge spotted form gliding beneath the waves. We passed it, noting that it was nearly as long as our forty-six-foot cruiser and nearly as large in girth as our boat was wide. The creature's back was bluish black with white blotches that were arranged in a checker-board pattern—a design that looked especially impressive with the ocean's blue superimposed on it. Behind the irregularly rounded head were two pectoral fins, rather like arms.

As I turned the boat and moved as close to the fish as I could, so that we could follow it and observe its habits, it showed no signs of panic. It seemed quite content to swim along slowly and continue its feeding. Several times we were near enough to it to jump from the boat to its back.

We realized we could not take in this fish alive, but since we did not want to kill it, we just kept pace with it for a few hours to take pictures of it with still and motion picture cameras and to study it. Although I had to look after the wheel, I also took pictures when I had a chance, and one of these was unusually successful. As the fish passed under the boat, about six feet below the surface, I just happened to click the camera. The result showed the pattern of the fish's skin very clearly. I was so proud of it that I have an enlargement hanging on my office wall even now.

We noticed that the whale shark fed on plankton by skimming the water with its great mouth open, its head half out, its dorsal fin mostly out, and its tail cutting the surface. Its favorite feeding place, we noticed, was along what is called a tide rip, where two different currents in the ocean come together. You can easily see a tide rip because it is usually marked by a collection of floating seaweed and flotsam (floating objects cast off or swept off from a boat). Drifting with one current and rejected by the other, the seaweed and flotsam are endlessly tossed between them. At such a junction plankton abounds.

Although this was a day without the thrill of battling a game fish or landing something of record size, I still remember it for one of my greatest fishing successes.

What I brought home was not something I could hang up on the pier, but an experience shared by all too few. If I ever manage to capture a small whale shark (it is not possible to bring home a large one), many more people will better understand the meaning of my adventure.

But to realize fully the awesome quality of the whale shark it is necessary to see one fully grown. It is the size of whales, I think, which is so fascinating to men. Moby Dick's massiveness, as well as his whiteness, amazed the crew of the *Pequod*.

Perhaps whales themselves don't always know how to handle their bulk. At any rate a story told to me by a friend of mine suggests this.

It was off Brown's Bank, eighty miles out from Nova Scotia, on a June night in the early 1930s that the incident he related occurred. A schooner, captained by my friend Henry LeBlanc, had hove to for the night; LeBlanc and six members of his crew were enjoying a good sleep below while one man on deck stood the watch.

Suddenly the schooner was struck from below by a shock which tossed all the men from their bunks to the floor.

In the confusion that resulted, they thought that somehow the schooner had been rammed. When they all scrambled up on deck, however, they saw a huge whale thrashing furiously about in the water near the boat. After shaking its head and turning round, it disappeared beneath the surface and was seen no more.

Apparently it had risen to the surface to breathe—as whales must do—directly under the schooner. It was that impact which caused the great shock. The whale then lifted the vessel almost entirely out of the water before it plunged over on its side and fell back into the sea. This caused the schooner to rock so violently that the man on deck watch nearly fell overboard.

I imagine that the poor creature, which only wanted a breath of air, was just as amazed as the men by what its bulk had done.

Luckily the whale had not damaged the propeller, so the crew started up the engine as quickly as possible and headed into Yarmouth. There the boat was put into dry dock. No damage to the bottom of the boat was found, which is not surprising because the back of a whale is soft and flexible. If it had bumped against the rudder, shaft, and propeller, however, it might well have broken one or all three.

21

Jonah and the Whale

FROM THE HOLY BIBLE

If it seems odd that a story about a whale should be included in a book about sharks, bear in mind that the story of Jonah and the whale is a very odd story.

It seems unlikely that Jonah was swallowed by a whale—the passage in the Bible merely says that it was a "great fish." I think that we can assume that even in those unenlightened times men knew the difference between a whale and a fish.

The words "a great fish to swallow up Jonah," to my way of thinking, mean just that, but was the "great fish" a shark? Sharks sometimes do follow a ship in distress as though waiting for something to be thrown overboard, or perhaps the destruction of the ship itself. This is a definite characteristic of sharks which, to my knowledge, whales don't share.

Even as recently as sixty years ago, people found it difficult to believe that sharks would eat a human. In America, large sums of money were offered to anyone who could prove that a shark or a fish would actually eat a person.

In the light of this, it is quite understandable that even though the writers of the Old Testament had Jonah being swallowed by a fish, history has turned it into a whale—probably because it seems more acceptable. Even recent shark stories have been changed and distorted with the passage of time, the

teller adding alterations to make his story more
acceptable to his audience of the moment.

The story of Jonah and the great fish has a few
other loose ends, too. How did he breathe? Why
wasn't he digested along with the rest of the day's
dinner? However, I suppose that any fish which would
swallow a man whole and then vomit him up again on
the orders of the Lord, would have to be unique in
more ways than one. . . .

•

Now the word of the Lord came unto Jonah the
son of Amittai, saying, Arise, go to Ninevah, that great
city, and cry against it; for their wickedness is come
up before me.

But Jonah rose up to flee unto Tarshish from the
presence of the Lord, and went down to Joppa; and he
found a ship going to Tarshish: so he paid the fare
thereof, and went down into it, to go with them unto
Tarshish from the presence of the Lord.

But the Lord sent out a great wind into the sea, and
there was a mighty tempest in the sea, so that the ship
was like to be broken.

Then the mariners were afraid, and cried every man
unto his god, and cast forth the wares that were in the
ship into the sea, to lighten it of them. But Jonah was
gone down into the sides of the ship; and he lay, and
was fast asleep.

So the shipmaster came to him, and said unto him,
What meanest thou, O sleeper? arise, call upon thy
God, if so be that God will think upon us, that we
perish not.

And they said everyone to his fellow, Come, and let
us cast lots, that we may know for whose cause this
evil is upon us. So they cast lots, and the lot fell upon
Jonah.

Then said they unto him, Tell us, we pray thee, for
whose cause this evil is upon us; What is thine occupation? and whence comest thou? what is thy country?
and of what people art thou?

And he said unto them, I am a Hebrew; and I fear the Lord, the God of heaven, which hath made the sea and the dry land.

Then were the men exceedingly afraid, and said unto him, Why hast thou done this? For the men knew that he fled from the presence of the Lord, because he had told them.

Then said they unto him, What shall we do unto thee, that the sea may be calm unto us? for the sea wrought, and was tempestuous.

And he said unto them, Take me up, and cast me forth into the sea; so shall the sea be calm unto you: for I know that for my sake this great tempest is upon you.

Nevertheless the men rowed hard to bring it to the land; but they could not: for the sea wrought, and was tempestuous against them.

Wherefore they cried unto the Lord, and said, We beseech thee, O Lord, we beseech thee, let us not perish for this man's life, and lay not upon us innocent blood: for thou, O Lord, has done as it pleased thee.

So they took up Jonah, and cast him forth into the sea: and the sea ceased from her raging.

Then the men feared the Lord exceedingly, and offered a sacrifice unto the Lord, and made vows.

Now the Lord had prepared a great fish to swallow up Jonah, and Jonah was in the belly of the fish three days and three nights.

Then Jonah prayed unto the Lord his God out of the fish's belly, and said, I cried by reason of mine affliction unto the Lord and he heard me; out of the belly of hell cried I, and thou heardest my voice.

For thou hadst cast me into the deep, in the midst of the seas; and the floods compassed me about: all thy billows and thy waves passed over me.

Then I said, I am cast out of thy sight; yet I will look again toward thy holy temple.

The waters compassed me about, even to the soul: the depth closed me round about, the weeds were wrapped about my head.

I went down to the bottom of the mountains; the earth with her bars was about me forever: yet hast thou brought up my life from corruption, O Lord my God.

When my soul fainted within me I remembered the Lord: and my prayer came in unto thee, into thine holy temple.

They that observe lying vanities forsake their own mercy.

But I will sacrifice unto thee with the voice of thanksgiving; I will pay that that I have vowed. Salvation is of the Lord.

And the Lord spake unto the fish, and it vomited out Jonah upon dry land.

22

From *Shark-O*

P. FITZGERALD CONNOR

Basking sharks are similar in many ways to the giant whale shark. They grow almost as large, feed on plankton, and when left to their own devices have sluggish, inoffensive personalities.

Whale sharks are found in the temperate oceans of the world while basking sharks are found in the northern oceans of the Northern Hemisphere. Only one has ever been reported farther south than North Carolina.

They are frequently seen off the northeast coast of America, but are not hunted in these waters. On the other hand, in the early 1950s, there was a thriving industry going in the waters of Norway, Scotland, and Ireland.

Shark-O is a fast-moving and very well-written account of a season's shark fishing along the rugged west coast of Scotland. The excerpt takes the reader on a hunt. These men, unlike sports fishermen, rely on catching sharks for a living so that there is a desperate tenseness in their hunt unknown to sport fishermen. Mr. Fitzgerald Connor manages to convey this very well, for, from his book, it is apparent he is a writer first and a shark hunter second.

●

The Bosun and Ralph began scrubbing the decks; JB started inserting sticks into the newly assembled harpoons. It became rather warm in the wheelhouse.

Well, there's Arinagour again. And there's Eilean Ornsay and there are the skerries. A bit of surf breaking over those skerries now, and there's one I've never seen before. No—surely not. There's no skerry there. . . .

"Give me the glasses, Ralph."

Where was it now? Ah, yes . . . but that's strange. . . .

"Shark-O!"

Yes, a fin! Half a mile away—just off the edge of that tide rip sweeping round Eilean Ornsay. Not much of it showing; but still, a fin. It vanished.

Full speed we hastened toward the spot. "Pep her up, JB. Advance the mag." And then it surfaced again, a single, hesitant tip. "It's moving too quickly," I said in despair. "There's not enough feeding." JB nodded and took the wheel. Four hundred yards now.

And then it vanished entirely. No fuss, no commotion. Just a fin, and then no fin. We lay off for some time, but nothing broke surface.

Maddening!

A Coll lobsterman came up the coast in his boat.

"Did you not get him?" he shouted across the water; and then, seeing us shake our head, he added scornfully: "That shark's been up and down the whole afternoon. I could have been hitting him over the head with my oars."

But the sight had put us in good heart. If there was one shark there would be more. Except at the end of the season, sharks are by nature gregarious, only when they don't show at all does one suffer the anguish of wondering whether to stay or whether to leave. "Look at that," I said to Ralph. "We've burned gallons of fuel today, searching all over the place, and meanwhile here's this chap coming up three hundred yards from where we started."

"Let's stay around," suggested Ralph.

Indeed we would.

An hour passed. From the north, MacBrayne's cargo boat came into sight, approaching Coll on her weekly visit. And then as she swung round the buoy to turn into the bay, the Bosun gave a sudden triumphant shout and pointed.

No need to say what it was. And by now we all knew where to go and what to do.

Behaving in much the same way as the other had done, the fin sank, came up again; sank, came up again. Then it vanished.

"Steady, JB. Out of gear. Wait for it."

Behind me, the Bosun was standing down in the fo'c's'le hatch with only his head and shoulders above deck level: a good position. From there he could hold himself clear when I fired and afterward he could flick the coils of rope if they caught in anything. Meanwhile, I saw that the crew of the cargo boat were lining the deckrails in order to watch. I think we all had trouble breathing.

From nowhere, it seemed, twenty or thirty gannets arrived and started diving.

And then suddenly, astern, another black tip broke surface. We watched it all the way; it continued rising until the water was washing over the sides of the huge back underneath. And as we swung round and made full speed toward it, there in a moment were five or six more. No splash; no hurry. Just five or six black triangular sails that hadn't been there a moment ago.

"Slow down, JB. Dead slow, JB."

"Skips—look at that!" The Bosun spoke with bated breath, leaning over the gunwale while the *Cornaig Venture* slid forward. And there down below were tier upon tier of huge shapes. Nightmare shapes, weaving their bodies this way and that. Why, we were running them down as they surfaced!

"Stick to that one, JB. Don't chop and change. We'll get plenty shark now."

I pointed a tremulous hand at the nearest fin of a pair that was going away from us. If last year's observations were worth anything, I had an idea which sex that rear shark would be. Head to tail they cruised steadily forward while, with staring eyes, we crept up behind them—now in gear, now out of gear—going just a little bit faster than they were. "Ca-choo . . . three, four . . . ca-choo! Starboard, JB. Now port. Give her a kick ahead. Now straighten up. That's it."

Oh, look at that back—just as good as the one at Canna. That's the spot. There!

The gun roared, the mounting rocked; the top few coils leaped in the air past the Bosun's nose; and then the harpoon plunged right into that unbelievable shape below. But we were unable to see exactly where it had struck.

JB turned the wheel to starboard, swinging the stern away. The rope lay slack, dangling over the gunwale. And for a second or two nothing more happened.

Just in time, Ralph and I noticed the Bosun staring with open mouth over the side. He had one elbow on the pile of inert rope.

We both shouted: "Back, Bosun!"

The Bosun arched his body as if someone had stuck a pin in his bottom, and simultaneously the stricken beast below reacted in much the same manner. Only in this case, the pin was real and it weighed ten pounds, and the beast itself was as heavy as two elephants put together.

As if he were taking deliberate steps to swat some outside fly, the shark flung his tail first away from us to get the momentum, and then he brought it hard up against the bilges. The *Cornaig Venture* shuddered and moved bodily over to port; a surge of water came over the decks: it hadn't been a sharp crack, but a heavy pushing thud. And a second later the tail went up in the air and towered over the wheelhouse. For a moment that ten thousand-pound beast stood on its head. "Ca-choo . . . three, four." And then there was no shark on the surface. Only a whirlpool of water where it had been. But the coils of rope were peeling over the gunwale, coil after coil in front of the Bosun's awestricken face. He fluttered his fingers around them as they went.

"It's all right, Bosun. We'll get them back later."

MacBrayne's cargo boat disappeared round the point of Eilean Ornsay, with her crew lining the stern.

From overhead the gannets continued diving into the water while all around us sharks continued coming up to the surface.

We watched the coils rushing over. It was deep here, ninety fathoms or so, and the rope would probably run to the end if we let it.

"Come on, Bosun. Catch it up on the bitts."

"That's the job, Skipper. Don't want to let him get fancy ideas."

Rashly, the Bosun grasped one of the uppermost coils. He soon let go. But by then these hands were skinned and he was a lucky man that he hadn't gone over the side. Moving urgently, we took some rope from halfway down the coils that remained and made them fast in place of the end of the rope. The job was only just finished when the full force of the shark exerted itself on the bitts. The *Cornaig Venture* jerked, heeled over, swung round.

"Lively bastard, isn't he, Skipper?"

Indeed.

An extraordinary thing now. Even though we pursued an erratic course right in amongst that shoal of sharks, none of them showed any fear. One even had the temerity to follow us up—while from sixty fathoms down its less fortunate fellow towed us forward; then there came a change of direction from down below and we started moving backward, and the beast on our stern lunged off and disappeared into the depths. But the others remained. Intent on their business: paired off, head to tail.

"Yes, he is a bit lively," I answered, as if the Bosun had only just spoken. "I can't have got much of a shot."

A grinding noise from astern showed that JB had started the winch. Slowly the two drums in front of the wheelhouse revolved.

We'd been taken quite a distance out by now. Why not heave him up straight away? It was getting late, but if all went well there might be time for another before nightfall.

"Let's reel him in, boys."

There was no doubt about this shark being lively. If we had not known it before, we knew it once we started to heave on the winch. The other three, of course, had no yardstick by which to measure it, but from last year's experience I knew that this shark had been hit in a place that had left him all the power in his body. A foul-hooked grilse can feel like a twenty-pound salmon: a five-ton shark is big—yes—but thirty-horsepower geared down to one in eight, as the engine was in the winch, takes a lot of stopping. Yet with four turns of the rope on the drum the engine would have stalled if we hadn't allowed the rope to ride for the heavier lunges.

The bows plunged. I saw the doubt in JB's eyes. Would the rope stand it? Would the decks lift? And what would happen when we got him alongside? A harbor launch. . . .

Yet, in spite of all doubts, we were exultant. The gun hadn't misbehaved; the barbs, although they were certainly taking some punishment, hadn't broken; the rope, bar tight and stretched to half its natural width, hadn't parted. For every two fathoms lost we gained five.

"That's it, Ralph-boy. Brace your legs on the wheel-house." . . . The sea. That gratification of masculinity. In a small boat. . . . Under the circumstances this was by no means a one-sided battle.

Slowly the drums revolved; slowly the pile of rope on deck grew larger. Ready now for our wild west act with the chain sling, the Bosun and I peered over the bows, while between us the rope came up, thumping and grinding the fairlead. Mighty forces at work. Was that the boat's shadow down there? No, it's El Sharko!

"Now then, Bosun, he's going to heave us around a bit, but as soon as his tail breaks surface—out and around with chain sling. I'll say, 'One—two—three.' Chuck it out on the 'three.' Here he comes. Whoops, dearie—hold on to the gun for a minute. Keep the winch turning, JB! Get him right up to the stem. That'll do—hold it, JB. Hold it! Now then, Bosun—ready?"

"Skips, he's as big as the boat. . . ."

"One—two—steady up, man. It's only seawater. Now, one—two—three!"

Oh heavens—we've missed. And look where the harpoon is right in the softest part of his back! Never mind—get the chain in, quick.

"This time, Bosun. Never mind that—the boat can stand plenty of those sort of thumps. Hold him, JB —hold him! Ralph, give him a hand. Now, Bosun, next time up."

"Okay, Skips. You say when."

"One—two—oh my God, look at that!"

We dropped our arms in dismay. The chain sling fell from my hands. Ralph and JB left the winch and joined us up in the bows.

"He's gone, Skips."

To be quite correct he hadn't yet gone. But as far as we were concerned he had gone just as much as JB's brace and bit had gone this afternoon, although it had seemed to lie so tantalizingly close. With the *Cornaig Venture* lunging around on his back, the shark had finally torn the harpoon out of the soft part of his body, and now, bewildered by unexpected freedom, the great beast lay there in front of us. He rolled his eyeballs upwards—those eyes that someone had made into ashtrays. Then bewilderment over, he gave one lash of his tail and standing up on his head, he went straight down. Silent, we watched the turmoil of water subside. It was all over. Now—yes—now he had gone.

VII

CATCHING SHARKS

●

You may well wonder why stories of catching sharks
are presented here separately from big-game fishing
stories when the motivation and end result are
basically similar for both. Before doing the research
for this book, I would have thought the same; however,
there is a world of difference. Zane Grey—with his
big boat, burley trails, game fishing rod, etc. can hardly
be compared to a native who swims up to a shark
and slips a noose over its tail.

There are many methods of catching sharks and
they appear all throughout this book.

Twice, Ron and I have accidentally caught a great
white in the steel trace attaching our cage to the boat.
The first time we thought it was a freak experience, the
second had us being very careful to avoid a third.

Selkirk, the South African who caught his big shark
from the shore and played it by running over the
rocks, is not alone with this technique. Sharks are
often caught by shore fishermen in many parts of
the world.

Mr. Dows, a neighbor of ours when I was a teen-
ager, caught a small wobbegong shark in Port Hacking
near Sydney. I was watching him pull his struggling
catch over the water-covered sand flats when a much
larger wobbegong emerged from the bottom and, with
one gulp, swallowed the baby shark. Mr. Dows,
undeterred by this, kept winding away on his rod. We

actually began wading out through the shallow water, for the second shark was about five feet long.

Mr. Dows feared his light line would break under the excessive strain of holding the shark's weight. Eventually we were knee-deep in water on the edge of the sand flat. The sand fell down to a depth of three feet. There, lolling crossly around, was the big wobbegong with Mr. Dows's line protruding from its mouth. A few experimental tugs on the line brought forth a sudden twitch; then the shark settled down to wait us out. (Wobbegongs are bottom dwellers whose long sharp teeth have no serrations; the line was between its teeth and not likely to be severed.)

Mr. Dows soon tired of this. He gave the shark a few pokes with his rod. Nothing happened, so I waded ashore and picked up a rock weighing about seven or eight pounds. I waded back, carrying my burden, and, with great care, tossed the rock out on to the shark. It seemed to sink rather slowly but eventually came to rest on the wobbegong's head. For a second, the shark did nothing, then, suddenly, he moved a little, spilling the rock off. Then he sort of coughed a bit, and out came the little shark, still very much alive. Mr. Dows reeled in his coughed-up catch and the bigger wobbegong swam casually off into deep water. The little shark ended up on the barbecue that night and was considered delicious eating by the Dows family.

So, you can see there can be a big difference between catching one shark and another. Mr. Dow's catch could hardly be included in a section covering big-game fishing, just as Zane Grey's exploits would look very out of place next to Mr. Dows's.

Compared to the carefully calculated system used by the big-game fishermen who indulge in the sport, other types of shark fishermen seem to be an incredibly varied lot with an even more varied end result to their efforts.

23

From *Fangs of the Sea*

NORMAN CALDWELL AND
NORMAN ELLISON

This true story of shark fishing as an industry, off the
east coast of Australia, shows the fragility of the shark
population when harvested by man.

Ron and I have a holiday home at Seal Rocks, where
much of the action takes place, so we know the area
very well and even today, forty-five years after
commercial shark fishing in the area ceased, sharks
are uncommon, though occasionally we find a few
gray nurse out near the rocks, and the wobbegong, or
carpet shark, is relatively plentiful.

One thing that this account of Norman Caldwell's
brings home to us is the huge number of potentially
dangerous sharks that can inhabit an area frequented
by swimmers, without contact between the two.

There is no doubt that the sharks off Newcastle, if
they so desired, could have attacked and eaten every
surfer in the water. They simply weren't interested.
Today the locality, where, in 1926, Bill Young and
his crew meshed sharks so successfully, has not
changed all that much, but the marine life has been
depleted. This is not only because of commercial
fishing but industry and people pollution as well.

Caldwell's account is similar to that of the shark
fishers of Scotland. The sharks are different and so are
the methods, but there is a similarity in the men. They

were tough, hard-working individuals, accepting disappointment and hardship as readily as good weather and easy catches.

Commercial shark fishing is still viable in some Australian states, but mostly the catches are of small edible sharks destined for the fish-and-chip market. The days when Norman Caldwell and Bill Young hauled in the big ones off Seal Rocks are long gone, but Ron and I still like to believe that there are a few big sharks left out there somewhere, patrolling the blue black depths as they patrolled forty-five years ago.

●

In August 1926 I left England for Australia to make preliminary arrangements. Three senior members of the company's staff came out a few months later. They were Captain G. R. Turner, the field head of the company, his right hand, Captain Bill Young (who has since put the shark in print with his *Shark, Shark,* published in America), and James Steadman. Then came a break with our English headquarters. The four of us resigned. But we were still sharkishly inclined; still convinced that shark fishing could be made into a money spinner. Several well-known Sydney men liked the idea so much that they provided working capital and formed a company—Marine Industries, Ltd.

We did a lot of reconnaissance work. We secured tangible proof that sharks abounded at many places. But accessibility was an all-important aspect. Eventually we decided on Pindimar as our headquarters. Pindimar is a tiny little fishing village in Port Stephens, New South Wales, about twenty sea miles north of Newcastle. The Port's hundred miles of shoreline are sparsely populated. The "capital" of the Port had no more than a hundred inhabitants; and when all the fisher-folk and oystermen were at home, Pindimar could not muster more than sixty people. The company was lucky enough to lease part of the old Government Trawling Depot, which several years previously was . . . well, it was a government trawling depot.

In May 1927 we opened our shark-catching station.

A dock was built adjacent to the Pindimar main jetty, and brine tanks, winches, oil rendering plant, and two hot-air dehydrating plants were set up.

All in all, your average shark weighing, say two hundred and fifty pounds, will beat, in financial value, a porker of the same weight, with the added commercial advantage of costing you nothing for fodder, nothing for care, nothing for land, and almost nothing for transportation, excepting as a finished product. And the shark is yours for the catching.

"Yours for the catching." Ah, there's the rub: the catching! For although anyone, anywhere along the Australian coastline, is likely to have a shark snap his bait, there's a big difference between fluking, yes, or even catching, a shark on a line or rod, and commercial shark fishing. To begin with, hand-lining or rod-fishing would never pay. And you cannot get sharks in commercial quantities by the usual methods of trawling or netting. Even dynamite is ineffective. You might kill some by a well-placed depth charge, but by the time you had hauled a few into the boat, the others would have sunk; for the shark lacks the air bladder possessed by most fish. When it is dead it promptly sinks. So Marine Industries had to evolve a different way of catching our bread and butter. We used huge gill nets.

After we started to treat our first haul of sharks, some of the Pindimar locals raised a lusty protest. Our sharks stank, they said, with adjectival trimmings; we were creating a nuisance. Well, I am not going to say that a dead shark is attar of roses; but I think the Pindimar objectors were laying on the olfactory color a bit thick. Fortunately for us, the authorities appealed to thought more of a new industry than a few oversensitive nostrils. We stayed put at Pindimar.

However, the matter of smell was only a minor trouble. Our real headaches were with the nets. Bill Young was the net expert. It was decided to have the bunt or body of ten nets made in Sydney. They were to be one thousand feet long and twenty feet deep. They were the biggest nets ever made in Australia.

That was something of a triumph, but when we hung the first net our complacency gave way to perplexity.

How the deuce were we going to buoy the thing? What were to be the floats? Tin cans of pint size were tried. They were a failure—when the nets were set in deep water, the underwater pressure caused the tins to collapse. Finally, we decided on five-inch glass floats. With hemp coverings (to protect them against knocks) they proved thoroughly effective. But first we had to find out the exact number of floats necessary to keep the net upright in the water. Trial and error gained that information.

In the meantime we had rigged the nets. The float or top line was two-and-a-quarter-inch manila rope. From it hung the bunt of the net. Along the bottom of this was the lead line, so called because of the lead weights set along it at regular intervals. The idea of the weight —there were also two sixty-pound anchors—was to keep the bottom of the net on the seabed. It's about time I explained the whys and the wherefores of the design of the net. You see our shark net was to take up a position on the seabed, just like a tennis net. The lead line and the anchors hold the bottom of the net down, and the floats hold the rest of the net upright. To enable the net to be lifted easily—perhaps I should say as easily as possible—a line is attached to each top corner of the net, and this runs to a buoy on the surface. The two anchors have similar surface communication. Yes, my dear Doctor Watson, the buoys serve as location markers.

Before we went into action, we had another marine headache. This time our boats were responsible. They were staunch thirty-footers, each with a twelve-horsepower diesel engine. They were built in Sydney and shipped to Pindimar. But when we tested them outside Port Stephens, we came back very wet and disconsolate. They were open boats and when loaded with two tons of net each, they shipped a lot of water in dirty weather. I'm not quite sure our choice of names had been appropriate—we called them the *Devil* and the *Demon*. In any case open boats were not fit for our work. So we took the *Devil* and the *Demon* over to the shipyards at Tea Gardens. A few weeks later, the launches were decked.

When we hung our first net at Pindimar, there were broad smiles among the local know-alls. When we mentioned our intention of setting the nets inside the Port, there was outright laughter. Sharks were rarities up there, we were told. We mentioned Salamander Bay as a likely meshing place. The laughter increased. What in the world makes you think that there are sharks in Salamander Bay? We explained to those skeptics who really wanted to be helpful that results in other parts of the world have proved that sharks abounded in spots with the same characteristics as Salamander Bay. So why not here? We were quite confident. Every man Jack of us was an enthusiast.

Captain Turner was managing-director of the company, Bill Young, fishing superintendent, Jimmy Steadman had charge of the dock, and I was factory manager. The skippers of the boats were Eric Beach and Frank Winsor. Beach had as mate James Cowdry and a local hand, while Ted Morante and a boy were Winsor's crew. The dock staff consisted of Bill Ping, a first-rate beamer and skinner of sharks, his brother, and several other relatives. All good men at their jobs, and not afraid of work. The men took to the new work with rare aptitude. And, said Captain Turner, who was an excellent judge of men:

"They'll be just as much at home in the handling of sharks." They were.

I broke the shark fishing ice, by capturing a nine-foot whaler shark off the end of the jetty. That afternoon we had set our first net in Salamander Bay; set it and left it there until next morning. It had been a big day for us, and after our return from the bay, I could not resist the temptation to do a bit of hand-line fishing. After an hour's wait, I caught the whaler. The catch seemed a happy augury.

Netting for sharks is different from any other form of netting, the cause being not so much the size of the shark, but the size of his brain. I've yet to find a shark with a brain bigger than an egg cup; and that tiny supply of gray matter is an indication of the intelligence of a shark when faced with a netting problem. Sharks are bottom feeders. Oversea experience and local research had proved this. So we set our net on the bottom. The idea was that our victims were to come prowling along and bump into the net. Then the rest was up to the shark.

You see, besides being small-brained, the shark has two other physical failings; he is short-sighted, and he has a disproportionately large liver. Altogether he's a stubborn, ill-tempered brute. Whereas most other fish would shy off when they touched a foreign substance, such as the mesh of a net, the shark apparently believes in going through obstacles. He hasn't sufficient sense to back water when he hits a net. The slits that serve him as gills get caught in the net; and finally he suffocates. Yes, he actually drowns in his own element just as a man would become asphyxiated in the free, open air if he could not use his respiratory organs.

The mesh of the net is soft and pliable, being made from seventy-two soft-laid cotton thread. The mesh varies in bars from six to twelve inches. In single strands the mesh is mere gossamer to any shark over six feet long. But there are hundreds of strands, interlaced, and when these get twined about head, gills, or fins, the matter of extricating itself is too big a job for nearly all sharks. The more the shark tries to push forward, the more the net twists about it. We have netted sharks up to twenty feet long, and up to a ton in weight; and, although there have been instances, not a few of them, when the net has been the worse for wear, there never has been an occasion in my experience of the netting of thousands of sharks when one has got away after it had blundered into the net. Our kind of net, that is.

But to return to Salamander Bay, and our Australian debut. Our little crew were amazed and smiling happily when the morning after we set the net we hauled it back on to the boat. For that netting yielded thirty sharks, ranging from one hundred to five hundred pounds—and all whalers. All Pindimar turned out *en fête* to witness the wonder that had come amongst them. We tried to appear nonchalant when we pulled into the wharf with our catch. I, for one was jubilant, and the skeptics were evidently nonplussed. With finger and toe, they prodded those sharks, almost as if they were determining whether the sharks were real. Then our shore gang got to work. It was a busy scene. Out came the skinning knives to be sharpened. The long arm of the dock derrick swung out, a steel hook was forced into the gaping jaw of a large whaler, and the shark was hauled aloft and on to the jetty. The platform scales were run into position, and the shark weighed. When it came off the scales, the pump was started and the blood and slime washed off the carcass. Then knives flashed. Cutting away the fins and opening the skin was hard work. The edges of the knives coming into contact with the denticles, or the outward covering of the shark, were dulled with each cut, and required frequent sharpening.

The fins were cut away first. The next operation, and the most important one, was the handling and cutting open of the hide. Only certain cuts must be made; one false cut decreases the value of the hide. It takes much practice before one gets proficient in the art of skinning a shark. Billy Ping grew to be expert. A queer chap Bill; part Malay, part aborigine, but a great worker. As the hides were to play an important part in the leather industry—at least we hoped so—they had to be as nearly faultless as possible. After the hide was taken from the carcass, it had to be "beamed" or cleaned of any adhering flesh. This again was Ping's job.

The whaler shark, probably the most numerous of all Australian sharks, has a hide of medium thickness, with a characteristic grain that lends itself, after treatment, to many purposes in the leather world. The hide of the tiger shark is heavily ingrained, and the resultant leather can be used for all kinds of bag work and motor car upholstery. The gray nurse shark has a hide unique in every way. It is extremely tough, yet pliable, while the grain stands out more boldly than in any other species. But these differences are not disconcernible at first sight. No. Most sharks look the same until the heavy shagreen on the outer surface of the hide has been removed. This is done by a specialized tanning process. So we left that to the tanners. Incidentally, American tanners are very keen about the hides of the gray nurse.

After Bill had cleaned the hide, it was trundled along to the factory, where, coated with salt, it remained until ready for the tanner. In those early days of our new industry, a lot had to be done before that event came to pass.

Another important by-product is the liver oil. A shark has two livers, each ranging in size from one foot to twelve feet in length, and in weight from five to two hundred pounds. The weight depends upon the size of the shark and the amount of food he has eaten. A well-fed shark produces rich, oily livers; a badly fed or hungry shark supplies little oil. We have got as much as eighteen gallons of oil from the livers of a thirteen-foot tiger shark. The oil is extremely rich in vitamins A and D on which cod oil is dependent for its therapeutic values. In color it varies from almost white to a pale yellow. Apart from its medical value, the oil is excellent for rearing and fattening calves—as a substitute for cream when added to skim milk.

There is no secret in the rendering process. After the livers were cut away from the shark and washed they were cut into foot lengths, and dumped into a large steam-jacketed kettle. The heat opened the oil cells, the oil being drained off to keep it free from stearin and liver residue.

This residue, when dried, made a meal which contained a protein value of 37.9 per cent. How do I know? Well, the Sydney Technological Museum has the figures; the tests were made there. When pressed into cakes, the residue is an excellent fattener of pigs and other stock. The Americans have made great strides in this direction, several of the leading New

York merchants holding large stocks of the meal. Our company was asked if we could supply them.

You've heard of shark fin soup? Yes? Well, back on our dock, Ping is on the first stage of getting this Chinese delicacy under way. Generally speaking there are two kinds of shark fins—black and white. Actually the white fin is drab-colored and the black fin is dark gray. The main culinary attraction of shark's fin is its gelatine: in proportion to size there is more gelatine in a shark's fin than in any other living thing. The fin also has medicinal value; it contains vitamin D. Medical men in Europe and America are showing an ever-increasing interest in this by-product of the shark.

The Chinese call the large white fin *chu sit,* and the large black fin *tua sit.* Commercially, all shark fins are valuable. The dorsal fin, the mark of the beast which cleaving the water within the vicinity of surf beaches sets the shark bell tolling and with it a frantic rush from the water by surfers, fetches up to three shillings per pound when dried. The pectoral fins are those which project from the shark's body behind and below the gills. These fetch three shillings per pound. The lower lobe of the tail fin is especially valuable. It is a mass of gelatinous fibers, loses no weight when drying, and fetches at the Chinese auction sales up to five shillings per pound. Drying is done by exposure to the sunshine. Large fins generally take about two weeks to cure, and lose about forty per cent of weight in the drying process. Today, the importation into China and Malaysia of shark fins runs into hundreds of tons a year, with an increasing demand. As a matter of fact, the market could easily absorb double or thrice the amount ordinarily available.

As I said before, Port Stephens is a good place; but in a very short time we were forced to lay our nets outside the heads. Systematic netting soon exhausted the supply of sharks in the bay. Unlike the cattle or sheep man, the fisher for sharks cannot see his prey, cannot look down upon his herds and pick out a place where he will round them up for branding or slaughter. Experience, however, taught us that the shark is a migratory bird, and just as much at home in deep as in shallow water. Some days our nets would go down in the most likely places, and remain there empty. Then a net would be lowered in a corner that looked barren of fish life or other fish food and we made an excellent haul. It was comparatively easy to lower a net off the boat into a fishing position in the water, but raising and emptying a shark net at sea is no easy matter, especially if the weather is rough and trying to tear the net out of the hands of the crew; very often they have to let go, with the result that the net has to be sought for afresh. Netting, as we did, off a rocky coastline, increased our difficulties; but it was there we caught the largest number of sharks. One week's catch off Morna Point, just north of Newcastle, was two hundred and twenty-nine sharks. We collected sixty-five of the best in one net—over eight tons of tigers, whalers, gray nurse, and pointer sharks.

If there was a sea running, the motion of the water combined with the backwash from the shore demanded lots of skill, a quick eye, and quicker legs. To be in a thirty-foot boat in a heavy sea, with a monster shark weighing over half a ton in the net, and to get him aboard without getting swamped or breaking the mast ... that, my masters, is a grueling, thrilling job.

Our first netting off Seal Rocks was a memorable one. The Rocks are twenty-five miles north of the entrance to the Port. One of the boats left headquarters early in the morning. By dusk the nets were set off the rocky headland crowned by a lighthouse.

Overnight the little boat sheltered in the bay. Next morning when the first net was hauled, the crew were jubilant. There were twenty sharks in the net; and the second net yielded fifteen more. Thirty-five sharks in one haul was indeed good. But the surge about the rocks made awkward the job of stowing away the catch. The hatch was soon filled, and the remainder of the catch had to be stowed on top of the nets and lashed down. A heavy load. The sharks weighed, approximately, five tons, and the wet nets two tons. And remember, ours was only a thirty-footer with a twelve-horse-power engine.

We were almost down to the scuppers as we turned for home. The boat behaved like a perfect lady in the long easterly roll. But the load was altogether too heavy. On the last stage of the home run we intended to set the two nets in the sheltered water off Broughton Island, a few miles from the entrance to Port Stephens. That would ease the weight strain very considerably. But halfway on our fifteen miles' run to the island a snorting southerly buster swept down. With this and the easterly swell, great sheets of water were soon sweeping us fore and aft. We battened down the hatch. The wind strengthened, the white caps grew bigger and angrier, and the pump could not cope with the water that was pouring aboard. The skipper decided to turn and run back to the Rocks. As he attempted to turn, a wave swept over us broadside. We bailed frantically while the skipper headed us into the wind. But the waves were raking the deck.

There was only one thing to do. We set about jettisoning the cargo. It was a heartbreaking job. First we dumped the six sharks on the deck. That was comparatively easy. But when we set about the others in the hatch, Old Man Trouble came aboard. The moment the hatch cover was lifted a big gust tore it from our hands and whisked it overboard. And as if they knew of the breach in our defense, the waves whipped into a harder attack. The water poured into the hatch. We had been at pains to stow the sharks as closely as possible; space was valuable. Now, the sharks were jammed so closely together that, with the violent movement, we found it impossible to yank out the brutes by hand. We had to use the winch and the mast derrick.

Have you ever tried to haul a sixteen-foot tiger shark, nearly a ton of it, lifting it high from a derrick boom, and lowering it into a big sea that is smashing against your boat, and tilting it into all kinds of crazy positions? No? Well, take my advice and don't. It's bad for nerves, language, and muscles.

The skipper could not lend a hand. With engine,

helm, and sea, he had his work fully cut out. A white shark, a monster eighteen feet long and of huge girth, was hauled from the hatch, tail first, the mast bending under the strain. The man at the winch did his best to help his mate, who was trying to get a hold on the swaying brute, and push it over the side. But the sea took command of both the boat and the shark, the latter swinging like a pendulum, a movement that threatened to capsize the boat. The man at the winch found the pawl had jammed, and he could not lower the shark. It called for some rapid thinking on the part of the winchman. A quick leap and he was astride the swaying derrick arm. A knife thrust cut the rope sling about the tail, and the shark took a header back to the sea.

The increased fury of the gale (as it was now) made it seem almost impossible that the boat would go any further without swamping. The bulldog way in which the two men fought on, waiting their opportunity when the boat rolled to drop or push a shark over the side was . . . well, fishermen are like that.

You should have seen the hands of the crew! One can shave the hairs off one's arms with the tooth of a tiger shark. The teeth of a whaler are like triangles with saw edges. The fangs of a gray nurse resemble crooked stilettos. And the hides of most sharks have a covering of shagreen like very rough sandpaper. And there were violent and unexpected movements by the boat, and the derrick arm. No choosing a place to grab the shark. You caught the brute wherever your hand landed. None of those chaps would have been able to play the piano for a few weeks. But they got the boat back in one piece—two days late. They had to shelter off Broughton Island until the gale had finished.

Now that we were getting sharks, our big problem was the tanning of the hides. Or rather how to remove the denticles. These no more resemble ordinary fish scales than armor plate resembles the tin foil wrapper of a piece of chocolate. The denticles, usually known as shagreen, cover the entire surface of the outer skin. Once these denticles are removed, the hide is ready for the tanner. Captain Turner is essentially a man of action. He set about the problem of shagreen removal. There were many experiments and, eventually, with the cooperation of F. A. Coombes, of the government tanning school, a successful process was evolved.

Then just as things were beginning to go along swimmingly, Bill Young ran foul of a director of the company and resigned to return to America. A month or so later, Jimmy Steadman resigned in order to return to London. And Captain Turner was sent to London by the board of directors, with leather samples, etc., for the formation of a large parent company. After a long period of waiting on our part, his negotiations fell through. The burden of running the industry fell on my shoulders. At first it was heavy going; especially when our board set out on an economy campaign. The staff, with the exception of a few local men, was changed, and I was able to use only one boat. But, thank goodness, the catches were still good. My staff were loyal to the backbone. They now consisted of Frank Winsor and his son, Bill Ping and his brother, Tommy Priestly (a splendid type of Australian boy and a great worker), and Steve Manton. They worked hours that would make a rabid unionist froth at the mouth. Winsor, his son, and Ping's brother did the fishing. Bill Ping, Tommy, and Steve Manton worked the docks. In my spare time I attended to the oil plant, the skinning, and the stowage of hides.

Things seemed to be going well. Hundreds of hides were collected. Fins were dried in large numbers, bagged, and shipped to China. There was rejoicing when a cable came from the company's agents in the East, to the effect that our first six bags of shark fins had realized £96 at auction. Other consignments steadily followed. The oil, which we filtered and purified, was sold to Sydney firms at 2*s*. 9*d*. per gallon. We sold several tons of it. Now that the tanning process had been perfected we shipped the hides in bulk to our tanners in north Sydney.

They got busy, and a month later, sample hides were ready. Mine was the job to find a market for them. I left Pindimar with perfect confidence. The work of catching and treating of sharks and hides was in good hands. And I was soon to learn there was a most encouraging market for shark leather. Some of the biggest shoe manufacturers and bag makers in the Commonwealth placed orders. Our leather was being converted into men's and women's shoes, bags, and suitcases. We were getting 5s. 3d. a square foot for ordinary leathers and 10s. per square foot for carpet shark hides. Yes, it looked as if our company was headed toward a really big success.

Then came a big setback. Winsor and his son threw in their jobs and went to Sydney for another firm. Here was a gap that was going to prove hard to fill. Netting ceased. I went up to Pindimar and, after a long yarn with our little staff, decided to run the shark boat myself. There were only four of us and, believe me, none of us needed sleeping powders. Often we took the boat out at two in the morning in order to get to the nets before the wind became too strong; and there were times when we did not return with the catch until midday. Then we had to do the skinning, finning, and beaming, and rendering down the livers, and salting the hides. We worked far into the night, seven days a week. Yes, they were grueling times. But there were those grand chaps pulling every ounce of their weight. And there were other folks at Pindimar who proved themselves friends indeed: such as Charlie and Mrs. Priestly of the post office, and Fred and Mrs. Evans of the ice works.

We had now fully mastered the science of commercializing the shark.

One thing I needed badly at the factory was a plant to treat the flesh of the shark. The wood-burning, hot-air driers were only suitable for drying shark flesh in strips (one hundred and eighty pounds to the ton when dried), and not in bulk conversion into meal. The whaler flesh is 88.9 per cent protein, and makes a wonderful white meal for cattle when dried and ground.

We made huge hauls of large stingrays, Port Jackson

sharks (too small for general use other than meal or fertilizer), and other inedible fish in the shark nets—all of which went to waste through lack of proper gear to convert them into an asset. I kept in touch with the overseas buyers of fishmeal. They were satisfied with the samples and analysis submitted; they wanted large stocks. Hundreds of tons of good meal-making flesh had to be dumped back into the sea. The plant I required was an expensive one, and the directors could not see their way to purchase. I carried on, catching sharks for hides, fins, and oil.

24

From *Fishing in Many Waters*

JAMES HORNELL

Fishing in Many Waters is an interesting work in that it investigates in a most unsensational manner just about all types of fishing with all types of tackle and bait.

The chapter on shark fishing, included here, tells of the methods used by three different island races to catch large sharks. Each of the methods is a variant of the same general method even though the fishermen are from widely different localities—Melanesia, Micronesia, and the Malabar coast of India.

Mr. Hornell's observations about using a rattle to attract sharks is an interesting one. I don't know whether it works or not. I have seen Pacific Islanders using coconut shells as rattles and we have tried it ourselves.

It is true that we did get several gray whaler sharks to come up to the stern of the boat, but at least one other person on the boat was successfully line fishing. The sharks may have been attracted by the vibrations of her struggling fish.

I haven't seen anyone lasso a shark alongside a boat, but it would certainly be very easy to catch a shark this way. In Australia, a three thousand-pound white shark was caught by a lasso over her tail. The whitetip reef shark, *Triaenodon obesus,* can often been seen asleep on the ocean floor with his head stuck deep into a cave, but with his tail sticking out. Any diver who approached gently would be able to slip a noose over the tail before the sleepy shark realized what was happening. Often, when I have seen one of these tails protruding from a cave, I have given it a hard pull, generally causing the startled shark to struggle out in a cloud of sand.

The supposition that a shark will attack a light-colored object while ignoring a darker-colored one has been mentioned by a number of shark authorities and our experience is that some species seem to prefer light or warm colors. I would certainly feel nervous if I were the only pale object in with a group of darker ones, if a hungry shark were in the area.

•

The voyage from Samoa to Tonga had been disappointingly slow. Ten days had passed since we had said good-bye to Apia and nothing had happened to relieve the monotony of idle days. True, I had signed on in the capacity of purser (on a nominal wage of fifty cents a month), but as I had to pay the captain a substantial sum for the privilege, the job was a sinecure.

The ship, laden with a cargo of lumber and rigged as a four-masted schooner, was a sluggish sailer. The twin auxiliary Diesel motors, provided against emergencies, were equally sluggish; the crew declared there was an understanding between the two "coffee mille," as the sailors called them, that there should be no competition; if one was in action, it was tactily agreed that the other should be given a rest. But there were, unfortunately, occasions, usually critical, when both desired to rest at one and the same time!

When at last we rounded the north end of Vavau, northernmost of the Tongan group, and met a strong head wind, lassitude and depression took a firmer grip upon the ship's company until one of the sailors called out that four big sharks were following the ship. The prospect of a spell of shark fishing cheered up everybody. A decaying piece of salt pork was conjured forth by the cook, skewered on a hook, and thrown over the rail at the end of a stout line. The sharks proved a greedy crowd. No sooner did the odor of the dainty morsel begin to diffuse than our lithe attendants sprinted forward and the bait vanished.

A few minutes later the winner of the race was dragged aboard, lashing out furiously with its tail. Hardly did it touch the deck when the carpenter, ax in hand, leaped forward and severed the tail from the body.

Here our Chinese cook intervened; swooping on the tail, like a hawk on a cowering bird, he carried off his prize, intending later to convert it into savory soup. The first mate would have liked to affix it to the end of the jib-boom, to ensure good luck and good weather for the rest of the trip, but the cook gained the day; the bait had been provided by him, and this gave him prior claim.

After the tailless carcass had been thrown overboard, a number of Tongans who were carried as deck passengers began to bewail this as woeful waste, declaring that shark flesh is first-class *kai-kai*. To console them another baited hook was put out and a second shark was hooked; we failed to land it, for it bit clean through the wire trace. A third try was made and this time the floundering monster was safely landed and duly handed over to the Tongans to their great delight, on the understanding that the cook should have his perquisite—the fins. And that night there was high revelry around the fo'c's'le galley.

Experience gained after our arrival at Neiafu, the port of Vavau, confirmed all that our passengers had said about shark flesh as a local dainty, and about the methods employed to capture these fishes. At one particular season, round about the latter part of April and throughout May, fishermen set out in little outrigger canoes to fish for sharks off the northwest coast where sharks then congregate. When the fishing ground is reached and sharks are sighted, one of the crew stands in the bows with a piece of meat none too fresh dangling from a short line at the end of a pole. Holding this in one hand, his other is busy vigorously shaking a rattan hoop on which coconut half-shells are strung in pairs, with the convex sides turned toward one another.

The large size of the threading holes permits of considerable movement and a loud clattering noise is made when the shells are jangled half in and half out of the sea. The men believe that this noise has an attraction for sharks, so when the bowman is shaking his rattle, the while he apostrophizes a shark to come and pay his good friends a visit, a second man gets ready to noose the fish; he stands with a stout lasso in his hands, ready to drop the running loop over the shark's head as it rushes alongside, eager to seize the bait. The lasso is made by plaiting together narrow strands of split rattan cane.

When a shark decides to make a rush, the bowman and the steersman must cooperate closely, the one to play the bait in the right way, drawing it slowly and temptingly along one side of the canoe, from the stern toward the bow, the while he utters soft persuasive words to the shark, and not from any other direction.

If these moves be properly coordinated the man who holds the lasso will be given a good opportunity to drop the running noose over the shark's head, a split second before the bait be reached.

This is the critical moment; if the noose be placed adroitly and in the right place and then drawn tight the shark's head should be brought into such a position as will permit the steersman to drop his paddle, seize a club and deal the shark a stunning blow between the eyes. If the shark be large and powerful and likely to prove riotous, a second noose is passed around its tail if possible.

Clever fishermen count on landing several big sharks as the day's work of one canoe.

When inviting a shark to pay a visit to his friends, he is addressed in the most respectful terms and called by some polite name such as "Hina." Should a small shark come alongside in response to the call and the clatter of the shell rattle, the fisherman requests it to oblige them by going in search of a big relative and by telling it that some kind people have prepared a feast to which it is invited. The men who relate this declare that it is usual for the little fellow to return after a short time, escorting a big shark well worthy of their attention.

A variation upon this method, common also in Samoa, is found almost everywhere in the fishing villages of the Bismarck Archipelago, lying off the northeast coast of New Guinea. The differences are partly in method but more particularly in the gear used, for the lasso is here provided with a large propeller-shaped brake or drag upon its free end.

In these islands, of which New Britain and New Ireland are the largest, when the shark fishers reach the fishing ground, the bow paddler picks up his rod, a long and supple bamboo, baits the line with a fish, and plays this bait just under the surface of the water. He lets it drift aft and dances it about merrily by delicate twitches of the rod. A second man stands next to the rod fisherman shaking a coconut shell rattle vigorously in the water.

When a shark, attracted by the bait or by the clattering of the rattle, comes nosing along, the first man draws the bait slowly toward the bow where he stands. If this succeeds in inducing the shark to make a rush, the bait is whipped smartly out of the water just before it is reached; his companion, who has meanwhile exchanged the rattle for a plaited lasso, slips its running loop into the water exactly in the place where the bait had been a second before.

If all goes well, the shark's head passes through the loop thus cunningly substituted; a jerk on the rope tightens it and away the shark goes, carrying off the lasso complete with its propeller-shaped drag, which is thrown overboard as soon as the loop is tightened. The fish tears along at great speed in the vain endeavor to shake loose from the incubus of the wooden "retarder." Every attempt to gain relief by swimming away or by grounding is hampered and slowed down by the drag attached to the end of the lasso. The direction of this slow flight is also indicated by the splashing made by the retarder. This the fishers follow up, and when they judge the fish to be sufficiently exhausted, they pull the canoe alongside.

It is now the turn of the young men in the canoe. Eager to show their prowess, they seize their clubs and rain a shower of blows on the shark's head, until it ceases to struggle.

When the canoe, with its prize safely aboard, returns to its village, its success is heralded by blasts upon a conch trumpet made from the shell of a large triton.

On the Malabar coast of India, shark fishing was formerly a thriving industry; today it finds employment for few men. The smallest of dugout canoes are used manned by a crew of two. In search of a catch they go farther seaward than any of the men who fish for the regular run of food fishes.

They fish with hand-lines made fast near the fore end of the canoe. When a fish is hooked, they play it in such fashion as to convert the canoe itself into an even more efficient brake on the wild rush of their victim than the propeller-retarder used in the Bismarck Archipelago. When the fish is tired out they paddle alongside and dispatch it. Now the men seem to face an exceedingly difficult problem: How to get the big carcass into a canoe not much bigger than itself?

To these men it presents no hardship; they jump into the sea, rock the canoe till it fills with water up to the gunwale. Canting it over on to its beam-ends, they slither the shark's carcass into the canoe and then begin to bail out the water aboard. When this has been partially accomplished, they scramble aboard, finish the clearance of the water, and head for home, content with their day's work.

The three methods above described appear to form a developmental series. Most primitive is the Malabar method. Next comes that employed in the Bismarck Archipelago where an artificial "retarder" replaces the canoe as the drag upon the fish which entails its eventual exhaustion. Finally, in the Tongan method we find that the great skill of the fishermen enables them to dispense with any form of braking device.

Two forms of the rattle are in use. In Tonga and Samoa the pairs of coconut half-shells are strung upon a single hoop of rattan cane; in the Bismarck Archipelago the fishers use the loop doubled and of a smaller diameter.

When a propeller-shaped retarder is employed, the length varies from 4 to 4½ feet.

The noise made by the rattle is said to be mistaken for the excited cries of a flock of sea birds feeding on and hovering over a shoal of fishes, by any sharks that may be in the vicinity; hearing the sound they hasten toward it, eager to participate in the feast. Another reason given is that the noise resembles the sound made by a traveling school of horse-mackerel—fish which sharks are fond of.

Finsch says that this coconut rattle is also used in shark fishing in the Trobriand Islands; from the context he appears to indicate that the shark is caught with a line armed with a wooden hook, 1½ feet in length.

In the Gilberts the shark is sometimes hunted in its own element by a diver armed with a long knife; the same writer describes how Rarotongan fishers at Aitutaki are accustomed to watch for a shark enjoying a siesta at midday with its head and most of its body withdrawn within one of the cavernous hollows common on the ragged and undercut margin of a coral reef. When the fisher sees a tail protruding from one of these, he slips overboard from his canoe; swimming quietly down he slips a noose round the tail and signals the fact to his friends above, who haul the shark to the surface and spear or club it to death.

The same story comes from other parts of the Polynesian island world; I found it current in Fiji, and Hadfield records this way of fishing sharks as practiced in the Loyalty Islands, lying off New Caledonia; the same writer adds that a precaution sometimes taken by divers in the South Sea is to bind something dark-colored over the white soles of their feet.*

Sharks with flesh of good, edible quality being plentiful in the waters off the southern coast of Arabia, a

---

*From my own observations in India and Ceylon, I am satisfied that sharks seldom attack dark-skinned divers; instances of attacks by sharks on the native divers employed in the pearl and chank fisheries of India and Ceylon are extremely rare; of these, several of the alleged instances which engaged my personal attention were discovered to have been caused

long-established trade in sun-dried shark flesh, cut into
long baton-shaped pieces, continues. . . . The fishermen
engaged in this industry inhabit the Kuria Muria Islands
and the numerous villages scattered here and there in
the coast lands of the mainland opposite, between Ras
Sharbut and Ras Nus. These people, who belong to the
Bautahara and Beni Janaba tribes, are fearless and in-
defatigable hunters of the shark, for this is the main-
stay of their livelihood. Wood being scarce and expensive, these poverty-stricken folk are driven to continue
the primitive procedure of their forefathers without
change or improvement; hence we find them employ-
ing their inflated waterskins, made from the pelts of
sheep or goats, as a makeshift device to go afloat in
pursuit of their quarry. With the aid of such buoyant
floats, these Arab fishermen put to sea without fear
and seldom return without a satisfactory catch; happily
the temperature of the sea along this coast is high and
there is little hardship if they have to remain afloat
and swimming for several hours should success elude
them for some considerable time.

The use of inflated skins on this coast is of high
antiquity; the Periplus of the Erythraean Sea (first
century A.D.) records that frankincense was transported
on "rafts held up by inflated skins after the manner of
the country and in boats . . . to Cana," probably the
modern Bir Ali, a harbor about 240 miles east of Aden.
And if inflated-skin rafts were used, we may be certain that skin-swimming floats existed concurrently.

---

not by sharks as reported, but by the savage barracuda; the sharp teeth
of those of large size can inflict very severe wounds. Conversely, in waters
where native divers work with almost complete immunity, white men are
exposed to much danger when they swim in the same waters; witness the
fatalities which occurred in Colombo harbor when soldiers bathed from
troopships moored there during the war of 1914–18.

25

From *Shark! Shark! the Thirty-Year Odyssey of a Pioneer Shark Hunter*

WILLIAM E. YOUNG

Reading *Shark! Shark!,* which was first published in 1934, brings home with tremendous impact how drastically the shark population has been reduced, especially around the large population centers.

To harpoon nine tiger sharks and boat five of them in Honolulu Harbor now would be impossible, yet that is what Bill Young did in the space of a few hours.

Over the past few years I have dived around the Hawaiian Islands several times and have not seen a shark. Companions on these dives, who were all locals, said that they seldom see sharks.

One thing that the segment included here points out very clearly is the role of the shark as a scavenger. The dead horse, which would have become a stinking, rotten mass in a few days, would have been completely devoured by the sharks had they been left alone. Sharks have their appointed place in nature's scheme and garbage collection happens to be one of their functions.

Young's book is interesting, too, in that it affords us a insight into numbers and distribution of sharks forty years ago, so that we can compare it with today.

●

Because the mouth of almost every common species of shark is situated "underneath his chin," it is a firm belief of every landlubber and almost every fisherman that sharks must turn on their backs to bite.

Now it so happens that with one or two exceptions, all sharks' eyes are located at the side of the head so that vision directly forward is almost an impossibility if the object regarded is very close. When attacking a surface bait or prey, the natural tendency for the shark is to twist or roll his head, enabling him to see the object before the actual snap of the teeth.

Yet not all sharks will roll in this manner. I have observed many a shark, swiftly bearing down on the floating bait, with nose out of water, rise and gulp it while remaining on a normal keel.

And, of course, in the depths all attitudes are the same to the shark when he is about to bite into his food.

It is, then, possible for a shark to roll when taking a bite, as he very frequently does, but it is by no means essential that he do so.

Sailors have long claimed that the shark and the porpoise are deadly enemies. Many are the tales told in substantiation of this quaint assertion.

But the porpoise is the enemy of its food fish alone, for it has no weapons. Teeth in a porpoise are like a cow's: sharp in youth and dull in age. But these mammals are among the fastest things in the sea; nothing that swims can catch them.

I have never seen porpoises play around sharks, but if they did, the sharks could not catch them and the porpoises do not hurt the sharks.

Porpoises, with the aid of their transverse tail, zip along under the bows of a ship, jumping out of the water for the fun of it, then like a flash they are gone —ahead of the fastest steamer, ahead of fish, ahead of everything, the playboys of the seas.

Near the Red Sea once, as we were going across the Gulf of Tajura from Djibouti to Obok one morning about dawn, suddenly without any warning there were thousands of porpoises in the air. In a flash they were gone and the sea was calm again.

They had driven a school of bonita toward shore and

finally into the air, and then caught them on the fly. And bonita are swift fish.

Porpoises are the kittens of the sea in their love of playing; they are inoffensive and make good eating, although it seems like slaughter to kill these warm-blooded animals.

At Fernandina we served smoked porpoise meat to a Norwegian who had been brought up on smoked reindeer. We could not convince him that he was not eating venison. Dr. Allan Rogers, the famous chemist, some time ago introduced porpoise meat in the Brooklyn fish market. Under that name it did not sell very well, but when they called it sea venison, it sold out.

The most famous porpoise in history was an albino of clear white, known as "Pelorus Jack." This animal lived outside of Wellington Harbor, New Zealand; it was his custom to meet every incoming steamer, piloting them in through the reefs to safe moorings. Pelorus Jack was the pet of the sailors in those waters, and later on was officially protected by legislation, but eventually he died after long and honorable service. This was the only fish in history ever to be recognized by legislative enactment.

Do sharks eat men?

Many people claim that they will not. If this is true why is it that sharks, according to one popular belief, will follow a vessel carrying a human body, in the hope that they will be on hand at the time of the sea burial?

Well, the truth is that sharks have no way of determining whether or not there is a body aboard any vessel. A body buried at sea with the proper ceremonies is shrouded in stout canvas and weighted at the feet with a heavy grate bar. The descent into the depths is so sudden that no shark could possibly attack the body, even if it were not protected by strong canvas.

It is extremely improbable that anybody buried on the high seas ever was touched by sharks. But sharks will hound a boat during very calm weather, whether or not it carries live or dead men, because of the food that is cast overboard as garbage.

At the boathouse we had to take care of our quota of foolish questions. A guest of the hotel, a man named Knute, came along one day and expressed extreme skepticism about the presence of sharks in the waters just off the harbor entrance.

"Bill," howled Herb, "here's a man says there ain't any sharks in the harbor out there. What'll we do with him—throw him in?"

The gang looked up and grinned. Jack and I came over and introduced ourselves. "You say you think there are no sharks out there?" asked Jack, digging me with his elbow. "Hear that, Bill? No sharks. I always suspected it; you and your stories of catching man-eaters right in the harbor! Why, I'm ashamed of you!" Herb looked at me severely. "Bill, if you can't go out there today and scare up some sharks, I'll know you've been lying to me. What are you goin' to do about it?"

"Well maybe we'd better go catch some if we can." And the hunt was on. Knute and I boarded the *P.D.Q.* and ran out to a good place, towing out a horse carcass. For the rest of the morning we waited, towed the bait around and around, swore, looked vainly for shark, and grew thoroughly disgusted.

"Seems like you can't catch sharks here," said someone. "Mr. Knute, what do you think of shark fishing?"

Lunchtime soon came, without any sharks coming to lunch. "Tell you what we'll do, Mr. Knute," I decided. "We'll run in for lunch, but send out a man with the launch while we eat. Then, if he sees some sharks, he can hoist a white flag and we'll come a-runnin'."

About three that afternoon Mr. Knute was a confirmed cynic about sharks. He knew there was no such "animule"—at least, not in Honolulu waters. Puffing away at a big cigar, he expatiated at some length about his ability as a fisherman, provided any fish were in the water.

I can remember to this day how his hand was sweep-

ing majestically as he described some record catch
when his mouth opened and stayed that way.

"Flag—flag," he said weakly, pointing. True enough,
the launch had raised her flag and it was bobbing up
and down at the masthead frantically.

It didn't take us long to get on the scene. Harpoons
were ready, and Knute, iron in hand, was to have the
thrill of his life and spear a giant of the sea all by himself. The horsemeat was being torn to ribbons by the
savage lunges of fifteen-foot monsters, so busy that
they did not heed our quiet approach. Knute half rose,
quaking with shark fever.

"All right," was the guarded signal, "let him have
it!"

Knute threw with all his strength. The harpoon disappeared into the water. In his excitement, Knute nearly
fell overboard. Missed!

We pushed him aside and commenced to hurl the
irons. One caught a tremendous scavenger just back of
the gills, and in short order he was dead from a stab
with the keen-edged spade. The harpoon was cut out
and two more were thrown, both taking effect.

Knute was like a chicken with his head off, hopping
excitedly up and down, bobbing about the boat in a
furious endeavor to see all that there was to see. I'll
wager he found more sharks off the harbor that afternoon than he had ever dreamed of before.

He got in everybody's way, suggesting, giving advice,
groaning at his hard luck in missing a prize trophy and
begging for another chance, but he kept us in good
humor for the rest of the day.

The dead sharks were secured with a line around the
tail and made fast to the stern cleat. Before we made
for shore we had killed nine, four of which sank to the
bottom as a dead shark always will. But a catch of five
tiger sharks was not so bad, particularly such big specimens, and already Knute was begging for us to tell the
newspapermen that he had killed them all.

We hung them all up on the wharf, tail first, and
took a picture of them. Knute did not get credit for

catching them all, but he posed, happily in front of the "Big Five," as we came to call them, for his photograph. And if that picture hasn't established his place as premier deep-sea fisherman back home in Keokuk, I'll eat the next shark I catch.

Some motion-picture men happened to be on shore at the time, and suggested that they secure an exciting newsreel based on the "Big Five." We were willing, and went through an elaborate pantomime of fishing and harpooning sharks which were already high and dry on shore.

Because we had neglected to kill all the sharks we harpooned that afternoon before we secured them alongside, several had threshed and rubbed against the sides of the boat with their shagreen skins, some even leaving the imprint of formidable teeth on the bow of the boat. Sides and bottom, we found later, were literally sandpapered to a high polish by the shark-skin contact, barnacles, moss and paint being cleanly removed.

In the old days, cabinetmakers and ships' carpenters used shark skin for smoothing wood instead of sandpaper, the keel on the denticle making a double tool. When rubbed one way it acted like sandpaper and in reverse it smoothed with microscopic fineness.

Herb and Jack were busy on the boathouse wharf one day when they spotted a big tiger shark swimming in the harbor, the first that we had seen so far inside the breakwater. They made for a small boat, harpooned the shark, and had to be chased in another boat across the harbor before the sixteen-foot tiger could be brought up and killed with a spade.

The fight and capture were not observed by a group of soldiers from a transport which had only recently dropped anchor not far away. These boys were intent on going swimming, each of them picking out a redwood plank from a nearby schooner for use as a surfboard. By and by the swimmers came to our wharf on their way to town. But when they saw what it was that we were hoisting up tail first at the wharf they beat it out of the water in as fine a race as you could imagine, leaving behind the planks which came in handy for us later on.

The shark was a female, and happened to give birth to her little ones as we hoisted her. They remained swimming playfully about in the shallows. Each one was perhaps eighteen inches in length, and showed no fear or ferocity when we scooped them up in a basket. The soldiers, curious, stayed around until a doctor had dissected the mother shark to see what was inside, and then they departed, but not in the water this time. No more swimming there for them. As a parting gift we let them take home a baby shark or two apiece. The litter numbered about twenty-seven.

26

From *Battles with Giant Fish*

F. A. MITCHELL-HEDGES

Mitchell-Hedges is a man who loves fishing. He writes about his experiences with just about everything from garfish to man-eating sharks.

This excerpt from his *Battles with Giant Fish* tells how he went about catching a man-eating shark in Kingston Harbor, Jamaica.

I found it interesting that Mitchell-Hedges, on finding that the shark had damage to its nerve center, came to the conclusion that the fish could have been insane. This, coupled with its abnormal shape, must have caused it to live differently than most other sharks of its species who rely on speed and flexibility for survival. The deformity may have caused it to seek easy prey and turned it into a man-eater.

The mass of excited spectators at the shore shows just how people react to sharks (especially ones which have reputations as man-eaters)—fear tinged with hysteria.

We all realize that the chances of being taken by a shark are exceedingly remote, but it is the horror of having chunks bitten from one's body while still alive which evokes fear out of all proportion to the actual danger.

Mitchell-Hedges wrote this book in 1922. He was one of the pioneers of big-game fishing and had to design much of his own tackle. He approached his fishing with scientific attitude and much of his catches ended up in museums in the United Kingdom.

I couldn't work out his relationship with Lady Richmond Brown, though!

•

During the first fortnight of March, I was compelled to go slow, the fights with these giant fish, coupled with the tropical heat, having strained my heart pretty badly. This entailed a visit to Kingston, where the doctors warned me seriously that I must go easy, so I was perforce compelled to rest, and occupied myself in my research work among the reefs.

On the fourteenth, I made up my mind to leave Black River and sail on the following Monday for Port Limon en route for Panama. We commenced the packing of all our specimens, when, in the middle of it, I received a telegram from Kingston informing me that a tragedy had taken place there. The message was very brief, simply stating that a girl, whilst standing in the water, had had her leg bitten off by a shark.

On the fifteenth another telegram arrived stating the girl had died in the hospital. This was followed by many more telegrams asking me to come up to Kingston immediately and endeavor to rid the harbor of this menace to bathers.

We hastened our packing, and, taking the whole of our baggage, on the seventeenth bade good-bye to Black River with feelings of much regret.

The little town gave us an excellent sendoff, and after catching the train at Maggoty station we were very much surprised to find that wherever we stopped en route many people were assembled to wish me the best of luck in my attempt to catch this lurking and deadly peril.

My trusty henchman, Griffiths, accompanied me, and on the arrival of the train at May Pen I obtained the morning paper, to find it full of accounts of the tragedy, together with the announcement that I was coming up from Black River specially for the purpose of trying to catch the shark.

It was with feelings of considerable embarrassment that I found, when the train pulled into Kingston, an

enormous crowd awaiting my arrival ou
tion. At first it seemed as if I would not
through. My old school friend Lieutenant
D.S.C., R.N.R., the harbormaster and on
sportsmen it has ever been my good fortu
together with Mr. Archibald McInnes, the
and Lloyd's surveyor, with the help of one or two of
the police, managed to steer me through the throng
into a waiting motorcar.

On paying a visit to the locality where the tragedy
took place, I found the front seething with people,
though what they expected to see was beyond me.

I was then given the first authentic details of what
had actually happened.

Miss Adelin Lopez, who was not quite fifteen years
of age, together with a little boy, Tom Bray, were bathing in Kingston Harbor between the Myrtle Bank Hotel
and the Yacht Club, in only a few feet of water—in
fact Miss Lopez was actually standing in the sea—
when suddenly, to their amazement, Mr. Lopez and
several people who were close on shore heard a pierc-
ing cry of "Father, father!" coming from the direction
of the water. Realizing that his daughter was in distress, he rushed in, and on lifting her out, was confronted with the dreadful sight that her right leg had
been completely severed close to the body. Three doctors arrived on the scene in a very short space of time,
but in spite of their medical skill all efforts to save her
were unavailing and the poor girl died within twenty-
four hours. The little boy who was with her was fortunately not attacked, though naturally terribly frightened.

I have always expounded the theory that a person
standing or floating in the water is in far greater danger
of being bitten than when swimming. Later on I will
give instance of how big sharks will come right in on a
beach after a motionless object.

Colonel Eden Clarke, inspector-general of the police,
and Lieutenant Harry Owen now rendered most valuable service in the attempt to capture this terrible
creature. The constabulary on land cleared the mob

e waterfront, and on sea the water police drove e natives that were assembled in boats, thus leaving an open space; and without delay, with the help of Lieutenant Owen and my trusty Griffiths, I ran out five empty 50-gallon oil drums moored to the bottom with lines attached, on the same principle as I related when catching the big shark off Parattee Point.

These were laid on Saturday afternoon, the eighteenth March, and I baited two with dead dogs, and four with fresh fish called yellowtail, weighing about 5 or 6 pounds.

Early on Sunday morning messengers came rushing up to the house where I was staying with Lieutenant Owen to say that one of the buoys was violently agitated and that a great fish was hooked. We ran down as fast as we could toward the beach, but long before we reached it we knew by the roar rising that a vast crowd assembled. Thousands of natives were pouring in from every direction, and it became a matter of virtually fighting through a solid phalanx of people to get there. A few police were doing their utmost to control the people but were overwhelmed by numbers. We managed to reach the water's edge at last, and ultimately, with the aid of a boat, the buoy, which had been moored close to the spot where Miss Lopez had been attacked, was dragged ashore, and at the end of the line, played out, appeared one of the ugliest brutes of the shark species I have ever seen. It was dragged up, and it will give some idea of the immense jaw power of these creatures when I state that as the big hook was being cleared from the mouth, its jaws closed in a convulsive snap, and subsequently, on its being completely withdrawn, I found that the barb had been bitten into the steel almost as if it had been welded.

On this big fish being brought to land, the police present were entirely swept aside by the multitude, which now numbered several thousands. Pressing forward, it almost looked as if we would be forced completely into the harbor. There was a small wooden pier jutting out alongside. This also became rapidly packed

with natives. Filled to its utmost capacity, it began to
show signs of giving way, the planking in several cases
cracking and breaking, and as the crowd still surged on
to it many were pushed into the water, dropping off the
edge like flies. For a time it looked very much as if
another tragedy might occur, when fortunately the police were reinforced by a detachment of water police
and further sections of the Jamaica constabulary.

Lady Richmond Brown and Mrs. Owen (wife of the
harbormaster), who up to now had been utterly unable to pass through the crush, by dint of hard work on
the part of the police eventually had a path cleared for
them so that they might take photographs of the big
fish now lying motionless, but as Lady Brown commenced to do this, in spite of the numbers of police employed the crowd again surged forward and we were
all actually driven down to the water's edge. Had the
police not used their batons trouble would certainly
have occurred.

To attempt to move the shark through the solid
wall on land was out of the question. The government
boat therefore came in and the carcass was hoisted
on board of it, and we embarked from the end of the
little jetty, traveling down the harbor with our gruesome occupant to the water police station. Here it was
hoisted on a railway truck by a crane and moved into
the shed. We were not to be left undisturbed, however,
for the crowd rushed from the place where the fish had
been landed, streaming down Harbour Street and completely surrounding the shed where we were assembled
to perform the autopsy. Here again the police rendered yeomen service and probably prevented the sides
from being driven in.

The stomach of the fish was protruding completely
from the mouth, and in its struggles as very often occurs
with this species, it had completely emptied its interior.

The autopsy disclosed several singular features which
were most interesting. There were three young about a
foot in length, quite alive when they were removed,
and a considerable number of infertile ova. On removing the backbone, surrounding it for a distance of a foot

and a half was a large calcinated growth—I think one might safely call it osteoma. This had produced a rigidity of this section, with attendant paralysis, and by destruction of the nerve center (I merely venture this as a theory) has possibly produced a species of insanity. This fish was quite abnormal: although only 11 feet in length, its girth was 8 feet 6 inches, and it weighed approximately 700 pounds. The logical deduction following the proved condition of this creature would be that it would no longer possess the activity necessary to enable it to capture its normal food, *i.e.,* various fish, and therefore it would probably become a garbage feeder, consuming almost anything that would not entail undue exertion in capture. Apart from the diseased vertebrae, its bulk alone would have precluded any swift motion.

I carefully preserved the backbone, and it has been on view, together with other specimens, at Messrs. Selfridge's, as well as many other places.

When the examination was over, I was again very embarrassed by the exuberant goodwill of the people when I left the shed, and I shall always look back on the tribute paid to me by the *Gleaner* newspaper as one of the most pleasant incidents in my life.

At the time I believed this fish to have been the one that attacked and killed Miss Lopez, but Mr. Gerald Abrahams, who lived in the immediate vicinity of the tragedy, after the capture still cherished the belief that other monsters lurked in the vicinity, and with commendable perseverance continued to bait and put out a shark line, being richly rewarded about a week later by the capture of a large tiger shark. This, one of the most ferocious inhabitants of the sea, one would certainly not expect to find so far away from the main ocean as where it was caught—high up in Kingston Harbor.

I do not know whether Mr. Abrahams's efforts have been properly appreciated by the people of Kingston, but I should like here to pay him a personal tribute for ridding the waters there of a fish which I venture to state was an actual menace to bathers, and would sooner or later have taken toll of human life, as to my certain knowledge one of these fish, 12 feet 6 inches in length, attacked a man (also standing in the water) off Morro Island, Pacific, about six months later.

In view of the capture of this fish by Mr. Abrahams, I must certainly modify my idea with regard to the fish caught by myself. I believe the length of his shark was over 13 feet, and I would like to remind bathers in Kingston Harbor that there still remain others.

27

From *A Pattern of Islands*

ARTHUR GRIMBLE

There is something lighthearted and utterly charming about the attitude Polynesians have toward sharks. Although no doubt reflecting their carefree outlook on life in general, it is such a change to read about people who accept the presence of sharks as something perfectly normal.

I feel there is a great deal we could learn about sharks and their behavior from the Polynesians, for it is quite apparent they have a better understanding of these creatures than we do.

Arthur Grimble's account of a native swimming toward a tiger shark and causing it to move aside is undoubtedly true. As I state several times in this book, most sharks are used to other creatures swimming away from them, not the reverse. This approach must be very confusing to a shark, particularly a dangerous one who is normally given right of way.

Most Polynesians hunt sharks for food. Sharks are good to eat and one average-size shark feeds a lot more people than one average-size fish, so it is understandable that knowing about sharks and hunting them in spite of the potential danger involved is a way of life to the Pacific Islanders.

Ron and I once spent some time on the island of Wuvulu in the Bismarck Sea. This island is surrounded by a narrow reef which drops down vertically 2,000 feet or more. Every day, the islanders stand on the

248

reef edge fishing over the drop off. Usually they wade out when the tide is low, carrying a long bamboo rod and a woven fish bag. Once at the edge, they fish for hours. There are plenty of fish over the dropoff. There also are hundreds of sharks.

We hardly ever went diving without seeing whaler sharks swimming past, yet the fishermen of Wuvulu have never been attacked. Even when the tide is in and all that can be seen of the islanders is a row of brown heads and long poles, the sharks seem to stay away. These men are catching fish. Although they kill their catch instantly with a quick bite on the head, there is always the initial flapping and struggling before the fish is pulled in.

To the people of Wuvulu, fishing this way is an everyday occurrence. To me it seems an almost suicidal method of catching fish, and something I would never have the courage to try.

Most of us have a vision of the islands of the South Pacific as being paradise. *A Pattern of Islands* shows us that even paradise can be dangerous, that life is not always tranquil.

The excerpt chosen relates the islanders' attitude toward two of the sharks that frequent the waters of the Gilbert Islands. Their regard for the tiger shark reflects that of most experienced divers today, as does their cautious behavior in relation to the *rokea* which seems to be the great white or mako. If nothing else, it shows that the Pacific Islanders have long known what civilized researchers are just beginning to find out: Some sharks are dangerous and other dangerous-looking sharks are not.

Arthur Grimble wrote of the Pacific Islands and the islanders lovingly, with humor and compassion, but he personally had little time for sharks and, in that, reflects the attitudes of most people. While I don't agree with him on the subject of tiger sharks, I do think that his descriptions of his own efforts to catch one are some of the finest writing on the subject that I have ever read, and perhaps the funniest.

There is one line in Grimble's book which we would

all do well to remember. He writes, "I gave up fishing after a few years because I found my heart too often aching for the beauty and courage of the things I caught."

I have never met this man but I like him just from his writing and the way he sees things.

•

Although safety first is the rule when tiger shark are about in numbers, plenty of Gilbertese are ready to fight a lone prowler in its own element. Owing to his great girth, a tiger cannot turn quickly; once launched on its attack, it thunders straight forward like a bull; there lies the hunter's advantage in single combat. Out sailing with a Tarawa friend one day, I pointed out a cruising dorsal fin. "That's a *tababa*," he said, "watch me kill him."

We lowered sail and drifted. He slid overboard with his knife and paddled around waiting to be noticed. He soon was. The fin began to circle him, and he knew he was being stalked; he trod water; it closed in gradually, lazily to fifteen yards.

He held his knife right-handed, blade down, the handle just above the water, his crooked right elbow pointed always toward the gliding fin. He would have a split second to act in when the charge came. It came from ten yards' range. There was a frothing swirl; the fin shot forward like an arrow; the head and shoulders of the brute broke surface, rolling as they lunged. My friend flicked aside in the last blink of time and shot his knife into the upswinging belly as it surged by. His enemy's momentum did the rest. I saw the belly rip itself open like a zip-fastener, discharging blood and guts. The tiger disappeared for a while, to float up dead a hundred yards off.

That kind of single combat used to be fairly common. It was rather like a nice score of fifty at cricket in England; the villagers applauded but did not make a great song about it. But the feat of Teriakai, another Tarawa man, became a matter of official record.

Tariakai was a guest of His Majesty's at the time, having got himself into trouble for a rather too carefree interpretation of the marriage laws. He was an exceptionally welcome guest; his vital, stocky frame was the equal of a giant's for work, and the bubbling of his unquenchable humor kept his warders as well as his fellow prisoners laughing and laboring from morning to night. A happy prison is a tremendous asset to any Government Station. Whenever there was a special job to be done, he was the man we always chose to do it. It followed naturally that when the captain and chief engineer of S.S. *Tokelan*—lying beached for cleaning in Tarawa lagoon—wanted to go out for a sail in weather that threatened to turn nasty, Teriakai went also to look after them.

The southeast trades have their treacheries on the equator. Though they breathe steady at twenty-five miles an hour for months on end, you can never afford to forget how suddenly the wind can slam round to the north and blow a forty-mile gale. If the northerly buster takes your mainsail aback close-hauled to the south-easter you are capsized before you know what has hit you. The Tarawans call that particular wind *Nei Bairara,* the Long-armed Woman. She caught Teriakai and his friends just after they had put about for the homeward run. They were spilled into the lagoon ten miles from their starting point and eight miles from the nearest land on Tarawa's northern arm.

Two chief dangers threatened them then: tiger sharks were all around them, and they were near enough to the ocean reef to be sucked out to sea when the tide began to fall. Teriakai attended to the sharks first of all. He started by hacking the mainsail adrift with gaff and boom complete. (His Majesty's guests are not supposed to carry sheath knives, but he had one, bless his impertinence). The canvas, buoyed at head and foot by its spars, made a fine bag under water, into which he ushered the captain and engineer: "Stay inside this," he said, bridling their refuge by a length of halyard to the upturned boat, "and the *ta-*

baba won't smell you." Then he looked for the anchor. The chain had fortunately been made fast to a thwart, but it took him an hour of diving and groping to get everything unsnarled so that the anchor reached bottom. "I'll go and get help now," he said when that was done: "If I can get past those *tababa,* we shall perhaps be meeting again."

He swam straight at the ring of tigers—the captain and engineer watched him—and the devils let him through. I asked him afterwards if he had any notion why. He replied, "If you stay still in the sea, the *tababa* will charge you. If you swim away from them in fear, they will smell your fear and chase you. If you swim without fear toward them, they will be afraid and leave you in peace." So he chose his shark, swam full speed toward it, and lo! the line melted away before him. There was absolutely nothing to it except a courage that passes belief.

He had gone about four miles before anything else happened. I have an idea it need not have happened at all unless he had wanted it to. He said the next *tababa* just attacked him, but he never could explain for laughing why he trod water and waited for this one instead of trying to shoo it off like the others. It is a good guess that he was overcome by the thrill of wearing a sheath knife again and the delight of feeling himself, after months of prison, alone and free for a little in his loved lagoon. Then again, the *tababa* was a male. I do not know how males and females are distinguished from a distance, but the Gilbertese fisherman knew, and they valued the genital organ of a bull tiger very highly. They said a man who had the right magic could appropriate its virile qualities to his own quite unspeakable advantage as a squire of dames. Teriakai made a nice job of the *tababa,* extracted the priceless organ from its ventral slot, tucked it into his belt, and swam on.

The swift night of the equator fell on him in the next half hour. The moon was not yet up, repeated busters from the north were whipping the water to fury.

In the welter of waves about his head, he missed his direction and swam into a maze of reefs off the coast to left of his objective. The breaking seas flung him on cruel edges, rolled him over splintering coral branches, sucked him into clefts bristling with barbs, spewed him out again stabbed and torn until more than a quarter of the skin (so the doctor reported) was flayed from his body. But he got through still conscious, swam a mile to shore, waded and walked two more to a white trader's house, and collapsed on his verandah. The trader brought him round with a tot of rum, but refused to take his boat out to the rescue on a night like that.

Teriakai's answer was better than words. He grabbed the bottle of rum (forbidden by law to natives) from the man's hand and ran with it out into the night. He had another five miles to struggle to the next trader's house; I doubt if even his gay courage could have made it but for the liquor. In any case, it would be pettifogging to carp at the good cheer of his arrival. He awoke Jimmy Anton with a stentorian song about *tababa,* and himself, and girls, and capsized white men, beating time for himself on the front door with whangs of the thing he had cut from the shark. In his left hand was an empty rum bottle. He streamed blood from head to ankles, but a smile of pure rapture shone through the torn mask of his face.

Jimmy Anton, the son of an Austrian father and a Gilbertese mother, was not the man to refuse a risk either for him or his boat. He called out his Gilbertese wife, and between the three of them they got the boat launched at once. His wife brought coconut oil for Teriakai's wounds, blankets and brandy for the rescued. They set out together. The moon had risen by then. They found the capsized boat just before dawn. The captain and engineer had been in the water twelve hours, but they were still safe inside their canvas bag. Teriakai was awarded the bronze medal of the Royal Humane Society. Before that arrived, he had acquired a uniform to wear it on, for we discharged him from prison at once and made a colony policeman of

him. Nobody ever found out what he did with the
trophy the shark gave him. It disappeared from official
ken the moment we got him into the hospital.

There is just one kind of shark that really does scare
the Gilbertese. They call it the *rokea*. It is a giant as
slim as a panther, that doubles on its tracks at full
speed. Fortunately, it never haunts lagoons, being a
deep-sea hunter, but when the bonito hold their an-
nual swarming over the forty-fathom banks outside
some lagoons, the *rokea* are there too in their scores.
The biggest of them run well over twenty feet long.
You never see them lurk or prowl, for their dreadful
quickness exempts them from any need of stalking.
They flash like hurled lances through the water, and
they can leap bodily from the sea, using tails as well
as jaws to kill.

I had hooked a bonito outside Tarawa one day when
there was a jerk followed by a deadness at the end of
the line. I started reeling in, but my canoe mate
jumped forward and without a by-your-leave cut the
line. "A *rokea* has bitten your fish in half," he said
then, "give it the rest." He explained that if the half-
fish had been hauled aboard, the enraged *rokea* might
have attacked the canoe, and that would have been the
end of us.

I did not really believe him then. It was only a
couple of years later that I saw what he meant. My
canoe with a dozen others was trolling for bonito off
Nonouti when we heard a thud and a crack from a
craft not sixty yards off.

As we looked up, there came another thud; a vast
tail had frothed from the water and slammed the canoe's side. A second later, the whole fish leaped, and
there was a third smashing blow. We saw the hull cave
in and start sinking. The *rokea* leaped again, and one
of the two fishermen on board was swept off the foun-
dering deck by that frightful tail. We saw him butch-
ered as we raced to rescue the other man. While we
hauled the survivor aboard, the sea near us boiled with
sharks as other *rokea*, attracted by the victim's blood,

fought each other for fragments of his body. The survivor, a boy of seventeen, confessed with tears that he was to blame; he had whipped a bonito aboard as a *rokea* was after it; the demon's attack followed in the very next instant. There was no more trolling there that day. They said the *rokea* would now connect every canoe keel with human flesh, and attack unceasingly. We made off at once for other grounds, sailing bunched together for safety.

I gave up fishing after a few years, because I found my heart too often aching for the beauty and courage of the things I caught. But there were two terrors of the sea whose death I never could mourn—the octopus and the tiger shark. These seemed to me as little worth pity as any prowling bully, and I felt no sense of guilt in killing them.

In the early days at Tarawa, I did want just one *tababa* all my own. I could not get the brutes to take any kind of trolled bait or cast lure, so I had to fall back on the villagers' technique with a one-man canoe, a twelve-inch ironwood hook bought as a curio, and a lovely loaded club. My cook boy immediately doubled up with laughter when I announced my intention to him. I asked him why all that mirth, but he only clutched at his stomach and staggered some more around the verandah. He found further entertainment in watching me attach the hook to a trace of steel dog-chain, and in putting up an idiotic burlesque of magic ritual over the finished work. His antics had the other servants hooting with him in the end. They clung to my arms, gurgling, "O, the Man of Matang . . . the Man of Matang, o-o!" to show no offense was meant. But nobody would tell me exactly what was the great joke behind it all.

The next day, when we got to the sandspit where my little canoe lay waiting, it became clear that the whole village had been warned of the event. The beach was crawling with sightseers. They were all immensely courteous, but the shining of their beautiful eyes gave them away. I was wafted on to the canoe and pushed off in a silence that throbbed with joyous expectation. I found this more than a little embarrassing, but it was nothing to what followed.

Eighty yards offshore I dropped the baited hook, made the line fast and, following instructions, set the canoe drifting beachward with a paddle stroke or two. I had certainly hoped for a quick bite, if only to save my face, but I was altogether unready for the fulminating success that fell upon me.

I was not yet settled back in my seat when the canoe took a shuddering leap backward and my nose hit the foredeck. A roar went up from the crowd as I was drawn whizzing away from it on my face. I picked myself up with much care and was in the act of sitting again when the shark reversed direction. The back of my head cracked down on the deck behind me; my legs flew up; my high-riding bottom was presented to the sightseers shooting at incredible speed toward them.

In the next fifteen minutes, without one generous pause, that shark contrived to jerk, twist, or bounce from my body for public exhibition every ignoble attitude of which a gangling frame, lost to all self-respect in a wild scrabble for hand-holds, is capable. The climax of its malice was in its last act. It floated belly up and allowed itself to be hauled alongside as if quite dead. I piloted it so into the shallows. There I tottered to my feet to deliver the coup-de-grace. But it flipped as the club swung down; I missed, hit the sea, somersaulted over its body, and stood on my head under water with legs impotently flapping in the air.

This filled the cup of the villagers. As I waded ashore, there was not a soul on his feet. The beach was a sea of rolling brown bodies racked in the extremity of joy, incapable of any sound but a deep and tortured groaning. I crept silently from their presence to the seclusion of my home. When my cook boy was able to stand, he staggered back and told me the point of it. A Gilbertese youth is trained to sit in a bucking canoe about as carefully as we are taught to ride. It takes him a year or so to master the technique. That was why the villagers had turned up expecting some innocent fun from me, and gone away fulfilled. But they dispatched the shark before leaving. Their *kaubure* brought along the liver that evening as a reward for my cook boy. A few days later, the jaws, beautifully dried and cleaned, were sent to me, the champion of the wooden hook, as a consolation prize.

28

From *Saltwater Angling in South Africa*

ROMER ROBINSON AND
J. S. DUNN, C.B.E.

South Africans must be among the keenest fishermen in the world. While working out from Durban on the film *Blue Water, White Death*, Ron and I were amazed at the number of anglers who lined the harbor breakwater.

We were told that a great many big sharks, including several white pointers, had been hooked and landed by fishermen off this breakwater, and it was stories like this which gave us encouragement and hope in the months that followed.

Next to Australia, South Africa has the most recorded cases of shark attacks, so it is not surprising that in his book *Saltwater Angling in South Africa*, Romer Robinson continually refers to the sharks as man-eaters.

This story of a fight between angler and sharks makes exciting reading. The fisherman, Mr. Selkirk, showed great skill and knowledge hooking and successfully playing a large shark from the shore.

Once again, I am struck by the continual deriding of the shark as it fights with all its strength to live. I am not criticizing Mr. Selkirk's efforts, for the fight no doubt taxed his strength and endurance to the limit, but the lack of feeling, so common in fishing

258

stories, for the poor, dumb brute on the end of the line
fighting away his life for the pleasure of a man who is
in no danger of anything more than a few stiff
muscles amazes me.

I found the telling of Mr. Selkirk's fight with the
shark more interesting than the usual "man catches
shark" stories. He was at a disadvantage working
from the shore and I liked the description of the shark's
tactics as it fought for freedom and how Selkirk
outmaneuvered him by running around the rocks.

Although I cannot help but feel sorry for the shark,
Mr. Selkirk really deserved his catch and all the
glory that went with it.

●

Shark is classified as vermin, but for the angler in
search of strenuous sport and tremendous thrills, the
shark is a formidable quarry.

From the breakwater of the famous fishing harbor
at Kalk Bay many grim conflicts with sharks have
taken place in the past, and numerous trophies, in the
shape of monstrous jaws, figure among the collections
of fishermen who have played these powerful fish to
the death. There is also a hardy school of shark fight-
ers at Durban, where the sport is carried on, as a
specialized form of angling, from the north and south
piers.

Of the famous fishing marks along the Cape coast,
the village of Hermanus is, perhaps, the only locality
where the capture of man-eaters on rod and line from
the rocks has been reduced to a specialty. This form
of sport is practiced by a local angler, Mr. W. Selkirk,
whose numerous captures of record fish, of all varieties,
entitle him to rank as a prince among fishermen. His
record catches include some wonderful specimens;
amongst them a 106-pound red steenbras, brought
to the gaff on six cord line—no mean achievement in
a locality where the sharp reefs and shelving ledges
favor the fish more than the angler. But a record specimen landed is never the acme of achievement. It

merely sets a higher standard to be attained, and thereby imparts that wonderful quality of adventure which is so characteristic of the sport.

Influenced by this spirit, Mr. Selkirk accepted the daring challenge of the large sharks that haunt the sheltered waters of Walker's Bay at certain seasons of the year. The honors of the first exchange ended all in favor of the fish, but from a close study of their movements and habits, an effective method of handling them on rod, reel, and line was evolved. At present no fewer than twelve of these great fish, weighing from 500 to 800 pounds each, have fallen to the rod of the Hermanus angler.

Though the gear for fighting the man-eaters is, perhaps, a little primitive, it is admirably adapted to this strenuous form of sport. The rod is a stout bamboo, about 12 feet in length, equipped with a large reel containing 500 yards of fifteen cord line. An ordinary four-gallon paraffin or petroleum tin is employed as a float. To resist the varying pressures imposed upon the tin when it is submerged by the sharks, it is filled with air, pumped into it through a bicycle tube valve soldered into the top of the tin. Attached to this effective air-tight float is a 6- to 9-foot trace of thick wire, with a hook sufficiently large to take a fish bait weighing from 6 to 10 pounds. The wire trace is extended for some length on the rod side of the float, in order to take the heavy blows of the shark's tail when it lashes out in frenzied efforts to free itself. In order to avoid injuries to the angler, a bucket is worn to support the butt of the rod, while a shoulder strap takes up some of the strain. A hand pad is also used to brake and control the reel, which runs on ball bearings, without any mechanical check whatever.

It need hardly be mentioned that the fights with the big man-eaters are of the most exhausting nature, and it is no exaggeration to state that the angler who hopes to be successful in carrying the struggles through to victorious conclusions requires to be in a state of physical training verging on that of an international rugby forward in his prime. The sensations of fighting the man-eaters with the gear described can be best conveyed by an authenticated description of a combat off the Hermanus rocks.

When the northwest wind is blowing, that is, when the breeze comes from the shore and the waters round the little fishing cove at Hermanus are clear and calm, the large sharks frequently come close inshore to pick up anything in the way of food. It was the writer's good fortune to observe the visitation of one of these great scavengers. Something like a long dark shadow was seen moving slowly over the sea bottom just beyond the picturesque headland that abuts the fishing harbor. This long sinister shape was a giant man-eater on the prowl, and some boys of the village, always eager for sport, reported the presence of the shark to Mr. W. Selkirk, the sturdy angler whose specialty is the slaying of these fish. He came down posthaste, with his gear and equipment in order, tin float and all. A large bait, in the shape of a whole fish, was lashed to the hook and the buoyant float was slowly lowered into the water immediately below the headland. Sitting daintily on the calm surface, the air-tight tin was slowly blown seaward by the gentle land breeze. The large bait could be distinctly seen dangling in the clear water. It was not long before the lurking shark spied the attractive bait. Heedless of the angler and the numerous spectators gathered round on the headland, the man-eater approached the bait. It nosed it for a moment, hesitated, and then swerved away at a wide tangent, with a flash of speed that caused ruffles on the smooth surface of the sea. As though playfully biding its time with the bait, it repeated this dashing maneuver perhaps half a dozen times and then swam away for some distance to cruise about cautiously, as if suspicious of the lure. From the rocks, each movement of the monster was plainly discernible—its lightning turns, its powerful swiftness in the water, the wicked flash of its white belly, and the cruel point of the snout. Suddenly it turned, came in at lightning speed, and at one gulp took down the bait in its open jaws. Immediately the tin began to move rapidly along the surface. As the speed increased the float furrowed up a wake of foam in its path, until it was taken under with a sudden swirl. The top of the stout rod swayed and quivered, bending heavily to the strain. The line from the reel hissed through the rings in a fierce and burning rush, which only stopped when the float reappeared about 200 yards from the shore. From the direction in which it was traveling, it at once became apparent that the shark was heading for a group of jagged rocks jutting out to the left of the harbor. Observing this, and realizing that the man-eater's maneuver would eventually foul the line, Mr. Selkirk made for the reef, holding his rod high to avoid obstacles, running over rough and sharply sloping ground for a considerable distance, taking in and paying out line, according to obstructions which barred his way. He reached the rocks in good time to defeat the shark's movement, and by determined handling turned it from the rocks. With another wild burst, it returned to the deep water, where it dived again. The float completely disappeared for what seemed like a few minutes, but the fierce bending of the rod, the rapid revolutions of the reel, and the cutting swish of the taut line in the water showed how terrifically the fight was being waged below. A struggle of this kind is no ordinary trial of endurance. It tests to the utmost the skill of the angler, requires keen watchfulness and prompt decision, besides entailing a considerable exertion of physical strength. The task of continually braking the reel, in order to tire out the shark in its abandoned rushes, is in itself an exhausting business, though it gradually produces its effect upon the vigor of the quarry.

After its second long run from the reef, the shark came to the surface nearly 400 yards from the shore, and at once resorted to different tactics. It leaped out of the water, as though deliberately seeking to crush the tin float under the weight of its falling body. It lashed out at the wire trace, the blows of its powerful tail resounding loudly on the water. It thrashed the sea into white foam all around it, gyrated, bored and twisted its lithe body. These efforts failing, it endeavored to seize the float so as to crush it in its jaws, but the steady pressure from the rod, and the frequent tactic of deftly jerking the tin out of the reach of the monster's mouth began to tell upon its powers of endurance. For a few minutes it seemed to relax its efforts. Temporarily exhausted, it came close up to the rocks. It appeared completely docile now, swimming in until it was within a few feet of the angler. A local fisherman, standing by with a harpoon, poised himself on a favorable spot, in readiness to administer the coup de grâce, but the angler would not allow this, knowing from experience that the shark was very far from having spent its powers and that it would take the combined strength of many men to hold the fish on the harpoon. His judgment was not at fault. After cruising for a brief spell in the deep water at the foot of the rocks, the quarry once more gathered speed and rushed out to sea, submerging the float to a great depth, judging by the amount of line played out. As quickly it came up again. It skimmed along close under the surface of the water at an incredible speed, taking out yard upon yard of line, rolling and twisting in frantic efforts to entangle itself so as to snap the frail chain between itself and the rod, but these desperate tactics only served to absorb more and more of its strength, and for the second time it lay still, apparently exhausted. It was merely a lull in the fight. Pausing far out for a while, it swam round majestically in a wide semicircle, heading for the harbor entrance, thereby causing Mr. Selkirk to run over the rocks again, to counteract the possibility of his line fraying on the sharp ledges. This time the shark, in its desperation, came directly into the fishing harbor, where it reached such shallow water that it appeared aground at the very feet of the angler and the eager, clamorous crowd of onlookers. The excited spectator with the harpoon again stood by, but still the angler would not permit the use of the weapon. The monster was yet too strong to handle with safety. With a vicious swirl, it turned again, rushed out fiercely, and the struggle was renewed. In this way the minutes passed into hours, with the shark fighting desperately all the time, but coming nearer to the end of its strength, owing to the remorseless pressure from the rod. After three hours of this grueling play, the angler, though palpably tired, and aching in shoulders and arms, slowly established his mastery, and reeled in, yard by yard, until the shark, almost completely played out, rolled over on its side. It recovered momentarily, made a last futile burst, and then finally turned over, white belly upward. There was no need for the harpoon now. The exhausted quarry was slowly pulled in to shallow water, and the quietus was administered with a long lance, to put the victim out of the way of doing any harm. It was hauled up on the rocks, and the enormous jaws were cut out to be dried and retained as a trophy of one of the many memorable combats conducted from the rocks of Hermanus.

It is needless to add that not all the man-eaters hooked have been landed in this way. One or two of them have rushed at the tin float, seized it and crushed it in their jaws, a disaster which has robbed the angler of his only chance of playing the monsters. Others have entangled themselves in the line, snapped it, and succeeded in breaking away with float and wire trace. One of the sharks, having snapped the line, could not rid himself of the float, and careened round the bay. The angler gave chase in a boat, but the frail skiff was immediately attacked by the shark, which rushed the boat on three occasions, striking the gunwale with its dorsal fin in one of these mad rushes. With admirable skill, and clever maneuvering, the angler was able to reattach his line by casting over the float, and, incredible as it may seem, he finally landed the man-eater, after an hour and a half's play from the boat.

VIII

GAME FISHING
FOR SHARKS

●

When people think of sharks, one of two things appears to be foremost in their minds: shark attacks or catching sharks. I have based this statement on the questions I am asked most often regarding sharks.

Game fishing for sharks is a most popular sport enjoyed by thousands of enthusiasts all around the world. People from all walks of life now participate in big-game fishing, but it was once predominantly a sport for the wealthy. The average man simply could not afford the boat and expensive trappings required to belong to a club and fish for big game on a regular basis.

Lucky indeed is the town or city that has good game fish in its local waters. Game fishing attracts thousands of tourists and fishermen to an area, and with the tourists come trade and affluence. Cairns, on the north coast of Queensland, Australia, is one such place. Honolulu is another. And the island of St. Thomas yet another. All these places cater to the game fisherman.

Once marlin and sailfish were the main quarry. Sharks were considered not worth the bother. Today, some species of sharks (unfortunately for them) are also considered good sport. The mako shark, in particular, is a great fighting fish with a lot of heart.

Tiger sharks, as Zane Grey found out, can give an

angler a good battle. The great white shark, on the other hand, is considered a good game fish only because of his enormous bulk and weight.

Alf Dean, world record holder for the biggest white shark on rod and reel, claims it's mainly a matter of power and technique to pull a white in once he is hooked. Ron saw Alf catch five great whites and the longest it took to boat a shark was 45 minutes from the time it was hooked.

Never having done any big-game fishing, I know very little about the sport. Several times we have gone out with game fishermen hoping for some action to film, but always without any luck as far as catching sharks is considered. It seems a lot of patience is needed for all the waiting around when the sharks won't oblige.

Once we saw a marlin jumping and, at first, thought he was hooked, but the fish was just jumping for joy or perhaps to tantalize Peter Goadby, who was also on board. Another time, a fine shark swam past completely ignoring our baits, which must have been very disheartening for the game fishermen, who had been burleying for half a day.

I have seen sharks caught on a line and hauled in, but never played on a light line. Somehow, I think I would end up rooting for the shark, but, even so, it must take considerable skill to feel the shark on the line and anticipate his next move over and over again for hours on end.

When making the selections for this book, I certainly had a surplus of game fishing stories to choose from. Big-game fishermen not only like catching sharks but also seem extremely apt at recording how they actually caught the shark and all the details surrounding the action.

29

Mako, Blue Dynamite

PETER GOADBY

Well known to game fishermen from all over the world, Peter Goadby is considered to be one of the most knowledgeable men in his field. Game fishing and sharks are his great love and take up much of his time and talent. All his books have been written on those subjects. This story is not from any of Peter Goadby's books, but was specially adapted from one of his magazine articles for inclusion here.

Goadby has great admiration for the mako, a shark Ron and I have never been fortunate enough to see in the open ocean. Judging from the lack of stories I could find regarding these fish, few other people have seen it either, and it worried me a little that this most famous of game-fishing sharks would not be well represented here.

Although many hundreds of other shark species are also missing, they are generally rarely seen or small harmless varieties not very interesting to the general public. As anyone reading Goadby's story will see, the mako does not fit into this category at all. While not an attacker of man, the mako will often defend itself to the limits of its strength and endurance, not giving in until dead.

Makos have the long pointed teeth of a fish eater, not the wide, triangular teeth common to sharks who eat larger marine creatures such as seals, whales, and, occasionally, man. Like all fish eaters who hunt in the open ocean, makos have to be fast and agile, two qualities essential in a good game fish. They possess exceptional courage as well.

I like the way Goadby describes himself being lifted and propelled headfirst, like a 200-pound live cork from a champagne bottle, into the water by a mako he had on his line. It is difficult to imagine a fish having such strength, for Peter Goadby is certainly no weakling and also a man well used to fishing for sharks.

This story speaks for itself. There is little I can add, for I don't personally know the mako. I am very grateful to Peter Goadby for making this story available and giving the reader a better insight into this wonderful shark.

Books written by Peter Goadby include *Sharks,* a publication covering attacks, habits, and species and *Big Fish and Blue Water,* his very well-known book on game fishing.

•

Mako—this Maori word sums up the sea itself— blue, warm, explosive, unpredictable, and dangerous. Mako is the name now used, understood, and accepted right around the world for a truly great shark. No more is the prosaic English "blue pointer" used to describe the shark that is rightly respected and often feared by offshore fishermen everywhere.

To the warlike and advanced Polynesian inhabitants of New Zealand, the Maoris, the unique curved, razor-sharp tooth of the big mako was a symbol of honor, of prestige, and of courage worn by chiefs and great warriors. Centuries before anglers knew of the mako as a sporting fish and centuries before there were saltwater sport fishing enthusiasts to be aware of the challenge of the mako, the sea-roving Polynesians acknowledged that here was a superb animal of the sea, something different from other sharks and fish.

Courage and explosive power captured by cameras and factual writers have earned the mako its modern reputation as "blue dynamite." For the fishermen who are familiar with the mako, "blue dynamite" has become a synonym for the mako which is the shark that has most often caused damage to boats and humans. It is the most likely shark to create action that is reminisced about with fact and legend intertwined forever. The respect and admiration the mako has earned is not lightly bestowed by the world's great fishermen. Many of those fishermen who regard the great billfish and giant tuna with something like adulation express the opinions that, whilst sharks per se are not worthy of anglers' effort and recognition, makos are something different.

Ernest Hemingway, Zane Grey, and Kip Farrington, Jr., all great anglers and great authors, found the blue dynamite worthy of their attention and worthy of their writing. This shark has a mystique, a charisma, which is not always associated with even the two mightiest of giant shark predators, the fearsome white pointer and the pugnacious tiger. What other fish, after struggling and succeeding to escape from hook and line, will return to the boat, black eyes gleaming and long curved teeth snapping to attack, maul and strike back? There is no need to add to proven facts about this shark. Makos will jump clear of the water upward of twenty feet. They will attack boats. They will chop tails from billfish (even the mighty broadbill swordfish). At boatside makos will sometimes make every effort to come inboard after fishermen. Makos are indeed great fish.

Of all the sharks, the mako has established a unique intrusion into fishermen's lives. Sure, the mako is a shark, but somehow it is different. Fishermen of all nationalities have a spirit of communion with this blue explosive fish hunter. This spirit does not evidence itself between fishermen and other sharks, in fact between fishermen and most other fish. Makos are not monsters; they are predators, just as man himself is a predator. Like man, and unlike most other sharks and fish, when makos are hurt, they strike back viciously. These sharks are mean, cunning, fearless, and dangerous to men who cross them. Makos today have the same effect on sophisticated, modern fishermen as they did on the ancient Polynesians. The fish dominate and the wise man watches with respect and caution.

The late Ernest Hemingway, great fisherman and superb writer in tune with nature, described the mako this way: "The only fish that I have ever seen keep their heads completely while attempting to escape and then, when captured, attack their captor viciously and cold-headedly, are the mako shark, the moray eel, and the gray snapper. The mako shark, which can jump as high as any fish, run faster than most and pull as hard as any, seems to me to be a true fighter. He will deliberately leap at a man in a dory who has him hooked on a handline. I have authenticated many instances of this among the commercial fishermen of Cojimar. . . ." Often, through his writings, Hemingway who is so descriptive in his loathing of ordinary sharks, shows his feelings for the mako.

Not all makos fight. Not all makos jump. Not all makos cause damage to boats and fishermen. But because they sometimes do these things, sensible fishermen everywhere watch the makos, ready for the explosion from latent to real danger. Makos were long ago recognized by European scientists and explorers. The Latin name, *Isurus oxyrinchus,* goes back to 1810 and published references in the nineteenth century were relatively common. The teeth were worn proudly by Maori and other Pacific royalty and used on their weapons, so there was no way Europeans, explorers, scientists and historians, could remain unaware of this shark. It was, however, only in the twentieth century, with the growth of recreational fishing, of fishing to rules, balanced tackle, and communication, that the mako really came into its own.

The famous Bay of Islands Swordfish Club in New Zealand was originally the Bay of Islands Swordfish and Mako Club. The club badges proudly displayed the mako equally with the marlin swordfish, as marlin were called in the 1930s.

The high-flying mako was one of the reasons why anglers traveled halfway round the world by ship and rail to fish New Zealand's fabulous waters. New Zealand has long been acknowledged as having the world's biggest makos. This is proved by the permanent residence in New Zealand waters of the all tackle world records for this species. This shark has the unique distinction of being the only one of the giant toothy critters to be often classed as a game fish and rated alongside and equal with the legendary giant billfishes and tuna. The great S. Kip Farrington, while having a real repugnance for sharks as a class, expressed himself about the mako this way: "It is a beautiful streamlined fish, with a fine blue back and silver belly. Makos are likely to fight on or near the surface and into the air—higher than any fish, either when hooked or loose . . ." Kip also warned of the danger at boatside and never to bring them into the cockpit and ". . . naturally, many guides and fishermen are nervous about them, and you can't blame them, for makos are unquestionably mean actors." Kip relates, "But by far the best story I have ever heard about the mako shark concerned four milk drivers who went school tuna fishing off Montauk Point with an inexperienced guide. They were trolling feather baits when something grabbed one of the baits and made a good run; the skipper thought he had hooked a white marlin and pulled the clutches. The fish doubled back and then leaped out, very close to the boat, and they got a look at the mako which they solemnly swear wasn't a pound under 800. He was so close that the splash threw water all over them and into the cockpit. They were so unnerved that the man with the rod rushed into the cabin and got as far away as he could—which was in the toilet in the bow—and the other three followed shaking at his heels. The petrified boat captain clung to his wheel and moved full speed ahead, and the fisherman—with the rod and reel still in hand—lost all of his line while standing in the toilet."

Kip Farrington and the other dedicated billfishermen would not have ever expressed admiration for any other sharks, in fact their loathing and repulsion is most evident. An exception to this common reluctance to tangle with, to know, to actually fish and hunt for the other sharks was Zane Grey. Zane Grey was an exception because of his intuitive understanding of nature, of the primitive, of the lonely, of the wilderness, of remote, unexplored areas, of the very challenge nature itself presents. However, Zane Grey's interest and fighting responses involving whites, tigers, and other monster species was undoubtedly kindled by his crossing swords with the blue dynamite mako early in his fishing career, with the honors generally ending up with the shark. In his paper on makos, published in 1934 by the American Museum of Natural History, Zane Grey said: "My bag of mako, to use an English sporting phrase, numbered somewhere in the neighborhood of seventy in all. Naturally, I lost a good many, especially the first year. The mako is a fish that often gets away. I had kept strict account of the larger ones, over 300 pounds; and I have caught ten of 400 or over, and one of 580 pounds.

"The last began to get into a class with big mako. I have hooked and lost several larger than that. And I have seen almost as many as I have caught myself, caught altogether by my brother, R. C., by my son Romer, and Captain Laurie Mitchell. Romer's big mako weighed 609 pounds, a really big one, an ugly brute in this case, cut and scarred by fights with his own and other kinds of fish. And he never showed once during the battle, fighting deep and doggedly for two hours. R. C. caught a grand leaper off the Great Barrier Reef Island, a shark well over 300 pounds, and one that exemplified all I claim for this class of fish. Captain Mitchell's famous strike of a 1,200-pound mako at Cape Brett and the loss of this line after two magnificent leaps I have written about elsewhere. Altogether, I have had a varied and full experience with mako sharks."

This Zane Grey paper reproduced what were then and still are the most fantastic collection of photographs of makos in aerial action ever published, but let's look at the action in the words of the master: "This mako, weighing some 400-odd pounds, leaped pretty close to twenty feet higher than Captain Mitchell's boat. I saw another, at a distance of two miles, flash white as snow as it shot above the same boat to a height of many feet. Both these mako escaped. At Cape Brett I saw one hooked by C. Alma Baker—a 503-pound shark that leaped six times behind the boat, all leaps from close to the same place, the second higher than the first, the third highest, and nearly thirty feet, and the remaining three graduating down. This shark turned over twice in the air at the top of his jump—on the second and third jumps—a performance that I would give much to record in motion pictures.

"I had one do almost the same for me. Mako leap every way under the sun. . . . Flying spray from our bow spoiled my view until the *Frangipani* slowed up and turned to run close to the *Avalon*. Whatever had been doing was over. One angler sat in his fishing chair, sort of red in the face, and popeyed; and his rod lay limp over the gunwale at right angles with a slack line floating on the water. The boatman, Cook, appeared to be bandaging his hands, and the boy, Vic, stood staring into vacancy. I hailed Wilborn: 'Hello there, Lone Angler. We say you'd hung a fish. What was it?' 'It wasn't a fish,' declared he. 'No, what then?' 'It was one of those flying devils . . . blue and white . . . with a mouth like a subway entrance spiked gates.' 'Mako. I thought so. He looked pretty husky. Where is he?' 'I've an idea he had an engagement in the China Sea. He was in something of a hurry.' 'I see. Broke off. Only an incident of New Zealand angling. He busted your rod.' 'I should say not. It was your rod.' 'Fine. I'm tickled pink. What else did he do?' 'Well he knocked that small gaff skyhigh.' 'You should have used the big detachable with the long rope.' 'We did.' 'Oh. Missed him, eh?' 'No. He took that gaff with him.' 'Not my big detachable,' I ejaculated incredulously. 'We needed a mile of rope.' 'So. I'm sure glad I didn't give you one of the expensive gaffs to practice with.' "

Zane Grey's crews were not the only ones damaged in New Zealand, or hurt with nearly fatal misses with makos. There was the Whangoroa incident where the hooked mako jumped clear of the water, suspended like a great blue eagle with angry black eyes and deadly white talon-teeth and landed plumb in the center of the cockpit (which had luckily and hurriedly just been evacuated by angler and crew), then demolished the fishing chair and scarred the decks and coverboards. A small Cairns mako of 160 pounds that the *Avalon* crew brought in after being played was wired and brought in through the transom door. This small mako took over *Avalon*'s cockpit, lashing at the fishermen with slashing teeth and flashing tail and preventing entry for over thirty minutes.

Other Australian crews have had many close shaves with death and injury. Frank Lipanovich, on successive weekends, had makos over 600 pounds jump into his boat, *Adriatic II,* causing damage to hull and deck woodwork and stainless steel bowrail. John Kellion was another Australian who knew how to find, attract, and hook the big makos. Two of these live in Australian fishing history in truth, not legend. It happened this way. One shark was around 800 pounds and was wired, then double-gaffed and should have been a sure capture. This Sydney mako bore down, rolled off one gaff, tore the other free in a flash, then sounded under the boat before it showed high and clear in a jump with gaff rope trailing clear over an aluminum skiff with two fishermen anchored nearby. The line parted and once again the shark was the winner.

The second incident, just four weeks later, was even closer to total victory for the mako with me as a fatal accident statistic. This second mako we mistook to be a 1,000-pound-plus white shark and treated casually, far too casually. An experienced crew such as ours should have been alerted by the fact that record size makos are relatively common at Port Stephens whereas big white sharks are less regular visitors to those waters.

I had the leader wire in hand quickly, brought the

big shark to boatside, lifted the pointed shark head clear of the water for gaffing, then realized that the massive gray shape (gray perhaps because of age and size) was in fact a monster mako, not a white shark. Two strong flying gaffs, one each side of the jaw, should have held that mako. But they didn't. Suddenly it cleared the water as if jet propelled. The mako's full length was out of the water and then it fell back into the same welter of white water. The full force of the unleashed power came to me through the wire wrapped onto gloved hands to lift and propel me headfirst into the foam and depths like a 200-pound live cork from a champagne bottle. Before a safe return could be made back into the cockpit I had to swim forward clear of the twisted brass rubbing strips and torn timber and then lift back inboard to safety. We didn't weigh that mako either. The lunging jump beside the boat cleared one gaff, broke the leader, and then the mako rolled clear of the other gaff and sounded, rolling all the time until only the limp 80-pound line and shambles of the port side of the boat reminded us of what we had seen. Death had indeed been close that day. The closest of many bruising and bloody encounters with blue dynamite in packages of various weights from 20 pounds to 1,000 pounds.

Alfred Glassell, the great American billfisherman, is another whose experience rates some makos near the top of all marine fishes. Alfred landed one at Bay of Islands, towed it around for half a day, then came into Otehei Bay for weigh-in. The "dead" mako cleared the weighing station, tore free from the scales and weighing gantry and fell back into the water, leaving Otehei Bay and stunned disbelievers on shore.

It was from Otehei Bay that Jim Whitelaw, his mate, and I thought we had done everything right with a 400-pound mako by playing it out, wiring, and gaffing it. Then all hell broke loose as again it cleared the water, changed direction on landing to wrap all of us in flying gaff rope. A broken fishing chair, blood and bruises on all three of us and memories of nearly another man overboard were reminders, if we needed any, of what happens when the fuse burns down in the "blue dynamite."

Where do makos get their explosive power? Their ability to jump a certain twenty feet clear of the water from an almost standing start? To run fast and long? One explanation of the speed and power of makos and their cousins, the white pointers, is that they are, in fact, warm-blooded species similar to bluefin tuna. Research has disclosed that the power available from muscles increases markedly if the fish blood temperature is high, and it is estimated that in fish with this characteristic, up to three times the power is available than from the muscle structure of cold-blooded fish.

It is a most sobering experience for fishermen to watch juvenile makos of around only ten to fifteen pounds dealing with live or whole fish baits. These little blue "rats" zoom in on live bait and chop off the tail, just as adult mako do when feeding and attacking broadbill and giant billfish. It is incredible that this characteristic instinct of killing and survival is built into every mako from the moment of birth. What a contrast between two predators at birth—the baby of man and the baby mako. One helpless, the other complete and swimming, killing and living in the world's cruelest, most deadly and unforgiving environment.

Makos have been caught in quick time on light as well as heavy tackle, sometimes without the fishermen ever having the adrenaline-pumping thrill of even one jump. Somehow quick times for these and other great fish do not do justice to the fish or human endeavor. The fish that we remember with honor and pride are those that have fought hard, given of their best and had an equal or more than equal chance for freedom because of their power and the sea itself.

The mako in any ocean is the same. Whether pronounced as in New Zealand, "marko," or in other places more commonly, "mayko," everyone understands what it stands for and what it means. Nothing more needs to be added. Nature has done it all. Once again Zane Grey expressed it best: "He was overcome but not beaten. He had the diabolical eye of a creature that would kill as he was being killed. And as Reuben lassoed the waving tail, the mako lurched out with snapping jaws, halfway up to the gunwale, to sink his teeth on the side of the boat. That was his last gesture."

30

From *An American Angler in Australia*

ZANE GREY

Zane Grey is remembered mostly for the books that he wrote with a Western theme, but he was also one of the most famous big-game fishermen of his day.

He visited Australia twice, the first time at the request of the New South Wales government to help promote the tourist industry. This excerpt is taken from a book written after this first visit.

While Grey had a great regard for marlin as a game fish, he regarded all sharks as vermin, not worthy of catching. This attitude changed considerably during his Australian trip. The big tigers and whalers he caught off the eastern Australian coast sometimes proved more than a match for Grey's skill as an angler and he came to respect their power, strength, and fighting ability.

Big sharks are still to be found off the New South Wales coast and the game boats still leave Sydney Harbor. Ron and I have been out after them with well-known big-game fisherman Peter Goadby. We have waited off the Heads, riding the oily swell, while the giant albatross feed noisily in our burley flow. Unlike Grey, we didn't catch a record tiger shark; in fact, we didn't catch any sharks at all, but the day was the same as Grey describes so well—hot and beautiful.

I find it sad that Grey could look at his dead tiger shark, that had fought so long and so hard for its life, and see it as a vicious brute. The great shark had not been trying to destroy Grey whereas Grey, from the safety of his boat, had been trying to destroy the shark.

We have always found tiger sharks, in their natural element, even when feeding, to be rather placid in nature. It would seem that they act like vicious brutes only when trapped, in pain, and fighting for life.

I would like to have met Grey when he was alive and shown to him these monster sharks he caught and killed with such pride, as they really are when free and unmolested in their own world. Grey lived in those days when the only good shark was a dead one, and he was responsible for plenty of those.

Besides catching sharks, Grey caught many other big-game fish and became a legend in his own time for the fish he fought and the records he held. I think he will be best remembered for his simple powerful writing about the sea, the men on it, and the giant fish in it.

●

The sun was hot, the gentle motion of the boat lulling, the breeze scarcely perceptible, the sea beautiful and compelling, and there was no moment that I could not see craft of all kinds, from great liners to small fishing boats. I sat in my fishing chair, feet on the gunwale, the line in my hand, and the passage of time was unnoticeable. In fact, time seemed to stand still.

The hours passed, until about midafternoon, and conversation lagged. Emil went to sleep, so that I had to watch his float. Peter smoked innumerable cigarettes, and then he went to sleep. Love's hopes of a strike began perceptibly to fail. He kept repeating about every hour that the sharks must be having an off day. But I was quite happy and satisfied.

I watched three albatross hanging around a market boat some distance away. Finally this boat ran in, and the huge white and black birds floated over our way. I told Love to throw some pieces of bait in. He did so, one of which was a whole bonito with its sides sliced off. The albatross flew toward us, landed on their feet a dozen rods away, and then ran across the water to us. One was shy and distrustful. The others were tame. It happened, however, that the suspicious albatross got the whole bonito, which he proceeded to gulp down, and it stuck in his throat.

He drifted away, making a great to-do over the trouble his gluttony had brought him. He beat the water with his wings and ducked his head under to shake it violently.

Meanwhile the other two came close, to within thirty feet, and they emitted strange low, not unmusical, cries as they picked up the morsels of fish Love pitched them. They were huge birds, pure white except across the back and along the wide-spreading wings. Their black eyes had an Oriental look, a slanting back and upward, which might have been caused by a little tuft of black feathers. To say I was in a seventh heaven was putting it mildly. I awoke Emil, who being a temperamental artist and photographer, went into ecstasies with his camera. "I can't believe my eye!" he kept exclaiming. And really the lovely sight was hard to believe, for Americans who knew albatross only through legend and poetry.

Finally the larger and wilder one that had choked over his fish evidently got it down or up and came swooping down on the others. Then they engaged in a fight for the pieces our boatman threw them. They ate a whole bucketful of cut bonito before they had their fill, and one of them was so gorged that he could not rise from the surface. He drifted away, preening himself, while the others spread wide wings and flew out to sea.

Four o'clock found us still waiting for a bite. Emil had given up; Peter averred there were no sharks. Love kept making excuses for the day, and like a true fisherman kept saying, "We'll get one tomorrow." But I was not in a hurry. The afternoon was too wonderful to give up. A westering sun shone gold amid dark clouds over the Heads. The shipping had increased, if anything, and all that had been intriguing to me seemed magnified. Bowen, trolling in Bullen's boat, hove in sight out on the horizon.

My companions obviously gave up for that day. They were tired of the long wait. It amused me. I remarked to Peter: "Well, old top, do you remember the eighty-three days we fished without getting a bite? And on the eighty-fourth day I caught my giant Tahitian striped marlin?"

"Right, sir," admitted Peter.

Love appeared impressed by the fact, or else what he thought was fiction, but he said, nevertheless: "Nothing doing today. We might as well go in."

"Ump-umm," I replied, in cowboy parlance. "We'll hang a while longer."

I did not mention that I had one of my rare and singular feelings of something about to happen. My companions settled down resignedly to what seemed futile carrying-on.

Fifteen minutes later something took hold of my line with a slow irresistible pull. My heart leaped. I could not accept what my eyes beheld. My line slowly payed off the reel. I put my gloved hand over the moving spool in the old habit of being ready to prevent an overrun. Still I did not believe it. But there—the line slipped off slowly, steadily, potently. Strike! There was no doubt of that. And I, who had experienced ten thousand strikes, shook all over with the possibilities of this one. Suddenly, sensing the actuality, I called, "There he goes!"

Peter dubiously looked at my reel—saw the line gliding off.

"Right-o, sir."

Love's tanned image became radiant. Emil woke up and began to stutter.

"It's a fine strike," yelled Love, leaping up. "Starts like a tiger!"

He ran forward to heave up the anchor. Peter directed Emil to follow and help him. Then I heard the crack of the electric starter and the sound of the engine.

"Let him have it!" advised Peter, hopefully. "It was a long wait, sir . . . maybe . . ."

"Swell strike, Peter," I replied. "Never had one just like it. He has taken two hundred yards already. It feels under my fingers just as if you had your hand on my coat sleeve and were drawing me slowly toward you."

"Take care. He may put it in high. And that anchor line is long."

When Love and Emil shouted from forward, and then came running aft, the fish, whatever it was, had out between four and five hundred yards of line. I shoved forward the drag on the big Kovalovsky reel and struck with all my might. Then I reeled in swift and hard. Not until the fifth repetition of this violent action did I come up on the weight of that fish. So sudden and tremendous was the response that I was lifted clear out of my chair. Emil, hands at my belt, dragged me back.

"He's hooked. Some fish! Get my harness," I rang out.

In another moment, with my shoulders sharing that pull on me, I felt exultant, deeply thrilled, and as strong as Samson. I quite forgot to look at my watch, which seemed an indication of my feelings. My quarry kept on taking line even before I released the drag.

"Run up on him, Peter. Let's get close to him; I don't like being near these anchored boats."

There were two fishing boats around, the nearer a little too close for comfort. Peter hooked up the engine and I bent to the task of recovering four hundred yards of line. I found the big Kovalovsky perfect for this necessary job. I was hot and sweating, however, when again I came up hard on the heavy weight, now less than several hundred feet away and rather close to the surface.

I watched the bend of my rod tip.

"What kind of fish?" I asked.

"It's sure no black marlin," answered Peter, reluctantly.

"I couldn't tell from the rod," added Love. "But it's a heavy fish. I hope a tiger."

Emil sang out something hopeful. I said: "Well, boys, it's a shark of some kind," and went to work. With a medium drag I fought that shark for a while, watching the tip, and feeling the line, to get what we call "a line" on him. But it was true that I had never felt a fish just like this one. One instant he seemed as heavy as a rock, and the next, light, moving, different. Again I lost the feel of him entirely, and knowing the habit of sharks to slip up on the line to bite it, I reeled like mad. So presently I was divided between the sense that he was little, after all, and the sense that he was huge. Naturally I gravitated to the conviction that I had hooked a new species of fish to me, and a tremendously heavy one. My plan of battle therefore was quickly decided by that. I shoved up the drag on the great Kovalovsky reel to five pounds, six, seven pounds. This much had heretofore been a drag I had never used. But this fish pulled each out just as easily as if there had been none. I could not hold him or get in any line without following him. So cautiously I pushed up the drag to nine pounds, an unprecedented power for me to use. It made no difference at all to the fish, wherefore I went back to five pounds. For a while I ran after him, wound in the line, then had the boat stopped and let him pull out the line again.

"I forgot to take the time. Did any of you?"

"About half an hour," replied Emil.

"Just forty minutes," said Peter, consulting his clock in the cabin. "And you're working too fast—too hard. Ease up."

I echoed that forty minutes and could hardly believe it. But the time flies in the early stages of a fight with a big fish. I took Peter's advice and reduced my action. And at this stage of the game I reverted to the conduct and talk of my companions, and to the thrilling facts of the setting. Peter held the wheel and watched my line, grim and concerned. Love bounced around my chair, eager, talkative, excited. Emil sang songs and quoted poetry while he waited with his camera. Occasionally he snapped a picture of me.

The sea was aflame with sunset gold. A grand golden flare flooded through the gate between the Heads. Black against this wonderful sky the Sydney Bridge curved aloft over the city, majestic, marvelous in its beauty. To its left the sinking sun blazed upon the sky-scraper building. The black cliffs, gold rimmed, stood up boldly far above me. But more marvelous than any of these, in fact exceedingly rare and lovely to me, were the ships putting to sea out of that illuminated gateway. There were six of these in plain sight.

"Getting out before Good Friday," said Peter. "That one on the right is the *Monowai,* and the other on the left is the *Maunganui.* They're going to come to either side of us, and pretty close."

"Well!" I exclaimed. "What do you think of that? I've been on the *Monowai* and have had half a dozen trips in the *Maunganui.*"

These ships bore down on us, getting up speed. The officers on the bridge of the *Maunganui* watched us through their glasses, and both waved their caps. They must have recognized the *Avalon,* and therefore knew it was I who was fast to a great fish right outside the entrance of Sydney Harbor. The deck appeared crowded with curious passengers, who waved and cheered. That ship steamed hissing and roaring by us, not a hundred yards away, and certainly closer to my fish than we were. The *Monowai* passed on the other side, almost even with her sister ship. Naturally, being human, I put on a show for these ships, by working hard and spectacularly on my fish.

Close behind these loomed a ship twice as large. She appeared huge in comparison. From her black bulk gleamed myriads of lights, and vast clouds of smoke belched from her stack. Peter named her the *Rangitati,* or some name like that, and said she was bound for England via the Panama Canal. Then the other ships came on and passed us, and soon were silhouetted dark against the purple sky.

All this while, which seemed very short and was

FROM *AN AMERICAN ANGLER IN AUSTRALIA*   285

perhaps half an hour, I worked on my fish, and I was assured that he knew it. Time had passed, for the light-house on the cliff suddenly sent out its revolving pierc-ing rays. Night was not far away, yet I seemed to see everything almost as clearly as by day.

For quite a space I had been able to get the double line over the reel, but I could not hold it. However, I always tried to. I had two pairs of gloves and thumb stalls on each hand; and with these I could safely put a tremendous strain on the line without undue risk, which would have been the case had I trusted the rod.

By now the sport and thrill had been superseded by pangs of toil and a grim reality of battle. It had long ceased to be fun. I was getting whipped and I knew it. I had worked too swiftly. The fish was slowing and it was a question of who would give up first. Finally, without increasing the strain, I found I could stop and hold my fish on the double line. This was occasion for renewed zest. When I told my crew they yelled wildly. Peter had long since got out the big detachable gaff, with its long rope.

I held on to that double line with burning, painful hands, and I pulled it in foot by foot, letting go to wind in the slack.

"The leader—I see it!" whispered Love.

"Whoopee!" yelled Emil.

"A little more, sir," added Peter, tensely, leaning over the gunwale, his gloved hands outstretched.

In another moment I had the big swivel of the leader in reach.

"Hang on—Peter!" I panted, as I stood up to release the drag and unhook my harness. "Drop the leader—overboard . . . Emil, stand by . . . Love, gaff this fish when I tell you!"

"He's coming, sir," rasped out Peter, hauling in, his body taut. "There! . . . my Gawd!"

Emil screeched at the top of his lungs. The water opened to show the back of an enormous shark. Pearl gray in color, with dark tiger stripes, a huge rounded head and wide flat back, this fish looked incredibly beautiful. I had expected a hideous beast.

"Now!" I yelled.

Love lunged with the gaff. I stepped back, suddenly deluged with flying water and blindly aware of a roar and a banging on the boat. I could not see anything for moments. The men were shouting hoarsely in unison. I distinguished Peter's voice. "Rope—tail!"

"Let him run!" I shouted.

Between the up-splashing sheets of water I saw the three men holding that shark. It was a spectacle. Peter stood up, but bent, with his brawny shoulders sagging. Love and Emil were trying to rope that flying tail. For I had no idea how long, but probably a brief time, this strenuous action prevailed before my eyes. It beat any battle I recalled with a fish at the gaff. The huge tiger rolled over, all white underneath, and he opened a mouth that would have taken a barrel. I saw the rows of white fangs and heard such a snap of jaws that had never before struck my ear. I shuddered at their significance. No wonder men shot and harpooned such vicious brutes!

"It's over his tail," cried Love, hoarsely, and straightened up with the rope. Emil lent a hand. And then the three men held the ferocious tiger shark until he ceased his struggles. They put another rope over his tail and made fast to the ringbolt.

When Peter turned to me his broad breast heaved —his breath whistled—the corded muscles stood out on his arms—he could not speak.

"Pete!—good work. I guess that's about the hardest tussle we've ever had at the gaff."

We towed our prize into the harbor and around to the dock at Watson's Bay, where a large crowd awaited us. They cheered us lustily. They dragged the vast bulk of my shark up on the sand. It required twenty-odd men to move him. He looked marble color in the twilight. But the tiger stripes showed up distinctly. He knocked men right and left with his lashing tail, and he snapped with those terrible jaws. The crowd, however, gave that business end of his a wide berth. I had one good long look at this tiger shark while the men were erecting the tripod; and I accorded him more appalling beauty and horrible significance than all the great fish I had ever caught.

"Well, Mr. Man-eater, you will never kill any boy or girl!" I flung at him.

That was the deep and powerful emotion I felt— the justification of my act—the worthiness of it, and the pride in what it took. There, I am sure, will be the explanation of my passion and primal exultance. Dr. Stead, scientist and official of the Sydney Museum, and Mr. Bullen of the Rod Fisher's Society, weighed and measured my record tiger shark. Length, thirteen feet ten inches. Weight, one thousand and thirty-six pounds!

IX

SHARKS
THAT ATTACK

●

One thing that all authors of shark attack stories have in common is that they have to rely on second- or thirdhand accounts as to what actually took place.

People's memories do differ: What one witness believes he saw can often be different from what other claims to have seen. It is to the credit of the experts who assess this information that when the final picture emerges, while not exactly correct in every detail, it certainly must be close to the truth.

Often, when I read the details surrounding an attack, particularly if by a shark whose habits are familiar to me, the possible motivation causing the incident is recognized. The reason for attacks on divers spearing fish are fairly apparent to most people. It is the smell of blood coupled with the vibrations of the wounded dying fish that attract the marauder who, by the time he reaches his quarry, has already begun to fall into a feeding pattern.

It is interesting that, while most spear fishermen I know have had speared fish torn from their floats, relatively few have been attacked themselves. This proves that the shark is not attracted to the human but rather to the fish which would be his natural prey. However, mistakes do occur and then we have a shark attack. The shark that bit Rodney Fox let him go and took the fish on his float line. It did not continue to attack.

In most cases, something must attract the shark to the potential victim. Sharks, not even the great white, don't swim around thinking that a human would be a nice animal to eat. If sharks really considered us to be good eating, in Australia at least, anyone entering the ocean would do so only at great risk. Surfboard riders often have their boards damaged by sharks, yet they themselves for the most part survive unmarked. I believe that sharks are curious about the large dead-looking objects floating on the surface and could go to investigate. Generally, they decide it's not what they want and swim away. Swimmers often fight off sharks. This would be impossible if the shark really meant business. With the majority of individual attacks recorded, it would seem that the attacker was merely investigating a strange object.

However, there are a number of cases where the shark attacked with a most positive attitude, tearing its victim to pieces, even when resistance had been strong. I feel the shark who attacks in this way is a very hungry shark whose desire to eat overrides all other instincts.

When a shark attacks a human, whatever the motivation is behind the attack, it is a terrible experience. The victim is hardly likely to care whether he was attacked by a hungry shark, a curious shark, or one who simply made a mistake. The horror and terror surrounding the act is always the same.

31

From *Sharks and Shipwrecks*

HUGH EDWARDS

Hugh Edwards has published many books about the sea. A journalist by profession, he is a diver by choice.

Sharks and Shipwrecks is a collection of true adventure stories involving the ocean. Hugh said that the idea came to him one day when he was thinking about different friends and the exciting lives they led. His thought was that they all had a story to tell, so he set off around Australia visiting all the people he had chosen for his book, writing down their tales. It is an interesting book, each story a personal account of adventure and experience.

"The Great Shark of Jurien Bay" is the story of Bob Bartle's fatal encounter with a great white. Every story of shark attack has its horror and heroism. Bob's is no different.

He was a friend of ours, and, as an Australian would say, "a real good bloke." In those days all the active divers knew one another, so Bob's death was a terrible shock to us all.

Other friends have been attacked while spearfishing, but most have fought off the shark and survived. Bob never had that chance; he didn't see the shark before it attacked.

There are other stories in the book, including Ron's and mine. Ron talks of filming the great white and I, to be different, of my pet moray eels.

Sharks and Shipwrecks has been successful—it went
on sale in the United States and Australia in 1975
and has just been reprinted. It is a good true adventure
book.

●

The Great Shark of Jurien Bay

A team of two, and a good team, they were the
Western Australian State pairs spearfishing champions
in 1967.

Bob was twenty-four, short but strongly built and
with a pleasant manner which won friends easily. He
was dedicated to diving and was the secretary of the
Western Australian Council of Underwater Activities
and an organizer to the Australian Spearfishing Championships held at Busselton, Western Australia, in December, 1967.

Lee was twenty-six. An ex-schoolteacher who made
a living from diving for crayfish and from spearing fish.
He had a tremendously powerful physique, very blue
eyes, and a black bushy beard. He was the more bril-
liant diver of the two, but Bob had the best endurance
and concentration. As a combination of strengths they
were highly effective at their sport.

In August 1967, Bob Bartle and his bearded diving
partner Lee Warner traveled the red dusty road to
Jurien Bay 240 kilometers north of Perth in a Volkswagen with their spear guns.

They were going to compete in a spearfishing meeting. As competitions went, it was a minor one. But
they regarded it as important. It was practice for them
for the Australian Spearfishing Championships in four
months' time.

In 1967, having learned hard lessons in gear and
techniques in previous championships, Warner and Bartle had the national pairs title as their goal. On their
home territory they knew they had a good chance of
winning against divers from the Eastern States—provided they had a solid grounding of months of hard

diving practice to build stamina and sharpen techniques.

So—though the cold and sullen winter waters of Jurien Bay were hardly inviting—they were looking forward to the meeting as a test of the progress they were making. Saturday, August 19, was listed as a practice day—a chance for visiting divers to look over the ground and adapt their gear to local conditions. The actual competition, the fish spearing, would be held the next day, on Sunday the twentieth.

On the practice day Bob swung his Volkswagen off the track and braked to a halt on the high grey bluff of North Head at Jurien Bay, overlooking the area where the competition would be held.

He and Warner looked out over the reefs and breaking bomboras [submerged reefs] of the bay with practiced eyes. The best ground looked to be a reef a mile or so offshore, and, with a few wry jokes about the weather, they got their gear out and began shrugging into their rubber wetsuits. Other divers from other cars were similarly getting into their gear, and they dressed quickly from long familiarity with their suits and equipment.

Lee had on a full-length black neoprene rubber wetsuit to his ankles, while Bob's short suit went only to his knees. Both men wore close-fitting helmet hoods, and they carried the standard floats with diver's flags (red, with a white diagonal stripe) which they tow for identification and from which they would hang their speared fish from a wire toggle.

They walked down the bluff's steep slope to the water's edge, carrying their masks, flippers, lead belts, and big single-rubber spear guns, and after a quick look around, walked into the water, rinsed their masks and—with a grimace at the weather—began swimming.

They swam out from the grey limestone headland, heading for the deeper water about a mile offshore, looking for big fish like kingfish, groper, jewfish, as well as the smaller fish which counted for points in competition. They swam with the hard-kicking style of professionals, working hard to get warm and cover ground.

They had no thought of sharks, though both had seen plenty on the offshore reefs. Warner had kept himself in pocket money as a youth by shooting gray nurse and whalers for fish shops, and had had a brush or two with bigger sharks.

Bob had also been involved in shark incidents, like most of the deep reef spearfishermen, and had fought off a bronze whaler at Dunsborough in the south, jabbing it away with his loaded gun as it charged repeatedly.

After Dunsborough he had claimed, "If anyone asks me if I'm scared of sharks I won't shrug my shoulders."

Most sharks were regarded as summer fish, active when the seawater was warm. At Jurien that August, as they swam for the far-out reefs, they thought it would be too cold, much too cold, for sharks.

The bottom was weedy and featureless, until about 700 meters off the headland they came across a hole or depression in eight meters of water. It was about twelve meters across with overhanging ledges—the sort of place for jewfish.

"Might as well have a look," Bob said.

Lee Warner nodded agreement. "Right-o," and Bob went down in a shallow glide, spear gun in front of him and dropping the lead sinker of his float line so it would not tangle as he swam through the caves under the ledges.

There were no jewfish. They prepared to move on, and Bob dived again for his float lead. He reached the bottom, picked it up, and as he was beginning to rise, Warner turned and began to swim on.

Suddenly an enormous black shape hurtled below Warner's flippers. It was a shark so big and moving so quickly that Warner—who had seen many sharks but nothing like this—gasped involuntarily.

Without slackening speed the shark hit Bartle, seizing him between shoulder and thigh, and striking with an impact which knocked his mask off. It began to shake him violently from side to side.

For an instant Warner remained frozen by the swiftness and unexpectedness of the attack. Instinct was to flee, but Lee was not lacking in courage.

He had killed sharks before, though nothing of this size. But he knew that a spear in the tiny brain could immobilize even a giant.

Warner dived down toward the struggling shapes on the bottom, aiming his spear gun as he dived.

"I went straight down and put a spear in the top of the shark's head right where I figured the brain should be. It hit with a solid clunk. But it didn't seem to affect it, except that it attracted the brute's attention to me. It sort of shook its head, then bit Bob in half and rose up at me. . . ."

The shark swam upward through a cloud of blood, the lower part of Bob still in its jaws, flippers protruding.

"Christ!" said Warner to himself, eyes bulging in horror behind the mask.

As it came at him he pushed himself away from it with the unloaded gun, jabbing at the great black eye with the butt. The eye rolled white. "I didn't think sharks could do that." His mind was curiously detached for a moment. But he was soon brought back to reality.

"Never in my life have I seen anything so chilling than watching that shark circling around me with the body of Bob still in its huge jaws. From less than one meter I could see the terrible wounds inflicted. I was helpless. I could see Bob was dead. That was only too obvious. I thought I was soon to follow. I simply cannot describe the terror which flowed through me. . . ."

The water was now dark with blood and shapes were distorted and indistinct—grotesque in the twilight of darkened water. The enormous shadow moved through it all.

"It kept circling about eight feet from me. Its body looked about five feet thick from top to bottom. I didn't really get a good idea of its length—I couldn't see the extremities and don't remember seeing the tail. All I could see was the eye and what it had in its mouth."

He had a moment of mesmerized indecision.

"Then out of the corner of my eye I saw Bob's gun which was still loaded and floating just below the surface. I grabbed it gratefully, and swinging it around tried to belt the spear into the shark's eye. But the eye was set close to the top of its head and somehow the spear just whistled harmlessly over the top of its head. It was the worst shot of my life. I don't know how I could have missed, and I've cursed myself for it a thousand times since.

"That was my last real chance to get back at the shark.

"It kept swimming round and round and started getting caught and tangled up in all the lines. It was tied to my gun by the line from the first spear and my gun picked up the float lines. There was just one big tangled mess. I was scared of getting caught up in the lines myself.

"The shark was black on top and white on its guts. A sort of mottled pattern. It looked weird in the bad winter light and the blood-reddened water. I could see its jaw was much wider than the body—the jaw must have been a meter wide at least. Maybe more.

"I knew Bob was dead. And there was the thought of other sharks.

"A little bronze whaler came and began darting around in the blood. Were there any more big ones? I swam backward, fast. From 100 yards away I looked back and saw the shark still moving around tangled in the lines and floats on the same spot.

"I felt pretty bloody helpless, I can tell you. But once I lost sight of it I began free-styling for shore. It wasn't too far but it seemed miles. Now and again I looked back to convince myself the shark was still back there. I was still frightened.

"I swam away from a friend and diving companion of seven years, and that's something I'll never forget. Not as long as I live."

Warner reached the shallows and ran from the water stumbling. When he looked back he could see one or two flags and floats of other divers far out at sea, unaware of the tragedy that had taken place so close to them. It all seemed unreal—in fact the sense of nightmarish unreality never left him.

He searched for the keys to Bob's Volkswagen, parked up on top of the bluff at North Head, and couldn't find them. But he found a key to one of the other cars and drove, skidding around the corners, ten kilometers along the dirt track to Sandy Cape, a crayfishing settlement, to gasp out his story and ask for a boat to get the other divers out of the water.

The season was over, but one or two boats still swung on the moorings with silent engines. Harry Holmes's *Gar Fan* was one, a thirteen-and-a-half-meter steel boat. Harry agreed at once to go to North Head and in a short time they were off the grey headland, with the cray boat rolling in the winter swell.

They could see the two divers' floats and the tangle of lines, and something dark below them. The shark was still there.

There was something else floating too. A human torso cut through across the breastbone by the teeth of the giant shark.

Bob still had air in his lungs. Death must have been very quick, for he had not even cried out. It may be that he was never aware of what had happened, and his diving friends have always hoped so.

When they took hold of the tangled lines in the hope they might catch the beast, the shark—that vast, indistinct shape on the bottom—began to swim slowly away. It was incredibly strong. The cords snapped one by one. The metal fittings on the spears, straightened out. Then it was gone.

The divers went back to Jurien Bay and held a wake that night. Next day they held their spearfishing competition as it had been planned. It wasn't bravado, and it was something other than plain courage.

"Bob would have wanted it that way," they said.

A massive hunt was launched for the shark and rewards were offered for its capture. But it was never seen again.

No one was quite sure even what kind of shark it was. It is a measure of the horror of that day that Warner—normally a meticulous observer of marine life—was unable to remember clearly anything about it except the great dark eye and what it had in its mouth.

The argument has never been resolved about whether it was a huge tiger, black-backed with age, or that known killer and maimer of divers, the great white shark.

The presence of breeding seals on nearby islands might explain the attack. The shark—like the one which attacked Henri Bource in Victoria three years earlier—may have mistaken Bob Bartle for a seal. But why did it pass under Lee Warner's flippers to attack the man on the seabed? That is a question which still occasionally faces Warner in his nightmares.

At Jurien Bay today there stands a simple memorial to Bob Bartle.

32

From *Shark Attack*

H. DAVID BALDRIDGE

H. David Baldridge's book *Shark Attack* is the most up-to-date, comprehensive collection of shark attack accounts available to the general public that I know of.

The case histories cited in this book have been collected from all over the world, and the information studied with the aid of a computer.

Baldridge was director of the United States Navy International Shark Attack File. This file was compiled with the aid of the marine division of the Smithsonian Institution.

They studied 1,652 cases which contained sufficient information to be of use to the computer study. Of these, Baldridge chose about two hundred for the book.

Shark Attack also contains a good deal of other interesting scientific information about sharks of all species. A few lines that appear in the middle of page 223 (not from this selection) are so true, yet the opposite to common belief, that I must repeat them here.

Baldridge writes: "Only about one-fourth of all attack victims received wounds of a nature and number to suggest that hunger might have provoked the attack. Sharks repeatedly strike their victims in a wild, frenzied fashion only about 4% of the time."

All our experience with sharks has shown that they are not man-eaters in the true sense of the word,

and it is gratifying to find an expert of the caliber of
Baldridge agreeing with our observations.

Shark Attack, although a collection of facts about
a serious scientific study, has been written in a simple
easy style that makes enjoyable reading. It is having
a success with the public not usually associated with a
scientific publication.

The following excerpt is typical of the honest and
to-the-point manner in which Baldridge has presented
the information he compiled.

•

Approximately two-thirds of all documented shark
attacks have occurred since 1940. The average of
about 28 cases per year is far below the estimate of
100 often stated in scientific and popular literature as
the worldwide yearly incidence of shark attack. Keep
in mind that the likelihood of an attack being reported
would surely depend upon the degree of injury received
by the victim. Fatalities are usually given widespread
publicity, and, except for some wartime cases and those
happening in the most remote regions of the world,
accounts of attacks in recent years resulting in death to
the victims would very likely be on file.

The peak year for attacks in modern times was
reached with 56 cases reported in 1959. It is probably
more than a coincidence that the Shark Research Panel
was established in 1958 and that a great amount of effort was devoted shortly thereafter to building up the
SAF (Shark Attack File). It seems reasonable that
the attendant publicity would have produced a sharp
increase in efficiency of reporting attacks. On the other
hand, there is also the possibility that we actually have
been enjoying since 1959 a period of decreasing incidence of shark attack for which there is no ready explanation. During the period 1941–1958, reported attacks increased at an average rate of about 1.2 cases
per year. But since the peak year of 1959, known attacks have fallen off at the approximate rate of 2.0
cases per year, with only about 23 expected for 1973.

Mortality rates have generally decreased (dropping an average of about 1 percent per year) from 46 percent in 1940 to an estimated 16 percent for 1973, with an overall mortality rate of 35 percent for the SAF as a whole. The general decline in death rates could be due to a number of factors, the most obvious of which would be a steady rise in the availability to attack victims of early, more advanced medical attention. Another important factor could be that continuing improvements in world-wide communications have led to the reporting of ever-increasing percentages of attacks involving nonfatal injuries.

There is no evidence at all to link incidence of shark attack with gross variations in shark populations or general turns by sharks toward more or less aggressive behavior. Instead, attack rates are more likely related to the ballooning human population and the extent to which people make themselves available for attack by their use of the sea for recreational purposes.

Now, if the incidence of shark attack is truly strongly dependent upon the number of people exposed to attack at any particular time, then it would be expected that attacks would happen more often at those times when people are more likely to frequent beaches in large numbers. It took my son, David, to point out to me that weekends should provide the greater opportunity for encounters between bathers and sharks. Of those cases which have occurred since 1900, 729 could be identified as to day of the week. We found on the average that about 65 percent more attacks occurred on days of the weekend than on weekdays, strongly supporting the contention that shark attack was, and presumably still is, more likely to occur at those times when the greater numbers of people are in the water.

As I will do from time to time, let me add a word of caution in regard to interpretation of these data. Because of the total lack of consideration of control information, the above observation does not in any way point to Saturday and Sunday as being the most dangerous days to plan a beach outing. Nor is it necessarily implied that the danger is greater to any particular

individual when many people are in the water. To
evaluate the relative hazard potential as it would affect
individuals would require detailed knowledge of beach
populations (people actually in the water) both on
uneventful days and those associated directly with attacks. This sort of information simply is not available.

Now, how about the time of day as related to total
numbers of attacks? There is a steady rise in attack
rate beginning in early morning to peak around 11:00
A.M., falling off markedly around noon, followed by a
rise to a larger peak at midafternoon, and finally falling again to very low numbers at about nightfall. Our
own experiences tell us that this pattern of activity is
consistent with the way in which people in general
make use of the waters at beaches. The population
builds up during the morning hours followed by at
least a partial withdrawal from the water about lunchtime. The afternoon brings with it more people and
sends some of the noon picnickers back into the water.
As dusk approaches, the peak afternoon crowd heads
for home. Direct confirmation of this impression of
human habit patterns was provided by my colleague,
Edward Broedel, who actually counted people (a total
of 1,018) in the water, hour by hour, on a day of
heavy attendance at Myrtle Beach, South Carolina.

Here again, taken out of context and without consideration of control data, the high incidence of shark
attack during the afternoon hours could lead one to
conclude that for an individual swimming at a beach,
the greatest chance of encountering an aggressive shark
would be during the midafternoon. The data in no way
support this, for to evaluate the relative danger facing
any particular individual as a function of time of day
would require knowledge of numbers of people exposed
but not attacked, hour by hour, and on a worldwide
basis, information that would be essentially impossible
to obtain. Yet, the hourly pattern of attack does point
to a very important fact, especially when considered
along with the finding of higher incidence of shark
attack on weekends. Both observations indicate that the

rate of attack is strongly associated with the numbers of people in the water.

With these findings in mind, it seems reasonable to assume that shark attack can occur at any time in waters where populations of sharks (including a population of one) can come into contact with man. On a longtime basis, the incidence of attacks would be strongly related to those periods of time when potential victims are more abundant. Even though lack of control data prevents any inference concerning danger to a particular individual swimmer, the chance of at least some unspecified person being attacked at any particular beach would be expected to increase as the concentration of people in the water increases. The time periods for such correlations are long, and the above considerations do not in any way deny the possibility of short-term rashes of attacks at times of low beach population. Neither do they mitigate against periods of calm even though the beaches are flooded with people. Such is the way it is with statistics.

All but four reported attacks have occurred between latitudes of 47 degrees South and 46 degrees North. The exceptions all involved injuries inflicted upon fishermen by captured sharks and were thus considered to have been provoked. The most northerly was probably that on Hans Schapper (Case 770) who, in June 1960, was bitten on the right arm by a small shark that had been inadvertently brought aboard a trawler in a fishladen net. Although the victim was treated at Wick, Scotland, the exact geographical location of the accident was not reported. Another northerly provoked attack happened on 4 August 1960 off the South Devon coast in the English Channel not far from Dartmouth, England, when William Chapel (Case 786) had his arm sliced open from elbow to wrist as he was pulling on board an 80-pound shark that had been hooked by an angler.

The most northerly unprovoked attacks occurred not in oceanic waters, but in upper reaches of the Adriatic Sea near the Istria peninsula of Yugoslavia. Unfortunately, information about them is very skimpy. On 4 September 1934, eighteen-year-old Agnes Novak was fatally injured near Susak (Case 370). The London *Times* reported in July 1954 that a Hungarian refugee and a companion set out to swim from Pola (Pula) toward Fiume (Rijeka), and only one reached safety, the other being taken by a shark (Case 309). Seven years later, in September 1961, Sabit Plana, a nineteen-year-old student, was swimming about 75 yards from shore with seven other students near the Adriatic Sea resort of Opatija. A large shark surfaced, bit off his left hand and injured his legs. The boy died before a boat from shore could reach him (Case 946).

From those Adriatic waters also came the strange tale of Zorca Prince (Case 974). On 30 August 1934, the New York *Evening Sun* carried a story datelined Fiume, Yugoslavia. It told of a young girl who paid with her life because she did not believe in dreams. Her mother had pleaded with her in a letter not to swim far from shore, for she had had a dream that Zorca would fall victim to a shark. Exclaiming to her friends, "I don't believe in dreams," the young student, a strong swimmer, made for a fishing boat far out in the sea off Reotore. The fishermen heard a shriek and went to help the girl only to find nothing but bloodstained water. They reported that a shark had been seen earlier swimming around the edge of their nets. But for a followup article in another newspaper a few days later, the case would have gone on record as a bonafide fatal shark attack. With a dateline of Belgrade, 1 September, the second article read, "It is reported from Kraljevica in the Alvala District that the news published by certain foreign papers according to which a young Yugoslavian girl, Miss Prinz, was attacked and eaten by a shark off the Italian coast, is without foundation. Miss Prinz is actually at her parents' home in Ljubljana and intends to spend the coming month taking examinations for admission to the university of this town." So, fortunately for Zorca Prince, we have replaced the red fatality tag on our File 974 with a green one indicating serious doubt that anything at all happened. It remains, however, one of numerous examples of how quickly and with essentially no actual evidence people are willing to accept a tale of shark attack.

The most southerly shark attacks have occurred off South Island, New Zealand, almost directly opposite the Adriatic Sea on the surface of the earth. Only one attack has been reported from below the 46th Parallel, and this one was relatively minor. Norman McEwan, on 27 January 1962, received small but deep gashes on his wrist when he was seized by a 5-foot shark while swimming in waist-deep water off Oreti Beach at the southern end of South Island (Case 1088). Several very appalling attacks have occurred below the 45th Parallel in the waters off South Island. In the early years of this century, a Mr. Grant was floating on his back in the open sea near Oamaru when a shark grabbed him by the arm (Case 924) injuring it severely enough to cause later loss by amputation. At about the same period of time near Moeraki, a Dunedin businessman, W. M. Hutchinson, was standing in water up to his waist, while his son was playing by diving off his shoulders. The boy had dived twice and was getting ready for a third dive, when a shark suddenly bit right through the man's leg, mortally wounding him (Case 925). Three more fatal attacks have occurred off South Island in more recent years.

At approximately 7:00 A.M. on the morning of 5 February 1964, Leslie Jordan was enjoying his usual morning swim in the chilly (58° F) surf at St. Clair Beach, Dunedin (Case 1266). After swimming some 250 yards into the sea, he suddenly began to wave his arms wildly and cry for help. A man on a paddleboard about 50 yards away went to his assistance, thinking that Jordan had suffered a cramp. As the paddler pulled alongside, the swimmer said he had been attacked by a shark and raised a leg to show massive wounds that were by now deeply staining the water. Jordan half crawled and was half pulled across the paddleboard, with his legs still in the water from mid-thigh downward. The rescuer gave the raised-arm signal for assistance. Shortly before a second paddler arrived, the shark was seen at the surface near the board, its dorsal fin and tail out of the water, a foot or two longer than the 10-foot paddleboard. The victim was unconscious by the time the second board came alongside and was then pulled completely from the water across both boards. As they neared the shore, a breaking wave tossed them all into the surf. The two men carried Jordan to the beach and immediately commenced resuscitation. It was only then that they realized the extent of his wounds. The right leg had been amputated through the knee joint. Behind the leg just above the knee joint there was a gaping wound, the edge of which showed four teeth marks. There was also a grazing mark six inches long and three inches wide on the inner side of the left leg made possibly by the shark's fins. The inside calf of the left leg was deeply lacerated with what appeared to be tooth marks above and below the wound. There were also other small lacerations on the thigh of the left leg from the knee to the buttock. All efforts failed to elicit any sign of life, and the victim never regained consciousness. Later postmortem findings indicated that he had become unconscious from loss of blood and shock while being brought in, and in that state had inhaled a quantity of water leading to death by drowning. The first rescuer testified that the victim's right leg had been intact, with the exception of a piece missing from the thigh, when he first approached Jordan. He concluded that the shark must have made a second attack, taking the lower right leg, as they awaited arrival of the second paddler. All evidence indicated the attacker to have been a great white shark, 10 to 12 feet in length.

As it has happened in other places, the respite from shark attack that South Island had enjoyed for so many years prior to the attack on Jordan was again broken a few years later when William Black was taken by a shark at St. Kilda Beach, Dunedin, on 9 March 1967 (Case 1449). The water was murky and cold (55–57° F). A light rain was falling. The time was 7:15

P.M., a few minutes after sunset. Black was taking part in a belt race with a fellow life-saving club member and was leading his opponent by about 20 yards. Suddenly, a large shark appeared and the water around Black quickly turned dark with blood. Those on shore also saw the shark's fin and commenced to pull in the lines attached to belts worn by the swimmers. Black's line suddenly went slack and was reeled in quickly. The line was found to be severed, with the belt and Black missing. A surf canoe was launched, but the search was fruitless and had to be abandoned as darkness fell. Subsequent intensive searches failed to uncover any trace of the missing swimmer.

The line separating tragedy from good fortune is sometimes very thin indeed. And so it was for seventeen-year-old Gary Barton (Case 1583) on Christmas Day in 1968 at St. Clair Beach, Dunedin. It was at this beach that Leslie Jordan lost his life to a shark almost four years earlier. Barton was riding a surfboard in 58-degree water about 50 yards from the beach when he saw something of "whitey browny color with a black nose" in the water beneath him. Suddenly he was knocked from the board and left hanging on to it by his arms. He quickly drew himself back aboard and lay flat on his stomach. But then the shark rose from the water, hitting Barton in the face with its snout, knocking him back into the water. As chance would have it, the shark did not press its advantage, and Barton was able to climb back onto his surfboard and paddle safely to shore. The fiberglass board didn't fare so well, for it bore on each of its sides a set of tooth marks up to one-inch deep along with a deep gash some 5 inches long.

The chain of attacks off South Island was to continue, for on 15 September 1968, in 55-degree waters only about 30 yards off the entrance to Otago Harbor, a 14-foot great white shark fatally mauled a twenty-four-year-old spearfisherman, Graham Hitt (Case 1550). One of a group of five skin divers, Hitt, clad in a full black wetsuit, had been spearing fish some 100 yards from the seaward end of a jetty in relatively clear water which dropped off rapidly to a depth of about 50 feet. One of the divers was startled by a very large shark with an eye "as large as a baseball" as it suddenly swam past him at a range of about 8 feet. The shark left his field of view but quickly returned, appearing to be moving in an agitated manner, balancing and pivoting on the tips of its pectoral fins which were about 6 to 8 feet apart. Just as the shark seemed to the diver to be positioning itself for a strike, it heeled over and made directly for Hitt, who was then swimming at the surface in a horizontal position and not facing the shark as it attacked. In a tremendous flurry of foaming water, the shark grabbed Hitt, shook him, just as suddenly let him go, and, after making one more circuit, turned and swam away. His companions courageously responded to Hitt's cries for help, moving quickly to his side and bringing him into shore. But death had been quick; there being no sign of life by the time they reached safety. In apparently a single bite, the shark had cut through the left leg to the bone, severing the femoral and other adjacent arteries. There were also a few tooth marks on the right leg. Pathologists later removed several tooth fragments from grooves in the left femur, the largest of which was 28.7 millimeters long and clearly identified the attacker as a great white shark. It is interesting to note that the shark showed no apparent interest in floats, only 10 to 15 yards away, which held several previously speared fish. One official advanced the theory that the shark could have mistaken the shiny black suit of the diver for one of the seals which are common in the area.

Even though the above attacks occurred at the most extreme latitudes, both north and south, it should not be taken that they also were necessarily the ones associated with the lowest water temperatures.

The Southern Hemisphere has only a slight edge, 54 percent in the total numbers of reported and coded shark attacks. The distributions within each hemisphere follow the same general patterns, i.e. very few attacks near the equator, rising to a peak at the middle latitudes, and falling off rapidly at higher latitudes.

Although I have no actual data to support it, this pattern of attacks versus latitude generally follows what I would expect in terms of worldwide population distribution. Here again, it appears as if the availability of people rather than sharks may determine the incidence of shark attack, considering the probable omnipresence of sharks in general in waters between latitudes 46° N and 47° S. . . .

The heavy predominance of attacks reported from English-speaking countries is highly suggestive of a language barrier in the procedures for gathering information on such happenings in other localities. There seems to be a particular lack of communication with Latin countries, especially those in Central and South America from which only a total of 25 cases are held in the SAF.

33

"Feeding Habits of Large Sharks"

STEWART SPRINGER

Sharks and Survival, compiled by Dr. Perry Gilbert, (from which this excerpt originates) is an unusual publication. Based on the knowledge of many different shark experts, it gives a very complete view of what was known and believed about shark and shark attacks in the 1960s.

This segment, titled "Feeding Habits of Large Sharks," I found very well presented. The thought of studying the contents of so many sharks' stomachs is to me a most unappealing occupation, but Stewart Springer must have examined hundreds and questioned many shark fishermen before writing the excerpt presented here.

I am often asked what sharks eat and, with the exception of the few species I know well and have personally fed, it is not an easy question to answer. Each species would have to have a different feeding habit or the balance between supply and demand would be destroyed. Port Jackson sharks, for instance, seem to favor shellfish. Offer a Port Jackson an abalone complete with shell and he will snatch it from you very smartly. However, if all sharks ate shellfish as Port Jacksons do, it wouldn't be long before the shellfish population ceased to exist. This doesn't mean that other sharks won't eat shellfish. As Springer points out, tiger sharks often have conch in their stomachs.

310

Also, I am sure that a Port Jackson shark, while quite happy with shellfish, would not hesitate to eat a nice fresh fish if given the opportunity. Nature has given sharks the job of controlling different sections of the marine population and the sharks have evolved in the manner best suited for hunting and eating their different types of prey.

Stewart Springer writes about the bull shark, which is similar to our whaler shark, as being at times very docile. I have never seen whaler sharks as quiet as Springer describes his bull sharks to be. Actually, whalers always seem frisky, but now I am wondering if around Australia there is an area similar to Cat Island in Mississippi Sound where the whalers go to breed and become docile. Sydney Harbor is supposedly a breeding ground for sharks but, judging by the number of attacks on humans in this locality, they are anything but docile.

It seems logical that female sharks would lose their appetites after giving birth to live young; otherwise, the baby sharks would stand a very good chance of being eaten by their mothers. This also leads to another reason for sharks preferring to give birth in estuaries or tidal rivers rather than the open ocean. Many sharks, male and female, find other smaller sharks extremely palatable. While the female is giving birth and not hungry, the male could be devouring her offspring before they were big enough to fend for themselves.

Sharks are credited with eating an incredible variety of food, from a man in full armor to their own young. They are the garbage men of the sea, and, without doubt, do their job well.

●

Shark fishermen had two sources of information on the food preferences of sharks: the examination of shark stomachs and estimates based on comparative success with various baits. Florida shark fishermen, oriented to the capture of sharks of the accessory populations and tiger sharks, found that shark stomachs contained almost everything, and also that sharks would bite on almost any kind of bait—fish, fowl, or mammal—either fresh or partly decomposed. Fishermen oriented to fishing for sharks of principal populations found that sharks ate fresh fish, that fresh fish were successful bait, and that the stomachs of the species of sharks they sought usually contained fish.

Sharks of the accessory populations usually had livers with substantially higher vitamin A potencies than sharks of the principal populations. This encouraged a number of persons to engage in shark fishing after preliminary investigation and sampling of the product's value. The samples usually included only the more easily caught sharks—those of the accessory populations. Assays of liver oil from such samples suggested a higher potency for most species than would be found with production at a high level. In spite of the relatively higher value of their livers, sharks of the accessory populations were not numerous enough to support a continuing fishing operation, even by one vessel.

Giving the evidence from the economic side the greater weight, but also considering evidence from fishing records, the principal fishing company developed some standard operating procedures for fishing and for baiting and setting shark lines. These vary somewhat according to area and kinds of sharks sought. These methods were successful, and consistent deviation from them always resulted in economic failure of the fishing operation. It seems reasonable to assume that the methods had some valid basis from which deductions about feeding habits may be drawn.

The fishing company strongly recommended that all longlines be set in line with the tide or current and not across it, and that all lines contain at least one hundred hooks, each baited with not less than 1 pound nor more than 2 pounds of cut bait. Experience had shown that it was important to develop a concentrated chum streak, or line of diffusing bait juices, that would lead groups of sharks as well as single sharks to the line.

A scarcely less important recommendation was that

hooks be sharpened or brushed bright and smooth every day. The points of the hooks were never hidden, and bait was put on in such a way that the hook was not choked. In areas of good fishing, one out of about twenty sharks caught with bright, sharp hooks was snagged by a hook through a fin or through some part of the body away from the mouth. In addition, it was suspected from the frequency of sharks taken in clusters that the turmoil generated by a fin-hooked shark aroused interest in the area on the part of any other shark in the neighborhood. It was reasoned that big catches were likely when sharks were attracted to the set early and when the line became a center of turmoil.

The largest single longline fishing cost, aside from labor, was the cost of bait. One shark-fishing boat set a minimum of two hundred hooks each night and consequently required an average of 300 pounds of bait daily. Experience proved that the best bait for all sharks was freshly cut fish, and that bait frozen when fresh was next best. Of the species of fish available in southern Florida waters, the little tuna, *Euthynnus alletteratus,* or the Atlantic bonito, *Sarda sarda,* appeared to be the best bait. No doubt, other small tunas would have been equally successful had they been available. Whole fish of any kind seemed to make poor bait, so it was necessary to select fish weighing 2 pounds or more. Except for the small tunas, the only available first-quality fish for bait appeared to be the crevalle jack, *Caranx hippos,* and the great barracuda, *Sphyraena barracuda.* Many species were not tried, of course, because of their small size. Other species such as the dolphin, Spanish mackerel, and amberjack were used occasionally in small quantities by fishermen who caught them while trolling to and from shark longlines. Notably unsuccessful as bait were snappers, groupers, and mullet.

One independent shark-fishing crew operating entirely in the Gulf of Mexico used porpoise meat for bait almost exclusively and with considerable success. The operation specialized, however, in catching tiger sharks and bull sharks. It changed fishing areas frequently, sweeping the coast from Tortugas to mid-Louisiana, and stopped fishing entirely during slack seasons.

Another fishing crew working on the coast of the Guianas was quite successful in catching bull sharks. These were especially desirable from that region, but not from the Gulf of Mexico. This crew used fresh shark bait alternately with bait cut from frozen little tuna. Generally, the bull sharks appeared to be attracted by the tuna but bit on the hooks baited with shark meat. Lines baited exclusively with pieces of shark flesh were unsuccessful.

Too few white sharks, mako sharks, thresher sharks, or whitetips were taken by the Florida shark fishermen to provide much background for estimate of normal diet. By combining information from apparent bait preference, stomach examinations, and observation, estimates of feeding habits of some of the common Florida sharks have been formed and are given here.

Tiger Sharks. The tiger shark is completly omnivorous. It swallows individual large conchs, such as Fulgur or even the giant horse conch, whole, and those of moderate 6- to 8-inch length by the dozen. In some undetermined way the shells are removed in the shark's digestive tract. Perhaps the shells are dissolved by the hydrochloric acid of the shark's stomach. I have seen tiger shark stomachs full of conchs complete with shells and others full of conchs with neither whole calcareous shells nor any remnant of shell, but I have not found partly dissolved conch shells in tiger shark stomachs, possibly because the chemical activity, once started, may temporarily divert the shark from interest in a baited shark hook. Conch opercula are not digested but tend to accumulate in the posterior tip of the tiger shark's stomach past the pylorus. Conch opercula are more commonly present than not in tiger shark stomachs from the Florida Keys area.

I have also found large tiger shark stomachs full of horseshoe crabs, *Limulus,* as well as pieces of large sea turtles, porpoise heads or pieces of porpoise, sea birds, and pieces of large fish. Garbage and artifacts are commonly present. Apparently, anything small enough to be swallowed by the shark may be eaten. I once found, in a tiger shark, an unopened can of salmon (the salmon was judged in excellent condition by organoleptic test); at other times I found a good leather wallet with no money in it, a 2 pound coil of copper wire, various articles of clothing, assorted nuts and bolts, and other articles in the stomachs of various tiger sharks. They seem to eat small fish only rarely, and, although they are probably the most frequent attackers of other sharks caught on shark lines, little evidence was found from the examination of stomachs to indicate that tiger sharks are often successful in capturing unhampered and free-swimming small sharks.

Tiger sharks apparently do not feed regularly on the spiny lobster, *Panulirus,* but, occasionally, large numbers of tiger sharks taken in the Tortugas area have stomachs full of spiny lobsters.

Tiger sharks are not often seen in daylight, but they readily attack surface baits at night. Young tiger sharks are more often seen near the surface and give the impression of being less timid in light than the large ones. Aerial observations of daylight chumming tests once revealed a group of tiger sharks at the bottom in about 40 feet of water beneath a pack of blacktips, *Carcharhinus limbatus.* But the tiger sharks could not be induced to approach the surface, and verification of the identification was made only by lowering a baited hook to the bottom and hauling in a sample.

Two tiger sharks containing portions of men were taken by shark fishermen in 1942–43, one from the west coast and the other from the east coast of Florida. It was impossible to determine whether the men were casualties before the sharks got to them.

Bull Sharks. Bull sharks may reach a weight of more than 500 pounds. Stomach examinations show that they occasionally eat a wide variety of marine creatures. The chief diet appears to be somewhat specialized, with a predilection toward small sharks. This is the only species showing a preference for sharks as bait. Bull sharks were also taken regularly with porpoise pieces as bait.

Bull sharks are common in shallow water in the northern part of the Gulf of Mexico in summer, and they regularly enter estuarine waters to give birth to their young. Before I really accepted the possibility that bull sharks could be dangerous, I encountered some while I was wading in waist-deep water at Cat Island in Mississippi Sound, and I found them so docile that I was able to give a couple of them a shove. Now that I have had more experience with the power of these sharks, I realize that I was lucky not to get my ribs cracked or at least a severe abrasion from the meeting. Actually, these bull sharks were probably females that had entered the shallows to give birth to their young and were, at that time, inhibited from feeding. In view of the abundance of bull sharks on summer days near beaches of the northern Gulf of Mexico, it is remarkable that this is not an area of frequent attack on bathers. I attribute the lack of attacks, by the bull shark at least, to the feeding inhibition of females in nursery areas. It might also be of general significance that no large sharks in this area are permanent residents of inshore waters, and that such members of accessory populations as appear in the region stay in relatively deep water.

In southern Florida waters a few bull sharks belong to the "bank loafer" category.

Spinner Sharks, Blacktip Sharks, and Lemon Sharks. These three species may well be treated together, because in southern Florida waters all three are migratory and appear to feed primarily on fish and crustaceans.

An early-spring northward migration of spinners past Salerno, Florida, called forth substantial but unsuccessful efforts to catch these sharks in quantity. In this migration the sharks make spinning leaps regularly. By following them with a boat it could be seen that the leaps sometimes started below a school of very small fish, through which the sharks passed with their mouths open while following a course toward the surface. I am confident that the relatively small numbers of spinners that I have seen from distances of less than 30 yards were *Carcharhinus maculipinnis,* but spinning sharks were also rather commonly observed at greater distances and at a considerable distance from shore. I have no way of knowing whether all spinners observed were *C. maculipinnis.*

Spinners were taken in large numbers from inshore waters of the northeastern coast of Florida and along the coast of Louisiana in the early spring and through the beginning of summer. Young are born at this time, but the adults remain in the shallow waters for two to four months, where they feed on fish along beaches and follow shrimp vessels to pick up trash fish thrown overboard. It is possible that the spinners then move southward and spread out over deep water, at which time they are generally not caught with the kinds of fishing gear used.

These sharks seem to have somewhat more specialized feeding habits than blacktips. The spinner sharks, *Carcharhinus maculipinnis,* have appreciably smaller teeth than the blacktip, *C. limbatus,* although spinner sharks are larger. Blacktip habits are apparently somewhat similar to spinner shark habits, except that blacktips remain in inshore waters along the coasts of the United States for longer periods and seem to use the spinning technique for feeding less often or not at all.

Lemon sharks, *Negaprion brevivostris,* which are considerably heavier than either the spinner or the blacktip, were much more important to the shark fishery. Lemon sharks taken north of Jacksonville, Florida, or along the northern coast of the Gulf of Mexico appeared to be members of the accessory population. The principal population is West Indian, but its nursery range includes peninsular Florida, chiefly the Florida Bay–Florida Keys area. Stomach examinations indicate that lemon sharks are primarily fish eaters. Moreover, a definite preference for fish is shown by results from fishing with various kinds of bait. Off-season catches of a few lemon sharks with abnormally high vitamin A liver potency suggest the existence of a small accessory population in southern Florida. The lemon shark is also suspected of moving southward and occasionally offshore in winter, and a few observations but no captures in offshore waters beyond the edge of the continental shelf suggest that this species may use some special feeding techniques during its offshore excursions.

Hammerheads. All of the three large species of hammerheads in the western North Atlantic were taken off the Carolina coast. In this area, *S. zygaena* was taken frequently. *S. zygaena,* however, was represented only by relatively few half-grown examples in catches at Salerno. No specimens of *S. zygaena* were taken south of Salerno. The species is said to be present in cooler waters of the western Atlantic in both the Northern and Southern hemispheres, but, since no specimens other than those in the Salerno catches were taken by the shark fishery south of the Carolinas, it seems doubtful that various old records from the Gulf of Mexico, the West Indies, and the Caribbean are based on correct identifications.

An early summer run of hammerheads off Salerno was found to consist primarily of adult male, *S. lewini,* and adult female, *S. mokarran,* and included a few half-grown *S. zygaena.* Large hammerheads were the most valuable species available to the Florida shark fishery because they had the highest potency liver oil of any common species. Stomach examinations indicated that hammerheads less than 10 feet long eat small fish and crustaceans primarily, but that those more than 10 feet long, chiefly *S. mokarran,* eat a greater variety of food, including stingrays and small sharks.

Observations indicated that hammerheads were the first species to reach newly baited shark lines; haulbacks, while setting, produced more hammerheads than other species. After being hooked, the hammerheads died quickly and were among those sharks most likely to be eaten by other sharks. In the few instances when free-swimming sharks could be observed from the surface, hammerheads seemed to be avoided by other species. Great hammerheads, *S. mokarran,* over 12 feet in length, were all females, and possibly most of them would fit our definition as members of an accessory population.

Ridge-Back Sharks, Carcharhinus. The Florida

shark-fishing operation was supported primarily by captures of six species of ridge-back sharks of the genus Carcharhinus. More than half of the sharks caught were sandbar sharks, and the bulk of the liver oil in the higher-potency range was obtained from dusky sharks. Of the ridge-back group, only the dusky shark could be taken in appreciable numbers on bait other than fresh or frozen fish. But the larger dusky sharks, weighing more than 400 pounds, frequently were found to have turtle remains, pieces of porpoise, or shark in their stomachs.

Dusky sharks of the principal population on the east coast of Florida are found most abundantly in large schools in depths of 300 to 150 fathoms. Shallow-water dusky sharks in this area appear to be an accessory population, since they are solitary and very sparsely distributed. Both dusky sharks and the silky shark, *Carcharhinus falciformis,* are found in greatest abundance along the edges of the continental shelf, but, of the two, only dusky sharks are found in the inshore accessory populations.

Nurse Sharks and Sand Sharks. Limited numbers of nurse sharks, which were useful to the local shark stations for their hides, were taken with anchored gill nets in a small summer fishery near Salerno, Florida. The nurse sharks frequent the shallow, rough-bottom areas in this vicinity, probably for mating, and successful fishing was carried out in depths of from 10 to 40 feet. Incidental to captures of nurse sharks, substantial numbers of sand sharks, *Carcharias taurus,* were taken. All of these were adults from 7 to 10 feet long. Most of them were females and were of little value for their hides because of the high incidence of courtship scars. Neither the nurse sharks nor the sand sharks produce oil of sufficient vitamin potency to make these species valuable. However, records of this fishing, supplemented by records of occasional captures of both species in experimental gill net sets in deeper water and on longlines, did provide some general information on sand shark distribution and feeding habits.

Adult female sand sharks are apparently common in

the shallow water near the shore. A few scattered captures from bottom-set lines between Cape Hatteras and the mouth of the Mississippi River in shallow coastal waters indicate a more widespread distribution of adults. Thus, since longline captures in the vicinity of Salerno were no more frequent than in other areas, we may conclude that adult sand sharks are not likely to be caught with baited hooks. Fish of various species constituted the only stomach contents found in sand sharks, and full stomachs were noted more frequently in sand sharks than in any other species. Furthermore, sand sharks represent the only species found with stomachs containing quantities of inshore game fish, such as channel bass or redfish, speckled trout, Spanish mackerel, and bluefish. Sand shark stomachs occasionally contained large sharksuckers, *Echeneis naucrates*. This is evidence that the penchant of that species for following sand sharks is a dangerous one.

34

"Anti-Shark Measures"

STEWART SPRINGER AND
PERRY W. GILBERT

Over the years, many people, scientists and laymen alike, have endeavored to discover a method of constantly repelling all kinds of sharks under different conditions. A variety of strange and unusual methods have been put forth, some of which are mentioned in this excerpt.

One idea, that of a bubble curtain keeping sharks at bay, could hardly be effective for any period of time. We have often seen potentially dangerous sharks swimming in white water (water full of bubbles due to breaking waves) without any noticeable concern.

Once, when snorkeling near a reef several miles from shore, I saw a shark about 6 feet long swimming in my direction. I moved closer to the rocks hoping the shark would pass on the seaward side, but the shark seemed to have the same idea. It was about 20 feet away when a particularly large wave broke on the rocks tossing me about and cutting underwater visibility down to nil. All I could think was, "Good grief, we are going to collide in this mess!" I didn't dare swim in any direction, but just hung there hoping for the best. As the bubbles dissipated, I saw the shark, behind me now, and still swimming along without showing any interest in either myself or the bubbles in the water.

Two weeks before the time of writing this introduction, I was diving with scuba near Seal Rocks in about 20 feet of water. Conditions were so poor that I was about to head back for the boat when my companion indicated he had seen a shark. I swung around, looking, but saw nothing until I looked up. There, directly above me, was a small whaler shark disappearing into the white submarine foam of a breaking wave. It seemed to be hunting a school of trevally and was completely unaffected by the bubbles from our scuba tank or the clouds of bubbles from the breaking wave.

I feel that where a curtain of bubbles may deter some sharks for a period of time, they would certainly not be deterred indefinitely and, in many instances, not deterred at all.

Shark meshing (described in this selection) has proven extremely successful in deterring shark attacks on meshed beaches. However, I was particularly interested to read that there had been two attacks on Merewether Beach (Australia) after meshing had been introduced. No details of the attacks were given. Not even the location of the beach was mentioned, other than Australia.

In all my dealings with sharks and shark people, I have been led to believe that there has never been an attack anywhere in the world on a meshed beach, so, although I feel sure the information is correct and that the attacks did occur, I also feel that there must have been some other unusual circumstances surrounding the attacks.

The most effective method of repelling a shark ever devised is, of course, the bangstick or powerhead. This simple invention has certainly proven its effectiveness over the years, not only for us but also for many of our friends. There are several different types of powerheads. For us, the most effective has proven to be a .303 rifle bullet in a small housing that screws on to the end of a conventional spear fired from a spear gun. The cartridge, upon contact with a firm object, is detonated by a firing pin and the full force of the shot ejects with immediate disastrous results. Perhaps more popular, but without the range or speed of a spear from a gun, is the shotgun cartridge on the end of a simple hand spear. This method works in a similar fashion to the spear gun system.

People diving in areas where sharks are prevalent normally carry one of these two explosive devices. They are inexpensive, efficient, and maneuverable. However, they are only suitable for divers who can see the shark approaching.

Recently there has been a lot of work done with colors. It appears that most sharks have a tendency to ignore cold dull colors, dull dark green, for instance. A green plastic garbage bag with a rubber flotation ring has proven very successful, not as a shark deterrent, but as something a shark simply ignores.

That a person threatened by sharks can reduce the threat by climbing into a plastic bag seems almost too simple to be true, but tests have proven that it works. Although this theory has only been tried with a limited number of shark species, it appeared to work extremely well and could possibly be the answer to keeping shipwreck survivors safe from shark attacks while they are waiting to be rescued.

We have tested the color theory on great white sharks and found that they most certainly have a preference for warm light colors such as orange or yellow even to the extent of ignoring food that is floating nearby and constantly attacking the yellow buoy holding the baits.

The person who discovers a perfect shark repellent will surely become an overnight millionaire, but it's going to take a long time, if ever, before something with the capacity to repel all sharks in all situations is likely to be discovered.

●

What kind of countermeasures can be taken? The kind of protective device useful to the lone man who for one reason or another faces a dangerous shark is limited in several ways. It must be light in weight and easily carried. It must be operable under water and function either all the time or when activated by the user. It must be safe for the user to carry and use under adverse conditions. It should be relatively inexpensive if it is to be widely used. And, finally, it must be reasonably effective in driving a shark away or in thwarting an attack. A .45 caliber automatic pistol is not satisfactory because it is not reasonably effective in driving a shark away and does not really meet any of these requirements.

Some qualifying statement should be made at the outset about protective devices. Some devices may be effective under special conditions or against certain kinds of sharks but still not be satisfactory for general use.

Explosives or special guns, for example, would, if widely used, be almost certain to kill or injure more men than sharks, although it is possible to carefully rig an explosive device so that a man in the water can use it to kill or repel sharks attacking singly in repeated trials, with reasonable consistency and with a fair margin of safety for himself.

If released by a man in the water, poisons or irritants of sufficient strength to promise protection against sharks are extremely dangerous to the man. Up to the present time no selective poison or irritant with strong specific and selective action against sharks has been found. Devices for injecting poisons into sharks have some of the disadvantages for general use already mentioned in connection with explosive devices.

One feature of the shark hazard needs special emphasis. Not all kinds of sharks respond to deterrent actions in the same way or in the same degree. Furthermore, there appear to be important individual differences among sharks of the same species. It is not possible at this time to predict with any certainty the types of response certain actions will receive from sharks. Electrical devices may eventually be so developed that they can produce predictable repelling stimuli to sharks, but, until now, attempts to deter sharks with such devices have been inconclusive or unsuccessful. Nothing beyond advice given in connection with the report *Shark Attacks in 1959* can be offered at this time as a countermeasure for the individual.

Our knowledge of effective methods for protecting commercial fishermen's gear against shark attack is slight. Repellent dye material is expensive and probably would have to be used in great volume to be practical for protecting large nets. Furthermore, it is questionable whether it would be effective under all conditions even then. The commotion of setting and hauling nets, the activity of fish within the net or gilled in the meshes, and the probability that the massed fish produce substances attractive to sharks' olfactory sense are all powerful stimuli.

In theory it should be possible to arrange a series of electrodes in the net to protect it and the catch by setting up repellent electrical fields. Not the least difficulty in such an arrangement would be the necessity to adjust the input to affect sharks without adverse results on the catch. Adequate tests of this kind of protection have not been made.

Fishermen are able to mitigate the danger to gear from sharks in various ways, none entirely effective. Trawler fishermen working among large sharks find that the cod end of the net is especially vulnerable to sharks on turns or when the net stops moving while they are hauling aboard and take such steps as they can to keep the gear moving at a steady rate. Longline fishermen try to avoid attracting sharks by drifting or by discharge of refuse near the starting point for the set.

Shrimp trawlermen sometimes use a protective sleeve of poultry fence wire or canvas over the cod end to reduce shark damage, a device reported to be partially effective.

Protecting swimmers and bathers at public beaches has been given special attention in some regions of the world. A complete fence is used to protect a bathing area at Fort Amador, Panama Canal Zone. This fence is effective, but it is installed across the entrance to a cove. The installation in this instance was less of an engineering undertaking than would be found for most public beaches. It can be seen that this shark fence is heavy and probably is an expensive device. Shark attacks have occurred in the immediate vicinity of the cove, and signs are erected to warn waders and bathers. To reduce the psychological impact without retracting the warning, a second sign with a humorous slant has also been installed in the same area.

Not all devices intended for beach protection are effective. In July 1960 two shark attacks occurred within ten days of each other at Sea Girt and Ocean City, New Jersey. These attacks received wide publicity in the press, and there was understandably considerable pressure on the part of public officials to find a means to "shark-proof" New Jersey bathing beaches. According to numerous press reports the magic answer was a curtain of bubbles rising from a garden hose punctured with a series of holes and attached to a portable air compressor. One report (*Perth Daily News*, West Australia, October 28, 1960) in the files of the AIBS Shark Research Panel states, "The sharks are so terrified by the 'shark fence' that they will not cross it even to get a juicy steak, according to inventor Frank Arpin." Reports which appeared in the *Sydney Daily Telegraph* (Australia, August 28, 1960), the *Montreal Star* (Canada, August 27, 1960), the *Natal Daily News* (Durban, South Africa, August 27, 1960), the *New York Herald Tribune* (August 27, 1960), the *Evening Standard* (London, September 15, 1960), and *Life* magazine (September 12, 1960) presented equally optimistic statements concerning the effectiveness of the bubble curtain as a barrier to large and dangerous sharks. In the November 1960 issue of *Fishing Gazette* (Vol. 77, No. 11, p. 21), the apparatus used at Sea Girt is described, and the effectiveness of the bubble barrier against sharks is summarized, as follows: "In tests of the prototype in an aquarium tank at Asbury Park, sixty large sharks (length not given) refused to crash past the barrier to reach food on the other side during a continuous five-hour test." In view of the wide publicity the bubble curtain received as a positive barrier to sharks, public interest in and enthusiasm for such a method of shark-proofing beaches was not long in coming. At Sea Girt, New Jersey, a perforated hose 350 feet long was placed on the ocean floor between two jetties, 200 feet offshore from a popular bathing beach, and, according to a local hotel manager, the bubbles proved to be "absolutely impenetrable" to sharks.

In the publicity the bubble curtain received as a positive barrier to sharks, no mention was made of the species of shark repelled, their approximate length, the distance of the bubble curtain from the wall of the aquarium tank in which tests took place, or the time of day or night during which tests were conducted. Clearly, a rigorous test of this type of shark barrier was needed before considerable sums were spent by resort areas of the world on bubble curtain equipment for shark-proofing bathing beaches.

During March and April 1961, one of us (Gilbert) had an opportunity to test the bubble curtain rigorously on several tiger sharks (*Galeocerdo cuvieri*) which ranged in length from 5½ to 13 feet and in weight from 95 to 900 pounds. The tiger shark is one of the most common dangerous sharks of the Florida–Caribbean area, frequently wanders in close to shore, and occasionally harasses bathers. The tests were conducted at the Lerner Marine Laboratory, Bimini, Bahamas, during the period March 29–April 4, 1961, in the south shark pen.

These unique pens for holding and operating on large sharks were constructed with funds provided by the Office of Naval Research and have been described by Gilbert and Kritzler in *Science*, 132: 424, August 12, 1960.

Tests showed conclusively that many tiger sharks would pass freely through the bubble curtain. It would appear then that the bubble curtain is ineffective as a barrier to tiger sharks. Test data reveal that the moderately high initial response to tiger sharks to the presence of the bubble curtain (thirty-one turned while fifty-one passed through) did not continue; the sharks quickly adjusted to its presence, and the majority ignored it after the first hour. It was also noted that one tiger shark approximately 9 feet in length was repeatedly turned by the bubble curtain during the twenty-six-hour test, and in certain of the ten-minute counts this was the only shark (of the twelve in the pen) which responded in this way. This latter observation points up the weakness of any program which employs only one or two individual sharks when testing a chemical or physical agent for its repellent properties.

Shark Meshing. Meshing is a method for the protection of beaches that has proved successful insofar as the record shows up to the present time. The purpose of the method is exactly the same as the purpose of the shark fence. However, it involves merely the systematic use of anchored gill nets near a bathing beach, but not as a complete barrier for approach to the beach area by sharks. The gill nets catch sharks as they approach the beach area or as they leave it.

Authorites of Durban, South Africa, began meshing operations in 1952 with several nets, each 450 feet long, placed parallel to the beach and about 1,500 feet offshore. At Durban no shark attacks occurred on "protected" beaches, after meshing was started. Australian experience in protecting beaches by meshing extends from 1937, excepting the period during World War II from 1943 to 1946, when equipment was not available. The record for success of meshing in Australia is almost as impressive, although two attacks occurred on Merewether Beach, one of about a dozen "protected" Australian beaches, within an eight-year period after meshing was introduced.

Both in Australia and in South Africa a great variety of methods to protect beaches were tried, including the use of complete wire mesh enclosures for swimming areas, but none was found to be as satisfactory as meshing.

In spite of the acceptance of meshing in South Africa and Australia it is difficult to evaluate the method for use in other areas, because it is not certain what factors produced the favorable record. The records do not show that meshing operations drove sharks away from beaches or diverted them to other areas. The meshing removed a number of large sharks from the shark populations presumably resident in the beach areas during the shark season. This removal of sharks may have been sufficient to be immediately effective in materially reducing the probability of shark attack: however, since attacks are relatively uncommon and may, in some years, not occur at all on certain much-used but unprotected Australian and South African beaches in the danger area, it is not certain that meshing initially affected the probability for casualty in any significant way. It has been noted that catches of sharks by meshing decrease from season to season when carried out over a long period of time. This suggests the possibility that the incidence of shark attack may be reduced merely because the population of large and dangerous inshore dwelling sharks has gradually become depleted in the vicinity of "protected" beaches. Commercial shark fishing carried on in the United States before 1950 had the apparent effect of temporarily reducing populations of large sharks in some limited areas with comparatively little fishing effort, but this was not true of all areas. Regular migration routes were fished intensively for years without apparent effect on the numbers of sharks present.

Meshing is essentially the same kind of operation as fishing for sharks with a gill net, and the objective is to catch all of the large sharks that regularly or occasionally come near a "protected" swimming area. As in other kinds of fishing, the best results come when advantage is taken of all possible local conditions and of the habits of sharks. The amount of meshing effort necessary to provide protection has not been determined. It is not known whether the mere presence of nets on beaches tends to divert sharks from the area, but this is probably not the case.

Electrical barriers have been considered as a means

of excluding sharks from access to bathing beach areas. Important difficulties, not only in design but in cost, need to be overcome to make these practical.

The role of commercial shark fishing in control of the local or general abundance of sharks needs more attention. Active commercial shark-fishing operations might prove to be the most effective way to reduce the local populations of large sharks as well as to provide effective countermeasures in the control of management of more general problems involving sharks.

What should be done to develop more effective shark countermeasures? The element missing in all the foregoing discussion of countermeasures is sufficient knowledge of the shark and its biology in the broadest sense. For the most rapid, the best, and the least expensive solutions to the various shark problems, it is imperative that more be known about the basic facts of the systematics, structure, functional organization, physiology, behavior, and ecology of sharks. We should seek answers having broad application as well as solutions to narrowly defined problems. In discussing the implications of the competition between men and sharks for the desirable resources of the sea, we have barely enough information to formulate questions.

Concurrently with basic study necessary to any adequate program to cope with sharks, continuing attempts to make practical applications of old and new knowledge are needed to answer specific problems with sharks. In this connection, research into new ways to utilize shark products would be very important. The least expensive way in which shark population may be reduced is through fishing pressure, and a commercial fishery obviously needs to pay its way.

35

From *About Sharks and Shark Attacks*

DAVID H. DAVIES

Dr. Davies is the director of the Oceanographic
Research Institute and Aquarium in Durban, South
Africa. He is considered a world authority on sharks
and their behavior. His book *About Sharks and Shark
Attacks* is based on the sharks that infest the waters
surrounding South Africa. It is well illustrated with
excellent photographs (some of them quite gruesome)
and drawings.

Throughout his book Dr. Davies is extremely
thorough, but often the correct information regarding
the attack is confused and incomplete. This is
understandable, for at such a time neither victim nor
bystander are carefully filing away everything they
see for scientific use. Often in the horror and panic of
an attack, little, if anything, is remembered about
what actually took place. The picture that emerges at a
later date, while the best available, may not be
anything like the correct one.

The piece that I have chosen from the book covers
an attack which is an exception. The attack on
Michael Hely is one of the best documented reports
of a shark attack that I have ever read.

Dr. Davies managed to record the entire incident,
and all the particulars related to it, in fine detail. The
report of the medical procedures used has value for
everyone who could conceivably be involved in a
shark attack, sailors, divers and surfers alike.

At first, the ragged tooth shark (in Australia, the gray nurse) was blamed for the attack. It was not until a more detailed examination of the wounds and teeth fragments were made that the true culprit, the Zambesi shark, was identified.

This is a fair indication that many attacks are attributed to the wrong species and that all shark attack identifications are suspect. Many species look similar, making positive identification by nonexperts difficult, especially when the only sight of the fish is in the water during the confusion and panic of the actual attack.

●

Cases of Shark Attack in South Africa

A detailed knowledge of the circumstances of shark attack on humans is important in the understanding of what can only be regarded as an extraordinary phenomenon. Humans are not the normal prey of sharks and it is unusual for a shark to attack a human so that every well-documented attack has its value in relation to the study of the subject of shark attack. Authenticated accounts by trained investigators were not available prior to 1960, but it is of interest to present a list of attacks which occurred up to the end of 1959 off the coast of the Republic of South Africa as a record of what is known about attacks occurring during this period and in the hope that readers might know of additional attacks which do not appear on the list.

The Oceanographic Research Institute of the South African Association for Marine Biological Research was formed in 1960 and a program of investigation of individual cases of shark attack was drawn up early in that year. It was felt that full advantage should be taken of a situation in which trained scientists and doctors were available in an area in which the incidence of shark attack on humans was relatively high. A trained team for the investigation of shark attack was made available without delay at any time. The team was equipped with a camera, flashgun, measuring instruments, specially prepared data sheets, and other equipment.

As a result of the establishment of this procedure for the investigation of shark attacks, sixteen cases have been investigated off the coast of Natal (December 1963) and a great deal of extremely valuable information obtained. In addition, two cases were investigated in the Cape Province and four cases in Mozambique during the same period.

Shark Attack on Michael Hely

Michael Hely, a European male aged sixteen years was swimming in slightly murky water at Inyoni Rocks near Amanzimototi at 3:35 P.M. on 30 April 1960. The temperature of the water was 71°F (21°C). Michael, who was a bricklayer's apprentice at the time, was wearing a pair of homemade swimming trunks, colored yellow and red, and he wore a silver ring on a finger of his right hand. The color of his skin was light tan.

He swam into a channel in the surf zone approximately 10 feet deep and 30 feet from the shore and was "treading water" when he felt something touch his right leg. He thought that he had brushed against a stick or some other submerged object. Immediately afterward he felt pressure and a downward pull on his right arm and was dragged below the surface of the water. At that moment, he realized that he was being attacked by a shark and he began a desperate fight for his life. He recalled a frenzied underwater struggle with his assailant lasting a few seconds; he broke free and on coming to the surface began to swim toward the shore when he was again attacked and was bitten on the right side. The shark remained at his side during his swim to the shore. On reaching the shore, Michael staggered out unaided. It is interesting to note that up to this time he had not felt any sensation of pain.

He was carried to the Life Savers' Office and was attended within twelve minutes by a doctor from

Amanzimototi who found that his injuries were serious and that he was in a shocked condition.

Michael's injuries included bite wounds on the right leg, the right forearm and hand, a finger of the left hand, and a very extensive wound on the right flank with widespread removal of skin and the lateral abdominal wall. This resulted in exposure and perforation of the large and small bowel, exposure of the right kidney and the hip bone (the entire iliac crest), and the removal of most of the right gluteal muscles.

In spite of severe loss of blood and the extent of his injuries, he remained conscious, was given morphine, and was placed in a head-down position to ensure a good supply of blood to the brain. He responded well to this treatment and was quiet and rational when taken to the Addington Hospital in Durban—a journey of 16 miles which took 45 minutes.

An investigation of the bacteriology of the victim's wounds in the arm and leg was carried out and the same haemolytic paracolon bacillus was isolated that had been found on the teeth and in the mouths of living sharks as a result of a bacteriological investigation carried out previously by the Oceanographic Research Institute in collaboration with medical research associates. Infection by this organism could result in the death of a victim, but an effective antibiotic treatment had previously been devised and is now administered as a routine to shark attack victims.

Four months after the attack, all the wounds had healed extremely well without the need for skin grafting even for the extensive abdominal injury.

There is little doubt that Michael Hely owes his life to the effective emergency treatment he received on the beach and the very considerable ability of the surgeons of the Addington Hospital.

The case of Michael Hely was the first investigated by the Oceanographic Research Institute and at the time the species of shark found off the coast of Natal were not fully known.

Thorough investigation of the wounds revealed no fragments of shark's teeth and it was necessary to carry out a careful evaluation of the characteristics of the victim's wounds in order to try and find out what species of shark had been responsible for the attack.

The findings of a retrospective study of this kind can naturally never be stated with complete certainty and, in fact, led to the tentative conclusion at the time that the shark responsible was a ragged tooth shark, *Carcharhinus taurus*.

This conclusion was to a large extent based on the presence of bony lesions in the hip bone of the victim caused by the teeth of the shark. These consisted of two narrow grooves as deep as 3 centimeters in the iliac crest. Although the characteristics of the other wounds did not necessarily support this conclusion, it did not seem possible that any teeth other than the long, nonserrated, stilettolike teeth of the ragged tooth shark could have caused lesions of this type.

A subsequent investigation of the characteristics of Michael Hely's wounds, using the extensive photographic records together with measurements and other data collected at the time of the attack, has shown that the characteristics of the wounds conform to those found subsequently to have been caused by the Zambezi shark, *Carcharhinus leucas*, which has flattened, triangular teeth with serrated edges.

The leg wounds consist of rows of small lesions triangular in shape while the edges of the extensive abdominal injury are generally clean cut as in all bites from Zambezi sharks, rather than torn (the ragged tooth sharks are of the tearing type). An explanation for the deep grooves in the iliac crest can be found in the suggestion that the flat cutting teeth of the attacking shark swept edge-on across the bone, producing narrow grooves rather than shearing off the entire iliac crest. Some indication of the size of the shark may be obtained from the size of the sweep of the jaws as shown in the tooth marks on the right leg. Reference to the extensive collection of prepared specimens of jaws in the Oceanographic Research Institute suggests that the shark was probably about 7 feet in length and weighed in the vicinity of 200 pounds.

36

From *Shark Attack*

VICTOR M. COPPLESON

Shark Attack is a vivid account of a predatory white shark which makes *Jaws* seem even more possible. Again, fact is stranger than fiction.

It is interesting that both Rodney Fox and Brian Rogers were attacked during spearfishing competitions at Aldinga Beach. Sixteen-year-old Jeff Corner was fatally attacked at Cardcalinga twenty-two kilometers south of Aldinga, also during a spearfishing competition. The attacks were over three consecutive years, but there is a definite possibility that the same shark could have been responsible for all three attacks.

This series of attacks, in fact, fits Sir Victor Coppleson's "rogue shark" theory, which appears again and again in the different attacks described in his book.

So little is known about sharks. Some research has been done on the more harmless species, but the larger and better armed a shark is, the less scientists seem inclined to study it.

Many big-game fishermen feel that the great white shark has a territory which he patrols. Just how big the territory is is anyone's guess. It could take days, weeks, or even months for a single shark to complete the circuit of its particular territory, which could explain the differing intervals between attacks in related areas.

This is only a theory based on the observations of

a few shark fishermen, but, with regard to the great white shark, it is the best information available.

Coppleson's book documents shark attacks from all over the world and presents a massive amount of evidence to support his arguments. He divides the attacks into localities, types of attack, methods of defense, and repellents. The mass of information Coppleson collected was first printed in 1958 and, at the time, was one of the best documented publications on sharks and their behavior in relation to man.

●

This theory of cruising rogue sharks attacking over long distances might well have been flimsy, were it not for a series of attacks which occurred in July 1916 over a stretch of more than 60 miles of coastline along the eastern seaboard of the United States. It is hard to dismiss the claim that these were all the work of one killer and to the theorist they are the classic example of the activity of a long-range cruising rogue.

So serious were the incidents associated with the attacks that the entire United States was shocked and the matter was discussed by President Wilson and his cabinet. What the cabinet considered was one of the most remarkable series of shark attacks in world history. In ten days, attacks occurred along 65 miles of the Atlantic coast just below New York, killing four and injuring another.

At the time, it was generally believed in the United States that sharks were harmless. So strong was the disinclination to believe they could be man-killers that after the first attack, an authority, Dr. F. A. Lucas, said publicly that there was little danger of a shark attacking anyone. The facts of the attack were examined, and five days later Dr. Lucas retracted this statement.

The series of attacks by what was described as the "mad shark" began on 2 July 1916 at Beach Haven, New Jersey, a popular summer resort, about 70 miles south of New York and not far from Atlantic City.

A twenty-four-year-old man named Vansant was swimming in about 5 feet of water at 5:00 P.M.

There were only a few others with him. The nearest was about 40 feet away. Sheridan Taylor saw Vansant standing alone shoulder deep in the sea. He heard Vansant scream and saw him wildly beat the water. Taylor was almost immobilized for a second. Then he saw the water turn red and rushed toward Vansant. Taylor saw the shark clearly. Its fin and part of its back were well out of the water. Taylor grabbed Vansant and with the aid of others, who formed a human chain, began pulling him in. The shark came too, its jaws on its victim's leg.

Taylor could have touched it without any effort. They came right in until they stood in about 18 inches of water. The shark was still there. Then it turned and made off. On the sand a medical student applied a tourniquet above severe injuries on the man's left leg, but Vansant died a few hours after reaching hospital. This killer, observers said later, was bluish-gray and about 10 feet long.

On 6 July, four days later. Charles Bruder lost his life in a similar manner at Spring Lake, 35 miles farther north. His right leg was taken off just below the knee and the left leg amputated by the shark's teeth at the ankle. They were horrible injuries, and Bruder died a few minutes after being rescued.

Hundreds of men and women and many children were on the beach on the afternoon when Bruder, far out beyond the outer life lines, raised a cry for help. Two lifeguards, George White and Chris Anderson, who had been watching the swimmer closely because of his distance from the shore, launched a lifeboat and started for Bruder while the crowd on the beach watched. As the lifeguards drew near, the water about Bruder was suddenly tinged with red. When White and Anderson reached Bruder, he cried out that a shark had bitten him. He then fainted.

On the beach an attempt was made to bandage his wounds while a doctor was called. Before one arrived, Bruder was dead.

This second attack horrified people in the area. Motorboat patrols were instituted in a number of resorts.

Wire-netting enclosures were set up. The entire coastal area went into a kind of systematic and organized panic.

Bruder's death renewed the controversy that had raged for years as to whether a shark would attack a man. It was suggested at the time that a turtle or huge mackerel had killed him. In support of that theory it was pointed out that the victim's legs were torn and chewed as though something had hacked them, and not bitten with the clean, sharp bite supposed to be characteristic of shark. Colonel W. G. Schauffler, Surgeon-General of the National Guard of New Jersey, and a member of Governor Fielder's staff, who attended Bruder just before his death, described the wounds on the young man's body. Because of the question raised by some as to whether or not Bruder had really been attacked by a shark, Colonel Schauffler's description of the wounds is detailed.

Bruder's right leg, he said, had been taken off so that the bone stuck out to a point halfway between the knee and the ankle. The foot and ankle had been bitten off and were missing. The flesh was ripped as high as the knee, and the bone was denuded of flesh. The left leg had been bitten off at the ankle, the lower ends of the two leg bones protruding from the flesh fully one-third of the length of the leg. There was a very deep circular gash above the left knee, extending down to the bone. On the right side of the abdomen a piece of flesh had been gouged out.

After the attack at Spring Lake, experienced surf men and fishermen ridiculed the elaborate precautions taken, asserting that sharks had never been sighted although some small bluenosed sharks had been caught near the fish pounds at Asbury.

On the other hand, a shark fisherman, T. Hermann Berringer, Jr., said he believed the increase in the number of fish pounds had attracted more sharks to the area.

This fatality caused *The New York Times,* in an editorial, to say:

"If the 500 dollars offered some 25 years ago, by

Hermann Oelrichs, for proof of an attack by a shark on a living man, were still to be won, claims for it apparently more than plausible would now be coming in from Spring Lake, down on the Jersey coast. To be sure the accounts from there now at hand do not include the statement of any witness who saw a shark . . . and tales of exciting happenings off beach resorts are commonly to be accepted with caution. This tale, however, for a time at least, will considerably reduce the profits of a not-too-prosperous season. It certainly was not invented for advertising purposes and unless it was a shark that took off Bruder's leg, what could it have been? . . . a reckless imagination might suggest the propeller of a German submarine . . ."

Two days after the attack, Captain Frank Claret of the liner *Minnehaha* made a statement. He was astounded, he said, that man-eating sharks had been seen at Jersey beaches. It was the first time he had ever known man-eaters to go north of the Bahamas.

"The best thing to do if a shark comes at you," said Captain Claret, "is to shout as loud as you can and splash the water with your hands and feet." (It might be noted here that the effectiveness of such advice depends entirely on the disposition of the particular shark.)

Reports from incoming steamers supported a theory that man-eaters along the Jersey coast had been driven north by hunger. Skipper of the vessel *Atlantic* (Captain Brewer) said he had seen sharks swimming northward. Off Cape Hatteras his steamer had passed the largest school of sharks he had ever seen. Some were huge monsters.

After the attacks were investigated, Dr. J. T. Nichols, Curator of the Department of Fisheries of the American Museum of Natural History, retracted a statement he made on 8 July that there was very little danger of a shark attacking anyone.

Of course—it happens everywhere—bathers quickly forgot about sharks. Then on 12 July the nation was galvanized. The rogue shark cycle was completed. On that day a ten-year-old boy and a young man were torn to death by the ravages of a shark. Another youngster was torn from hip to knee by the same monster. It was this third and final tragedy that shook the nation and caused President Wilson to summon his cabinet to consider the menace.

Early on 12 July, Captain Thomas Cottrell, a retired mariner, saw a dark gray shape swimming rapidly in the shallow waters by Matawan Creek. The creek was only 30 miles by sea north of Spring Lake, but it was 20 miles from the ocean. Captain Cottrell recalled the two swimmers killed by sharks on the New Jersey coast. He hurried to town and spread the warning among the two thousand residents that a shark had entered Matawan Creek.

Everywhere they laughed at him. How could a shark get 20 miles away from the ocean, swim through Raritan Bay, and enter the shallow creek? Thus the townfolk reasoned, and grownups and children flocked to the creek as usual for their daily dip.

But Captain Cottrell was right. That night a body lay in the Long Branch Memorial Hospital. A dead child lay somewhere in the dark water and in St. Peter's Hospital, New Brunswick, doctors worked throughout the night maintaining the life of another lad torn about the hip.

It was unfortunate that the first victim, ten-year-old Lester Stilwell suffered from fits. When he was convulsed in the water and went below the surface, Stanley Fisher, son of the retired commodore of the Savannah Line, assumed the boy had taken a fit and raced to the center of the creek to his aid. Young Stilwell came to the surface as Fisher approached. The lad screamed and yelled and waved his arms wildly. His body swirled round and round in the water. Fisher was warned it might be a shark. "A shark here?" he said incredulously. "I don't care, anyway. I'm going after that boy."

When he got to the center of the stream there was no sign of the lad. Fisher dived once, twice. At last he came up with the bloodstained figure in his arms.

He was nearer the opposite shore and struck out in

that direction while Arthur Smith and Joseph Deulew put out in a motorboat to bring him back. Fisher was almost on the shore. When his feet touched bottom, the onlookers heard him utter a cry and saw him throw up his arms. Stilwell's body slipped back into the stream. With another cry, Fisher was dragged after it.

"The shark! The shark!" cried the crowd ashore, and other men sprang into motorboats and started for the spot where Fisher had disappeared. Smith and Deulew were in the lead, but before they overtook him Fisher had risen and dragged himself to the bank where he collapsed.

Those who reached him found the young man's right leg stripped of flesh from above the hip at the waist line to a point below the knee. He was senseless from shock and pain, but was resuscitated by Dr. G. L. Reynolds after Recorder Arthur Van Buskirk had made a tourniquet of rope and staunched the flow of blood from Fisher's frightful wounds.

Fisher said he was in less than three or four feet of water when the shark grabbed him, and he had had no notion of sharks until that instant. If he had thought of them at all, he said, he had felt himself safe when he got his feet on the bottom. He had felt the nip on his leg, and looking down, had seen the shark clinging to him. Others ashore said they saw the white belly of the shark as it turned to seize him. Fisher was carried across the river and hurried by train to the hospital at Long Branch. He died before he could be carried to the operating table.

At the creek, meantime, dynamite had been procured. Arrangements were being made to detonate it off, when a motorboat raced up to the steamboat pier. At the wheel was J. R. Lefferts. In a craft lay twelve-year-old John Dunn. With his brother William and several others, he had been swimming off the New Jersey spot where Stilwell and Fisher were attacked.

News of the accident had reached the boys and they had hurried from the water. Dunn was the last to leave, and as he drew himself up on the brick company's pier, with his left leg trailing in the water, the shark struck. Its teeth shut over the leg above and below the knee and much of the flesh was torn away. He was taken to a factory nearby, where Dr. H. J. Cooley, of Keyport, dressed his wounds, and then by car to St. Peter's Hospital, New Brunswick, where the torn leg was amputated. Two days later they found Lester Stilwell's body resting against the shore 100 yards upstream from the place where he was attacked. There were seven wounds, four on the body, two on the left leg, and one on the right.

After this tragedy one of the most intensive shark hunts in history began. Hundreds of hunters scoured the area in boats. They used nets, they laid steel meshes across the creek and they fired thousands of rounds of ammunition into spots where sharks might be hiding. Hourly catches were made and many sharks writhing and thrashing were dragged ashore.

Two days later, Michael Schleisser, a taxidermist, caught an eight-and-a-half-footer off South Amboy, New Jersey, about 4 miles north of Raritan Bay. When he opened the shark he found in its stomach a mass of flesh and bones weighing about 15 pounds. The bones were identified as human. They included portion of a shin bone which apparently belonged to Charles Bruder, who had been attacked nine days previously. Mr. Schleisser mounted the skin and placed it on exhibit, where Dr. J. T. Nichols, of the American Museum, saw it and positively identified the shark as the great white shark, *Carcharodon carcharias.*

After the capture of this killer, shark attacks ceased. Mr. Murphy, of the Brooklyn Museum, and Dr. Nichols investigated this remarkable series of tragedies and concluded that Schleisser's shark was a solitary one and the sole attacker of the men and boys.

There was no lack of theories to account for these killings. Some said it was a shark season. Others suggested the brute must have been suffering from a kind of shark rabies like a mad dog. There was another suggestion that owing to the interference with shipping—

nobody had forgotten there was a world war on—the sharks missed the food they were used to getting from ocean liners and sought other victuals. There was a theory that recent naval disasters had given sharks an acquired taste for human flesh.

37

From *Sharks and Rays of Australian Seas*

DAVID STEAD

David Stead compiled the information in his book
Sharks and Rays of Australia, in the early 1960s.
Many of the accounts he so carefully documented
regarding shark behavior and attacks are no longer
acceptable. For instance, a 15- to 20-foot gray nurse
shark tossing its victim around like a cat torturing a
mouse is, in the light of what we know about this
species today, quite improbable. The shark was
probably a light-colored great white, the only coldwater
shark I know of who could have the strength to toss a
human around on the surface. A very large gray nurse
shark could possibly measure 12 feet in length, though
I doubt that I have ever seen any longer than 10 feet
and I have seen hundreds over the last twenty-one
years.

I thought the secondhand account where Stead
describes a massive sea creature, claiming it to be a
shark, over 100 feet long very interesting. The
crayfishermen in the area are even today a tough,
no-nonsense bunch. Most are descendants of the old
fishermen who started the industry at the turn of the
century. If they came in and described to me a shark
of immense length and girth, I would certainly be
inclined to believe them.

We filmed a whale shark near Broughton Island.
Perhaps the men were terrorized by an albino of the
species. I saw a pilot whale once who was colored a

pale mottled cream, contrasting sharply with his black companion, so why not a mottled cream whale shark? We know so little about the sea and its inhabitants, working, as we do, only on the fringes of the ocean. Who can really know what great monsters lurk in the depths?

David Stead's book is full of interesting information about sharks and their close cousins, the rays. One thing that puzzles me, not only when reading Stead's book but also other similar publications, is the vast number of legs of pork that not only found their way into the ocean but were also eaten by sharks. It seems that, up to thirty years ago, pork was not only plentiful but not very expensive.

●

Though it is not my purpose in dealing with what might be termed dangerous sharks, or those which may truly be regarded as potentially dangerous, in Australian waters, to give details of shark attacks, I shall be obliged to mention certain cases when considering the whaler shark. The only one I shall mention here in relation to the white pointer—as there was strong presumptive evidence that it was the species involved—is a shocking tragedy which occurred at Brighton, near Melbourne, in February 1930. Though, as I have said, the white pointer is more especially a pelagic species, it is not uncommon in its occurrence in the wide waters of Port Phillip and the lower areas of Hobart outer harbor.

At half past four in the afternoon of 15 February 1930, a lad who had just dived in off the end of the Middle Brighton Pier was seized by a very large shark —estimated in press statements variously to be from 15 to 20 feet in length—in full view of hundreds of people who had gathered for an interstate sailing race. The shark dragged him down out of sight momentarily, and then he was seen again for an instant, apparently still in the grip of the shark as it swam out into the deeper water and disappeared with its human prey. Although search parties went out immediately to look for the lad's body, and continued the search in the days following, while the water was dragged for a great distance around, no trace of him was ever found. It was stated authoritatively at the time that this was the first shark tragedy in the locality for fifty-four years. Piecing together some of the eyewitnesses' accounts and discussing the matter with them on the spot later, I came to the conclusion that the monster was a great shark, probably about 18 to 20 feet long. The carrying of the body right away is quite an unusual feature of shark tragedies—with which, sadly enough, we have been only too familiar in our east coast waters, notably in the vicinity of Sydney and Newcastle.

I have mentioned this instance particularly because, however black the record of the White Death may be in the waters of the world beyond Australia, as I have previously indicated we have very little in the way of attacks on humans to pin on the monster. Nor in this case could the shark be identified with any certainty, as the flurry in the water prevented any observer from seeing it clearly.

The brief account that I have given of this shocking occurrence is founded upon the personal evidence of eyewitnesses who talked to me shortly after the tragedy. As is well known, press accounts frequently contain lurid exaggerations of these shark attacks, and are sometimes filled with fanciful details not noted by careful observers. There were several such accounts in some of the Australian newspapers relating to this Brighton attack. Dr. Schultz, in his excellent book *The Ways of Fishes* (1948), has introduced an account of the Brighton occurrence which, unfortunately, reads like one of these fanciful newspaper statements. I hasten to add that Dr. Schultz is well known to me as a careful and competent ichthyologist, who would not willingly lend himself to sensational journalism. Here is his account:

In 1930 an eighteen-year-old youth, bathing at Melbourne, Australia, was cruelly murdered by an enormous gray nurse shark, estimated to be 15 to 20 feet long. The fish seized its screaming victim in its huge jaws, gripped him at the waist with its sharp teeth, submerged him and emerged again ten times, tossing him about like a cat torturing a mouse. Each time the animal and the youth appeared above water, they were further down the bay, leaving a bloody trail. The scream became fainter and fainter and ultimately the shark carried its victim off and down for the last time.

It will be remembered that, in discussing some records as to the size attained by the white pointer in various seas, I said that there had been quite trustworthy accounts on the New South Wales coast indicating the existence of much larger sharks than those mentioned. The most extraordinary of these I shall relate. The first, is not so hard to swallow! But as for the second . . . !

In May 1939, during some discussions in the Sydney press regarding the stature of sharks, Captain J. S. Elkington of Queensland wrote to me to tell me of an observation that he made in the year 1894 of a great shark outside Townsville Breakwater. (I may mention that Captain Elkington spent a considerable part of his life in the service of the sea, and was always a keen observer of Nature.) He said that while the 35-foot launch he was in was broken down for half an hour this shark lay within ten feet of the launch, giving him ample opportunity for observation. "It was not a basker, (basking shark)," he wrote, "but a real white or yellowish sort, which projected a couple of feet at least beyond each end of the launch." This observer knew the basking shark and was sure that the one seen was the great white shark.

The second account that I shall give is regarded by me as the most outstanding of all stories relating to the gigantic forms of this fish that has ever come to light— I mean, of course, accounts which really appeared to be founded upon fact: In the year 1918 I recorded the sensation that had been caused among the "outside" crayfish men at Port Stephens, when, for several days, they refused to go to sea to their regular fishing grounds in the vicinity of Broughton Island. The men had been at work on the fishing grounds—which lie in deep water—when an immense shark of almost unbelievable proportions put in an appearance, lifting pot after pot containing many crayfishes, and taking, as the men said, "pots, mooring lines and all." These crayfish pots, it should be mentioned, were about 3 feet 6 inches in diameter and frequently contained from two to three dozen good-sized crayfish each weighing several pounds. The men were all unanimous that this shark was something the like of which they had never dreamed of. In company with the local fisheries inspector I questioned many of the men very closely and they all agreed as to the gigantic stature of the beast. But the lengths they gave were, on the whole, absurd. I mention them, however, as an indication of the state of mind which this unusual giant had thrown them into. And bear in mind that these were men who were used to the sea and all sorts of weather, and all sorts of sharks as well. One of the crew said the shark was "three hundred feet long at least"! Others said it was as long as the wharf on which we stood—about 115 feet! They affirmed that the water "boiled" over a large space when the fish swam past. They were all familiar with whales, which they had often seen passing at sea, but this was a vast shark. They had seen its terrible head which was "at least as large as the roof of the wharf shed at Nelson's Bay." Impossible, of course! But these were prosaic and rather stolid men, not given to "fish stories" nor even to talking at all about their catches. Further, they knew that the person they were talking to (myself) had heard all the fish stories years before! One of the things that impressed me was that they all agreed as to the ghostly whitish color of the vast fish. The local fisheries inspector of the time, Mr. Paton, agreed with me that it must have been something really gigantic to put these experienced men into such a state of fear and panic.

Personally I have little doubt that in this occurrence we had one of those very rare occasions when humans have been vouchsafed a glimpse of one of those enormous sharks of the White Death type which we know to exist, or to have existed in the recent past, in the depths of the sea. While they are probably not abundant they must yet be so. Lest the reader may still think me to be credulous I would like to say that I have seen actual teeth of a shark of this type which were no less than five inches (individually) across the base. They had been dredged up from the bottom of the Pacific Ocean. These, I believe, were not fossil teeth, such as are found in various tertiary deposits—from which large quantities of great teeth of the white shark type have been obtained. In my opinion they were so recent as to justify the belief that they had come from great sharks of a type which might still exist in the deep seas! Such a shark as that might readily take the whole of a crayfish man's outfit—pots, crayfish, lines and boat! A shark possessing such teeth would be from 80 to 90 feet long.

38

From *The Shark Arm Case*

VINCE KELLY

There are few Australians who haven't heard of the
shark arm murder case. It has been a standby on the
historical feature pages for years. It was a classic
case of thieves falling out.

It hasn't anything to do with sharks at all, other
than the fact that somehow a shark swallowed an arm
belonging to a murdered man. The rest of his body
was never recovered, nor was his killer brought to
justice.

The murdered man's name was James Smith. The
police reconstructed the crime in this way: Smith's
body was probably cut up by his murderer. The
parts of the body were placed in a tin trunk, which
was completely filled without the arm. Unable to get
this in, the murderer cut it off and attached it to the
outside of the trunk with rope, tying one end of the
rope round the wrist. The trunk and its contents were
then taken out to sea and dumped. The arm worked
loose and was swallowed by a shark.

At the inquest following identification of the victim,
expert witnesses, one of whom was Dr. Coppleson,
who later published a book on shark attacks, testified
that they thought that the arm was removed with a
knife, not torn off in a shark attack, even though the
arm had wounds caused by a shark's teeth on it.

●

The chain of events leading to the sensational explanation for James Smith's disappearance began in a humdrum fashion. On April 17 Bert Hobson was in his boat a mile and a half off Coogee Beach. He left a set line there after baiting it for shark with mackerel.

Next day he found he had caught not one shark but two. A small one was just being devoured by a 14-foot tiger shark which had tangled itself in the line. . . . Bert Hobson towed the catch to the beach, where it was quickly transferred to his brother's aquarium as the star attraction. Captive sharks have a macabre fascination for a city of surf lovers and the 14-foot tiger attracted crowds daily.

The aquarium proprietor, Charles Hobson, was pleased. He fed the shark on mackerel, but after the first four days it rejected food and wallowed sullenly in the water.

Bert Hobson was among the crowd watching its sluggish maneuvers at 4:30 on the afternoon of Anzac Day, the seventh day of its captivity. Like the others, he was intrigued when the shark suddenly began to surge violently about the tank as though demented.

When it disgorged pieces of rats, birds and fins, and a human arm, Bert Hobson's shouts brought his brother, Charles, who promptly phoned Randwick police station to report the gruesome find.

Detective Frank Head and Constable John Mannion got there at 4:45. Bert Hobson was still guarding the arm. Warily, his eye on the shark, Head hauled it out with a firm grip on a piece of rope. It was tied tightly about the wrist with two half-hitches. On the forearm was a tattoo of two boxers shaping up at each other. They were tattooed in blue-inked outlines, their shorts in red. For everyone who knew James Smith the arm was the answer to the mystery of his disappearance. But police were wasting no time in attempting to establish beyond doubt the identity of the arm's owner. Constable John Lindsay had been rushed from the fingerprint section of the CIB. The fingerprint impressions from the skin removed by Constable Lindsay were blurred in the case of most of the fingers, but those from the thumb and ring finger were found to match those in the police records in the name of James Smith.

The comparison was made by the fingerprint expert, Detective Ewing, and he satisfied himself of this beyond any doubt. The earlier prints had been taken and recorded by Constable Masters, of Balmain, in September, 1932, after police had raided Smith's Rozelle Sports Club and charged him with illegal betting.

Smith was convicted of the charge. It was not a very important crime, but that raid yielded fingerprints to support the evidence of the tattooed boxers that the arm belonged to the missing James Smith.

To Smith's brother, Edward, a Newtown rope maker, the additional evidence of the fingerprints was unnecessary. After reading the account of the finding of the arm and the description of the tattooed boxers he called at Newtown Police Station. He said there was no doubt in his mind that the arm was that of his brother Jim, who had been missing since April 8.

Edward Smith then called at the Gladesville home to talk the matter over with his brother's wife—or widow. She was with his mother-in-law, Mrs. Johanna Molloy.

In the family conference Smith's distressed relatives compared notes on when they had last seen him. They were all agreed that he appeared unworried and in the best of health.

Gladys Smith recalled that she had not seen her husband since April 7. He had escorted her to the tram stop at about nine o'clock that evening when she was leaving her home for a few days.

He had expected to go on a fishing trip before she left—"to drive Greg Vaughan and a party at 5 pounds a week." When she asked him why he hadn't gone she said he replied that they hadn't sent the money for his fare.

Her mother related that he had left home on April 8. On that morning she had heard him talking to a small boy at the front gate. She had not actually seen the boy, but she had heard their voices. When the boy had gone Smith came into the house and said he would be going fishing.

Mrs. Molloy said, "He told me they had sent the money for his fare this time and you weren't to worry. He left here about half-past nine that morning. He said he was to meet a man of independent means from another State."

Mrs. Molloy added that she had told him, "You be careful, Jimmy," and he replied cheerfully, "I'll be careful, Mum."

Edward Smith's recollection was that Jim had urged him to accompany him on the fishing excursion, but Edward was not anxious to go. He said he had told his brother, "I'm not keen on going fishing with strangers."

But there was another date discussed at the family conference. This was recalled by both Gladys and Edward Smith. The date was April 13.

It is important because what happened that day tried to make it appear that James Smith was still alive at least five days after police were to allege that he had been murdered by Patrick Brady, his close friend and fellow conspirator in a scheme to commit robberies by forgery.

It was one of two messages clearly intended to mislead investigations by police. On that date a neighbor relayed a telephone message to Gladys Smith. April 13 was a Saturday. The message was to the effect that her husband would not be back until the following Monday, and she was not to worry.

Gladys Smith remembered it. Her son, Raymond, eighteen, remembered it because he passed it on to his Uncle Edward in the Queen's Hotel, Enmore, on the same afternoon. He told his uncle, "Mum just got a telephone message to say Dad won't be home till Monday."

Edward Smith's comment had been, "That's funny. He knows where to find me, but he never let me know. Something must have happened."

His premonition of disaster was more soundly based

than he imagined, but it was not shared by his sister-in-law, who allowed another week to elapse before she initiated personal inquiries about her missing husband. On April 20 she phoned the Hotel Cecil, Cronulla, but was told only that he had been seen "about the place" a few days earlier.

Gladys Smith telephoned Vaughan on April 24—the day before the shark disgorged her husband's arm—and told him she had heard nothing from her husband for more than a fortnight. She had then asked him bluntly, "What's wrong with Jimmy?"

When Vaughan said he didn't know what she was talking about, she had been incredulous and said, "You're joking, aren't you?"

"No, Mrs. Smith, I'm not joking," replied Vaughan. "I don't know what you mean. He wasn't going fishing with me, but Jimmy did come here before he went to Cronulla. He said he was taking a boat or something to Cronulla."

These were the days of ordeal of Gladys Smith. She was taken to the morgue where she had to face the unnerving sight of the tattooed arm, which the stricken woman positively identified as her husband's.

The Government Medical Officer, Dr. Aubrey Palmer, had examined the limb at the morgue on the day after it was taken from the aquarium. Because of the report that it had been bitten from a body by a shark, he had specially requested his friend, Dr. Victor Coppleson, to inspect it with him. Dr. Coppleson was an accepted authority on sharks.

In evidence, Dr. Palmer was to say later that on April 26, 1935, he made an examination of a left upper arm identified to him by Constable Mannion at the City Morgue.

"I made a preliminary examination with Dr. Coppleson, later it was taken away. When I made an examination a piece of rope was attached to it. It was tight on the wrist, with an ordinary clove hitch. The arm had been disarticulated at the shoulder joint, a more or less circular incision."

Police Prosecutor Sergeant William Toole asked,

"From your examination of the skin of the arm did you form any opinion whether a sharp instrument had been used to remove it?"

DR. PALMER: Yes. A fairly sharp instrument I think.

SGT. TOOLE: And the cartilage covering the bone?

DR. PALMER: The cartilage covering the head of the arm bone had several scratches. A number of scratches and one small cut. The cartilage was soft in one place too.

SGT. TOOLE: Were there any other wounds on the arm?

DR. PALMER: Above the elbow in front there was a transverse wound five inches long. That is the wound showing above the elbow. For a good part it was fairly clean cut and in other parts more ragged. I think the raggedness was due to changes taking place after death.

SGT. TOOLE: Was the arm in a good state of preservation?

DR. PALMER: Comparatively a fair state of preservation. It had some smell of decomposition. The cut on the shoulder was fairly clean. At the first examination Dr. Coppleson was with me. Constable Raines signed for and took the limb and the limb was later returned to me.

SGT. TOOLE: Later did you submit the bulk of the soft tissues of the arm to the Government Analyst?

DR. PALMER: Yes, the report from the Government Analyst showed that no chemical preservation had been used to preserve the arm. And I thought also that it was unlikely that the person to whom the arm had belonged had died from poison, or at any rate from the more common poisons.

SGT. TOOLE: From your dissection of the arm did you arrive at any conclusion as to how the arm had been removed?

DR. PALMER: I took it that the arm had been removed from the body by a fairly sharp instrument.

SGT. TOOLE: Would you say it was done by a surgeon?

DR. PALMER: It was obviously not done by a surgeon. There were no flaps left. It was obviously not done by a surgeon in an operation.

SGT. TOOLE: Did you form any opinion as to whether the arm came from a living person or a dead body?

DR. PALMER: I would not be absolutely certain that it came from a dead body, owing to the changes that took place. The difficulty of deciding is largely due to the changes that took place after death partly owing to decomposition and partly possibly owing to digestion. But I could not conceive that the person from whom the arm was taken was alive, or still alive at any rate.

SGT. TOOLE: Did you notice if there was any blood in the tissues?

DR. PALMER: There was no blood effused, thrown out, in the tissues at the cut edges, but there was a little blood in the different vessels and through the limbs, in the nature of clots.

SGT. TOOLE: Did you form any opinion as to how long the arm had been removed from the body?

DR. PALMER: Not exactly; not more than a few weeks at any rate. An arm keeps better when severed from the body. It might be some weeks. But it is impossible to tell exactly.

SGT. TOOLE: Would it be possible for a man to remove his arm himself in the manner in which you found it?

DR. PALMER: I think it extremely unlikely that a man could remove it himself. It is not a thing he could do with one sweep, although it is remarkable what terrible wounds some people, lunatics, do inflict on themselves.

SGT. TOOLE: Have you had any experience in connection with the digestion of sharks?

DR. PALMER: Not personally but through the courtesy of Dr. Dakin, Professor of Zoology at Sydney University, I have learned a little.

SGT. TOOLE: From that did you arrive at any opinion as to a shark's digestion?

DR. PALMER: Yes. It is a cold-blooded animal and the digestion is slow, more especially in cold water. Some times they starve for some time and then when they have a feed it takes some time to digest, from days to weeks.

SGT. TOOLE: If the arm had been swallowed by a small shark and the small shark swallowed by a large shark, would that have any effect on the arm?

DR. PALMER: No doubt the digestion would be slower. There would be a certain amount of shark to be digested first, although there might be some digestive juices left in the swallowed shark. But I should think that there would not be much digestion by the swallowed shark, so the swallowed shark would have to be digested first.

But in any case, there would not be anything unusual about an arm remaining in a shark for a week without being digested.

Dr. Palmer said that on June 13 he saw Mrs. Smith at the City Morgue in the presence of the City Coroner, Mr. Evatt and Sergeant Toole and showed her two pieces of skin, with the tattoo marks on them. She told him what she expected to see if they belonged to her husband.

SGT. TOOLE: Have you the pieces of skin with you?

DR. PALMER: I have them, but I do not usually produce dead bodies, or parts of dead bodies, unless the court asks me to do so.

The two pieces of skin were tendered and marked for exhibit.

Dr. Palmer said that he had later read a treatise by a German professor, Dr. Ernest Weinhart, which appeared in *Zeitschrift fur Biologie*.

Mr. Clive Evatt, the barrister briefed for Brady, asked him, "Relying on this thesis of the German doctor I suppose you agree that it is conceivable that if as much of the human arm as existed in this case, if it were torn or cut off the trunk, that the individual could survive?"

DR. PALMER: That is so, I agree.

MR. EVATT: If met in train accidents, machinery and factory?

Again Dr. Palmer agreed that the evidence he relied on principally was "the state of the arm, that it came off after death."

MR. EVATT: Again there is grave difficulty on account of the fact that it would be on those portions that the digestive juices would commence to work?

DR. PALMER: That is so, and decomposition, too.

Dr. Palmer said he had discarded the possibility of poisoning. Had the person died of some of our well-known poisons at any rate, he would have expected to find traces.

Mr. Evatt was sticking to his trump card. An amputated limb did not prove its owner dead.

MR. EVATT: There are two conclusions that I put to you; that there is no evidence available as to how the man died, that is, assuming he is dead, and secondly, the individual from whom the arm came could still be alive today?

DR. PALMER: I would not deny the possibility, but I could hardly conceive that he would be.

Dr. Palmer's evidence was followed by that of Dr. Victor Marcus Coppleson, with whom shark fishing and observation was almost a lifetime study. He was also a wealthy specialist and resided in one of Sydney's exclusive suburbs, Point Piper. He told the court that he identified the arm and made an examination of it. He said it had been removed by a sharp instrument at the shoulder joint.

Sergeant Toole asked him, "Did you form an opinion as to whether it had been removed by a surgeon or otherwise?"

DR. COPPLESON: I formed the opinion that it had not been removed by a surgeon. In the first place, there were not flaps actually cut.

SGT. TOOLE: Did you form any opinion as to whether it had been removed from a living being or a dead body?

DR. COPPLESON: My examination was mainly from the surgical aspect and I formed the opinion from such evidence as there was. My chief point was not so much as to whether it was removed before or after death. Such evidence as there was appeared to show it was removed after death.

Mr. Evatt was still shrewdly adhering to the theory that Smith's tattooed arm did not prove that Smith was murdered or even dead. He asked Dr. Coppleson, "Your chief interest was to ascertain whether the arm was bitten off by a shark?"

DR. COPPLESON: I don't know. Dr. Palmer rang me and told me that he had an arm down there and he would like me to come down.

MR. EVATT: Dr. Palmer regarded you as having experience in shark bites at St. Vincent's Hospital?

DR. COPPLESON: Not necessarily at St. Vincent's. He knows I am interested in shark bites. I have seen shark bites at the morgue with Dr. Palmer.

MR. EVATT: You consider it was not a shark bite, neither that on the shoulder or on the arm?

DR. COPPLESON: There was evidence that this arm had been bitten in parts by a shark. There was evidence of shark's teeth marks on the forearm. On the back of the arm there were small marks which appeared to have been made by a shark's teeth. There were a number of small triangular marks . . .

MR. EVATT: What about this mark (showing on the photograph)?

DR. COPPLESON: I cannot remember that exactly, I would not say whether it was or was not. The wound over the elbow—there is some doubt whether that was caused by a knife or by a shark bite.

MR. EVATT: You agree that it is impossible to say definitely whether the arm came from a dead or a living person?

DR. COPPLESON: At the time of removal? I am of the opinion that it did come from a dead body, but I would not say for certain.

MR. EVATT: You did say that it was impossible to say for certain whether the arm was cut from a dead or living person?

DR. COPPLESON: That is so.

MR. EVATT: You agree generally with the conclusions that I put to Dr. Palmer: That the arm itself in no way revealed how death eventuated, assuming that the person is now dead from whom the arm came, either before or after death?

DR. COPPLESON: If it came from a dead body, there is no evidence how that person died.

MR. EVATT: Suppose it had been cut off by a machine?

DR. COPPLESON: That is different. A machine tears the arm off . . . pulls it off.

MR. EVATT: And in other cases it is cut off?

DR. COPPLESON: I can't say that I have heard of a person living after that. But in a tearing injury it is possible that a person might live. In a tearing the arteries react differently.

MR. EVATT: I am putting it as a theory.

DR. COPPLESON: With immediate attention, a person could survive, provided the arteries and vessels are tied . . .

MR. EVATT: Have you ever known an arm to be torn off by a shark in that manner?

DR. COPPLESON: Yes, in the Sydney Hospital. A boy there had his arm taken off at the shoulder. The boy died.

Both doctors agreed that the arm appeared to have been severed with a knife or some blade instrument rather than a shark bite although they noted scars on the forearm and accepted them as wounds caused by teeth of a shark.

But were they? Quite a different explanation for them would have been claimed by the defense had Patrick Brady's trial for murder not been halted by the judge with his direction to the jury to acquit Brady.

X

FICTION

●

Sharks often appear in fiction, but rarely are the stories about the shark itself. *Jaws* and Ernest Hemingway's *The Old Man and the Sea* are, of course, two exceptions. Even so, it was only after considerable searching that I found the selections presented in this book. They are four truly delightful stories and, with the exception of *Ti-Coyo and His Shark* could all quite possibly be true.

Dr. Charles Holder's fictitious great white shark could almost be real, yet I know that it would be impossible to follow the movements of a live shark in the ocean for any length of time in the way Holder describes. However, I cannot help but wonder if the ending to his story is not based on fact. Perhaps there is a great white shark on display in the British Museum with a wound or notch on the dorsal fin. If I ever visit the British Museum, I will certainly find out for myself.

Fascinating as true shark adventures may be, fictitious shark stories are easily as exciting to read and, in some cases, even more interesting.

39

From *Tiger Shark*

Written for children, *Tiger Shark* is a fictitious adventure story about a family who go to sea on their yacht the *Sea Witch*. It is a story everyone who has an interest in the creatures of the sea should read.

Edwards is a diver who knows the marine world and how its inhabitants behave in their natural element. He has used this knowledge brilliantly. Everything that happens to the creatures in his book is based on fact, making his writing both entertaining and educational.

The crippled tiger shark is beautifully portrayed. It is obvious that the writer has had a good deal of personal experience with these giant fish.

The story is mainly about a wounded and hungry shark who menaces Sam, the eldest of the three Masterson children, and then proceeds to turn what started out as a happy, carefree holiday into a nightmare.

I have chosen the last chapter for inclusion here, mainly because it is one of the few stories I could find that had a happy ending for everyone, including the shark.

I can well understand Sam feeling sorry for the captured shark, even though it had tried to eat him. In similar circumstances, my feelings would have been the same.

Ron and I have twice freed a captured great white.

365

Both times we felt only pity for the helpless, frightened shark.

One other nice touch in the Edwards book—he has dedicated it to his three children, Christopher, Caroline, and Petrana.

●

The Moment of Truth

As he stood staring down at it, Sam felt only pity for the shark. He saw the bent and rusted turtle harpoon injuring its shoulder and blocking the gill. He could imagine the pain it caused.

"Poor shark!" he whispered. "What a terrible way to die."

He put his hand out and touched the iron experimentally. The shark flinched, but it was lashed so tight with Joe Benson's knots that there was little it could do.

The ropes were biting deep into its body and it hung between the lashings, its body humped, fins trailing, quite helpless. Waiting to be killed.

Sam touched the iron again. It was loose in the wound and he saw that if he could twist the harpoon head, he might be able to pull it out.

"Steady, boy," he said to the shark. "This is going to hurt a little!"

He turned the iron and gave a quick jerk. It stuck for one agonizing moment, and then came out cleanly in his hand. He dropped it with a light clatter on the dinghy floor. The shark shuddered a little as the iron came out.

Sam leaned over and touched the spot where the iron had turned one of the gills inside out, blocking the others. He noticed that already they had returned to shape and place, and the trailing fin was noticeably higher. The gills gradually opened and began functioning for the first time since the terrible impact of the hurtling harpoon so long ago!

It was ironic. Sam thought, that now the shark was halfway to being healed, it was about to be killed.

"Who's going to shoot it?" he heard Michael's voice. "The rifle's in the wheelhouse!"

A wave of pity welled up in Sam. He saw the huge black eye watching his movements. He put out a hand toward it, and the white membrane rolled up over it like an eyelid, just as a man expecting a blow would close his eyes and shrink away from it.

The eye opened again, rolling desperately, and Sam saw something else there. The shark looked terrified.

"Poor shark," said Sam again. He took out his knife and slowly lifted it high.

For a long moment he held it there, spellbound and looking into the shark's eye. Without realizing it he moved his face closer and closer to the great head.

"Sam!" he heard his father's shout from the cockpit of the boat.

"Sam!" the voice came again, this time more sharply. "Sam! What the devil do you think you're doing, boy?"

He knew he had little time.

"I'll be quick, shark," he promised.

"Don't kill it with the knife, Sam," Michael yelled. "Use the gun. Wait for me!"

Amanda put her hands over her eyes.

"Get back, Sam, he'll jump the ropes!" Joe shouted. "He's dangerous, boy. Get away from him!"

Sam ignored them all. With one quick slash he cut the tail lashings. Then he leaned forward and one by one cut the loops around the great head and shoulder. As they fell apart he saw the deep grooves the ropes had made.

The shark hung there, seemingly unaware that it was free.

Sam heard Michael's furious voice, the sound of running feet on the decks and a confused noise behind him. He did not look back.

Instead he put his hand out.

"Go on, shark!" he said softly. "Go. Get back to the ocean where you belong. And get well . . . and keep out of the way of men. They can be more dangerous than sharks . . ."

The shark rolled beside the dinghy, its gills flaring like a breathless man gasping for air.

It wriggled its body experimentally, and shook its head like a groggy boxer. Sam could sense all the stiff and agonized muscles from the fight against the line and the drums and being lashed against the boat. It turned in a slow circle beside the dinghy as though testing its balance, and rolled on its side so that its eye and half its huge head was out of the water. Sam leaned toward it and put out his hand again.

The horrified watchers saw the mouth open slightly showing the white teeth. The great tail began to coil like a spring.

"My God!" cried Joe. "It's going to strike!"

"Get back! Get back!" shouted his father.

No one had time to move. It all seemed to be happening in slow motion.

Sam leaning forward with his head and his hand now only centimeters away from the great shark.

Then a strange thing happened.

Instead of throwing its head across in the terrible sideways crashing, bone-crunching snap that had shattered the dinghy oar, the shark seemed to pause and look at Sam for a moment.

Sam put out his hand once more and this time the eye did not blink. It looked back directly at him and their gaze fused for a moment.

Sam pushed the shark's shoulder again.

"Go," he said gently, and this time the shark did go.

It sank slowly below the surface and as the sea covered its back, it began to swim with long powerful strokes of its tail.

Sam waited until it had disappeared into the dim blue depths and the last ripples had gone. Then he wiped the knife, coiled the severed lines, and pulling himself aboard *Sea Witch*, stepped down past them into the for'ard cabin without a word to anyone.

"The shark knew Sam was its friend," said Amanda. "That's why it didn't bite."

"A shark can't think like that," replied Joe. "They only know how to bite and kill."

"What about the jaws?" wailed Michael. "All that work for nothing!"

"Shh!" said Amanda crossly. "The shark attacked Sam and it was up to him to do what he liked with it. And anyway," she said, her blue eyes flashing angrily, "the poor shark had a harpoon put through his back by some stupid human . . . why wouldn't he attack any person he saw in the water? Besides he was starving!"

"Steady down," said Alan Masterson. "I think Sam's made the point for all of us."

Joe nodded and began whistling and whittling away with his knife at the broken oar blade, and Michael started untangling the remains of the shark line. After a while their father stood up and went below. Sam was lying on his bunk with the sheet pulled over his head. His father touched him gently on the shoulder.

"You were right about the shark, boy," he said softly. "Two wrongs don't make a right in our world or theirs. But never put your head near a shark's jaw again."

"He wasn't frightened then."

"Maybe not," said his father. "But I was."

"Sorry, Dad," said Sam, understanding at last. As his father climbed the stairs to the deck, Sam called, "Dad."

His father stopped and turned. "Dad, Joe's not angry with me?"

"What for, son?"

"Well, he went to all the trouble of catching the shark."

"I don't think so. I'm sure he understood." At the moment Joe's form darkened the companionway.

"Brought you down a souvenir," he said brightly. "There's two, actually, because you'd better keep the bent harpoon. But I thought you'd like this as well."

It was the oar blade and broken haft with the shark's teeth embedded in it. Joe had put a turk's head knot round the haft and another round the blade, and in beautiful lettering had carved in the wood:

"To Sam—From His Friend the Shark"

"Thanks, Joe," said Sam, eyes shining. "I'd rather have that than the jaws any day."

"Yes," Joe agreed. "Better than the jaws."

As he climbed the companionway again he saw his turtle rod lying on the deck and picked it up. "Never did get them turtle eggs," he said to himself, scratching his beard.

Next morning, Joe, Michael, and Amanda took the dinghy ashore and, after Michael had tied the anchor line knot very carefully, they collected a fresh bucket of eggs.

Then they raised *Sea Witch*'s anchor and sailed for the west lagoon.

"That's where the pearl shell is, Amanda," said Joe. "You'll probably find another pearl there like the Star o' the West," and he hummed a sea shanty under his breath as the wind caught *Sea Witch*'s sails and they steered for the lagoon pass and the open sea.

Michael wondered if the real reason for moving anchorage was that Joe and Mr. Masterson really thought —despite Sam's firm belief to the contrary—that the shark might still be dangerous and might still come back to the lagoon.

He was about to ask Joe if this was true, but instead he asked: "How far to the west lagoon, Joe?"

As they rounded the point of the reef with the backs of incoming turtles dotting the blue water, Sam looked back and wondered what the tiger shark was doing.

Deep down, and far away, the shark was swimming steadily.

His tail was high now that the pain which had paralyzed his right shoulder was gone, and his pectoral fins jutted sharply out from his body evenly balancing the sweeps of his giant tail. The sea slid through his part-open mouth and out again through his wide gill-slits, bringing oxygen to his bloodstream. His eye was clear and bright and he felt his new strength as he swam.

Ahead of him flickered three pilot fish he had picked

up in the lagoon and behind him—a little nervous at first—was a new friend; a cobia kingfish keeping station below him. The king had new courtiers and a new life.

40

From *Big Game at Sea*

CHARLES F. HOLDER

Big Game at Sea was written at the turn of the century by Dr. Charles F. Holder, who was founder of the world's first game fishing club and a man of considerable imagination, as this excerpt shows.

From a predominantly factual book, I have chosen this story of an old shark, one far past his prime. It is the story of all aging creatures whose senses dim and whose movements slow. This segment, obviously, is not a true story, but who can say that it did not happen, for no man has yet traced the movements of a shark from birth to death.

One passage irritated me—the description of the white shark's eyes. Small, gray, beady they are not; large, black, bottomless would describe them more correctly. This error in describing the shark, which was correctly depicted in every other way, is surprising, for Dr. Holder not only knew his shark but knew it very well.

I enjoy Dr. Holder's writing. He has a feeling for the sea and its inhabitants that comes across wonderfully, be his subject shark, fish, or fisherman.

•

The man-eater could not be induced to take a baited hook, and it was believed by many of the men that he followed the vessel waiting for a wreck; and when a certain ship disappeared in a hurricane and went down

372

with all on board in the Florida Strait, it was said that
"Old Bill" went down with her. In any event, he disappeared for months. He was now eighteen feet long, of
enormous bulk. He rarely went north of Hatteras and
then only in summer, when he followed the shad
schools north, making the turn at Long Island in June
and the coast of Maine some time later in summer.
His habits had changed. He preyed upon dead animals, had become a scavenger, and would follow a
cattle ship halfway across the ocean to feed upon a
dead steer. He appeared to be too heavy to run down a
horse mackerel, and the smaller fishes evaded him altogether, though occasionally he found a school of
mackerel surrounded by a net and would dash into
them, crazed by the scent of blood and slime, and gorge
himself with them.

He was utterly insensible to pain, as while entangled
in a net he was lanced several times by an infuriated
fisherman; but the men noticed that he did not stop
eating, paying no attention to the wounds; and when
his size was seen the skipper ordered the men aboard
the schooner. On another occasion, when entangled in
a net near Gloucester, five miles offshore, he destroyed
it, rolling over and over, biting the net, tearing it into
countless pieces. A doryman attacked him with a harpoon, upon which he turned savagely, gripped the cut-
water in his teeth, nearly crushing it and lifting the boat
several feet. The men pulled off at a glimpse of his
size, and the next day some of his teeth were found
in the planking.

One summer he came up the coast searching for
some cattle steamer, but finding none he swam on,
and attracted by the fishing boats, followed several.
Food was scarce. Horse mackerel eluded him. One
day he ate a huge jellyfish in desperation, and next
seized and rent a mass of kelp in which a dead fish
was wound, which brought on a frenzy for food and
blood. A schooner was fishing nearby, and as the men
hauled up fish, he would take them off, carrying away
the lines and filling his mouth with hooks to which he
paid little attention. Finally the fishing stopped and

he came to the surface some distance off and seeing a dory anchored, swam up to it, then circled around it. His appearance must have terrified the man, for he grasped an oar and struck at the shark, shouting for help. It was said later that the shark deliberately tried to tip over the boat by rising beneath it; but it is an historical fact that over a dozen men and women on the schooner saw the man-eater rush at the dory, rise over it amidships, saw the unfortunate man waving his arms, then saw him strike at the shark with the oar; but the man-eater fell partly on the dory, crushing it down, and then both disappeared. This incident occurred off Nahant, and for several summers the shark haunted the New England coast and the Gulf of Maine. He repeatedly attempted to capsize boats off Boon Island, and terrorized the dory cod fishermen and others by rising beneath them and swimming about their boats. The "Big Shark," under which alias he was known, is still remembered by the old fishermen of the coast.

The shark had earned his title of "man-eater" beyond question, and his nature changed with the acquirement. Though starving at times, he haunted vessels, paying little attention to the large migrating schools of fish which most sharks follow up and down the coast. In his soggy brutal mind he associated ships with this new game, and the small gray eyes had learned to distinguish between the animate and inanimate parts of a vessel; a floating, rippling flag over the stern or a propeller did not deceive or attract, but men who were hanging in the chains or over the rail painting or scraping a ship sometimes saw a strange but mighty shadow below them and crawled aboard, terror stricken, with an undefined fear.

The man-eater had at one time been quick of motion, a swift hunter. He had learned the tricks and customs of the fishes. He knew when the bluefish migrated, the millions of shad came in from the deep submarine plateau upon which they wintered, and with others he had followed them, lurking about the mouths of rivers, often creeping, in devouring other sharks or eating the hundreds of shad in nets. He lurked about the Gulf Coast islands for some time and lay in wait for the silver kind, the tarpon that came up from the South American coast in February, and he soon learned to watch until a fisherman had hooked a tarpon, and more than one will recall feeling a sudden strain and seeing a huge white-bellied figure rise five feet with the tarpon quivering in his maw. Again he followed the horse mackerel in the spring, lurching along far beneath them, yet keen on their scent, following the peculiar oily exudations from their scales which followed them for miles, as a hound would a fresh trail, making rushes at night and often running a school inshore, losing them on the sands where the fishermen lanced them and wondered why they came ashore.

This and more the great shark had done, but now his enormous bulk, his slow movements suggested a different life; the huge creature had reached the demonical climax of his development. He had fourteen or more rows of white serrated, knifelike teeth; he moved with great deliberation, and was apparently incapable of rapid movement; but this was not altogether true, the shark was really capable of a type of activity. He could dart ahead or from side to side, or turn upon his side with matchless grace, but he rarely did; he now plowed slowly along searching for the objects which suggested the game of his choice.

It was this change of habit that made the great white man-eater an ocean wanderer. He avoided the shore and attached himself to a large ship which sailed from Boston to Liverpool; trailed it, like a hound on the scent, for days; laid by it in storms and calms; and every bucket of refuse thrown over brought the man-eater up from astern with a rush. He finally lost the trail of this ship in chasing something which was thrown over, and was a thousand miles or more at sea. He swam in every direction, hoping to pick up her scent or wake; now madly, again swimming slowly. He dived down a quarter of a mile, searching for the bottom which was three miles beyond, but was driven up by the cold to swim along the surface on calm days.

The marvelous turquoise tints of the ocean's heart,

its splendid virile life, its strength, its ponderous movements, its silvery tracery, the frosting of the sea as it broke made no impression upon his sodden brain. The wonderful illumination of the sea at night, its real comets and constellations of vivid phosphorescence were not seen by him as he moved along. It mattered little to this blood hunter that the ocean was a realm of beauties, that each crystal drop was buoyant with life and countless lovely forms. He failed to note the splendors of the huge jellies whose tentacles of living lace brushed over him in a cloud of color—lavender, blue and pink—all were unseen by this incarnate appetite without sensation or desire beyond carnage.

Swimming aimlessly along one day, the shark crossed a familiar scent. Several Mother Cary's chickens were fluttering over the surface after some substance foreign to the clear waters. At once the great bulk shot into action. It rushed across the line, caught the scent, lost it, turned savagely and caught it again, then dashed on into the wake of a great ship bound for Rio. For days he followed, now astern, again lurching along the quarter with one ugly eye cast upward; again sailing along the surface, his big dorsal fin cutting the water. He was fired at; hooks were tossed over baited with salt pork, but the man-eater paid no attention to them. He crossed the line with the ship, grew gaunt and ugly, and was forced to catch a porpoise or starve, so well did the wind hold, and finally entered the harbor at Rio and failed miserably in an attempt to capsize the boat of a pilot.

Meeting an outgoing steamer, the man-eater trailed it up the coast of Barbados. Here he found a small sailing vessel bound to the westward, and so reached Aspinwall in the Caribbean Sea. The water was intensely hot and he lay out in deep water, cooling his massive bulk during the day, going inshore at night, occasionally chasing the great rays whose leap from and return to the water sounded like the discharge of a cannon.

One day the shark entered the harbor late in the afternoon and swam in the direction of the anchorage, a huge uncanny menace. The crew of one ship were in bathing. They had a top gallant sail overboard and were swimming in it, suspecting the presence of sharks. The man-eater swam beneath and around it and was seized with a frenzy at the scent that drifted away. He began to swim rapidly, first in one direction, then in another, circling the ship about twenty feet below the surface, then rising. At this time one of the sailors, more venturesome than the rest, swam out into the channel, and the shark, catching the scent, swung its tail from side to side and darted upward, baring its notched fin to the sunlight.

"Ahoy there!" came from the foretop. "Come aboard!"

The lookout did not utter the word shark, but the swimmer turned and struck out.

"Way third cutter!" rang out from the quartermaster.

The boat struck the water with a crash, naked men fell into her and seizing the oars gave way. Men never pulled like this before; yet the man in the bow, boathook in hand, urged them on in God's name. The swimmer was still twenty feet away when the shark shot ahead assuming a titanic shape. He turned slightly though not upon his back, and for a second the man in the bow saw its ghastly form against the blue, then in a moment of horror realized that he was too late.

The white shark with the notched fin was noticed at Aspinwall's several months where desperate efforts were made to capture him, then he attached himself to a northbound steamer and followed her through the Straight of Florida, by Cuba, up the Bahama Banks, leaving her by a singular fatality where he was born, near Cary's Foot Light on the Florida coast. Here he was attracted by a fleet of wreckers. He lingered here a few weeks, then dogged a tramp steamer to Bermuda, and one day went to sea on the trail of a British cruiser. But she was only going out for gun practice, and as the huge sullen brute came boldly to the surface and circled about the vessel glaring at her with his beadlike eyes, the big lateenlike dorsal cutting the water, one of the men asked permission to fire at him, and cleverly sent a ball through his gills.

Then came the culmination in the career of this insatiate monster, wounded to the death, but so insensible to injury that the scent of his own life blood reached his brain before the sense of pain, his first move being not alarm, but desire. Frenzied by the lust for blood, rapine, and slaughter, the man-eater turned and dashed through the deep red cloud, and was rushing savagely from side to side in search of himself, when a second shot cut the soft spinal marrow. The great mass dropped inert. For the first time the powerful tail did not respond; the huge lips gripped tightly, the rows of gleaming teeth stood erect for a moment, then the small expressionless eyes convulsively turned inward, the pilot fishes darted wildly about the dropping head and open gills, the black and white remoras were along his tawny sides hard and fast; the man-eater was dead.

In one of the great British museums is the mounted and splendid specimen of a shark. The length is given as twenty-five feet, and the card attached to it states that it is an adult specimen of the white shark or man-eater, *Carcharodon*. It was donated by the officers of one of His Majesty's ships. It is a perfect specimen of this rare shark, if we except the wound or notch on the dorsal fin.

41

From *Ti-Coyo and His Shark*

CLEMENT RICHER

Ti-Coyo is a strange tale, but it is refreshing to find an author writing of a shark which, while retaining all of his sharklike characteristics, has a friendly personality and a rather endearing manner.

It is a pity that sharks aren't really like this—it would make swimming a great deal safer. In real life, sharks lack feeling and the playfulness which are two of Manidou's most endearing qualities.

Clement Richer's tale of a boy who finds his very own shark, helps and befriends it, is a delightful story and one that I enjoyed reading, if only because it is the exact opposite of our own experiences with these creatures.

I like to read happy shark stories even if they are not true. The poor sharks of this world suffer from being forever presented as dreadful man-eating monsters. Ti-Coyo's shark, for a change, is a happy sweet man-eater, one I would personally love to meet.

●

Fair weather returned, but with it, for Ti-Coyo, many anxieties.

For a whole week the village had lived in constant dread of some new cataclysm. But Heaven was tired and wanted a rest. At dawn on the eighth day the volcano ceased to rain its cinders over a circumference of sixty miles and life became normal once again.

The shameless little stream had been the first to feel the change and, much to its regret, had returned to its natural bed, from which all hoped that it would never again emerge. The animals had wandered back to their pastures, and Joe had managed to patch up his collapsed dwelling.

The sea seemed now so calm that it was difficult to believe that only a week earlier it had been lashed to such a pitch of fury that everything not standing high enough to escape it had been submerged. So freshly did the breeze blow, so gaily did it set the leaves dancing, so sweet were the scents of the earth, so gay was the sound of bird song that one might have been tempted to believe that Nature, filled with remorse, was trying to make the survivors forget her recent indulgence in anarchy.

But Lucie, seeking solitude, wept silently for those whom she would never see again, and Dora, her mind full of the house on the sea-front at Saint Pierre, sobbed with bitter resentment.

"Wisdom is not to be found in books," the hunchback reminded her sententiously (he had got over his earlier emotion and was pleased to think how he had got away with all his money intact). "The shark who never went to school realized more clearly, and far earlier than all the men of science, that the time had come to escape from Saint Pierre."

"True enough," agreed the boy, who had just come up, "but where is he now?"

"Where is who?"

"The shark," said Ti-Coyo with a worried look.

Manidou had put in no appearance since the catastrophe, and the boy was feeling anxious about him. True, on the morning when the tidal wave had swept down on the island in the violent manner described he had found no trace of the shark and had therefore assumed that, guessing what was about to happen, it had made off on the previous evening. But, in that case, it had probably gone a long way, since the effects of the tidal wave had made themselves felt at a considerable distance from the source of the disturbance.

Ti-Coyo walked down to the little creek in a very bad humor. He was quite determined, if necessary, to set off in his canoe to explore every corner of the Caribbean Sea for traces of Manidou.

He was, however, spared the tedium of such an enterprise. He had lain down for a moment on the sand to consider where best he might start his search. As he pondered with folded arms and a heavy heart (he was stretched on his back, and was following with his eyes the movement of a cloud whose shape reminded him of Manidou), he heard the faint sound which usually accompanies the drawing up of a boat on the sand. Turning sharply, he saw, only a few inches from his head, the shark's cavernous maw. Manidou's face had that crestfallen expression which it always assumed when it found itself out of its natural element.

Ti-Coyo gave a shout of delight and dashed, fully clothed, into the sea, pursued by the shark. Then he dived and dived again until he had no breath left, caught a cockle which was ambling unconcernedly among the seaweed and at once withdrew into its shell (one of those shells on which the fishermen blow when surprised by a storm, in order to summon aid), shot to the surface with his trophy, flung it from him with a shout of triumph which echoed under the rocky arch so that the sound of it was carried far out to sea, and dived again in an effort—though in this he exercised the greatest care, for the thing was as sharp as a knife —to lay hold of the shark's tail close beside him.

At last he came to shore and sat on the sand with his legs in the water, while he set about cleaning his friend's body. This was the moment for which Manidou had been waiting impatiently. The barnacles that clung to his skin incommoded him abominably, and set up an intolerable itching. He stretched himself out in the shallow water in such a way that his back was partially exposed.

The skin of the shark is delightful to the eye and still more delightful to the touch. To prove the truth of this assertion it is necessary to wait only until its possessor has quitted its natural covering—and its life.

This skin is at once very supple and extremely tough, and the makers of shoes and handbags all over the world value it highly. With the aid of his knife, Ti-Coyo proceeded to loosen one by one the barnacles of every kind which clung, firmly fixed by the secretions of their bodies, to the mottled back and the immaculate belly.

All sorts of shellfish appeared to have sought the hospitality offered them by the shark which, in consequence, as it lay there motionless, had taken on the aspect of those long, wet rocks which show above the water at low tide, especially on the coast of Martinique, where they are the terror of all sailors. The case is recorded of one young fisherman who was deceived by the resemblance until the shark made him change his opinion, by which time the knowledge thus acquired was no longer of any use to him.

The monster turned over and over in the shallows in response to the pushes administered to him by the boy, who had his work cut out to cleanse, lengthwise and upwards and downwards, an animal of such vast dimensions.

At the end of an hour Ti-Coyo was sweating profusely. But not one single barnacle remained on the shark's body. The boy took a short walk along the beach apparently looking for something he did not find, for he very soon entered the water and dived. He brought a number of stones from the seabed, and these he threw away impatiently, only to bring others to the surface, of which he disposed in the same manner. Manidou showed much curiosity at his proceeding, which was, apparently, new to him. What Ti-Coyo had been in the habit of fishing from the depths had glittered brightly, but the shark could see that there was nothing of that sort here. Consequently, he followed the boy closely, thrusting his great snout here and there, for all sharks are inquisitive by nature and from necessity.

At last Ti-Coyo found what he was looking for—a large piece of coral with which he set about scrubbing the shark's back which was covered with white spots where the barnacles had stuck to it. He did not stop till he was out of breath, and until the animal's skin had once more become smooth and shining.

Then he opened the large, crooked mouth, and thrust his two arms into the cavity—the shark being careful to retract his teeth—in order to remove the odds and ends of cloth, wood and glass (a shark is quite capable of swallowing a bottle or two when it can find them) which had got caught between the cruel fangs. But Manidou, who had—and he made no bones about it—a special liking for human flesh, never for one moment, dreamed of closing his powerful jaws on the hands which were routing about in his throat.

42

From *The Old Man and the Sea*

ERNEST HEMINGWAY

What can anyone say about *The Old Man and the Sea?*
It is such a perfect story. Ernest Hemingway tells a
complicated tale simply, with a minimum of dramatics
but a lot of drama.

The sharks are central to the defeat of the Old Man.
At the same time, they are in every sense minor
characters. Few descriptions of a shark are better than
his page or so describing the mako.

I don't believe that it is as easy to kill sharks from a
boat with primitive equipment as Hemingway suggests,
but there is no denying what it adds to the story.
That he had watched sharks attacking a fish alongside
a boat, as described in the following excerpt, is obvious.
Ron has filmed sharks tearing chunks from another
shark in just the way that Hemingway describes.

The Old Man and the Sea is one of the best
fictional novels of the sea. It is also the one book of
Hemingway's that a lot of people seem to dislike.
I can't understand why. I like the Old Man, and
his battle with the great fish, the sea, and
the sharks.

●

They sailed well and the old man soaked his hands
in the salt water and tried to keep his head clear. There
were high cumulus clouds and enough cirrus above
them so that the old man knew the breeze would last

all night. The old man looked at the fish constantly to make sure it was true. It was an hour before the first shark hit him.

The shark was not an accident. He had come up from deep down in the water as the dark cloud of blood had settled and dispersed in the mile deep sea. He had come up so fast and absolutely without caution that he broke the surface of the blue water and was in the sun. Then he fell back into the sea and picked up the scent and started swimming on the course the skiff and the fish had taken.

Sometimes he lost the scent. But he would pick it up again, or have just a trace of it, and he swam fast and hard on the course. He was a very big Mako shark, built to swim as fast as the fastest fish in the sea and everything about him was beautiful except his jaws. His back was as blue as a sword fish's and his belly was silver and his hide was smooth and handsome. He was built as a sword fish except for his huge jaws which were tight shut now as he swam fast, just under the surface with his high dorsal fin knifing through the water without wavering. Inside the closed double lip of his jaws all of his eight rows of teeth were slanted inwards. They were not the ordinary pyramid-shaped teeth of most sharks. They were shaped like a man's fingers when they are crisped like claws. They were nearly as long as the fingers of the old man and they had razor-sharp cutting edges on both sides. This was a fish built to feed on all the fishes in the sea, that were so fast and strong and well armed that they had no other enemy. Now he speeded up as he smelled the fresher scent and his blue dorsal fin cut the water.

When the old man saw him coming he knew that this was a shark that had no fear at all and would do exactly what he wished. He prepared the harpoon and made the rope fast while he watched the shark come on. The rope was short as it lacked what he had cut away to lash the fish.

The old man's head was clear and good now and he was full of resolution, but he had little hope. It was too good to last, he thought. He took one look at the great fish as he watched the shark close in. It might as well have been a dream, he thought. I cannot keep him from hitting me but maybe I can get him. *Dentuso,* he thought. Bad luck to your mother.

The shark closed fast astern and when he hit the fish the old man saw his mouth open and his strange eyes and the clicking chop of the teeth as he drove forward in the meat just above the tail. The shark's head was out of the water and his back was coming out and the old man could hear the noise of skin and flesh ripping on the big fish when he rammed the harpoon down onto the shark's head at a spot where the line between his eyes intersected with the line that ran straight back from his nose. There were no such lines. There was only the heavy sharp blue head and the big eyes and the clicking, thrusting all-swallowing jaws. But that was the location of the brain and the old man hit it. He hit it with his blood-mushed hands driving a good harpoon with all his strength. He hit it without hope but with resolution and complete malignancy.

The shark swung over and the old man saw his eye was not alive and then he swung over once again, wrapping himself in two loops of the rope. The old man knew that he was dead but the shark would not accept it. Then, on his back, with his tail lashing and his jaws clicking, the shark plowed over the water as a speed-boat does. The water was white where his tail beat it and three-quarters of his body was clear above the water when the rope came taut, shivered, and then snapped. The shark lay quietly for a little while on the surface and the old man watched him. Then he went down very slowly.

"He took about forty pounds," the old man said aloud. He took my harpoon too and all the rope, he thought, and now my fish bleeds again and there will be others.

He did not like to look at the fish anymore since he had been mutilated. When the fish had been hit it was as though he himself were hit.

But I killed the shark that hit my fish, he thought.

And he was the biggest *dentuso* that I have ever seen. And God knows that I have seen big ones.

It was too good to last, he thought. I wish it had been a dream now and that I had never hooked the fish and was alone in bed on the newspapers.

"But man is not made for defeat," he said. "A man can be destroyed but not defeated." I am sorry that I killed the fish though. Now the bad time is coming and I do not even have the harpoon. The *dentuso* is cruel and able and strong and intelligent. But I was more intelligent than he was. Perhaps not, he thought. Perhaps I was only better armed.

"Don't think, old man," he said aloud. "Sail on this course and take it when it comes."

But I must think, he thought. Because it is all I have left. That and baseball. I wonder how the great DiMaggio would have liked the way I hit him in the brain? It was no great thing, he thought. Any man could do it. But do you think my hands were as great a handicap as the bone spurs? I cannot know. I never had anything wrong with my heel except the time the stingray stung it when I stepped on him when swimming and paralyzed the lower leg and made the unbearable pain.

"Think about something cheerful, old man," he said. "Every minute now you are closer to home. You sail lighter for the loss of forty pounds."

He knew quite well the pattern of what could happen when he reached the inner part of the current. But there was nothing to be done now.

"Yes there is," he said aloud. "I can lash my knife to the butt of one of the oars."

So he did that with the tiller under his arm and the sheet of the sail under his foot.

"Now," he said. "I am still an old man. But I am not unarmed."

The breeze was fresh now and he sailed on well. He watched only the forward part of the fish and some of his hope returned.

It is silly not to hope, he thought. Besides I believe

it is a sin. Do not think about sin, he thought. There are enough problems now without sin. Also I have no understanding of it.

I have no understanding of it and I am not sure that I believe in it. Perhaps it was a sin to kill the fish. I suppose it was even though I did it to keep me alive and feed many people. But then everything is a sin. Do not think about sin. It is much too late for that and there are people who are paid to do it. Let them think about it. You were born to be a fisherman as the fish was born to be a fish. San Pedro was a fisherman as was the father of the great DiMaggio.

But he liked to think about all things that he was involved in and since there was nothing to read and he did not have a radio, he thought much and he kept on thinking about sin. You did not kill the fish only to keep alive and to sell for food, he thought. You killed him for pride and because you are a fisherman. You loved him when he was alive and you loved him after. If you love him, it is not a sin to kill him. Or is it more?

"You think too much, old man," he said aloud.

But you enjoyed killing the *dentuso,* he thought. He lives on the live fish as you do. He is not a scavenger nor just a moving appetite as some sharks are. He is beautiful and noble and knows no fear of anything.

"I killed him in self-defense," the old man said aloud. "And I killed him well."

Besides, he thought, everything kills everything else in some way. Fishing kills me exactly as it keeps me alive. The boy keeps me alive, he thought. I must not deceive myself too much.

He leaned over the side and pulled loose a piece of the meat of the fish where the shark had cut him. He chewed it and noted its quality and its good taste. It was firm and juicy, like meat, but it was not red. There was no stringiness in it and he knew that it would bring the highest price in the market. But there was no way to keep its scent out of the water and the old man knew that a very bad time was coming.

The breeze was steady. It had backed a little further

into the north-east and he knew that meant that it would not fall off. The old man looked ahead of him but he could see no sails nor could he see the hull nor the smoke of any ship. There were only the flying fish that went up from his bow sailing away to either side and the yellow patches of Gulf weed. He could not even see a bird.

He had sailed for two hours, resting in the stern and sometimes chewing a bit of the meat from the marlin, trying to rest and to be strong, when he saw the first of the two sharks.

"*Ay*," he said aloud. There is no translation for this word and perhaps it is just a noise such as a man might make, involuntarily, feeling the nail go through his hands and into the wood.

"*Galanos*," he said aloud. He had seen the second fin now coming up behind the first and had identified them as shovel-nosed sharks by the brown, triangular fin and the sweeping movements of the tail. They had the scent and were excited and in the stupidity of their great hunger they were losing and finding the scent in their excitement. But they were closing all the time.

The old man made the sheet fast and jammed the tiller. Then he took up the oar with the knife lashed to it. He lifted it as lightly as he could because his hands rebelled at the pain. Then he opened and closed them on it lightly to loosen them. He closed them firmly so they would take the pain now and would not flinch and watched the sharks come. He could see their wide, flattened, shovel-pointed heads now and their white-tipped wide pectoral fins. They were hateful sharks, bad smelling, scavengers as well as killers, and when they were hungry they would bite at an oar or the rudder of a boat. It was these sharks that would cut the turtles' legs and flippers off when the turtles were asleep on the surface, and they would hit a man in the water, if they were hungry, even if the man had no smell of fish blood nor of fish slime on him.

"*Ay*," the old man said. "*Galanos*. Come on, *galanos*."

They came. But they did not come as the Mako had

come. One turned and went out of sight under the skiff and the old man could feel the skiff shake as he jerked and pulled on the fish. The other watched the old man with his slitted yellow eyes and then came in fast with his half circle of jaws wide to hit the fish where he had already been bitten. The line showed clearly on the top of his brown head and back where the brain joined the spinal cord and the old man drove the knife on the oar into the juncture, withdrew it, and drove it in again into the shark's yellow cat-like eyes. The shark let go of the fish and slid down, swallowing what he had taken as he died.

The skiff was still shaking with the destruction the other shark was doing to the fish and the old man let go the sheet so that the skiff would swing broadside and bring the shark out from under. When he saw the shark he leaned over the side and punched at him. He hit only meat and the hide was set hard and he barely got the knife in. The blow hurt not only his hands but his shoulder too. But the shark came up fast with his head out and the old man hit him squarely in the center of his flat-topped head as his nose came out of the water and lay against the fish. The old man withdrew the blade and punched the shark exactly in the same spot again. He still hung to the fish with his jaws hooked and the old man stabbed him in his left eye. The shark still hung there.

"No?" the old man said and he drove the blade between the vertebrae and the brain. It was an easy shot now and he felt the cartilage sever. The old man reversed the oar and put the blade between the shark's jaws to open them. He twisted the blade and as the shark slid loose he said, "Go on, *galano*. Slide down a mile deep. Go see your friend, or maybe it's your mother."

The old man wiped the blade of his knife and laid down the oar. Then he found the sheet and the sail filled and he brought the skiff onto her course.

"They must have taken a quarter of him and of the best meat," he said aloud. "I wish it were a dream and that I had never hooked him. I'm sorry about it, fish. It makes everything wrong." He stopped and he did not want to look at the fish now. Drained of blood and awash he looked the color of the silver backing of a mirror and his stripes still showed.

"I shouldn't have gone out so far, fish," he said. "Neither for you nor for me. I'm sorry, fish."

Now, he said to himself. Look to the lashing on the knife and see if it has been cut. Then get your hand in order because there still is more to come.

"I wish I had a stone for the knife," the old man said after he had checked the lashing on the oar butt. "I should have brought a stone." You should have brought many things, he thought. But you did not bring them, old man. Now is no time to think of what you do not have. Think of what you can do with what there is.

"You give me much good counsel," he said aloud. "I'm tired of it."

He held the tiller under his arm and soaked both his hands in the water as the skiff drove forward.

"God knows how much that last one took," he said. "But she's much lighter now." He did not want to think of the mutilated under-side of the fish. He knew that each of the jerking bumps of the shark had been meat torn away and that the fish now made a trail for all sharks as wide as a highway through the sea.

He was a fish to keep a man all winter, he thought. Don't think of that. Just rest and try to get your hands in shape to defend what is left of him. The blood smell from my hands means nothing now with all that scent in the water. Besides they do not bleed much. There is nothing cut that means anything. The bleeding may keep the left from cramping.

What can I think of now? he thought. Nothing. I must think of nothing and wait for the next ones. I wish it had really been a dream, he thought. But who knows? It might have turned out well.

The next shark that came was a single shovel-nose. He came like a pig to the trough if a pig had a mouth so wide that you could put your head in it. The old man let him hit the fish and then drove the knife on the oar down into his brain. But the shark jerked backwards as he rolled and the knife blade snapped.

The old man settled himself to steer. He did not even watch the big shark sinking slowly in the water, showing first life-size, then tiny. That always fascinated the old man. But he did not even watch it now.

"I have the gaff now," he said. "But it will do no good. I have the two oars and the tiller and the short club."

Now they have beaten me, he thought. I am too old to club sharks to death. But I will try it as long as I have the oars and the short club and the tiller.

He put his hands in the water again to soak them. It was getting late in the afternoon and he saw nothing but the sea and the sky. There was more wind in the sky than there had been, and soon he hoped that he would see land.

"You're tired, old man," he said. "You're tired inside."

The sharks did not hit him again until just before sunset.

The old man saw the brown fins coming along the wide trail the fish must make in the water. They were not even quartering on the scent. They were headed straight for the skiff swimming side by side.

He jammed the tiller, made the sheet fast and reached under the stern for the club. It was an oar handle from a broken oar sawed off to about two and a half feet in length. He could only use it effectively with one hand because of the grip of the handle and he took good hold of it with his right hand, flexing his hand on it, as he watched the sharks come. They were both *galanos*.

I must let the first one get a good hold and hit him on the point of the nose or straight across the top of the head, he thought.

The two sharks closed together and as he saw the one nearest him open his jaws and sink them into the silver side of the fish, he raised the club high and brought it down heavy and slamming onto the top of the shark's broad head. He felt the rubbery solidity as the club came down. But he felt the rigidity of bone too and he struck the shark once more hard across the point of the nose as he slid down from the fish.

The other shark had been in and out and now came in again with his jaws wide. The old man could see pieces of the meat of the fish spilling white from the corner of his jaws as he bumped the fish and closed his jaws. He swung at him and hit only the head and the shark looked at him and wrenched the meat loose. The old man swung the club down on him again as he slipped away to swallow and hit only the heavy solid rubberiness.

"Come on, *galano,*" the old man said. "Come in again."

The shark came in a rush and the old man hit him as he shut his jaws. He hit him solidly and from as high up as he could raise the club. This time he felt the bone at the base of the brain and he hit him again in the same place while the shark tore the meat loose sluggishly and slid down from the fish.

The old man watched for him to come again but neither shark showed. Then he saw one on the surface swimming in circles. He did not see the fin of the other.

I could not expect to kill them, he thought. I could have in my time. But I have hurt them both badly and neither one can feel very good. If I could have used a bat with two hands I could have killed the first one surely. Even now, he thought.

He did not want to look at the fish. He knew that half of him had been destroyed. The sun had gone down while he had been in the fight with the sharks.

"It will be dark soon," he said. "Then I should see the glow of Havana. If I am too far to the eastward I will see the lights of one of the new beaches."

I cannot be too far out now, he thought. I hope no one has been too worried. There is only the boy to worry, of course. But I am sure he would have confidence. Many of the older fishermen will worry. Many others too, he thought. I live in a good town.

He could not talk to the fish anymore because the fish had been ruined too badly. Then something came into his head.

"Half fish," he said. "Fish that you were. I am sorry that I went too far out. I ruined us both. But we have killed many sharks, you and I, and ruined many others. How many did you ever kill, old fish? You do not have that spear on your head for nothing."

He liked to think of the fish and what he could do to a shark if he were swimming free. I should have chopped the bill off to fight them with, he thought. But there was no hatchet and then there was no knife.

But if I had, one could have lashed it to an oar butt, what a weapon. Then we might have fought them together. What will you do now if they come in the night? What can you do?

"Fight them," he said. "I'll fight them until I die."

But in the dark now and no glow showing and no lights and only the wind and the steady pull of the sail he felt that perhaps he was already dead. He put his two hands together and felt the palms. They were not dead and he could bring the pain of life by simply opening and closing them. He leaned his back against the stern and knew he was not dead. His shoulders told him.

I have all those prayers I promised if I caught the fish, he thought. But I am too tired to say them now. I better get the sack and put it over my shoulders.

He lay in the stern and steered and watched for the glow to come in the sky. I have half of him, he thought. Maybe I'll have the luck to bring the forward half in. I should have some luck. No, he said. You violated your luck when you went too far outside.

"Don't be silly," he said aloud. "And keep awake and steer. You may have much luck yet."

"I'd like to buy some if there's any place they sell it," he said.

What could I buy it with? he asked himself. Could I buy it with a lost harpoon and a broken knife and two bad hands?

"You might," he said. "You tried to buy it with

eighty-four days at sea. They nearly sold it to you too."

I must not think nonsense, he thought. Luck is a thing that comes in many forms and who can recognize her? I would take some though in any form and pay what they asked. I wish I could see the glow from the lights, he thought. I wish too many things. But that is the thing I wish for now. He tried to settle more comfortably to steer and from his pain he knew he was not dead.

He saw the reflected glare of the lights of the city at what must have been around ten o'clock at night. They were only perceptible at first as the light is in the sky before the moon rises. Then they were steady to see across the ocean which was rough now with the increasing breeze. He steered inside of the glow and he thought that now, soon, he must hit the edge of the stream.

Now it is over, he thought. They will probably hit me again. But what can a man do against them in the dark without a weapon?

He was stiff and sore now and his wounds and all of the strained parts of his body hurt with the cold of the night. I hope I do not have to fight again.

But by midnight he fought and this time he knew the fight was useless. They came in a pack and he could only see the lines in the water that their fins made and their phosphorescence as they threw themselves on the fish. He clubbed at heads and heard the jaws chop and the shaking of the skiff as they took hold below. He clubbed desperately at what he could only feel and hear and he felt something seize the club and it was gone.

He jerked the tiller free from the rudder and beat and chopped with it, holding it in both hands and driving it down again and again. But they were up to the bow now and driving in one after the other and together, tearing off the pieces of meat that showed glowing below the sea as they turned to come once more.

One came, finally, against the head itself and he

knew that it was over. He swung the tiller across the shark's head where the jaws were caught in the heaviness of the fish's head which would not tear. He swung it once and twice and again. He heard the tiller break and he lunged at the shark with the splintered butt. He felt it go in and knowing it was sharp he drove it in again. The shark let go and rolled away. That was the last shark of the pack that came. There was nothing more for them to eat.

The old man could hardly breathe now and he felt a strange taste in his mouth. It was coppery and sweet and he was afraid of it for a moment. But there was not much of it.

He spat into the ocean and said, "Eat that, *galanos*. And make a dream you've killed a man."

He knew he was beaten now finally and without remedy and he went back to the stern and found the jagged end of the tiller would fit in the slot of the rudder well enough for him to steer. He settled the sack around his shoulders and put the skiff on her course. He sailed lightly now and he had no thoughts nor any feelings of any kind. He was past everything now and he sailed the skiff to make his home port as well and as intelligently as he could.

In the night sharks hit the carcass as someone might pick up crumbs from the table. The old man paid no attention to them and did not pay any attention to anything except steering. He only noticed how lightly and how well the skiff sailed now there was no great weight beside her.

She's good, he thought. She is sound and not harmed in any way except for the tiller. That is easily replaced.

He could feel he was inside the current now and he could see the lights of the beach colonies along the shore. He knew where he was now and it was nothing to get home.

The wind is our friend, anyway, he thought. Then he added, sometimes. And the great sea with our friends and our enemies. And bed, he thought. Bed is my friend. Just bed, he thought. Bed will be a great thing.

It is easy when you are beaten, he thought. I never knew how easy it was. And what beat you, he thought.

"Nothing," he said aloud. "I went out too far."

When he sailed into the little harbor the lights of the Terrace were out and he knew everyone was in bed. The breeze had risen steadily and was blowing strongly now. It was quiet in the harbor though and he sailed up onto the little patch of shingle below the rocks. There was no one to help him so he pulled the boat up as far as he could. Then he stepped out and made her fast to a rock.

He unstepped the mast and furled the sail and tied it. Then he shouldered the mast and started to climb. It was then he knew the depth of his tiredness. He stopped for a moment and looked back and saw in the reflection from the street light the great tail of the fish standing up well behind the skiff's stern. He saw the white naked line of his backbone and the dark mass of the head with the projecting bill and all the nakedness between.

He started to climb again and at the top he fell and lay for some time with the mast across his shoulder. He tried to get up. But it was too difficult and he sat there with the mast on his shoulder and looked at the road. A cat passed on the far side going about its business and the old man watched it. Then he just watched the road.

Finally he put the mast down and stood up. He picked the mast up and put it on his shoulder and started up the road. He had to sit down five times before he reached his shack.

Inside the shack he leaned the mast against the wall. In the dark he found a water bottle and took a drink. Then he lay down on the bed. He pulled the blanket over his shoulders and then over his back and legs and he slept face down on the newspapers with his arms out straight and the palms of his hands up.

He was asleep when the boy looked in the door in the morning. It was blowing so hard that the drifting-boats would not be going out and the boy had slept late and then come to the old man's shack as he had come each morning. The boy saw that the old man was breathing and then he saw the old man's hands and he started to cry. He went out very quietly to go to bring some coffee and all the way down the road he was crying.

Many fishermen were around the skiff looking at what was lashed beside it and one was in the water, his trousers rolled up, measuring the skeleton with a length of line.

The boy did not go down. He had been there before and one of the fishermen was looking after the skiff for him.

"How is he?" one of the fishermen shouted.

"Sleeping," the boy called. He did not care that they saw him crying. "Let no one disturb him."

"He was eighteen feet from nose to tail," the fisherman who was measuring him called.

"I believe it," the boy said.

He went into the Terrace and asked for a can of coffee.

"Hot and with plenty of milk and sugar in it."

"Anything more?"

"No. Afterwards I will see what he can eat."

"What a fish it was," the proprietor said. "There has never been such a fish. Those were two fine fish you took yesterday too."

"Damn my fish," the boy said and he started to cry again.

"Do you want a drink of any kind?" the proprietor asked.

"No," the boy said. "Tell them not to bother Santiago. I'll be back."

"Tell him how sorry I am."

"Thanks," the boy said.

The boy carried the hot can of coffee up to the old man's shack and sat by him until he woke. Once it looked as though he were waking. But he had gone back into heavy sleep and the boy had gone across the road to borrow some wood to heat the coffee.

Finally the old man woke.

"Don't sit up," the boy said. "Drink this." He poured some of the coffee in a glass.

The old man took it and drank it.

"They beat me, Manolin," he said. "They truly beat me."

"He didn't beat you. Not the fish."

"No. Truly. It was afterwards."

"Pedrico is looking after the skiff and the gear. What do you want done with the head?"

"Let Pedrico chop it up to use in fish traps."

"And the spear?"

"You keep it if you want it."

"I want it," the boy said. "Now we must make our plans about the other things."

"Did they search for me?"

"Of course. With coast guard and with planes."

"The ocean is very big and a skiff is small and hard to see," the old man said. He noticed how pleasant it was to have someone to talk to instead of speaking only to himself and to the sea. "I missed you," he said. "What did you catch?"

"One the first day. One the second and two the third."

"Very good."

"Now we fish together again."

"No. I am not lucky. I am not lucky anymore."

"The hell with luck," the boy said. "I'll bring the luck with me."

"What will your family say?"

"I do not care. I caught two yesterday. But we will fish together now for I still have much to learn."

"We must get a good killing lance and always have it on board. You can make the blade from a spring leaf from an old Ford. We can grind it in Guanabacoa. It should be sharp and not tempered so it will break. My knife broke."

"I'll get another knife and have the spring ground. How many days of heavy *brisa* have we?"

"Maybe three. Maybe more."

"I will have everything in order," the boy said. "You get your hands well, old man."

"I know how to care for them. In the night I spat something strange and felt something in my chest was broken."

"Get that well too," the boy said. "Lie down, old man, and I will bring you your clean shirt. And something to eat."

"Bring any of the papers of the time that I was gone," the old man said.

"You must get well fast for there is much that I can learn and you can teach me everything. How much did you suffer?"

"Plenty," the old man said.

"I'll bring the food and the papers," the boy said. "Rest well, old man. I will bring stuff from the drugstore for your hands."

"Don't forget to tell Pedrico the head is his."

"No. I will remember."

As the boy went out the door and down the worn coral rock road he was crying again.

That afternoon there was a party of tourists at the Terrace and looking down in the water among the empty beer cans and dead barracudas a woman saw a great long white spine with a huge tail at the end that lifted and swung with the tide while the east wind blew a heavy steady sea outside the entrance to the harbor.

"What's that?" she asked a waiter and pointed to the long backbone of the great fish that was now just garbage waiting to go out with the tide.

"Tiburon," the waiter said, "Eshark." He was meaning to explain what had happened.

"I didn't know sharks had such handsome, beautifully formed tails."

"I didn't either," her male companion said.

Up the road, in his shack, the old man was sleeping again. He was still sleeping on his face and the boy was sitting by him watching him. The old man was dreaming about the lions.

Acknowledgments

Grateful acknowledgment is made for permission to use the selections included in this anthology, as follows:

From *Blue Meridian* by Peter Matthiessen. Copyright © 1971 by Peter Matthiessen. Reprinted by permission of Random House, Inc., and Candida Donadio & Associates, Inc.

From *Jaws* by Peter Benchley. Copyright © 1974 by Peter Benchley. Reprinted by permission of Doubleday & Company, Inc. and Andre Deutsch Limited.

From *Sharks Are Caught at Night* by Francois Poli, Published by Henry Regnery Company. Copyright © 1957 Presses de la Cité. Reprinted by permission of Contemporary Books, Inc. (formerly Henry Regnery Company) and Les Presses de la Cité.

From *Shark: Unpredictable Killer of the Sea* by Thomas Helm. Copyright © 1961 by Thomas Helm. Reprinted by permission of Dodd, Mead & Company, Inc. and John Farquharson Ltd.

From *Heaven Has Claws* by Arthur Conan Doyle. Reprinted by permission of John Murray (Publishers) Ltd.

From *Sharks, Sea and Land* by "Sinbad," published by Blackfriars Printing & Publishing Co., 1889.

From *Lord of the Sharks* by Franco Prosperi, translated by Camilla and Guido Roatta, published by the Hutchinson Publishing Group.

The Vanishing Grey Nurse by Valerie Taylor, reprinted from *The Australian Women's Weekly* by permission of the author.

From *The Arcturus Adventure* by William Beebe. Copyright 1926 by William Beebe; renewed 1954 by William Beebe. Reprinted by permission of G. P. Putnam's Sons.

From *Sharks and Other Ancestors* by Wade Doak, published by Hodder & Stoughton, Auckland, N.Z. Copyright © 1975 by

Wade Doak. Reprinted by permission of the author and the publisher.

"Sharks That Ring Bells" from *The Lady and the Sharks* by Eugenie Clark. Copyright © 1969 by Eugenie Clark. Reprinted by permission of Harper & Row, Publishers, Inc.

From *The Coast of Coral* by Arthur C. Clarke. Copyright © 1956 by Arthur Charles Clarke. Reprinted by permission of Harper & Row, Publishers, Inc., and David Higham Associates Limited.

From *Men Beneath the Sea: Conquest of the Underwater World* by Hans Hass. Copyright © 1975 by Hans Hass. Reprinted by permission of St. Martin's Press, Inc. and David & Charles Ltd.

From *Kon-Tiki* by Thor Heyerdahl. Copyright 1950 by Thor Heyerdahl. Published in the United States by Rand McNally & Company. Reprinted by permission of Rand McNally & Company and George Allen & Unwin Ltd.

From *Creatures of the Sea* by William B. Gray (Funk & Wagnalls). Copyright © 1960 by William B. Gray. Reprinted by permission of Thomas Y. Crowell Company, Inc., and Frederick Muller Ltd.

From *Shark-O* by P. Fitzgerald Connor, published in 1953 by Secker & Warburg. Reprinted by permission of the author and A.M. Heath & Company Ltd.

From *Fangs of the Sea* by Norman Caldwell and Norman Ellison. Copyright © 1965 by Jean Caldwell and Norman Ellison. Reprinted by permission of Angus and Robertson Publishers, Sydney.

From *Fishing in Many Waters* by James Hornell. Copyright © 1950 by James Hornell. Published by Cambridge University Press and reprinted by their permission and that of Mrs. D. A. Davies.

From *Shark! Shark! the Thirty-Year Odyssey of a Pioneer Shark Hunter* by William E. Young. Published by Gotham House, N.Y., 1934.

From *Battles with Giant Fish* by F. A. Mitchell-Hedges. Reprinted by permission of Gerald Duckworth & Co. Ltd.

From *A Pattern of Islands* by Arthur Grimble. Reprinted by permission of John Murray (Publishers) Ltd. (1952).

From *Saltwater Angling in South Africa* by Romer Robinson and J. S. Dunn, C.B.E. Published 1923 by Robinson and Co., Ltd., Durban, South Africa.

Mako, Blue Dynamite by Peter Goadby. Adapted from "Mako—the Explosive Blue Dynamite" in *Modern Fishing*. Copyright © 1976 by Peter Goadby.

From *An American Angler in Australia* by Zane Grey. Copyright 1937 by Zane Grey. Reprinted by permission of Zane Grey, Inc.

ABOUT THE EDITORS

VALERIE and RON TAYLOR are two of the foremost photographers of sharks in the world. Together with PETER GOADBY, a third Australian, they know as much about sharks as can be known; all three have spent their lives studying the sea and its inhabitants. The Taylors have done live shark photography on the *Jaws* films and on *Blue Water, White Death*. Their underwater television series, "Ron and Valerie Taylor's Inner Space," has been shown all over the world and a new one is now in preparation.